Norman Bel Geddes

CULTURAL HISTORIES OF DESIGN

SERIES EDITORS

**Grace Lees-Maffei of the University of Hertfordshire, UK and
Kjetil Fallan of the University of Oslo, Norway**

The Cultural Histories of Design series presents rigorous and original research on the role and significance of design in society and culture, past and present. From a vantage point in the heart of the humanities, the series explores design as the most significant manifestation of modern and contemporary culture.

FORTHCOMING TITLES

Modern Asian Design by D. J. Huppatz of Swinburne University, Australia
Norman Bel Geddes by Nicolas P. Maffei of Norwich University of the Arts, UK
Soviet Critical Design by Tom Cubbin of the University of Gothenburg, Sweden
Open Plan by Jennifer Kaufmann-Buhler of Purdue University, USA

Norman Bel Geddes

American Design Visionary

NICOLAS P. MAFFEI

Bloomsbury Academic
An imprint of Bloomsbury Publishing Plc

B L O O M S B U R Y
LONDON · OXFORD · NEW YORK · NEW DELHI · SYDNEY

Bloomsbury Academic

An imprint of Bloomsbury Publishing Plc

50 Bedford Square	1385 Broadway
London	New York
WC1B 3DP	NY 10018
UK	USA

www.bloomsbury.com

BLOOMSBURY and the Diana logo are trademarks of Bloomsbury Publishing Plc

First published 2018

© Nicolas P. Maffei, 2018

Nicolas P. Maffei has asserted his right under the Copyright, Designs and Patents Act, 1988, to be identified as Author of this work.

Series: Cultural Histories of Design
Series editors: Grace Lees-Maffei and Kjetil Fallan

British Library Cataloguing-in-Publication Data
A catalogue record for this book is available from the British Library.

ISBN:	HB:	978-1-4742-8459-2
	PB:	978-1-4742-8461-5
	ePDF:	978-1-4742-8457-8
	ePub:	978-1-4742-8458-5

Library of Congress Cataloging-in-Publication Data
Names: Maffei, Nic, author.
Title: Norman Bel Geddes : American design visionary / by Nic Maffei.
Description: New York : Bloomsbury Academic, An imprint of Bloomsbury
Publishing Plc, 2018. | Series: Cultural histories of design | Includes bibliographical references and index.
Identifiers: LCCN 2017043790 | ISBN 9781474284592 (hardback : alk. paper)
Subjects: LCSH: Geddes, Norman Bel, 1893-1958. | Designers–United States–Biography. |
Design–United States–History–20th century.
Classification: LCC NK1412.G43 M34 2018 | DDC 745.2092 [B]–dc23 LC record
available at https://lccn.loc.gov/2017043790

Cover image © Bettmann/Getty Images

Typeset by Integra Software Services Pvt. Ltd.

Dedicated with love to Grace,
Jay, and Laurel for their patience and inspiration.

Contents

List of Illustrations

List of Plates

Acknowledgments

This book would not have been possible without the assistance and generosity of numerous individuals and institutions. First, I am thankful to my parents, whose passion, encouragement, and collection of design-related artifacts piqued my initial interest in industrial design history. This fascination was developed and refined at the University of Texas, Austin, where Jeffrey L. Meikle patiently guided my research of the Harry Ransom Center's (HRC) Normal Bel Geddes Papers. My professors and classmates at the University of Delaware, Newark, helped me hone my skills as a historian. The archivists and curators and other staff at the HRC, in particular Rick Watson, Helen Adair, and Kathy Henderson, deserve special thanks for their time and generosity. I am equally appreciative of the support of the many individuals who aided my searches and acquisition of images and permissions, including Christopher M. Leich, Kenneth Hamilton Sather Bruguiere, and those at the Edith Lutyens and Norman Bel Geddes Foundation, the Museum of Modern Art, New York, the New York Public Library's Department of Rare Books, Special Collections and Preservation at the University of Rochester River Campus Libraries, the Yale University Manuscripts and Archives, the Library of Congress, the Theosophical Society in America, the Austrian Frederick and Lillian Kiesler Private Foundation, Vienna, Fondacion Le Corbusier, Paris, Hearst Communications Inc., Getty Images, and Scala, Florence. I am hugely appreciative of the inspiring tutors and thoughtful colleagues I met while I was a PhD student at the Royal College of Art, London, in particular my supervisors, Penny Sparke and Jeremy Aynsley. I have benefited hugely from those who read drafts of this book, including Jeffrey L. Meikle and Kjetil Fallan. Financial support was provided through the Graham Foundation, Chicago, the Hagley Museum and Library, the Harry Ransom Center, and the Norwich University of the Arts, which also provided essential research leave. The editors at Bloomsbury, Claire Constable and Rebecca Barden, have been unfaltering in their assistance. Finally, I am most grateful to my wife Grace who has provided constant encouragement, loving support, and astute commentary on my research on Bel Geddes.

Introduction

Norman Bel Geddes (1893–1958) was perhaps the most influential of America's first generation of industrial designers, which included Henry Dreyfuss, Raymond Loewy, Walter Dorwin Teague, and Harold Van Doren. Through his grand schemes, immense imagination, and even greater sense of self, Bel Geddes significantly contributed to the development of the industrial design profession, which in turn played a crucial role in America's transformation to a consumer society. *American Design Visionary* investigates Bel Geddes's startlingly visionary designs of teardrop-shaped cars, trains, and planes, along with his genius for publicity, which helped secure streamlining as *the* design style of the 1930s and indelibly stamped the industrial design profession as one of unbridled vision and machine-age optimism.[1] His 1929 design for Air Liner Number 4, a nine-deck-high-flying wing, exemplifies the monumental scope and imaginative reach typical of many of Bel Geddes's designs. With its 528-foot wingspan, the unrealized Air Liner Number 4 included a nightclub for 300 persons, four tennis courts, and a glassed-in promenade along the length of the wing. His design triumph, the General Motors Futurama exhibit at the New York World's fair of 1939, combined the logic of Le Corbusier with the imagination of H. G. Wells. An educational amusement ride, it depicted a vast miniaturized model of the future dominated by superhighways and tower cities. Visited by tens of millions of people, it profoundly shaped the American notion of the world of tomorrow. While the economic depression of the 1930s provided a catalyst for escapism and technological fantasy,[2] Bel Geddes's redesign of everyday goods stimulated consumer desire.[3]

After an illustrious career as a leading practitioner of the New Stagecraft, a European and American avant-garde stage design movement that emphasized visual unity and the mood of a play, Bel Geddes opened one of America's first industrial design offices in 1927.[4] According to Bel Geddes, it was during this year he became the "first designer to establish a specialized service with a supporting organization in 'Industrial Design',"[5] and "Founded [the] profession of Industrial Design."[6] While he mentored many of his future industrial design competitors, including

Dreyfuss and Russel Wright, his large and highly systematized office became the training ground for numerous others, including Eliot Noyes, and senior members of the Van Doren office. For the first three years of his professional life, Dreyfuss was Bel Geddes's "apprentice, office boy, and then assistant."[7] In 1946, Bel Geddes claimed that of America's "hundred leading designers ... at least half" apprenticed in his office, "two of my six leading competitors are among this group," and in "the office of my leading competitor six of his eight highest paid men are of this category."[8]

This book explores Bel Geddes's lifelong effort to present himself as a pragmatic visionary and the attempts of his contemporaries to brand him a genius and a dreamer. Despite Bel Geddes's bold creations, unswerving idealism, and inflated ego, Dreyfuss considered him the "only authentic genius this [industrial design] profession has ever produced."[9] George Nelson, in his 1934 *Fortune* article on the emerging field of industrial design, described Bel Geddes as a "dynamic, volubly articulate individual," and, referring to the nineteenth-century circus entrepreneur, "a born showman, the P. T. Barnum of industrial design," a "bomb-thrower" who "cost American industry a billion dollars" through retooling and "join[ing] the redesign movement."[10] Seven years later, at the height of Bel Geddes's industrial design success, the *New Yorker* offered a similar portrait of an "intense, wild-haired," "super-salesman" who "moves from one grandiose venture to another, leaving chaos, and usually an awed but somehow satisfied client," noting that his critics considered him "impractical and visionary" compared to his "businesslike" contemporaries.[11] Bel Geddes, however, spent a lifetime developing a very different image: one of logic, vision, and expertise—the industrial designer as organizational mastermind and creative seer who infused mass-produced goods with an aura of glamor and optimism (Plate 1, Figures I.1 and I.2).

Although many of his visionary designs were never realized, whether futuristic cities or streamlined vehicles, they stimulated the emerging profession more immediately than those of his more pragmatic contemporaries.[12] Despite the Bel Geddes office's association with speculative design, it championed consumer research, realized numerous design jobs, and maintained an impressive stable of clients, including Texaco, IBM, Chrysler, Shell Oil, General Motors, and dozens of others, helping the firm to achieve both national and international recognition, while identifying the industrial designer as a rational and indispensable expert. Many of Bel Geddes's manufactured products, including the architectural Manhattan cocktail service, the bullet-shaped Walter Kidde seltzer bottle, and the all-metal bedroom furniture for the Simmons Company, have become well known to design cognoscenti and the wider public through their appearance in books, auctions, and exhibitions (Figures I.3 and I.4).[13]

American Design Visionary charts Bel Geddes's conceptual influences whether aesthetic, ideological, or philosophical, placing him within the shifting intellectual currents of the first half of the twentieth century. Primarily self-educated, Bel Geddes dedicated himself to discovering the secrets of imagination and creativity, resulting in a lifelong commitment to making the imagined ideal into a material reality—extending this doctrine of transformation to the self and the world. To this end Bel Geddes maintained an extensive library, exploring a range of intellectual and spiritual ideas, including psychoanalysis, scientific management, Bolshevism, clairvoyance, Theosophy (a religious philosophy based on Eastern thought and mystic concerns), and machine-age proselytizing (popular writing which promoted the machine as the symbol and savior of the era).[14] As early as the mid-teens, Geddes, who would add Bel to his name after April 1916, had found inspiration in the writings of the philosopher Friedrich Nietzsche, who recognized ambition as a human drive, and the founder of Christian Science, Mary Baker Eddy, whose mind-over-matter, spiritual attitude emphasized optimism, physical restoration through prayer and self-realization. In the 1920s,

FIGURE I.1 Bel Geddes posing with his stage-set model for the unrealized production of Dante Alighieri's *The Divine Comedy*. In the background are sanguine on-paper scene renderings of the stage settings, *c.* 1920. Photo by Vandamm Studio, © Billy Rose Theater Division, The New York Public Library for the Performing Arts.

FIGURE 1.2 Bel Geddes with model of the "City of Tomorrow" for a Shell Oil advertising campaign, *c.* 1937. Photograph probably by Frances Waite. Harry Ransom Center, University of Texas, and the Edith Lutyens and Norman Bel Geddes Foundation, Inc. 2016.

Bel Geddes became interested in Theosophy, especially its visionary emphasis, including attainment of higher consciousness through emotional and intuitive experience. Bel Geddes would later explore the industrial philosophy of Henry Ford, and adopt ideas from the modernist architect Le Corbusier and the futurologist H. G. Wells, thus bridging the spheres of modernism and mass culture.

FIGURE I.3 Bel Geddes's "Manhattan" cocktail service manufactured by Revere Copper and Brass, designed 1934–1935, produced 1937. Chrome-plated metal. "Skyscraper" shaker, 12 & 3/4 × 3 & 5/16 × 3 & 5/16 in. (32.4 × 8.4 × 8.4 cm); "Manhattan" serving tray, 3/4 × 14 & 1/4 × 11 & 5/8 in. (1.9 × 36.8 × 29.5 cm);. goblets: 4 1/2 × 2 3/4 in. (11.4 × 7 cm). Brooklyn Museum, Gift of Paul F. Walter. 83.108.14a-d. Creative Commons-BY (Photo: Brooklyn Museum, 83.108.5a-c_83.108.6_83.108.13_83.108.14a-d_bw.jpg).

The notion that modernity, characterized by rationality, bureaucracy, and science, was disenchanted and thus devoid of wonder and mystery can be traced to Max Weber's *Die Entzauberung der Welt* (1917). Historians now argue that modernity provides a space for both logic and enchantment, the latter surviving in magic shows, mass spectacle, and other phenomena, allowing individuals to experience wonder and delight, even in the midst of modernization.[15] Such scholars of modernity have understood the late nineteenth and early twentieth centuries as a period which "embrace[d] seeming contraries, such as rationality and wonder, secularism and faith" (3, 2009). Saler and Landy note that this period was "characterized by a fascination with spiritualism and the occult, a vogue for non-Western religions and art, and a turn to aestheticism, neo-paganism,

FIGURE I.4 Bel Geddes's seltzer bottles manufactured by Walter Kidde Sales Company *c.* 1935. Chromed and enameled metal with rubber fittings. Photograph by Norman Bel Geddes and Company. 10 × 4.5 × 4.5 in. (25.4 × 10.8 × 10.8 cm) Harry Ransom Center, University of Texas, and the Edith Lutyens and Norman Bel Geddes Foundation, Inc. 2016.

and celebrations of the irrational will." Unearthing interests in clairvoyance, Theosophy, and Christian Science, *American Design Visionary* evidences Bel Geddes's apparently antimodern pursuits.

Daniel Herman argues that spiritualists of the period through spirit knocking, séances, and so on "prefigured the electronic technology of spirit materialization in the twentieth century—telephone, film, radio and television." This in turn aided the development of a twentieth-century modernity, characterized by a therapeutic mass culture.[16] He writes, "It was spiritualism's capacity to fuse religion, therapy, and entertainment that separated it from earlier attempts to communicate with the dead and propelled its rapid success."[17] If we can view progress ideology—the belief in civilization's constant improvement—as a quasi-religious, technological fundamentalism, then Bel Geddes's designs, whether manifested in aesthetic streamlining or a faith in futuristic visions, can be seen as attempts to reenchant modernity. Whereas the spirit medium allowed séance-goers to access a parallel world of past deceased, Bel Geddes's visions of tomorrow allowed viewers to access a future world of technological improvement. Such fantasies could be accessed in the present through the purchase of streamlined goods or attending spectacles such as the Futurama, with their promises of technological progress especially in the economic chaos of the 1930s.

The years following the 1929 stock market crash witnessed a vigorous public debate over the economic, social, and moral issues of increased modernization within American capitalism.[18] Popular discourse of the interwar period articulated, on the one hand, a desire for cheaper goods and increased wages, and on the other, the dread of mechanized warfare and technological unemployment.[19] The business community reacted defensively to such attacks on industry and commerce, responding with public relations campaigns intended to forge appealing corporate images.[20] *American Design Visionary* investigates the significant role Bel Geddes played in reimaging his industrial clients as progressive, rational, and farseeing, especially in the depression decade. While Bel Geddes's expansive ego and superb skills of salesmanship appealed to industrial clients, who embraced redesign as an essential sales tool in an increasingly competitive market and depressed economy, the luster of the Bel Geddes name helped to associate his corporate employers with logic and foresight.

Bel Geddes's interests and activities reflected the social and cultural developments of his time. He experienced the chaos brought by war and the economy's devastating peaks and troughs. He read of metaphysical mysteries and of the subconscious, subscribed to industrial culture's gospel of order, and embraced the symbols of the machine age—the motorcar, the airplane, and the factory. Freud and Ford embodied the Janus-faced nature of the age: desire and order, the irrational and the rational, consumption and production, and the evolution of the self and the material world. This era, marked by intensive modernization and the science of the self, provided Bel Geddes with a fundamental belief in the dual importance of material and individual progress.

Modernity has been understood as a significant period of transformation—of individuals, societies, and the material environment. Bel Geddes hoped to transform himself, his consumers, and the designed world. Modernity witnessed the intensification of consumer culture, the wholesale alteration of the physical landscape, and the increased freedom to shape one's identity. A guiding attraction of twentieth-century consumerism was the possibility of self-realization through the purchase of goods.[21] The tendency to construct one's self, whether through shopping or social role-playing, "manipulating the self in order to manipulate others," is not unique to Bel Geddes's era, but has been recognized as a hallmark of modernity.[22] This study shows how Bel

Geddes harnessed the flexible nature of identity in shaping his image and those of his audiences, be they theatergoers, consumers, or visitors of the Futurama. His self-awareness of this process is evident in the 1954 draft title of his autobiography, *I Designed My Life*.[23]

In his professional life, he remade himself according to his varied audiences, advancing from one creative field to another including vaudevillian, portraitist, advertising artist, stage designer, "architecturalist," and industrial designer, even pursuing an architectural license in the 1930s.[24] Constructing and maintaining his public image was key to the success of his business. He presented himself as a visionary artist to his stage design students, a tough-minded businessman to industrialists, a hardened modernist to architects, and a technological prophet to the public at large. His knowledge of the irrational and the rational, his efforts to balance the two, and his career shift away from the artistic world of theater toward the logic of industry and manufacturing, echo a similar transformation within American culture during the first half of the twentieth century: in aesthetics—from expressionism to functionalism; in prophesying—from spiritualism to technological and consumer forecasting; in national direction—from westward expansion to the inward conquest of the self.[25]

At the height of the economic depression of the 1930s, publicity for Bel Geddes proclaimed, "Practical visionaries like Norman Bel Geddes are helping us to learn how to play the game of tomorrow."[26] Bel Geddes's fascination with imagination and pragmatism, however, extended much earlier. In 1912, he looked to the mystically infused writing of New Stagecraft theorist and stage designer E. Gordon Craig, who described "imagination" as "the most precious possession of mankind." "Mysterious" and "eternal," it is "this which heals, by which you see, by which you hear, by which you understand and are converted to the truth of life."[27] By 1915, Geddes wrote of the need for "living imagination";[28] and in 1922, he asserted, "'Imagination' is not synonymous with fantastic or fantasy. It means the devising of ideal constructions from concepts, free from practical limitations."[29] By 1924, Bel Geddes had developed the motto "Imagination creates the actual,"[30] which became his guiding design principle. In his copy of Le Corbusier's *The City of To-morrow and Its Planning* (1929), Bel Geddes underlined the architect's axiom, "What gives our dreams their daring is that they can be realized," and which he rewrote below as "A dream is an idea to be translated into a reality."[31] The concept of the practical visionary allowed Bel Geddes to don numerous guises, whether mystical artist, pioneering modernist, ingenious Yankee, or man of tomorrow. *American Design Visionary* explores how such strategies helped Bel Geddes to sell his image to a diverse audience, including theater creatives, culture elites, industrial clients, and the public. Bel Geddes appealed to an audience fascinated by stories of technological prophecy and invention, placing himself in the pages of the nation's popular media alongside H. G. Wells, Thomas Edison, and Henry Ford, celebrated for their vision: their machine-age insights and technological triumphs.

Bel Geddes's canny promotion of his designs of stage sets, buildings, products, and world's fair exhibits was fundamental to the construction of his image as a logical and visionary figure. While Bel Geddes highlighted the rational aspects of his projects and persona, he understood the need to promote consumer fantasy. Thus, his designs were guided by efficiency and logic, vision and drama, and expressive and rational modernism. Significantly involved in design for theater, retail, world's fairs, advertising, and industrial manufacturing, Bel Geddes was uniquely positioned to interpret the values of America's developing consumer culture.

American Design Visionary contributes to design historical discourse and method. It provides an example of an archive-based study that recognizes its subjective construction, viewing the archive and its contents as a predetermined tool designed to promote its subject in a particular way.[32] In addition, the study recognizes the subjectivity of its author: the unavoidable bias of the historian. However, attempting to seek a modicum of objectivity the investigation uses a conceptual trope developed by Bel Geddes, the "practical visionary," as a lens to understand his designs and promotional rhetoric. This seemingly contradictory phrase was chosen for its frequency in the historical evidence. It is not imposed to create a set of binaristic oppositions, but employed to explore the fluidity across the conceptual terrain traversed by Bel Geddes. Finally, *American Design Visionary* is a historical study which recognizes change from the macro to the micro levels, from the influence of global economics to the changes in corporate strategy, to the evolving techniques of the design studio. Within these methodological constraints, *American Design Visionary* provides a unique perspective on Bel Geddes's life, designs, and self-promotion, observing his shifting career emphasis from advertising to theater to industrial design, analyzing how he combined these practices to promote his design office, the products of his clients, and his own visionary persona. This study evaluates the evolving appeal of design vision in the first half of the twentieth century, from the interwar period with its mystical attraction, to the economic depression when it promised escape, to the postwar era when consumerism and managerial design witnessed its decline.

1

Becoming a Practical Visionary: Bel Geddes's Youth and Early Career

During the period of Bel Geddes's youth and young adulthood, America developed from a producer to a consumer culture, according to historian T. J. Jackson Lears, "from a Protestant ethos of salvation through self-denial to a therapeutic ideal of self-fulfillment."[1] The country experienced a cultural shift from an emphasis on "character" to that of "personality," where "self-fulfillment, self-expression," and "self-gratification" took precedence over moral imperative and "sacrifice" to "a higher law."[2] With his interest in constructed identity and consumer desire, Bel Geddes was a significant participant in this transformation. Fundamental to this cultural shift were the late-nineteenth-century, quasi-religious movements of Mind-cure and Christian Science, with their emphasis on healing, self-development, and positive thought.[3] This change was accompanied by the tensions of two competing forces of modernism and antimodernism. The former clung to logic; the latter valued irrationality—two values Bel Geddes precariously juggled, writing: "through [the] life of this human these two vital forces [reason and instinct] would be in opposition."[4]

The roots of these tensions and the origins of Bel Geddes's practical vision can be traced to his family upbringing. Norman Melancton Geddes, born in 1893 in the small town of Adrian, Michigan, was the son of Clifton Terry Geddes and Flora Luella Yingling (Figure 1.1).[5] Norman's grandfather, Norman Geddes, was successively a professor, attorney, mayor of Adrian, Michigan, director of a bank and insurance company, and, for twenty-six years, President of the Board of Trustees of Adrian College.[6] His grandfather's numerous roles provided a significant model for Geddes in reshaping his own image, and brought the young boy into contact with prominent artistic, industrial, and scientific figures, an experience that eased his future interactions with artistic leaders and men of industry.[7]

FIGURE 1.1 Flora Luella Geddes, with sons Norman (right) and Dudley, in Newcomerstown, Ohio, *c*. 1900. Photograph by unidentified photographer. Harry Ransom Center, University of Texas, and the Edith Lutyens and Norman Bel Geddes Foundation, Inc. 2016.

Luella found success in teaching music, and shared her enthusiasm for art, music, and drama with her sons.[8] The family's conservative religious values, however, may have encouraged the young Norman to later explore alternative forms of belief.[9] In this way Geddes participated in what has been viewed as America's transformation from a Protestant culture of self-denial to a modernist one of self-fulfillment.[10] In 1901, tragedy struck the Geddes family; Clifton lost the family fortune in a financial panic, initiating his long slide into economic and personal failure. The family struggled as he moved from one unpromising job to another, working mostly as a salesman.[11] To make ends meet, the young Norman sold newspapers and his mother ran a boarding house.[12] Eventually, Norman's parents separated.[13] After the breakup and years of personal failure, Clifton Geddes committed suicide on June 22, 1908.[14] Luella nevertheless managed to hold the family together, and they soon moved to Newcomerstown, Pennsylvania, where Norman spent the rest of his childhood doing odd jobs, making miniature theaters, drawing, and painting.[15] While Clifton's professional experience introduced Norman to salesmanship at an early age, a skill he would develop in his own career, his financial failure added urgency to Geddes's entrepreneurial ambitions. Clifton's suicide must have had a profound effect on Norman, perhaps encouraging his interest in the comforting optimism of Mind-cure, and initiating a lifelong obsession with realizing his dreams, something his father was unable to achieve.[16] The loss of his father encouraged a paternal bond between Norman and his uncle Frederick L. Geddes, a wealthy Toledo, Ohio, lawyer whose industrial contacts formed Norman's first clients.

Norman's interest in transforming the material world and the self is evident in his boyhood scrapbook *c.* 1903, which reveals a fascination with art, fantasy, illusion, and play-acting, concerns that would endure throughout his creative life. He sketched "funny pictures and paintings"[17] and filled his scrapbook with images of circus performers, masked robbers, magicians, vaudevillians, and American Indians, the latter fueled by his friendship with the family's Native American stable boy, Will de Haw (Figure 1.2).[18] Snapshots from this period portray Geddes in various heroic poses with long hair and dressed in indigenous garb: on horseback and standing with his hands outstretched to the sky. Such romanticized images reveal a desire to attain a primitive and wild masculinity during a period of increased modernization.[19]

As a boy Geddes read children's fiction and numerous dime novels.[20] He was "enthralled" by *Gulliver's Travels*, *Alice in Wonderland*, *The Wonderful Wizard of Oz*, and *Twenty Thousand Leagues under the Sea*.[21] These stories dealt with transformation of space and individuals. *The Wonderful Wizard of Oz*, by theosophist L. Frank Baum, is understood as "perhaps the best-known mind-cure text ever written," with its pro-consumer perspective, echoes of spiritualist séances, and emphasis on incarnation.[22] In *Twenty Thousand Leagues under the Sea*, rather than offering an alternate reality, Verne focused on technology, predictive thinking, and progress, themes Geddes would build a career around. A fascination with exaggerated scale, the imagination, and fantastic technology would endure throughout his creative life.

After dropping out of high school Geddes was drawn to conjuring while working as bellboy on a Great Lakes steamer, where the magician Howard Thurston (1869–1936), "a vaudeville headliner," illusionist, and card trick specialist, encouraged him to join the profession. "Magic, sleight of hand, mind reading, had never interested me, until now."[23] The emphasis on thought control at the heart of much magic correlates with the mind-over-matter teaching of Christian Science. The power of the mind is central to both. Likewise, there is a distinct overlap between Spiritualism, with its links with séances and the occult, and magic, with its emphasis on hypnotism, telepathy, and

FIGURE 1.2 Photographs of a young Geddes dressed as a Native American. No date. Photograph by unidentified photographer. Harry Ransom Center, University of Texas, and the Edith Lutyens and Norman Bel Geddes Foundation, Inc. 2016.

levitation. Geddes's boyhood love of magic sowed the seeds of his more elaborate illusions in his stage designs and the Futurama. At age 14, Geddes would have been keenly aware of the celebrity status of magicians and vaudevillians, as stage magic blossomed during the golden age of vaudeville from the 1890s to the mid-1920s (Plate 2).[24] Thurston fascinated the young Geddes, who in 1913 began a professional tour of small Ohio towns as Zedsky the Boy Magician on the Sun Gus vaudeville circuit. Around this time Sun Gus operated a chain of eight theaters in the Midwest and East, the two leading ones were in Springfield and Hamilton, Ohio, where Geddes most likely performed.[25] During 1914–1915, he revisited the circuit and, with the blessing of his mother, performed as a vaudevillian, employing costumes, music, and monolog and developing several characters, including Bob Blake, Eccentric Comedian, and Little Willie Green (Figures 1.3 and 1.4).[26] By adopting a variety of monikers, Geddes performed an important trick of self-invention, changing from a fatherless Germano-Scot into an alluring entertainer and illusionist. While this was an important act of self-transformation, Geddes was a flop in both guises.[27] In changing his name and persona, he shared the vaudeville tradition of illusionist and escape artist Houdini, and the strongman Eugen Sandow, who remade their identities to gain wider appeal and escape the burdens of their immigrant past.[28] While his vaudevillian-era name changing was both temporary and tentative, Geddes would later alter his name permanently.

FIGURE 1.3 Geddes as Bob Blake, eccentric comedian playing Little Willie Green, *c.* 1914–1915. Harry Ransom Center, University of Texas, and the Edith Lutyens and Norman Bel Geddes Foundation, Inc. 2016.

FIGURE 1.4 Geddes as Zedsky, boy magician, *c.* 1909. Photograph by unidentified photographer ("Zetski the Magician" is written on the reverse). Harry Ransom Center, University of Texas, and the Edith Lutyens and Norman Bel Geddes Foundation, Inc. 2016.

During his design career, Bel Geddes associated the magician with the industrial designer, and explained that the "well-known business man ... looks upon the [industrial] artist with the same perplexed admiration ... as the small boy looks upon the vaudeville magician."[29] This view presented the industrial designer as both modern and antimodern, a trickster-technician who combined deception and invention. The magician, whose illusions encouraged both skepticism and belief, has been recognized as a key figure in the shaping of modern culture.[30] During a period when science and technology dispelled superstition, uncovered fraud, and provided important inventions, the allure of the magician persisted alongside the popularity of the practical man. As an industrial designer Bel Geddes would attempt to personify both.

Bel Geddes's self-creation is evident in his own autobiographical accounts where he presented himself as a restless and driven individual who followed his creative passions and whose success often depended on enabling father figures, not unlike the rags-to-riches characters who populated the story books of his youth. An oft-repeated chapter in the story of his life describes his fateful expulsion in 1907 from ninth grade in Newcomerstown for creating chalkboard caricatures of school staff.[31] In his posthumous autobiography of 1960, *Miracle in the Evening*, he described how the *Cleveland Plain Dealer* cartoonist James H. Donahey, who had a similar experience, took Norman under his wing, encouraging him to enroll at the Cleveland Institute of Art, where he studied drawing and its theory for three months in 1911. Although Geddes found the experience disagreeable, he learned to "analyze a subject ... by studying its inner workings, whether actual or theoretical; then ... draw these in their simplest combination."[32] This approach would guide his design method, which emphasized simple forms determined by inner structure. It was while at the Cleveland Institute of Art that he made friends with Thundercloud, a touring life-drawing model and native of the Blackfeet tribe. Apparently, Thundercloud was in great demand. In April 1913, he was photographed in a Toronto studio by the prolific local amateur M. O. Hammond, who considered him "a dandy model, bright, talkative, effusive and sympathetic," and posed him in a "[creation of] my own ... a squat and dropped head suggesting disconsolate old age," reinforcing the myth of the noble savage popular in Western art and photography.[33] Sponsored by the Field Museum of Natural History, Chicago, Geddes would spend three months in the summer of 1912 at the Lame Deer Reservation near Sheridan, Montana, learning Native American philosophy and history, and drawing impressionistic images of the Blackfeet on horseback, in ceremonies, and in portrait (Plate 3).

Geddes's project was part of wider ethnographic, though not unproblematic, effort to record the culture of Native Americans, including Walter McClintock's narrative account, *The Old North Trail, or Life, Legends and Religion of the Blackfeet Indians* (1910) and, perhaps, most notably, Edward S. Curtis's twenty-volume photogravure study, *The North American Indian* (1907–1930), which romantically, and often fictitiously, represented Native Americans of the West, including the Blackfeet, as a proud, primitive, people in decline. Curtis's photographs were widely reproduced for a general readership in magazines such as *Century* and *Scribner's* from 1898 onward and resulted in numerous related projects in the following decades, including popularizing books, a documentary film, exhibitions, and lectures (Figure 1.5).[34] It seems unlikely that Geddes would have escaped the influence of such cultural representations. With its chiaroscuro and soft focus effect, his chalk drawing of a "Siouan Type" is not dissimilar to Curtis's portrait photographs of the first decade of the twentieth century.[35] These and his activities reflect a fiercely antimodern longing for an imagined American past. In a significant act of identification, Geddes decorated his own tepee in the Blackfoot style, and wrote: "No previous three months of my life had ever meant so much to me or brought me greater satisfaction."[36] Through such activities he participated in the wider cultural project of representing Native Americans as stoic warriors, after the systematic decimation of their populations through the importation of new diseases, scorched-earth policy of villages and fields, and forced resettlement, resulting in a population decline from around 5 million in 1492 to 250,000 by 1900.[37] In early 1913, the white, middle-class Geddes described how he employed empathy to visualize his Blackfeet drawings:

I try to put myself in the same mood the Indian was in when he walked these grounds before me. I always wear moccasins because they are more comfortable and noiseless than civilized shoes. Possibly I am stalking up a ravine as would an Indian in search of game and come across a spring in the rocks. I see an imaginary Indian, dressed as I am, nude but for a breechcloth and

FIGURE 1.5 "The Eagle Medicine-Man, Apsaroke." Photograph by Edward S. Curtis, *c.* 1908, appeared in *The North American Indian (1907–1930).* Library of Congress, Prints and Photographs Division, Edward S. Curtis Collection (reproduction number, LC-USZ62-117711).

moccasins, a quiver slung over his back, his bow and arrow in hand, and he, too, is stopping to drink ... I stare at my vision a few seconds, then out comes my sketchbook, to transpose the picture, as it were.[38]

Geddes's "vision," however, was absent of suffering. This Romantic self-projection is not unlike the pseudo-mystical activities he would later encounter through his interests into séance and Theosophy, which held that spirits "of dead people hover over the earth and can be reached readily at séances and through mediums."[39] He continued to visualize a subject before drawing it. In a series of stage design courses he taught privately in the 1920s, he stressed the importance of "seeing a thing clearly and having your mind thoroughly made up before you begin your drawing."[40] Geddes's Blackfeet drawings and paintings, of which he claims to have produced around 1,200, would soon land him a job at Barnes Crosby, a Midwestern advertising illustration firm, and a few months at The School of the Art Institute of Chicago, and his Native American experience would inspire the design of one of his first plays, *Thunderbird* (1917).[41]

The Romantic longing to escape civilization and return to a natural and primitive existence was a recurrent impulse in the nineteenth and early twentieth centuries. One of the most vocal promoters of this tradition was Ernest Thompson Seton, who cofounded the boy scouting movement at the turn of the century with Robert Baden-Powell. Seton believed that everyone should spend one month a year outdoors. Established by Seton in 1902, the goal of the Woodcraft Indians was "to make a man."[42] In 1915, Geddes's little magazine of art and ideas, *InWhich*, published an article entitled "Simplicity," which provided a list of "modern day," "great men," including Ernest Thompson Seton, Henry Ford, Woodrow Wilson, and Augustus Rodin, perhaps suggesting Geddes's desire to learn from men of nature, industry, leadership, and art (Plate 4). As *InWhich* was produced to promote Geddes and reflect his ideas, the list suggests his desire to fuse the practical man and artist within himself.[43] Seton represented natural regeneration, while Ford was associated with industrial transformation. As a young man, the worlds of nature, art, and industry appealed to Geddes. He wrote, "everything about the woods interested me ... I have often thought that the only reason that I did not become a professional naturalist was my deeper interest in design and theatre."[44] Filming insects and reptiles would later become a passion. For him, perhaps the accord between nature, technology, and art lies in the analogy of progress, each seeming to conform to evolutionary laws.[45] He would later view streamlining from a Darwinian perspective, championing the teardrop as the most evolved of forms.[46]

Portraiture and advertising illustration

After January 1913, Geddes met the Norwegian neo-impressionist painter Henrik Lund (1879–1935) at the Art Institute of Chicago, and at the artist's request studied with him for three weeks in Lund's Chicago studio.[47] This would prove fundamental in Geddes's development as an artist and adherent of modernism. With his interest in the mechanics of thought, Geddes was drawn to Lund, whose portraits explored the character of their subjects with "psychological insight." Lund, the "leader of the young Norwegian painters,"[48] was considered a "virtuoso," and was influenced in his early years by the Norwegian Edvard Munch and later by the French Impressionist Edouard Manet.[49] Lund's painting, however, failed to achieve the emotional intensity and experimental daring of Munch, to whom Geddes was attracted and likely discovered while studying with Lund. Munch's work is known for its powerful psychological subject matter, its attempt to reveal the subconscious mechanisms of the artist's mind, and as a precursor to modernist art movements, including Expressionism and Surrealism.[50] While Geddes's notes from this period describe Lund's work as intuitive, informal, charming, and restrained, he also includes a list of some of Munch's most emotionally compelling paintings: "The Scream" (1893), "The Madonna" (1893), and "Angst" (1894), above which Geddes wrote, "Style characterized by simplicity. Psychological—symbolical … Emotional expression. Experimentor."[51]

Geddes considered his studies with Lund "the most serious month of my life"[52] and called him "the greatest teacher I ever had."[53] Lund introduced him to significant avant-garde concepts, encouraging him to experiment, simplify, and represent inner thought and feelings. Geddes would later apply these lessons to his modern stage designs. Soon he would pursue a short-lived career in portraiture and advertising illustration while simultaneously engaging his main passion—stage design.

Prior to 1913, Geddes briefly attended classes at the Art Institute of Chicago, which like America's other training grounds for aspiring illustrators and painters—the Pennsylvania Academy of Fine Art, the Art Students League, and the National Academy of Design—provided lessons in anatomy, drawing, painting, and composition.[54] After spending only a few months at The Art Institute of Chicago, Geddes followed Lund's suggestion and gave up art schools for good, studying instead at the morgue, the lessons of which, as he explained in his published autobiography, "were profound."[55] By the middle of 1913, Geddes had begun a meager sideline as a portrait artist, using his family network to secure clients, including Edward Drummond Libbey, founder of Libbey Glass Works, Ohio, and Nina Stevens, assistant director of the Toledo Museum, who paid him $5 for a drawing. He met Libbey, the founder and first president of the museum, through his uncle Frederick L. Geddes. Fred Geddes was also friends with the museum's director, George W. Stevens, who had originally recommended Norman as a student at The Art Institute of Chicago.[56] Fred Geddes would later introduce Norman to the automobile manufacturer Ray Graham of the Graham-Paige Company, one of the designer's first industrial clients.[57] In the summer of 1915, a pencil drawing of the contralto Ernestine Schumann-Heink, according to the National Cyclopedia of American Biography, "attracted praise." From 1915 to 1917, Geddes would continue to draw and paint portraits, including those of the Progressive politician and novelist, Brand Whitlock, and opera singer, Enrico Caruso.[58]

From around 1913 to 1916, Geddes worked in advertising and illustration around Chicago and Detroit, two of the most active advertising agency centers along with New York and, Philadelphia.[59] While simultaneously developing theatrical ideas, he worked for numerous commercial art companies that provided engraving services for the advertising industries, including the Barnes Crosby Company, the Peninsular Engraving Company, the commercial art firm, Apel-Campbell, and the publicity agency Thorson-Seelye, which he formed with several other young admen.[60] Though Bel Geddes became art director at Peninsular and General Manager at Barnes Crosby, Detroit, he spent much of his spare time writing plays and building stage models.[61] After 1914, he brought his mother and brother to Detroit.[62] During this period, his illustration assignments included lettering for the Sears, Roebuck & Company catalog, numerous posters for the Dodge Brothers, Continental Motors, Packard, Hupmobile, and others, covers, and advertisements which appeared in magazines ranging from The Saturday Evening Post to Collier's Weekly.[63]

Michele Helene Bogart in *Artists, Advertising, and the Borders of Art* pinpoints the explosive expansion of the US publishing industry, especially magazines and newspapers, along with improved printing technology such as the halftone process after the 1890s as a key period providing increased opportunities for American illustrators. Inexpensive popular magazines including *Collier's Weekly* (1888), *Ladies' Home Journal* (1884), *McClure's* (1893), and *Saturday Evening Post* (1897) provided a wealth of opportunities for aspiring illustrators. Pictures were a significant selling point for these and other profusely illustrated magazines, made possible largely by the halftone process that allowed for detailed reproduction of pencil marks and brush strokes, imparting an atmosphere of fantasy to the medium. By the turn of the century, illustrated mass market magazines such as the *Saturday Evening Post* and the *Ladies' Home Journal* had helped to establish illustration as a well-paid, "prestigious and high-profile form of art and an attractive career option." Both magazines depended on illustrated fiction to maintain their appeal and sales. Therefore, the practice of illustration became strongly associated with the visual interpretation of fiction writing. Contemporaneous critics who valued authorial authority and the reader's imagination complained that illustrations were a detriment to readers, distorting narratives and manipulating thought.[64] Bel Geddes would face similar accusations in this own work, especially his fantastic visions of the world of tomorrow which offered their own fictions of the future.

Although the editors of the *Post* and the *Ladies' Home Journal*, George Horace Lorimer and Edward William Bok, respectively, raised the national profiles of representational illustrators such as Maxfield Parrish, and others (Bogart, 1995: 24), Bel Geddes preferred European artists, especially poster artists such as Toulouse-Lautrec and Ludwig Hohlwein, whose work represented for him the ideal poster which could be read at a glance.[65] His work had more in common with Hohlwein, and was often characterized by abstracted representational imagery and flat fields of color (Plate 5). While Bel Geddes developed his career in illustration, his understanding of human psychology was informed by recent advertising theory, which reflected psychological discoveries and later proved essential in his manipulation of his theater and design audiences.[66]

Christian Science and Fordism

For Bel Geddes, the influence of disciplined thinking, the power of imagination, and the mechanics of the subconscious became guiding concerns during the 1910s and 1920s. "The matter absorbed a considerable amount of my thought at the time .... the fundamental aim of my life was the development of this inner spirit of expression."[67] During his advertising and theater period, Bel Geddes studied writing on the transformation of the self, others, and the material world, including texts on Christian Science and philosophy.[68] He owned many books by the founder of Christian Science, Mary Baker Eddy, including the founding text of the movement, *Science and Health: with a Key to the Scriptures*, a gift from his mother in late 1913, which he filled with copious notes and underlining. The Mind-cure doctrine of Christian Science provided Bel Geddes with an important set of beliefs to negotiate the challenges of modernity. Mind-cure followers rejected the more restrictive traditional religions in their search for a belief in accord with contemporary values of rationality, secularism, and commerce. With its emphasis on empiricism and faith, Christian Science taught that the practical and the visionary, the scientific and the metaphysical, were inextricably linked. The transformation of the self and the shaping of the mind and the body—the evolution of thought and the use of prayer in health—were key concerns of Christian Scientists.[69] Mind-cure, guided by the idea that individuals directed their own future and willed their own happiness and health, harmonized with Bel Geddes's notion of the practical visionary, whose optimistic forecasts of the world of tomorrow were rooted in science and commerce.[70] In *The Varieties of Religious Experience* (1902), the era's leading theorist of practical thought, philosopher William James, proclaimed that Mind-cure was America's "only decidedly original contribution to the systematic philosophy of life."[71] In his discussion of the American popularity and power of Mind-cure, he outlined its key features, including "idealism" and "progress," identifying its origins in the Four Gospels, American Transcendentalism, "Spiritism," "Hinduism," and "popular science evolutionism." However, he considered its most characteristic quality to be the "belief in the all-saving power of healthy-minded attitudes [...] in the conquering efficacy of courage, hope and trust, and a correlative contempt for doubt, fear, worry." It was this practical application of positive thought, especially to achieve physical healing, that most impressed James and related most strongly to his own notion of pragmatism.[72] In the first decade of the twentieth century, James popularized the philosophy of pragmatism, a doctrine that required philosophical inquiry to be understood in terms of experience (Suckiel, 1982: 5).[73] Bel Geddes would later define his notion of the practical visionary in pragmatic terms, not as the flights of unachievable dreams but making the imagined a reality, a personal philosophy he vigorously promoted throughout his career. Understandably, he immersed himself in the ideas of the American thinker and wrote that James "correspond[ed] more closely to my own viewpoint."[74]

Bel Geddes's mother practiced Christian Science since he was a boy, when he witnessed a "very moving and strange" series of events, including her use of prayer to heal his brother Dudley's leg.[75] Christian Science's emphasis on healing would have appealed to Bel Geddes. He suffered from debilitating "nervousness" in 1915 and high blood pressure and heart disease in his later years, eventually dying of a heart attack in 1958,[76] after his second wife, Frances Resor Waite, had fallen victim to tuberculosis in 1942. His first wife, Helen Belle Sneider, was an enthusiastic adherent of Eddy's and encouraged him to study her teachings. In a 1915 courtship letter to Norman, Belle explained, "We had a good many of the same interests, with Christian Science in common and the complete change of attitude that brings" (Figure 1.6).[77]

Bel Geddes's copy of *Science and Health* contained numerous underlined passages on positive thinking, controlling one's thoughts, and self-transformation, including Eddy's call to "Hold thought steadfastly to the enduring, the good, and the true and you will bring these into your experience proportionally to their occupancy of your thoughts."[78] Eddy viewed Christian Scientists as artists whose greatest achievement was the perfection of their own mind. "We are all sculptors, working at various forms, moulding and chiseling thought."[79] The idea of shaping the intellect into an ideal form would have appealed to Bel Geddes, who aimed to develop both a perfect mind and ideal designs. His later forays into streamlining illustrate his goal of achieving what he considered the ultimate form. The Christian Science emphasis on flexible identity and the influence of the mind would help him to shape his own image and to understand audiences, thus assisting his selling of a product or idea. The optimistic outlook at the root of Christian Science and its emphasis on truth, universality, and the realization of ideals guided his design ethos, while harmonizing with modernist tenets of utopianism, honesty and evolutionary theory.

Writing on both efficiency and Christian Science emphasized straight thinking and self-improvement. Bel Geddes's numerous books on efficiency in business and industry included

FIGURE 1.6 Geddes with paint set and Helen Belle Sneider with camera, *c.* 1915. Photograph by unidentified photographer. Harry Ransom Center, University of Texas, and the Edith Lutyens and Norman Bel Geddes Foundation, Inc. 2016.

Getting the Most Out of Business (1917), a Mind-cure text for the businessman, covering issues of clear thinking, efficiency, and foresight, and a well-thumbed copy of Henry Ford's *My Philosophy of Industry* (1929), in which he would find echoes of Mind-cure belief.[80] Bel Geddes underlined Ford's passage on the shaping of individuals and the importance of disciplined thought, which developed an analogy between the production of goods and the molding of people, "Just as a clean factory, clean tools, accurate gauges, and precise methods of manufacture produce a smooth-working, efficient machine, so clear thinking, clean living, square dealing make of an industrial or domestic life a successful one."[81] Efficiency and Mind-cure writing had overlapping, though divergent, emphases, focusing on efficient thought, evolutionary progress, self-transformation, and vision: whether clear thinking or accessing a higher plane of thought, trend prediction, or prophecy. It was this combination of the practical and the visionary that was a constant trope in Bel Geddes's intellectual pursuits.

InWhich magazine

Bel Geddes's canny skills of self-promotion and the influence of his recent studies were revealed in his little magazine *InWhich*, produced monthly by him and Helen Belle Sneider from June 1915 to November 1916.[82] Hundreds of little magazines proliferated across the United States after 1912. Normally short-lived, they were "designed to print artistic work which for reasons of commercial expediency [was] not acceptable to the money-minded periodicals or presses," appealed "to a limited group of intelligent readers," and "[came] into being for the purpose of attacking conventional modes of expression."[83] *InWhich* illustrated Geddes's belief in the interdependence of art and spirituality, the importance of vision in realizing one's dreams, and highlighted Norman and Belle's commitment to Mind-cure ideas and the avant-garde. The April 1916 issue of the magazine proclaimed: "*InWhich*—It believes in thots [*sic*], facts and common sense; It sympathizes with new movements; It wants simplicity,"[84] a philosophy in harmony with the proliferating little magazines of the period, such as the *Little Review* (1914–1929) and *The Dial* (1920–1929), which sought to publish the latest in avant-garde ideas and art.[85] The first issue of *InWhich* proclaimed its mission was "to bring the newest and best ideas in art to those who understand and are striving to realize its connection with life."[86] Despite these lofty aims, Geddes used the magazine primarily to promote himself as a newly fashioned visionary artist (Figure 1.7). In the sixteen-page magazine, he introduced his recently hyphenated name, Norman-Bel Geddes. This act of self-invention was in keeping with his other metamorphoses, whether as Zedsky the boy magician, a Blackfoot warrior, or Maq Yohaan, Geddes's Nietzschean alter ego, a mystic poet who inhabited the pages of *InWhich*. Such a figure is depicted surveying the horizon, sitting atop a mountain on the September 1915 cover of *InWhich*. The bird's-eye view was a recurring trope in the designer's work, whether in *InWhich*, the Airliner Number 4, or the Futurama or the title of his 1932 book, *Horizons* (see Plate 14).[87]

In search of a blueprint and philosophy for *InWhich*, Geddes and Sneider were drawn to the Arts and Crafts Movement, which, in its reaction to nineteenth-century industrialization, sought spiritual harmony through the production of handmade goods, the removal of boundaries between the arts, and the search for simplicity in life. In particular, Geddes looked to Elbert Hubbard's arts and crafts magazine, *The Philistine* (1895–1915). Hubbard was America's most visible Arts and Crafts Movement leader, head of the East Aurora, New York, crafts community the Roycrofters, which modeled itself on William Morris's Kelmscott group of artisans. Hubbard had also been an important advertising man, who had worked for hundreds of advertisers and wrote promotional material for retailers and national corporations.[88] Geddes may have seen something of himself in Hubbard, who was flamboyant and unabashed in his self-promotion. Hubbard's little magazine rejected Christianity and peddled the Roycrofters's publications and handcrafted goods, while promoting Hubbard as a visionary leader.[89] In the autumn of 1915, Geddes and Belle spent two weeks in East Aurora, including "church and dinner at the Roycroft."[90] Consistent with Arts and Crafts Movement values, Geddes appreciated creative endeavor that evidenced the role of the hand, including illustration, painting, and production of limited-edition magazines. Like many modernist designers, he would adapt arts and crafts ideals—including simplicity in form and decoration, honesty in materials, and design as a spiritual and improving force—to the sphere of machine production.[91] However, whereas Morris recommended, "Have nothing in your [*sic*] houses that you do not know to be useful, or believe to be beautiful," as a design consultant Bel Geddes would use such utilitarian rhetoric to promote stylistic obsolescence.[92]

InWhich was almost entirely the work of Geddes, as "Editor," and included poems and articles on art, philosophy, and theater, as well as his lithographic and pen and ink compositions. Belle acted as the "Associate Editor," contributed articles, and, as Geddes explained, was a

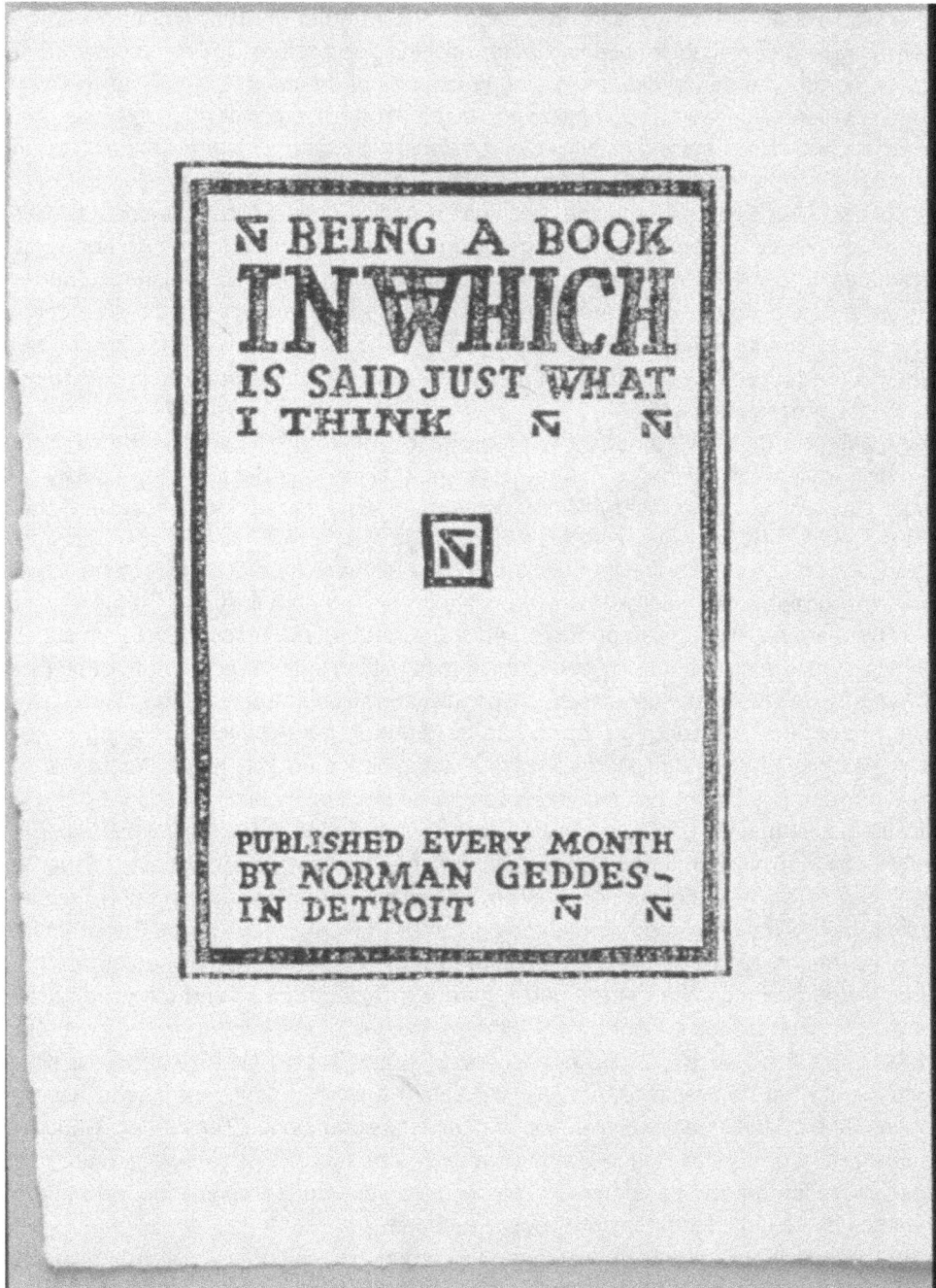

FIGURE 1.7 Page of *In Which* ("Being a book INWHICH is said just what I think") with NG monograms, *c.* 1915–1916. Harry Ransom Center, University of Texas, and the Edith Lutyens and Norman Bel Geddes Foundation, Inc. 2016.

necessary "literary" talent, without whom his own "ideas could not be carried out in a first-class way."[93] He would later continue to rely on collaborators, whether ghostwriters of his articles and books, or designers of his industrial and theater designs. His brother Dudley Geddes printed the magazine at home on a handpress, producing small runs of around 400. A key to the marketing of Geddes's personality was the magazine's distribution to prominent individuals from the spheres of art and commerce, including the renowned illustrator Edward Penfield; the retailer John Wannamaker; the editor of *The Masses* (1911–1917), a monthly little magazine of art and socialist politics, Max Eastman; and the wealthy theater dilettante Aline Barnsdall, who in 1916 gave Geddes an important break in his stage design career: she brought him to Los Angeles to stage productions for her Little Theater, offering him the post of scenic designer.[94] The range of recipients reflected the extent of his ambitions and is testimony to his skills of self-promotion. Later in his career, Bel Geddes would hone this public relations technique to perfection, strategically publishing his designs and ideas in articles, pamphlets, and books and sending copies to potential clients and influential supporters.

Geddes believed that the "most unique feature" of *InWhich* "is that it is personal. Being a book in which I say what I think ... it is the only book where one person rules—bodily puts his own personality." He explained that *InWhich* presently had no competition because of the death of Elbert Hubbard, who perished with his wife Alice in the 1915 sinking of the *Lusitania*, after which the Roycroft community fell into decline: "We even have it on the Roycrofters now and to prove how much bigger [sic] element a personality is than an organization, just look at the time the Roycrofters are having to keep on their feet."[95] Geddes's quote recognizes the importance of personality (or what might be termed celebrity) in maintaining an enterprise, promoting ideas and selling products. He would later develop both a popular and saleable personality and an organization that could promote it. The seeds of which can be found in his *InWhich* publishing project. His interest in personality extended to many of the self-made men and heroic figures of his era. He owned numerous biographical and autobiographical studies, including Hubbard's accounts of important historical figures (*Little Journeys*), Henry Ford's philosophy of industry, and Theodore Roosevelt's story of his transformation from a frail boy into a figure of vitality. Other studies included those of Michelangelo, William Penn, and Vladimir Lenin, who, like Bel Geddes, had renamed himself.[96] Geddes's interest in autobiographies of Frank Lloyd Wright, Benjamin Franklin, and Henry Adams, in particular, may have inspired his own lengthy unpublished autobiography.[97] Geddes collected clippings on different public figures including Edison and the adventure writer, Jack London, whose stories provided masculine messages of self-growth in the crucible of the wilderness.[98] Underscored passages in his copy of *Michelangelo* (1915) suggest a significant identification with the Renaissance man, as well as a refusal of artistic restrictions, according to the Christian Science belief in the dissolution of conceptual boundaries. They reflect Geddes's own traits, a desire for control, unbounded creative energy, and a belief in his own genius.[99] For him, these men represented self-transformation, as well as adventure, imagination, and ingenuity— characteristics he would adopt in his own public persona.

Geddes's fascination with historical and contemporary celebrity is consistent with the increased emphasis on personality in America in the early twentieth century. After the first decade of the century, the notion of the movie star emerged along with the industry of celebrity.[100] The management of persona as a means of shaping public perception would be famously scrutinized in *Public Opinion*, 1922, by Walter Lippmann, who wrote of "stage-manage[d]," "constructed personalities," "Great men ... known to the public only through a fictitious personality," resulting in "at least two distinct selves, the public and ... the private."[101] In a letter to *InWhich* business manager, Jacob Weitz, Geddes fashioned himself as a manufactured celebrity designed for public consumption. "By personal I mean this. Keeping Norman Geddes, who ever he is, in the book all the time. Make him felt. Keep it published by Norman Geddes instead of published by the InWhich publishing Co [*sic*] or words to that effect." The inner cover of each copy of *InWhich* read: "BEING A BOOK INWHICH IS SAID WHAT I THINK. PUBLISHED EVERY MONTH BY NORMAN GEDDES."[102] The phrase "who ever he is" suggests that Geddes was still constructing his evolving public persona. The first issue of June 1915 prominently presented a portrait of Norman Geddes with the title: "Poster portrait of himself by himself."[103] His carefully crafted personality would remain a fundamental aspect of his design organization throughout his career.

The construction of Geddes's alter ego, Maq Yohaan, is a remarkable example of a self-made historical celebrity. The January 1916 issue of *InWhich* projected Geddes into a spiritual and creative pantheon of the "great men ... Jesus of Nazareth, Beethoven, Martin Luther, Michael Angelo, Maq Yohaan, [and] Thomas Edison."[104] The true identity of Yohaan is revealed in his unpublished love poem to Belle signed "Maq Yohaan." In the margin, he scrawled: "I'll bet you'll like this better now. I wrote it on the typewriter [the] same day I wrote it in [the] letter to you."[105] There are numerous parallels between him and his alter ego, including an inflated sense of self, a love of imagination and clear thinking, an adherence to Christian Science, and an embrace of foresight and utility.[106] Geddes owned numerous books by Nietzsche, including *Thus Spake Zarathustra, A Book for All and None* (1911),[107] whose protagonist, like Yohaan, pondered the nature of humankind from his mountain view. Geddes wrote of the German philosopher's influence on his intellectual development and recommended his writings in *InWhich* in 1916.[108] Nietzsche has been widely recognized as a fundamental influence on modernism and pioneer modernist designers, especially Bruno Taut, Erich Mendelsohn, and Le Corbusier.[109] Geddes would adopt Nietzsche's visionary perspective and his emphasis on the transformation of the self and the world.[110]

While Geddes fashioned a singular identity for public consumption, he understood himself and his fiancé as an integrated personality. Following the Christian Science view of the unification of the feminine and the masculine, he considered their thoughts and identity one and the same.[111] In March 1915, Belle told Norman, "Until I met you and loved you, I never realized that one person can be a continuation of another and [a] really vital part."[112] The following year, in the weeks before their marriage, Geddes wrote:[113]

> You and I are going into life together .... socially—businessly [*sic*]—that is, with all we have ... Everything together—our love—our work .... No one can give credit to one of us with out [*sic*] the other—no one will know which of us did a certain thing ... —we both did it—it was done by Norman–Bel Geddes! That name will mean a fortune some day.[114]

An article entitled "Norman-Bel Geddes" introduced the April 1916 issue of *InWhich* and told of Norman and Belle's newly unified existence. "So now there is no Norman Geddes or Bel [*sic*] Sneider. Where you find one you find the other what one thinks the other usually does and always tolerates. They use the hyphen as an equal sign and will be known in the future as Norman-Bel Geddes."[115] Geddes would later drop the hyphen and prefer Bel Geddes.[116]

While Christian Science guided the union of Belle and Norman, its emphasis on science, faith, evolution, and universality informed Geddes's views of art. *InWhich* outlined an "evolution[ary]" artistic "process" where "certain effects take place in what we term 'matter' in response to spiritual stimuli." At the "moment of conception and creation the artist is one with the universal power."[117] The passage suggests that imagined ideals had a spiritual source. Invoking a larger mystical reality, in 1915 *InWhich* summarized a number of Geddes's key concerns.

> All great action is the act of dreams. The dreamer ... has dreamed himself into a maker of empire, an explorer, a composer, a sculptor. His dream is the spirit of possibility,—living imagination .... He goes from himself to a larger self, to the reality of a universal dream ... Our dreamers show a universe, a world of essentials, which turn to One.[118]

Geddes's copy of *Art for Life's Sake* (1913), a manifesto on the integration of art and life, by the prolific art critic and early supporter of European modernism, Charles Henry Caffin (1854–1918), may have inspired this approach, and perhaps laid the foundation for Geddes's belief in visionary thought. Caffin hoped to synthesize "Religion, Morality and Art" to achieve "the universal," and he believed that society could only be improved by a "dreamer"—a "practical man ... who has the vision of the idealist," "the faculty of intuition," and "prevision."[119]

Having announced his name change in April 1916 Bel Geddes would soon transfer his mystical views of life and art from the page to the stage. The last issue of *InWhich* appeared in November 1916. The magazine's staff felt that *InWhich* had achieved its primary goal, to promote Geddes.[120] Dudley Geddes had embarked upon a newspaper career, while Norman focused on his theatrical work. His obsession with "living imagination" may have reflected a greater desire to realize his theatrical goals. He would soon be given the chance to do just that. After being reprimanded by his Barnes Crosby employers for devoting too much time to his theater projects, Norman was given an ultimatum: he had twenty-four hours to choose between his job in posters and his career in theater.[121] He chose theater.

Bel Geddes then began a journey to Los Angeles where he hoped to stage *Thunderbird*, which had been purchased by Barnsdall. Frank Lloyd Wright had been working with Barnsdall on a plan for her Little Theater complex in Los Angeles, and by 1916 Bel Geddes had convinced Barnsdall to let him design its stage, thus engineering a significant opportunity to work with America's leading modernist architect.[122] Despite his lack of an architectural license, he was keen to engage in architectural design for Barnsdall and perhaps a collaboration with Wright. On his way to Los Angeles, he briefly met with Wright, but only discussed Wright's work and ultimately abandoned any collaboration.[123] Bel Geddes claimed, however, he was able to design and build the Children's Theater for the Little Theater.[124] He later considered Wright's theater for Barnsdall impractical, lacking in "flexibility," and overly dependent on "style," pointedly complaining this was "due to the architect's refusal to consider other viewpoints than his own."[125] Bel Geddes claimed that Wright innocently stole his theater design ideas, which the architect had probably learned from Barnsdall.[126]

In the end, *Thunderbird* was not produced, in part because of Bel Geddes's overly ambitious designs, the scale being too large for Barnsdall's Little Theater.[127] Despite his tendency for impractical and grand schemes, Barnsdall was impressed by his talent and hired him for two years to develop scenery, costumes, and lighting for eight plays. In the spring of 1917, the Los Angeles

Little Theater was discontinued, leaving him without any work. He soon found employment in California's nascent film industry, where he wrote and directed the patriotic, historical film *Nathan Hale* for the Universal Film Company, which, characteristically, he claimed was a first—a motion picture without subtitles.[128] The film, however, was a flop.[129] He described his experience in the "movie field" as a "fiasco."[130] Despite having a family to support, he left Universal after only six weeks.[131] Bel Geddes would, nonetheless, continue his interest in film. After 1926, as an amateur moviemaker he claimed he shot and produced over one million feet of film, including comedic skits in which he starred, compositions with theater personalities, and numerous studies of traffic, theater, reptiles, and insects. He even filmed "Helen of Troy" (1926) with ants as actors, fusing his love of nature and design.[132] Despite being offered a "position of director" of a permanent company to do "experimental productions," Norman would soon leave for New York to pursue an immensely successful career in stage design marked by innovative, large-scale productions. This would be followed by an even-more ambitious adventure in industrial and architectural design.[133]

Bel Geddes's early years as an entertainer, portrait painter, commercial artist, and publisher illustrate both the scope and scale of his personal and professional ambitions. His numerous guises manifested a modernist sensibility, an ease with self-making and a refusal of artistic boundaries. During his *InWhich* period, he became fascinated by the mechanics of the mind and the realization of dreams. As a young man, his intellectual journey ranged from the philosophy of industry to the metaphysics of artistic creation, exemplifying a continuing interest in reason and intuition. In his efforts to harness his imagination and stimulate audiences, his intellectual pursuits led him to Theosophy, psychoanalysis, and the socialism of soviet Russia. As he entered the worlds of theatrical, architectural, and industrial design, he combined his knowledge of creativity and psychology to stimulate the thoughts and feelings of both theatergoers and consumers.

2

Transforming Audiences: Stage Design to Industrial Design

Bel Geddes hoped to transform consumers of theatrical, commercial, and architectural design by breaking down barriers between audiences and actors, workers and the bourgeoisie, and the purchaser and the product. As a designer he aimed to create objects and environments that would stir the emotions of theatergoers, shoppers, and users of buildings. Spaces and spectacles conducive to psychological or political transformation, Bel Geddes believed, might promote the purchase of a product or the embrace of an ideology. Extending the philosophical trajectory established in *InWhich*, this design approach reflected the tendencies of the New Stagecraft, Bel Geddes's interests in socialism, mysticism, and commercial enterprise, and the widely held view that design could alleviate a machine-age spiritual malaise.[1]

In the summer of 1917, a pivotal and oft-repeated chapter in the story of Bel Geddes's life unfolded. While sitting on a Los Angeles park bench, he noticed a copy of the *Literary Digest*. The wind blew the pages to the headline, "Millionaires Should Help Young Artists," an interview with the influential New York investment banker and patron of the arts Otto Kahn. He quickly spent most of his last few dollars on a telegram to Kahn, requesting a $400 loan to travel to New York to find work as a stage designer. As he recounted it, Kahn was impressed by the young designer, and telegraphed the money the same day.[2] A few months later Bel Geddes was in New York and Kahn soon recommended him to the Metropolitan Opera Company, where Kahn played a guiding role. Bel Geddes soon began designing his first operas, quickly developing a reputation as a talented theatrical designer. Over the next decade he would become one of America's leading and most ambitious stage designers, often creating prodigious and hugely expensive theatrical productions. From 1916 to 1942, Bel Geddes designed over seventy productions, including *The Miracle* (1924), *Jeanne d'Arc* (1925), *Lysistrata* (1930), and *Dead*

End (1935) His pioneering work significantly contributed to the New Stagecraft movement in America.[3] His successful stage design career and gregarious nature thrust him into New York's café society where he met many of the nation's intellectuals, artists, and celebrities. It was here that Bel Geddes would develop and maintain significant friendships with the influential theater commentator Sheldon Cheney, the German "expressionist" architect Erich Mendelsohn, who was visiting the United States in 1924 for research and to develop business contacts, and theosophist and designer Claude Bragdon, whom he met in 1921 and whose ideas perhaps accorded most strongly with his during the first half of the 1920s.[4] Despite Bel Geddes's efforts to paint himself as a self-made man, it was often through these social connections, along with family networks, that he developed his ideas and found business opportunities. His design ethos was increasingly shaped by New York's dynamic intellectual milieu, where he and his contemporaries explored mysticism, modernism, Marxism, and psychoanalysis, understanding the release of repressed feelings and access to alternative realities as an essential aspect of modernity.[5]

Bel Geddes's knowledge of Theosophy, psychology, and advertising

An insatiable intellectual magpie, Bel Geddes's knowledge of the mind and design was shaped by discussions with friends and a growing library, which included numerous texts on psychology, salesmanship, the occult, and architecture. Many of the authors read by Bel Geddes freely mixed psychology and design, such as the influential delineator of visionary architecture and adherent of Theosophy, Hugh Ferriss, whose *The Metropolis of Tomorrow*, 1929, called for "psychological" architecture;[6] and Egmont Arens and Roy Sheldon, whose *Consumer Engineering: a New Technique for Prosperity*, 1932, encouraged the combination of psychology and salesmanship.[7] Ferriss's book depicted luminous visionary cityscapes, including pedestrianized walkways above streets of traffic, a concept that would become key to Bel Geddes's models of cities (Figure 2.1). His understanding of the mechanics of the mind and spirit was greatly informed by his many books by Claude Fayette Bragdon (1866–1949). Bragdon, who considered the parabola a static and ideal form, may also have influenced his appreciation of streamlined design.[8] At a time when many modernists in Europe and America were exploring alternative belief systems, Bragdon combined ideas from Theosophy, Spiritualism, psychology, and fourth-dimensional mathematics to encourage the spectator's "ecstatic" experience, a life-altering and intense feeling of mystical absorption and rapturous transcendence.[9] Bragdon was an architect and a set designer, and wrote numerous books on Theosophy (Figure 2.2). The religious philosophy founded by Helena P. Blavatsky (1875) synthesized Darwinian, Christian, Confucian, Buddhist, and Hindu beliefs among others and scientific thought, and was concerned with inner evolution, karma, and reincarnation, proven concerns of Bel Geddes, who in the mid-1910s had purchased copies of the *Ramayana*, an ancient South Asian epic poem, and the *Mahabharata*, an Indian religious epic.[10] Bragdon's primary goal was to facilitate access to a higher consciousness, or fourth dimension, through the evolution of the self.[11] Bel Geddes was keenly aware of this project, and in his copy of Bragdon's

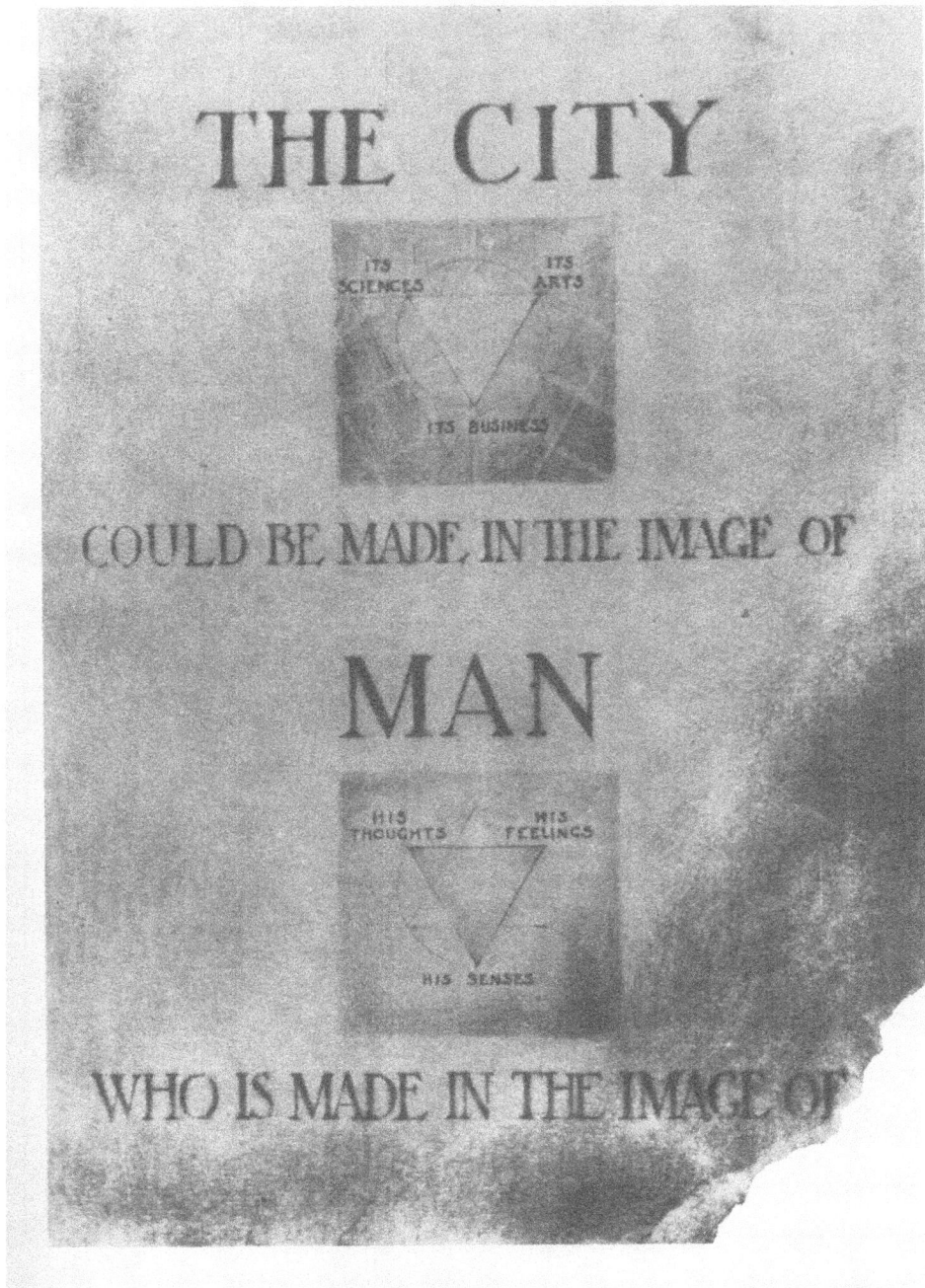

THE CITY

ITS SCIENCES   ITS ARTS

ITS BUSINESS

COULD BE MADE IN THE IMAGE OF

MAN

HIS THOUGHTS   HIS FEELINGS

HIS SENSES

WHO IS MADE IN THE IMAGE OF

FIGURE 2.1 Final page of Hugh Ferriss's, *The Metropolis of Tomorrow*, 1929. © Christopher M. Leich 2016.

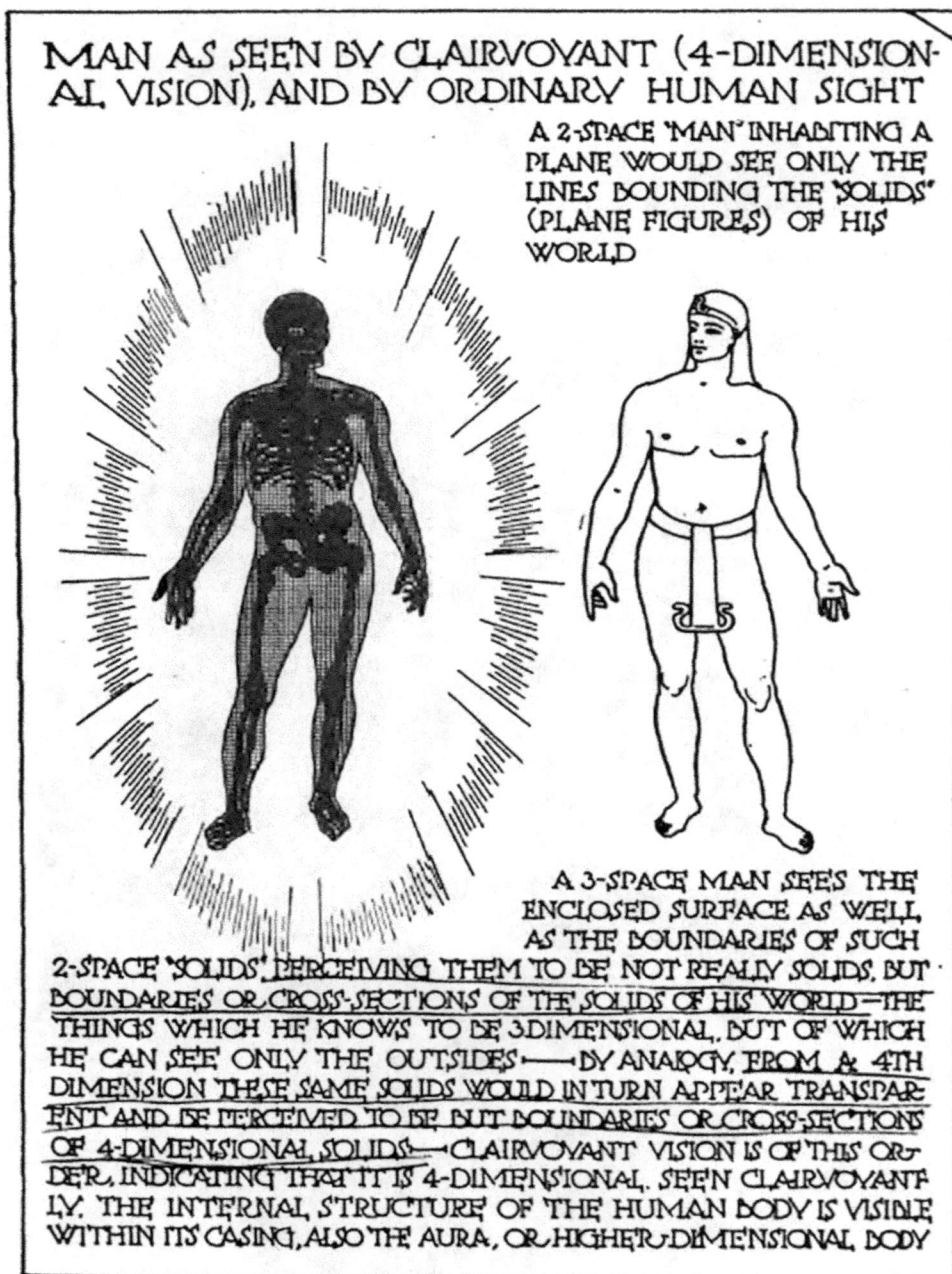

MAN AS SEEN BY CLAIRVOYANT (4-DIMENSION-AL VISION), AND BY ORDINARY HUMAN SIGHT

A 2-SPACE 'MAN' INHABITING A PLANE WOULD SEE ONLY THE LINES BOUNDING THE 'SOLIDS' (PLANE FIGURES) OF HIS WORLD

A 3-SPACE MAN SEES THE ENCLOSED SURFACE AS WELL AS THE BOUNDARIES OF SUCH 2-SPACE 'SOLIDS', PERCEIVING THEM TO BE NOT REALLY SOLIDS, BUT BOUNDARIES OR CROSS-SECTIONS OF THE SOLIDS OF HIS WORLD—THE THINGS WHICH HE KNOWS TO BE 3-DIMENSIONAL, BUT OF WHICH HE CAN SEE ONLY THE OUTSIDES——BY ANALOGY, FROM A 4TH DIMENSION THESE SAME SOLIDS WOULD IN TURN APPEAR TRANSPARENT AND BE PERCEIVED TO BE BUT BOUNDARIES OR CROSS-SECTIONS OF 4-DIMENSIONAL SOLIDS—CLAIRVOYANT VISION IS OF THIS ORDER, INDICATING THAT IT IS 4-DIMENSIONAL. SEEN CLAIRVOYANTLY, THE INTERNAL STRUCTURE OF THE HUMAN BODY IS VISIBLE WITHIN ITS CASING, ALSO THE AURA, OR HIGHER-DIMENSIONAL BODY

PLATE 19

FIGURE 2.2 "Man as Seen by Clairvoyant," an illustration in *A Primer of Higher Space (The Fourth Dimension)*, by Claude Bragdon, Manas Press, 1913. Courtesy of the Department of Rare Books, Special Collections and Preservation, University of Rochester River Campus Libraries.

A Primer of Higher Space (the Fourth Dimension), 1913, underlined the passage, "the whole evolutionary process consists in the conquest, dimension by dimension, of successive space-worlds."[12]

Before 1913, the Russian journalist and occult writer Peter Demianovich Ouspensky (1878–1947) read Claude Bragdon's *Man the Square* (1912), a theosophical parable on attaining higher spiritual consciousness. Ouspensky then republished his 1911 edition of *Tertium Organum* in 1915, which Bragdon discovered in 1918 and with Nicholas Bessaraboff translated into English in 1920.[13] In the late 1920s, Bel Geddes would advise his theater design course students to read Ouspensky's book. A mystic with an abiding interest in the fourth dimension, Theosophy, psychology, and Eastern religions, Ouspensky believed that humans could enlarge their consciousness to create a new state of awareness and thus be receptive to higher dimensional spaces, for example the fourth dimension.[14] Perception of the fourth dimension, Ouspensky insisted, could be developed through intuitive capability combined with an emotional element that Ouspensky identified most strongly with the sensitivity of the artist.[15] He saw this as an evolutionary stage in humankind. Writing in *Tertium Organum*, Ouspensky explained how only highly evolved individuals could perceive the hidden world ("noumenon") in the real world ("phenomenon"):

> Only that fine apparatus which is called the soul of the artist can understand and feel the reflection of the noumenon in the phenomenon. In art it is necessary to study "occultism"—the hidden side of life. The artist must be a clairvoyant: he must see that which others do not see; he must be a magician: must possess the power to make others see that which they do not themselves see, but which he does see.[16]

The notion of fine-tuning artistic perception to "see" beyond reality is consistent with Bel Geddes's interests in magic, clairvoyance, and psychology and may have encouraged him to master the practice of foresight and develop his role as a design visionary. As with Christian Science, and the disciplined thinking promoted by Henry Ford, the mind was central to Theosophy in its emphasis on developing one's "consciousness," as Blavatsky termed it, in a spiritual evolution. In addition to Bragdon's work, Bel Geddes possessed *Man Visible and Invisible: Examples of Different Types of Men as Seen by Means of Trained Clairvoyance* (1920), by the prolific publisher of theosophical books, C. W. Leadbetter.[17] Leadbetter coauthored *Thought Forms* (1905) with one of the leaders of Theosophy, Annie Besant. The book, illustrated with Leadbetter's colorful nonfigurative compositions representing different states of mind, is considered a significant influence on the development of modernist abstract art.[18] Like *Tertium Organum* both books emphasized seeing the "hidden side of life" (Plates 6–8). Having fully absorbed a range of alternative philosophies of perception, by 1927 Bel Geddes proclaimed [in his stage design courses] that potent art should originate from an "undefinable" [*sic*] inner source, a view he had outlined in *In Which* nearly ten years earlier, alternately referring to this source as "spirit," "God," and the "fourth dimension."[19] In 1929, Bel Geddes expressed his view that emotional drama was a necessary aid for traveling beyond ordinary experience, an idea consistent with expressionist theater and the writings of Ouspensky, Bragdon, and Freud.[20] Bel Geddes wrote, "What the theater needs is drama, not tricks. It needs minds capable of penetrating through the surface of life to its soul and giving out this expression."[21]

Theater Number 6: Merging the audience and actors

In 1928, Cheney wrote that recent avant-garde theater emphasized the unity of theatrical elements in order to achieve the "highest emotional intensity" for its audience. Cheney was the critic most responsible for giving impetus in America to the New Stagecraft, the reform trend inspired by European theater visionaries Craig and Adolphe Appia, who led a revolt against the tradition of painted and artificial scenery of the naturalists.[22] Lee Simonson, Robert Edmond Jones, and Bel Geddes dominated the new tendency in American theater which emphasized visual design, "simplified realism," a more unified theatrical space between the actors and the audience, and the integration of theatrical elements, including lighting, staging, and movement.[23] This unified approach demanded one interpretation and one interpreter whose aim was to express the primary mood or metaphor of the play.[24] This holistic approach to theater design was influenced by Richard Wagner, who promoted the idea of *Gesamtkunstwerk* or "total work of art" which aesthetically unified the various elements of a theatrical production.[25] Bel Geddes initially learned of the European trend through a visit to New York around 1915, where he viewed the German theatrical producer Max Reinhardt's spectacle-pantomime *Sumurum*, a revelation that seemed to confirm his nascent theater ideas.[26] About the same time, he purchased Hiram Kelly Moderwell's *The Theater of Today*, originally published in 1914, which introduced him to the Modern Movement in European theater. Bel Geddes was so excited by the book that he wrote to the author, who invited him to lunch and told him of Robert Edmond Jones, who soon became Bel Geddes's theatrical collaborator.[27] As an industrial designer Bel Geddes would later apply his knowledge of modernist theater, including the emphasis on organic unity, originality, abstraction, and simplification, to the designs of products, interiors, exhibits, and theaters.

Throughout his career Bel Geddes was involved in the design of dozens of theaters, whether collaboratively or as the sole designer.[28] After 1915 his designs were published and exhibited around the globe, garnering him considerable notoriety. Although it was unusual for theatrical scenographers to design the architecture of theaters, such boundary breaking was consistent with his holistic approach to design (Plate 9). Bel Geddes first presented his plans for Theater Number 6 in *InWhich* in 1915, refining the design by 1922, where it was promoted in Bragdon's article, "Towards a New Theatre" for the *Architectural Record*. The article employed urgent mystical prose to lavish praise on Bel Geddes, whose combined use of light, color, movement, and architecture would, Bragdon proclaimed, release "great primal orgiastic tides of thought and feeling," something Bragdon believed was "the very *raison d'être*" of ancient Greek theater and had since been lost to contemporary audiences.[29] Bel Geddes echoed Bragdon's views in his prophetic design monograph of 1932, *Horizons*, suggesting that a new and intense form of theater would "spiritually" awaken America's masses in the same way that Russian theater had provided a "relief for the pent-up emotional capacity" of its mass audience.[30]

Designed to remove any physical barriers between audience and actors, and thus encourage an emotional viewing experience, Theater Number 6 has been recognized as an early and influential example of the New Stagecraft (Figure 2.3). The 100-foot square plan contained a quarter circle stage centered on the diagonal of the plot. A flight of stairs ran the full length of the front of the stage, allowing contact between the audience and actors. The removal of balconies and boxes provided increased space for extra seating, while diminishing spatial and, by extension, class boundaries.[31] Sharing similarities with the Classical Greek stage, seating was along arced rows which were uninterrupted by transverse aisles. Audiences accessed their seats via the sides along the arcing longitudinal path created by the four and one-half feet spaces between each seat. In his article Bragdon was clearly aware that excluding transverse aisles may have ignored existing building laws, but argued that each longitudinal tier was essentially its own aisle, thus multiplying the access exits. The interior dome, which spanned both the auditorium and the surround behind the stage, was designed to receive dramatic light projections, including "mobile color" from the back of the auditorium and "sky effects" from a "lighting pit" behind and below the stage, thus intensifying the mood of the play.[32] Hydraulic platforms below the stage allowed for the movement

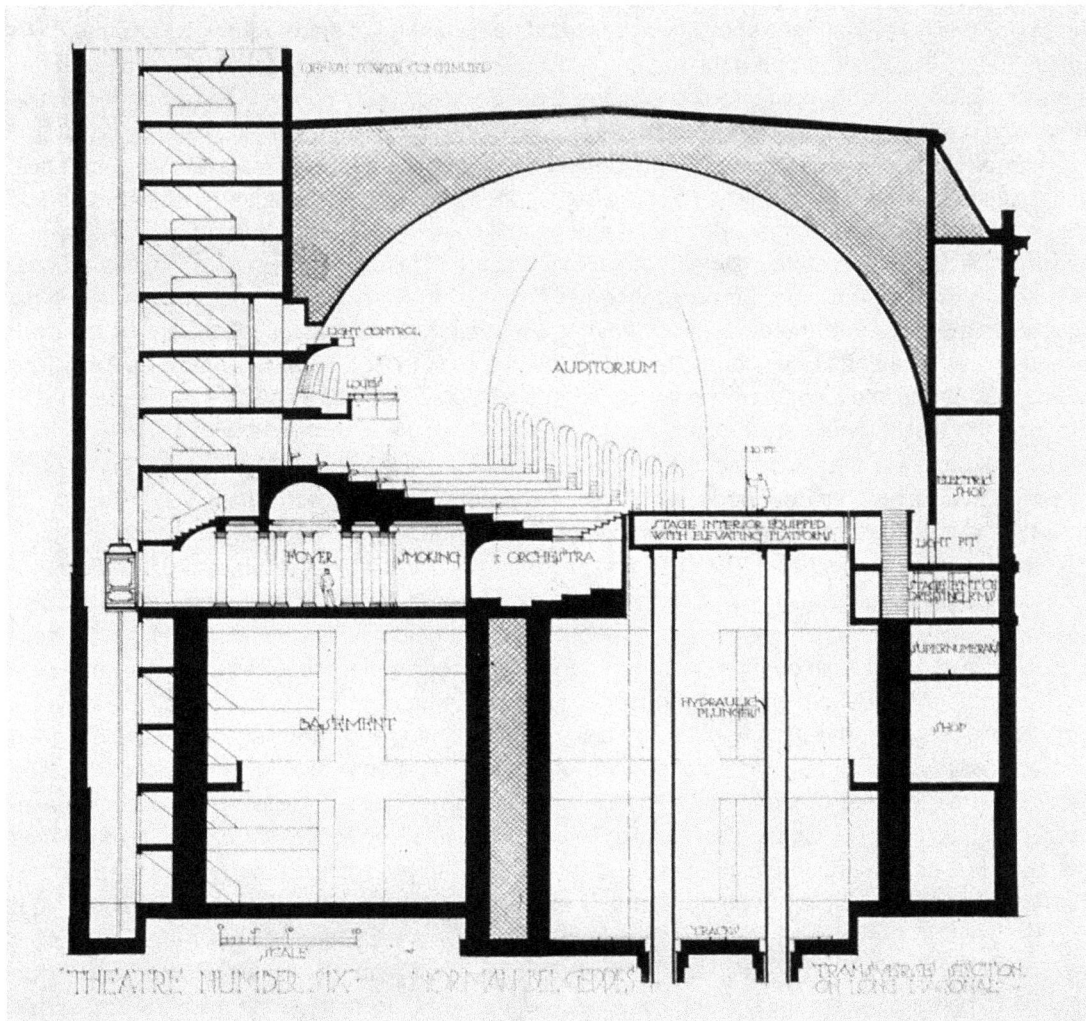

FIGURE 2.3 Cutaway view of Theater Number 6, *c.* 1922. Harry Ransom Center, University of Texas, and the Edith Lutyens and Norman Bel Geddes Foundation, Inc. 2016.

of stage elements between scenes, while removing the need for the usual tangle of ropes, crowding of curtains, and other appurtenances.

The plan synthesized many of Bel Geddes's key theatrical ideas, including the rejection of the traditional proscenium arch to integrate the audience and the actors, the projection of illumination from behind the audience for noninvasive, expressive effects, and hydraulic stages for seamless scenery changes. The theater historian Ian Mackintosh, however, has described Bel Geddes's theater plans as "breathtakingly beautiful but insanely impractical," noting that the acoustics of the huge dome would have made it impossible for the audience to hear the performance. [33] Bel Geddes has been recognized as a pioneer of stage lighting practice and theory. He claimed to have originated the use of 1,000-watt spotlights outside and above the proscenium. However, it is most likely that around 1914–1915, a time when problematic and intensely hot, sputtering arc lamps dominated,[34] his use of the 1,000-watt lens spotlight mirrored that of a handful of stage lighting innovators.[35] His lighting seems to reflect Appia's theories regarding light as a mood enhancer and a tool to define the three-dimensionality of actors and settings.[36] Bel Geddes would continue to rely on innovative lighting to create dramatic effects in his models, interiors, window displays, and exhibits.

Theater Number 6 may have been influenced by Bragdon's theosophical view of aesthetics, especially the unification of light and color. Bel Geddes owned Bragdon's book *Architecture and Democracy*, 1918, in which the theosophist argued that color, light, and movement had spiritual and healing effects.[37] The resulting synesthetic experience, the fusing of one's sensory perceptions, was key to Bragdon's project for an intense new form of theater. Bragdon understood theatrical lighting as a doorway to the dimension "beyond the tyranny of appearances" where he believed all human consciousness was connected.[38] "With light, as with God … 'all things are possible.' The drama may unfold itself, not in two, but in all dimensions, unrestricted by any confining boundary."[39] Bragdon felt that the new architecture and the new theater, through their emphasis on color and light, would express the "unconscious symbolization" of civilization's search for a "spiritual light."[40]

Bragdon believed that Bel Geddes's designs of Theater Number 6 illustrated the ability of light to act as an "emotional language, like music, with power to induce and maintain moods of the soul."[41] He was not alone in this belief. The critic and press agent Oliver M. Sayler praised Bel Geddes for "reaching out through metaphysical channels to a theater with deeper, more compelling emotional power."[42] Bel Geddes's stage design contemporaries, including Simonson, Jones, and Henry Dreyfuss, supported such a view and believed that projected scenery resulted in a mystical aura.[43] In his *Architectural Record* article, Bragdon wrote that the nearest things to such a theater were "the revival meeting, the prize fight, or the ball game," religious and commercial spheres Bragdon believed were only partially able to provide an intense response, albeit "perilously" "poised between creation and destruction, diabolism and ecstasy" (182). Revealing his knowledge of psychoanalytic theory, Bragdon claimed that Bel Geddes's theater would direct repressed feelings into outlets of creativity and inspiration, and wrote that the traumatic "psychic sublimations" of the First World War soldiers would eventually explode like the "great religious renewals of time past" (50, 57). "These great forces [repressed feelings] … are destined to re-enter life either in the shape of mob-violence—as a result of repression—or through inspiration to creative effort, if they find a prepared and natural channel such as theatre" (182). In accord with the New Stagecraft, Bragdon believed that the removal of physical barriers between the stage and auditorium would create a sense of communion between the spectators and the actors. This social unity, combined with the impact of the drama, Bragdon suggested, would promote a feeling of rapport, participation, and conduce to the generation of that indescribable common emotion which is perhaps a cosmic emotion under stress of which a dramatic representation becomes dynamic, poignant, rhythmic, exactly in proportion as the spectators become responsive, impressionable, enthusiastic, sensitive to every emotional overtone. (182)

It was this state of responsiveness and impressionability which was Bragdon's primary goal. Art, he believed, would encourage in the viewer a psychological and spiritual transformation.

Bragdon's article provided significant publicity for Bel Geddes's theater. It placed it squarely in the eye of the architectural profession, while bolstering hopes for a revolution in theater. In a letter of October 1922 to the *Architectural Record*, E. Gordon Craig defended Bel Geddes and berated the editors of the journal for what he considered their fickle agenda, declaring that Bel Geddes's Theater Number 6 "lacks nothing except sane living spectators... Yet he is not to blame:—the fault is yours:—Yours and the Public's. No architect can know what you modern folk want for you do not know yourselves ... no architect can fit you with a modern theater:—all he can do is to guess what ... will suit your everlasting metamorphosis. Obviously Mr. Bel Geddes has made a bold, pretty guess, and it is a scandal that you have ... forced him to guess wrong."[44] In 1923, the German publisher Ernst Wasmuth contributed to the praise, and informed Bel Geddes that his Theater Number 6 was "one of the most powerful proofs of the [third] dimension's character of all architectural production ... an example of the imperishable and deeply founded connection of ethical principles and architectural production."[45] In 1923, Wasmuth, which had earlier published the work of Frank Lloyd Wright, which proved extremely influential within European design circles,[46] published Bel Geddes's work in a folio of leading stage designers, thereby enhancing the designer's growing reputation.[47]

Bel Geddes's stage design course, 1922–1928

From 1922 to 1928, Bel Geddes elaborated his own theories of transformative drama in his New York stage design courses, where he trained a small, select group, including his future fiancée, Frances Resor Waite, and his future competitor Henry Dreyfuss.[48] Privately run, Bel Geddes's stage design courses were a source of both income and theatrical assistants. Many of his students became important designers, including Dreyfuss, who attended the course from the winter of 1922 to the spring of 1924 and remained to assist Bel Geddes on the setting of *The Miracle* and the intricate model of the *Divine Comedy*.[49] Dreyfuss, reflecting on his own career in theater, called Bel Geddes "genius #1 in my life."[50] According to Bel Geddes, his stage design courses were "entirely too successful."[51] Bel Geddes reckoned that up to 1924 the average enrollment was around eleven per session.[52] An advertisement of 1928 emphasized the pragmatic and progressive approach of the course: students would be taught the "practical problem" of designing a Broadway production and "the problem of experimenting with forms of staging that will not be accepted by Broadway ... for five years to come."[53] That same year Bel Geddes would extend his experimental approach in theater to the world of industry, devising a five-year incremental styling program for the Graham-Paige automotive company discussed below. In 1927, Bel Geddes sought to publish the stage design lectures as a book, but was ultimately unsuccessful due lack of time, poor writing ability, and difficulty with his "ghost writer."[54] A 1928 transcript includes the following lessons for the elementary course: "The Stage" (historical development of scenery, mechanics of the stage, stage direction and terminology); "The Objective" (Bel Geddes's philosophy of theater); "Visualizing the Setting" (Bel Geddes's approach to stage design); "Visualizing the Costume"; "The Working Plot"; and continued with a synthesis of the previous lessons into a practical scheme. Other lessons dealt with technical details of stage production, including the planning and realization of the settings, costumes, lighting, model, properties, makeup, rehearsal, and performance.[55] Lecture titles of a more advanced twenty-lesson course included "Art and the Theatre," "Architecture for Drama," "Ethics and Art—Religion and the Theatre," and "Creative Vision," indicating Bel Geddes's abiding interests in art, architecture, spirituality, and visionary thought.[56]

Since at least the middle of the 1910s, Bel Geddes had been aware of modernist design theories, especially those emanating from European theater. His stage design course reflected these principles, including organic unity, simplification, abstraction, originality, anti-historicism, and visionary thinking, tenets to which Bel Geddes remained committed throughout his career. In his lecture notes he recommended that the "Designer should consider [the] work from [the] standpoint of [the] whole."[57] He insisted that the new generation of designers, including himself, considered "Scenes and people" as individual "parts of the same mobile composition;"[58] and put "emphasis on simple design ... [and the] elimination of unessentials [sic]."[59] Regarding costume design, he warned: "Don't go to libraries. The least you know about historical costumes and the more you make historical costumes look like modern costumes, the better."[60] Bel Geddes demanded originality from his class, advising students to practice mental "courage," avoid "imitation," and seek ideas that are "wholly yours."[61] But, perhaps most importantly, Bel Geddes called for "vitality and imagination" and "breadth of vision."[62]

In a stage design lecture transcript of 1929, Bel Geddes wrote, "every person of vision, without exception, is fascinated by possibilities of this unknown, the unexplored, the state of emotion and ecstasy, which is psychological," echoing Bragdon's emphasis on intense feeling and Ouspensky's recommendation of combining intuition and emotion.[63] Bel Geddes taught that effective design depended upon the viewer's emotional and psychological metamorphosis, and defined "pure drama" as a "sequence of movement acting upon [the] mind & capable of stirring it emotionally."[64] Three years later in *Horizons*, Bel Geddes expressed his hope for an innovative form of theater capable of "rousing ... vast, overwhelming tides of thought and feeling in the masses," reflecting Bragdon's desire for a cathartic audience response and a return to the theatrical goals of Classical Greece.[65] Aware of the ancient Greek concept of "catharsis," the purification of the inner self through intense emotional experience, Bel Geddes wrote in 1929 that the contemporary dramatists, like the ancient Greeks, should play one theatrical element "against the other until from their own friction they would burst into flame, [and] drama would attain such power as it has never known."[66] In the same year, Cheney wrote that the "response" one "felt" after Greek tragedy was of being "purged by experience, taken beyond the world, left with a deeper ecstasy that clarified."[67]

Reflecting a boyhood interest in hypnotism, a fascination with psychology, and an enduring desire to elicit intense feelings from his audience, Bel Geddes wrote in a 1922 lecture: "The psychological effect of dramatic lighting on an audience has scarcely been considered. It can hypnotize them, arouse them, entrace [sic] them, awake them; free them from the dull backyards of their little lives into the great spaces of a sky of color and light and shadow and brightness."[68] Not surprisingly, when discussing the effects of color Bel Geddes credited Bragdon, and recommended to his stage design students his writing on colored light, Theosophy, and architecture, as well as Bragdon and Bessaraboff's translation of *Tertium Organum*.[69]

In his stage design course, Bel Geddes urged his students to "compose" with color using rhythm and crescendo, essential aspects of Thomas Wilfred's "color organ," or "Clavilux," a machine that projected brilliant patterns of dancing light, or "color symphonies," which captivated Bragdon and Bel Geddes in the early 1920s, and was performed at the Paris Exposition des Arts Décoratifs in 1925, an event later associated with the emergence of Art Deco. Prior to 1921, with the aid of patron Walter Kirkpatrick Brice a color music studio was set up on Long Island in cooperation with Bragdon and his Prometheans, a group of self-proclaimed color music visionaries who were interested in light as an emotional medium. It was here in 1921 that Wilfred developed his first Clavilux in close association with Bragdon (Plate 10).[70]

In the early 1920s, Bel Geddes became close friends with Bragdon and members of his artistic circle, including Brice and the musician Harry Barnhardt.[71] Barnhardt and Bragdon were interested in the therapeutic uses of theater, singing, and light. Bel Geddes described Brice as a "convivial and hospitable idle rich … Harvard man," who used his wealth to support Wilfred's Clavilux.[72] After meeting Bel Geddes, Bragdon told him, "Yours is the most constructive and original mind at play upon the problem of the theatre here in America … It meant a great deal to Mr. Brice, Wilfred and me that you thought so well of our light development. You are a Promethean already in fact and shall become one in name also."[73]

In Greek mythology, Prometheus was a demigod who made mankind out of clay, stole fire from Zeus, and taught human kind to use it creatively. His name is literally translated as "he who thinks in advance."[74] He is the archetypal deity of vision and creativity. "Prometheanism" has been identified by the historian of Russian culture, James Billington as a major characteristic of the "the cultural mood" of early-twentieth-century Russia.[75] Billington cites the writing of Ouspensky as representative of Prometheanism and defined the trend as "the belief that man—when fully aware of his true powers—is capable of totally transforming the world in which he lives."[76] While Bragdon associated his group of Prometheans with the creative use of light and color, it was perhaps also the will to transform that attracted Bragdon to Bel Geddes.

Bel Geddes considered his first meeting with Brice in January 1920 as "an important step in my life," because "up to that point I had done nothing but work." Bel Geddes soon began drinking absinthe, an anise-flavored spirit associated with Bohemian culture and thought to induce hallucinations, "nightly for four consecutive years."[77] The death of Bel Geddes's mother in 1919 may have contributed to his drinking. However, absinthe may have also expanded his already active imagination.[78] Meeting Brice and the others proved an intellectual turning point for him. The group stayed up late into the night discussing theater and other ideas. Bel Geddes stayed in Brice's guest room on a permanent basis, using it as a bedroom and studio, and to study Brice's extensive library.[79] At the same time, Belle Sneider was spending her time with a different group of friends, and by 1926 the couple had separated.[80] He blamed the breakup on Belle's inability to "keep up with him," her "dislike [of] the people he mixed with," and her "narrow minded purity." But, he also blamed his lack of affection and his immaturity. He was "shocked" and "hurt" by their breakup; he deeply valued Belle's contribution to his life and work, and wrote that she "greatly influenced" him.[81]

Originating in the Arts and Crafts Movement and the Bauhaus, the idea of combining various media into an expressive and unified art appealed to Bel Geddes and Bragdon who longed for an art of great force, unburdened by intellectual and aesthetic boundaries. They may have seen the Clavilux as an attempt to fulfill Craig's "prophesy" of a "new religion" of light.[82] In 1918, Bragdon wrote: "Indeed, with the aid of light, the theater may be the nursery of a new art-form altogether, a synthesis of sound, form, color, and mobility."[83] In describing the Clavilux as a portent of the "Art of the future," Bragdon revealed his distaste for the use of color and light in commerce, a sphere Bel Geddes would fully embrace. Bragdon asserted, the "Clavilux gave us the first faint actual intimation, showing what colored light might become when disassociated from all those ideas of corsets, chewing-gum, automobile tires, etcetera, the zeal of [which] the advertisers has [sic] succeeded [in] linking it up."[84] Significantly, it was on this point that he diverged from Bragdon. Bel Geddes had previous experience in advertising. And, by the end of the 1920s, he would increasingly engage in commercial design: including window displays for the Franklin Simon department store, automobile bodies for the Graham-Paige Company, an assembly hall for the J. Walter Thompson advertising agency, steel furniture for the Simmons Company, and weighing scales for the Toledo Scale Company.

After several years of stage design work, including lighting for Robert Edmund Jones, Bel Geddes developed his plans for the stage design and production of Dante Alighieri's renaissance masterpiece the *Divine Comedy* from 1920 to 1924, a period of few opportunities for the designer.[85] The commercially impractical, but highly influential, design proposal provided the first mature expression of Bel Geddes's approach to stage design, reflecting the tendencies of the New Stagecraft as well as the theories of Expressionism, abstracting and intensifying imagery in order to reveal an emotional and psychological reality beyond ordinary experience.[86] The project was planned entirely by him, including sets, stage, costumes, lighting, sound, and arrangement of dialogue and action.[87] It distilled Dante's story, removing the literal, local, political, and personal references in an effort to emphasize the spirit of the tale.[88] The plan of the unrealized *Divine Comedy* used innovative lighting in place of scenery, and emphasized the movement of large groups of actors with little dialogue.[89] For the project, Bel Geddes "designed perhaps the most monumental single stage setting and appurtenances ever planned." The bowl-shaped stage structure was 135 feet wide and 165 feet deep, rising to 50 feet at the rear and flanked by four huge towers. The towers and the crater-like stage setting accommodated the grand movements of hundreds of massed actors.[90] Using Francis Bruguière's photography of the model, the project was exhibited in Amsterdam in 1922, representing the bulk of the American submission for the International Exhibition of Theatrical Art. According to the historian of American theater design, Christin Essin Yannacci, its inclusion in the exhibition "ushered [Geddes] into a select crowd, assuring that his work would be seen by the leading international artists." She also notes that it helped to solidify Bel Geddes's reputation as a designer of visionary, rather than achievable, design.[91] The project was later published in 1924 as the book, *A Project for the Theatrical Presentation of The Divine Comedy of Dante Alighieri*, with atmospheric photographs by Francis Bruguière, the American experimental photographer of the New York theater community who drew inspiration from mysticism and Theosophy and, like Bel Geddes, was a member of Bragdon's circle of Prometheans.[92] Such systems of belief aided Bruguière's appreciation of the "spiritual power" in light, the "unification of mind and matter," and the "translation of emotions into abstracts shapes."[93] Thomas Wilfred's Clavilux performances of the early 1920s inspired Bruguière to explore light not as subordinate to another art, such as theater, but as its own unique medium.[94] The book itself was a remarkable creation: it combined innovative design and Bruguière's skillful photography of a model in which Bel Geddes installed up to 250 tiny costumed figures and plotted numerous lighting setups.[95] The project received immediate critical acclaim. Despite the fact Bel Geddes's *Divine Comedy* was never staged, its impact within the theatrical design community was perhaps as great as a major theatrical production.[96] Through such "superbly imaginative" plans, Cheney insisted, "Geddes had the most profound influence upon the budding American directors and producers."[97]

The proposal was so ambitious that it required its own theater, which Bel Geddes later designed for the Chicago World's Fair of 1933–1934 and published in *Horizons*. Similar to ancient Greek theaters and Theater Number 6, the Divine Comedy Theater combined an arced auditorium and round stage. It had no balconies, proscenium, or curtain to divide the auditorium from the stage, and employed a gigantic domed ceiling.[98] The success of the *Divine Comedy* in the mid-1920s helped Bel Geddes gain one of his most important clients, Max Reinhardt, who hired the designer for his next major production, *The Miracle*, requiring the physical transformation of a theater interior into a gothic cathedral, a project the young designer Russel Wright worked on as an unpaid apprentice. Like Bel Geddes, Wright would move seamlessly from a theatrical career to one in industrial design. A significant mentor of Wright's, Bel Geddes has been credited with teaching the young designer the value of approaching design in its broadest terms (Figure 2.4).[99]

Bel Geddes's stage settings and theater designs through their combined use of light, color, and movement, and the removal of barriers between the audience and the actors, were designed to elicit an emotional viewer response. Illustrating his knowledge of psychology and Theosophy, Bel Geddes proclaimed that theater design should be characterized by "Ecstasy above common life… Expressing the inner phenomenon of life—[and] appeal to [the] subconscious."[100] Equally applicable to the aesthete, the religious convert, or the consumer, the ecstatic experience—whether in artistic rapture, spiritual conversion, or the moment of the sale—required self-transformation. Like Freud and Joseph Breuer, whose talking cure was intended to promote well-being through the release of repressed emotions, Bel Geddes and Bragdon hoped intense drama would induce a cathartic change equivalent to psychological conversion.[101] While Bragdon advocated the use of intensity, light, color, and movement for primarily spiritual and therapeutic ends, Bel Geddes would soon use such knowledge for commercial ones.

Franklin Simon window displays, 1927–1930

With his designs of window displays for the Franklin Simon department store (1927–1930) Bel Geddes continued his move from theatrical to industrial design, applying his knowledge of drama to the sphere of consumer goods. He considered his work for the retailer "a significant training ground" and "the beginning of the momentous change" in his career, leading to his full immersion in design consultancy and the application of drama to selling goods. His "two years of handling consumer goods – clothes, furnishings, perfumes, interior decorations" helped him to develop an interest in "improving merchandise, making it more attractive, more serviceable, more economical to manufacture."[102] Bel Geddes's well-thumbed copy of *Contemporary Art Applied to the Store and Its Display* (1930), by the Austrian émigré and show window expert Frederick Kiesler, presented American window display as an "unprecedented" democratizing force, a significant

FIGURE 2.4 Bel Geddes's model stage set for *The Divine Comedy*. Photograph by Francis Bruguière, 1920. Harry Ransom Center, University of Texas, and the Edith Lutyens and Norman Bel Geddes Foundation, Inc.

venue for America's contribution to the world of "new art"—modern mass-produced goods.[103] He expressed his enthusiasm for Kiesler's viewpoint, scrawling vigorous marks next to the phrases: "CONTEMPORARY ART REACHED THE MASSES THROUGH THE STORE"; "THAT IS: IT WILL BE OF THE MACHINE."[104] Window display has been recognized as a key component of consumer society, and a significant site of fantasy, drama, and technological play during the early twenteth century.[105] Such elements were important to Bel Geddes's theatrical design and would beccme essential to his future commercial projects

In his designs for Franklin Simon, Bel Geddes treated the display windows like stage sets and applied the rules of drama to selling products. In 1932, he wrote: "The store window s a stage on which the merchandise is presented as the actors. The rules that apply to designing for the stage are in many ways true here."[106] The window must "arrest the glance; focus attention upon the merchandise; [and] persuade the onlooker to desire it."[107] Bel Geddes had developed the theatrical metaphor as early as April 1927 in discussions with the department store mogul Adam Gimbel, regarding window display work for Saks & Company, and in his article on window display in *Women's Wear Daily*, November 1927. In his writing he borrowed from Shakespeare, explaining that, "The Play's the Thing," including "the 'play' the merchant makes for the attention of the passerby."[108] In his book Kiesler discussed window display in the context of modernist theater, including that of Craig, Reinhardt, and the Russian Constructivists.[109] An even earlier precedent for the theatrical analogy belongs to the window display pioneer L. Frank Baum. Author of *The Wonderful Wizard of Oz*, founder of the National Association of Window Trimmers in 1898, and publisher of *The Show Window*, a leading monthly journal of window display, Baum had also been a salesman, retailer, theater director, and actor. Like Bel Geddes, Baum was attracted to Theosophy, relied on his experience in commerce and theater, and recommended the use of dramatic lighting and isolated merchandize to arouse consumer desire.[110]

In 1927, Kiesler had designed "simple, striking" window displays for Saks Fifth Avenue, using a "stark geometric backdrop against which a minimum of merchandise was displayed" (Figure 2.5).[111] While Bel Geddes's window display work for Franklin Simon continued with such an approach, it elaborated on it through the application of the theatrical metaphor and stage design techniques. According to Bel Geddes, the Franklin Simon work grew from his dissatisfaction with Fifth Avenue window display. He asked himself, "Why couldn't a big store window be fixed up like a stage, the object suggesting the action with which the merchandise will eventually be associated?"[112] Accordingly, his Franklin Simon window displays spotlighted one or a few products, creating a sense of theatricality by associating a limited number of goods with an alluring fantasy. To achieve his affect, Bel Geddes installed numerous "thousand-watt focus lamps in each window, with a varying assortment of interchangeable lenses and attachments."[113] With their emphasis on glamor, his displays reflected a wider trend of the 1920s: the use of atmosphere and modern design in advertising to create an aura of class (Figure 2.6). While associational window display had existed in the previous decade, most contemporary store windows continued to use cumbersome lighting and visual overcrowding well into the 1920s.[114] The Franklin Simon windows, on the other hand, employed a background that graduated from beige to dark gray, thus creating a neutral setting for the spot lit central character—the product. The display was based on an interchangeable set of background panels and triangular platforms, or "units" of varying form, material, and color. While wood units might be of ebony, walnut, or colored enamel, and metal ones of aluminum, brass, or blue steel, similar variations could be applied to glass and textiles.[115] Each unit was a multiple of four inches (264) and was painted one of thirty-six shades based on the primary colors (266). The range of colors, materials, and shapes resulted in "an endless variety of forms" and "geometric patterns," akin to looking through a "kaleidoscope" (264). Using scale models Bel Geddes's staff could quickly plan a display, produce working drawings, and rush them to the store's window trimming department (271–272). The window trimming department would then retrieve its display units from storage, having already produced them from instructions on a comprehensive card index system provided by him, which listed each unit's material, form, and color, including top, sides, and bottom, as well as "a diagram of the [component's] plan, elevation, dimensions and cross section" (265). Guided by his assistant, the window trimmers then arranged specific display units, merchandize, and lighting, according to the drawings provided (271–272). The standardization at the heart of the "unit system" would later be applied to Bel Geddes's designs of the Standard Gas Equipment Oriole and Acorn stoves (1930–1933) and plans for prefabricated service stations (1934) and houses (1940s).[116] He had initially offered his display concept to Saks

FIGURE 2.5 Window display for Saks Fifth Avenue, 1927. Designed by Frederick Kiesler. Photograph by Worsinger. © 2016 Austrian Frederick and Lillian Kiesler Private Foundation, Vienna.

FIGURE 2.6 Franklin Simon window display in *Horizons*, "Hat and Scarf," 1929. Photograph by Vandamm. Harry Ransom Center, University of Texas, and the Edith Lutyens and Norman Bel Geddes Foundation, Inc. 2016.

Fifth Avenue, which rejected it because the all-embracing system would render their present display equipment obsolete. According to him, the Franklin Simon window attracted huge crowds, and New York's big department stores, including Saks, quickly adopted the concept.[117] Reflecting on his Franklin Simon work in *Horizons*, Bel Geddes claimed that dramatic window display which effectively used lighting, color, and design had a "psychological" effect and was essential in selling products.[118]

J. Walter Thompson assembly hall, 1929

After initiating a career in window display, Bel Geddes continued his foray into the design of commercial spaces. In June 1928, Stanley Resor, the president of the immense J. Walter Thompson

FIGURE 2.7 J. Walter Thompson assembly room, view from meeting table toward auditorium, 1929. Unidentified photographer, possibly Mary Dale Clarke, 1930. Harry Ransom Center, University of Texas, and the Edith Lutyens and Norman Bel Geddes Foundation, Inc. 2016.

advertising agency, commissioned Bel Geddes to design the conference room of the company's New York office for $10,000.[119] Bel Geddes's commission coincided with the phenomenal growth of J. Walter Thompson during the 1920s. In 1922, its total annual billings were $10.7 million, and by 1926 they had doubled, eventually reaching $37.5 million in 1930, becoming the largest advertising agency in the world.[120] Bel Geddes's association with the agency was aided by his fiancée, Frances Resor Waite, the niece of the company's president (Plate 11). This family tie would prove instrumental in his career, helping him to gain new clients and facilitate a move toward the "wholesale designing idea," which he discussed with the wife of Stanley Resor, Helen Lansdowne Resor, founder of J. Walter Thompson's influential Women's Editorial Department, which interpreted women's desires for the agency's clients.[121] He met Frances Resor Waite in New York after he had finished his production of *Jeanne d'Arc* in Paris. She had seen his show in Paris and was eager to join his stage design class, which she attended for a year from 1927. She was quickly hired by him and was put "in charge of the costumes and clothes for all stage productions."[122] She would play important roles in numerous design projects, including overseeing the Franklin Simon windows.[123] By 1933, she had become Bel Geddes's wife and "business partner."[124] As a member of the Resor family, he landed a string of design assignments from J. Walter Thompson clients, including metal bedroom suites for the Simmons Company, stoves for the Standard Gas Equipment Company, an unrealized factory plan for the Toledo Scale Company, and the Shell Oil "City of Tomorrow" advertisement (1937), which would evolve into his most ambitious job, the Futurama (Plate 12).

Bel Geddes's conference room called for an "unusual" space that would create "a favorable impression" upon clients and board members (Figure 2.7).[125] The result was a large hall, eighty-by thirty-foot long and twenty-five-feet high, which used subtle lighting and elegant materials to create an impressive effect. Concealed ceiling lights operated by dimmers lit the two-story-high oyster gray walls. From floor to ceiling ran immense windows and turquoise curtains accented by brass strips and black Vitrolite.[126] Bel Geddes had successfully applied theatrical techniques to an architectural space, an approach consistent with his and Bragdon's theories, which emphasized the manipulation of the visitor's mood. He recognized the importance of using corporate spaces to impress clients, noting that a company's assembly hall "should put the visitor in a receptive, cooperative frame of mind."[127] Aware of its theatrical origins, a critic for *Theatre Arts Monthly* remarked on the room's "power and drama."[128] Bel Geddes would later use the design of his own office as a method of impression management. Upon arrival at his Rockefeller Center office, clients entered a dignified modern reception area where they could sit comfortably on simple elegant sofas surrounded by glass vitrines containing models of Bel Geddes's designs. Those who he deemed important enough could then enter the design consultant's thirty-foot-long, sparsely decorated office, which employed concealed filtered lighting to create an "atmosphere of warmth."[129]

From stage design to architecture: Plans for the Chicago World's Fair, 1933

The J. Walter Thompson assembly hall wasn't the only Bel Geddes project that blurred the boundaries between theatrical and architectural design.[130] Bel Geddes had long taken an "architectural" approach to his theatrical work as noted by Cheney in 1928.[131] In his 1932 book on stage design, *The Stage Is Set*, Simonson described Bel Geddes's theatrical settings as "purely architectural compositions."[132] Throughout his career he made contact with influential modernist architects. Having met Frank Lloyd Wright in 1916, in 1924 Bel Geddes befriended the pioneering German architect of expressionist buildings, Erich Mendelsohn, who gave him a copy of his book *Structures and Sketches* and a drawing of his Einstein Tower (Plate 13).[133] This was Mendelschn's first visit to the United States. It was made to develop business contacts and to witness and photograph America's industrial and modern architecture, including grain elevators, billboards, and the towering chasms of Wall Street for his book *Amerika Bilderbuch Eines Architekten* (1928). The book, through its often vertiginous and amateurish photographs of iconic modern structures, has been recognized as an important and early document helping to consolidate the formal vocabulary of the Modern Movement.[134] Bel Geddes and Mendelsohn maintained a correspondence until after the Second World War. In his introduction to Mendelsohn's work in the catalog for the 1929 New York Art Center's *Contempora Exposition of Art and Industry*, Bel Geddes associated the art of building with intense feeling and theatricality, asserting that the ideal architect "with the dramatist's instinct … adds the emotional quality that attracts and inspires humanity for all time."[135]

In July 1929, Bel Geddes was invited to develop an innovative theatrical program for the Chicago World's Fair.[136] In order to develop a noncommercial, avant-garde theater for a mass audience, he planned to showcase the work of leading theatrical artists within a group of theaters of his design. He immediately sent letters to eminent avant-garde artists, architects, directors, stage designers, and writers, asking them to dream up their own ideal theater.[137] Those contacted included Craig, Cheney, Reinhardt, Jean Cocteau, Jacques Copeau, Robert Edmond Jones, Eugene O'Neil, Pablo Picasso, Luigi Pirandello, Oskar Schlemmer, Constantin Stanislavsky, and Frank Lloyd Wright.[138] Bel Geddes hoped that this project might allow theater to develop as an independent noncommercial art and create a theatrical renaissance of global proportions.[139] "With two exceptions," Bel Geddes wrote, he received only "constructive replies" to his letters.[140] A supportive response came from his friend Cheney.[141] Walter René Fuerst, coauthor of *Twentieth Century Stage Decoration* (1928), was less enthusiastic. He was bothered by the idea of presenting experimental theater to a popular audience, and asked Bel Geddes whether such a public "ought to be instructed about" the avant-garde.[142] Bel Geddes saw no contradiction, believing his plan might bring intense theater and dramatic architecture to an even larger audience. However, after the 1929 stock market crash, his idealistic project was abandoned as the fair developed a more commercial emphasis.

By February 1930, the fair's Architectural Commission invited Bel Geddes as an advisor,[143] and asked him to design the exterior illuminations of the fair's buildings and landscapes and provide "concrete examples" of designs for restaurants and theaters.[144] Though he was hired as "Consultant for Illuminations," he was aware that his new job was a theatrical one. He explained that he was given the job in order to "dramatize the grounds."[145] In his plans for the illuminations, he wrote that the "fair should aim toward developing the qualities of a) Colosalism [*sic*], b) Novelty and c) Mystery." "Colosalism" would be achieved through "size and intensity," while "novelty and mystery," would be realized through glass panels, reflection, and the "concealment of the source of light." "Novelty," "colosalism," and "mystery" would become key components of Bel Geddes's design language.[146] His role at the fair provided an ideal opportunity to use light as a spiritual and dramatic expression of humanity. His lighting plans included a group of dramatically lit "great piers" upon which appeared the words "In the beginning there was light."[147] Another design illustrated a hydrogen-filled dome containing a "fountain of light," which distorted the "shadows" of the viewing crowds to create a passing "human panorama" "on the translucent surface."[148] Though never realized, Bel Geddes's world's fair illuminations illustrated his continued interest in dissolving the barrier between viewer and performer by integrating the audience with dramatic spectacle. At the same time, it sought to achieve the goals of Bragdon's Prometheans, of combining color, light, and motion to create soul-stirring emotional experience.

The therapeutics of color in interior design, *c.* 1930

The influence of stage design, dramatic lighting, and color therapy is found in design ideas for a house developed by Bel Geddes and Frances Resor Waite from 1930.[149] At the beginning of the 1930s, Bel Geddes and Waite drafted a series of articles on progressive interior design for *The Ladies' Home Journal*, which remained only partly published. Each article focused on a particular domestic subject, including the kitchen, the nursery, furniture, and lighting. Perhaps in an effort to extend their appeal, the planned articles rejected the extremes of the "French school," as Waite and Bel Geddes termed it, of modernist architecture exemplified by Le Corbusier and outlined a design approach characterized by a tempered modernism, the New Housekeeping, and a therapeutic element, emphasizing the healing use of light and color.[150] The therapeutic aspects of Bel Geddes and Waite's designs are apparent in their discussions of color in the home and the design of the nursery. Echoing Bragdon, and reflecting the Christian Science emphasis on healing, they wrote that humankind had only scratched the surface of light's full potential, "its more abstract aspects [as] an inducer of mood, as a curative treatment and as a mode of expression as eloquent as music, painting or literature." The article expressed a paradox of modernity—that contemporary life was debilitating, "unnatural," and sapped one's vitality, yet its fruits, the new technologies of light and electricity, were regenerative.[151] Bel Geddes's fascination with metaphysics would wane as he increasingly took a more rational approach to design. It was perhaps this appreciation of rationalization that drew him to soviet culture, which continued to engage the designer even as his list of capitalist clients grew.

Design proposal for the Kharkov Theater, Ukraine, 1931

After the Bolshevik Revolution of 1917, ideological mass spectacles, including ceremonial meetings, demonstrations, and festivals, were considered an essential part of soviet society, leading to the development of new forms of large-scale architecture and competitions for their design. During the 1920s and 1930s, leading architects from capitalist countries entered a variety of soviet architectural competitions, received commissions, or worked in soviet Russia, including Le Corbusier, Erich Mendelsohn, Bruno Taut, Walter Gropius, Ernst May, and Hannes Meyer. In 1931, Bel Geddes participated in an international competition for the State Theater, Kharkov, Ukraine (also known as the Massed Musical Performance Theater), recycling many of his ideas from Theater Number 6. The competition attracted 142 entrants, including Marcel Breuer and the pioneer Russian Constructivists, the Vesnin brothers.[152]

Reflecting a wider fascination with socialist ideology among American artists and intellectuals,[153] Bel Geddes owned numerous books on socialist theater, Lenin, and the Russian Revolution.[154] He explained that around the time of the First World War he first embraced socialism, which "effected my reading to a great extent. Especially in the direction of the downtrodden masses and before I knew it, I was a pro-Socialist, even to the extent of making speeches on street corners."[155] This early interest in socialism was expressed in *Horizons*, where Bel Geddes suggested that the economic answers to America's seemingly out-of-control business culture could be found in postrevolutionary Russian planning.[156]

Though Bel Geddes had a keen interest in Russian culture and its planned economy, the possibility of adapting the techniques of soviet mass spectacle to his own commercial work perhaps proved even more enticing. Through his participation in the design of the Kharkov Theater, he practiced a form of cultural and technological exchange.[157] By the 1920s Russia had imported American management theories and production technologies, in the form of Taylorism and Fordism, to improve its industrial and economic capacity.[158] Conversely, Bel Geddes looked to the monumentality and theatricality of revolutionary mass spectacle, employing techniques of propaganda in his designs for American corporations. In his commercial designs for mass audiences, such as the Futurama, he used architecture as an ideological tool, expressing capitalist ideology, encouraging automobile ownership, technological progress, and the shaping of passive spectators into active consumers.

Significantly, the design brief for the Kharkov Theater accorded with Bel Geddes's own design goals—the dramatization of an idea to provoke an emotional and intellectual response, and the unification of the theatrical product and its consumer. The prospectus for the theater competition opened with the words, "Workers of the World, UNITE!" and emphasized the need for a theater design that would "reflect in its architectural forms ... proletarian culture ... the industrialization of the country, [and] socialist reconstruction of all Public Economy and in all domains of culture."[159] It called for external balconies for orators, arrangements for lighting effects, and the mixing of actors and audience in "correspondence with ideological demands."[160] Bel Geddes's theater plan met the brief: it included the removal of the proscenium arch, an emphasis on lighting, but, most importantly, the merging of audience and actors, or, in this case, the proletariat and socialist ideology (Figure 2.8). The design was intended to excite, transform, and make audiences responsive to socialist ideology. In a draft of *Horizons*, Bel Geddes outlined his theory of influencing the audience. In "the ideal theatre," if the "audience cannot be induced into a state of restfulness ... of enjoyment, of receptiveness to entertainment, one cannot do with them what he wills"; "the audience must be made susceptible."[161] "There is no more emphatic way of bringing an idea to the attention of a mass audience and doing it with great force and conviction than in the theater."[162] Echoing his ideas for Theater Number 6 and reflecting the colossal scale of his theater designs for the Chicago World's Fair, Bel Geddes's Kharkov Theater combined three theaters into one structure, including a monumental "Mass Theater" with a seating capacity of 60,000 and the potential for up to 5,000 actors.[163] Consistent with the New Stagecraft the design of the indoor theater included a ramp allowing actors to merge with the audience.[164] All three stages allowed for illumination effects and sound amplification.[165] In a letter to the New York architect, Wallace K. Harrison, in 1957, Bel Geddes boasted that while the Vesnin brothers won the competition, according to him, his design earned second place, and the theater "as built, in 1936, followed my design almost in its entirety."[166]

FIGURE 2.8 Bel Geddes's model of his design for the Ukrainian State Theater and Opera House at Kharkov, Russia, submitted to the USSR competition, 1931. Photograph by Maurice Goldberg. Harry Ransom Center, University of Texas, and the Edith Lutyens and Norman Bel Geddes Foundation, Inc. 2016.

In October of 1931, shortly after receiving the Kharkov Theater competition details, Bel Geddes was invited to offer a design for the Palace of the Soviets, a center for political meetings and congresses built to celebrate the first five-year plan (1928–1932).[167] He was among a number of Western architects invited to participate, including Mendelsohn, Gropius, Le Corbusier, Berthold Lubetkin, and Hans Poelzig.[168] This was perhaps due more to his reputation than his lack of a professional standing as an architect. Like the Kharkov Theater, the design brief demanded prodigious architectural scale and a building that reflected socialist values.[169] Bel Geddes's monumental and ideological approach to architecture suggests that his Palace of Soviets design would have found a welcoming audience. However, he refused the offer to join the competition. With his characteristic orange crayon, he scrawled the word "Reject" after a clause in the design brief that denied his proprietary rights. His quick refusal of such a significant project suggests that his desire to maintain creative control overrode his keen interest in the Russian experiment.[170]

In 1932, *Horizons* expressed Bel Geddes's desire for an art and industry partnership that would benefit working people. In the book he outlined a scheme where industry would support the building of community theaters for immigrant workers in industrial towns, perhaps following the example of Russia's development of a network of amateur Proletarian Theatres after the Bolshevik Revolution.[171] The rhetoric of *Horizons* might have appealed to industrialists wishing to present their firms as socially enlightened. The plan also presented drama as a positive force, a way to provide a creative outlet that would benefit workers and bosses. Bel Geddes's plan reflected his socialistic concerns, harmonizing with Bragdon's desire for the cathartic outlet of the "mob"—a creative channel for the repressed feelings of the masses.

Architecture as a lively art

In *Horizons*, Bel Geddes described his architecture as part of a trend in American design opposed to historicism, tied to advertising, and one of the "seven lively arts," a term the cultural commentator Gilbert Seldes used in his 1924 book of the same name to describe what he considered popular American cultural forms, including jazz, slapstick, the circus, and comic strips.[172] Bel Geddes owned the book in which Seldes wrote, "unquestionably, a new liveliness is coming into architecture and we may hear of it as one of the Seven Lively Arts."[173] For Seldes the lively arts were popular, commercial, and entertaining. But, first and foremost, they were "intense."[174] In his book Seldes included Bel Geddes's stage designs as a significant contribution to the lively arts.[175]

Bel Geddes's designs of window displays and architecture drew from his knowledge of theater, with its emphasis on intense drama and the transformation of the audience. He believed that theater had a direct impact on individuals and provided an important form of mass entertainment and education. His theatrical aesthetic was derived from a variety of sources, including Christian Science, psychology, socialism, and Theosophy. Applicable to both to noncommercial projects and the realities of trade, Bel Geddes actively used his dramatic aesthetic to transform viewers into active consumers of spectacle, commercial goods, and ideology. His flexible approach to design, which saw few distinctions between theater and other artistic forms, aided his ability to move from the world of theater to that of industrial and architectural design.

Five years after America's first major industrial design offices were established, Seldes observed: "two of the most powerful influences" on the origins of industrial design were "advertising agencies and the makers of scenery for the theatre."[176] Loewy had worked in fashion illustration, Teague had for many years been a successful advertising illustrator, and Dreyfuss and Bel Geddes had maintained significant careers in stage design.[177] While Bel Geddes was quick to proclaim the relevance of his theater experience to his industrial design career, he was less vocal about his advertising past. He described his transformation from stage design to industrial design as a natural evolution and saw numerous commonalities between the two professions. He believed they both depended on detailed planning and seamless presentation and insisted that each must be "done with an eye to pleasing and intriguing the on-looker. Industry ... would be stagnant otherwise and certainly could not achieve popular success."[178] Bel Geddes's new direction was not surprising. Having embraced the notion of *Gesamtkunstwerk* many years earlier, he had seamlessly mixed theatrical and commercial design. While producing the artistic and philosophical *InWhich* magazine, he broadcast his services as a designer of personal monograms.[179] As a young advertising artist, he was obsessed with stage design. And, throughout his industrial design career, he maintained a substantial sideline in stage design. By 1927, he described industrial design as a hybrid profession, balancing the "opposites" of the businessman and the artist. Believing he possessed this "peculiar blending," he viewed his own mental discipline as key in combining "practical" and "aesthetic" thought. Reflecting the Mind-cure ideas, he explained that such equilibrium was all "a matter of consciousness," a "mind point of view which demanded clear thinking."[180] He recognized the need for imagination and fantasy in both stage and industrial design, explaining, "Once he [Geddes] dreamed in the make-believe world of the theater. Now he dreams in an industrial world of the future."[181] Believing that the theater "was not the center" of "national life," Bel Geddes "wanted to be in the thick of things … industrial designing,"[182] proclaiming, "I gave it [stage design] up to try something more important."[183] The new emphasis arguably represented a shift from the immaterial to the material: from the production of ephemeral events toward the design of consumer durables, from artistic idealism toward commercial reality. Accordingly, his promotional language altered from that of a dreamy artist to a hard-nosed businessman. While his stage design lectures emphasized aesthetic ideas based upon mysticism and Theosophy, *Horizons* presented a significant evolution toward machine-age rhetoric, while maintaining a visionary outlook. Thus, Bel Geddes fused the pragmatism of industry with the wishfulness of consumerism.

A weekend with his friend Ray Graham of the Graham-Paige Motor Company was pivotal in Bel Geddes's move to industrial design. Graham offered him $50,000 to design automobile bodies, hoping the large sum would tempt the successful stage designer. According to Bel Geddes, it was then that "designing for industry took a definite form in my mind." The invitation "sent the blood rushing… I burnt all over [*sic*] what an opportunity!" The excitement fired his imagination. Seeing the world through the eyes of a modernist, from his train window he viewed a "dozen reapers mowing down a wheat field almost at a single strip then … twenty [silos] in a row," and envisioned "numerous instances of introducing new ideas on a bigger scale in business toward economy." Bel Geddes would soon develop these ideas and images—the visual iconography of the Modern Movement—on a prodigious scale in his design monograph *Horizons*.[184]

3

Horizons: Publicizing the Visionary Designer

Throughout his industrial design career Bel Geddes published various promotional texts, whether articles, press releases, or books, to publicize himself as a forward-looking designer of boundless imagination. At the Bel Geddes office, it became standard practice to send his prophetic writing to business contacts in order to attract new clients and retain existing ones.[1] More than any of his promotional texts, *Horizons*, 1932, helped to secure his popular image as a technological prophet. Depicting both his unrealized and completed designs, his visionary book was the earliest monograph of America's first generation of industrial designers; those of Dreyfuss, Teague, and Loewy appeared years later (Plate 1).[2]

The book's cover gave some indication of its content: a message that American industry needed a courageous and modern design visionary. The word "HORIZONS" in bold sans serif, stretching the width of the book, proclaimed the book's emphatic and modern emphasis. The font itself, Kabel of 1927 by the German Rudolph Koch, was one of a spate of rectilinear modernist typefaces, including Futura in Germany (1927) and Gill Sans in Britain (1928). Consistent with Bel Geddes's embrace of both the allusive and neutral in modern design, Kabel with its angled forms and rigid geometries is both expressive and functional. The ten bold stripes which increase in width above the title suggested a limitless horizon. A series of stars across the top provided a firmament upon which to dream of tomorrow. Overall, this abstract representation of the "stars and stripes" implied a uniquely American way of visualizing the future. Finally, the name "Norman Bel Geddes" emblazoned across the bottom introduced the book's visionary protagonist.

Horizons is known primarily for its fantastic visualizations of streamlined ships, cars, trains, and planes (Figures 3.1 and 3.2). Its 293 pages burst with startling images of Bel Geddes's visionary designs and industrial products.[3] The book included his plans for monumental buildings and ambitious engineering projects, such as the Aerial Restaurant (a gigantic three-level, rotating

FIGURE 3.1 Motor Coach Number 2, *c.* 1932. Photograph of rendering. Harry Ransom Center, University of Texas, and the Edith Lutyens and Norman Bel Geddes Foundation, Inc. 2016.

tower restaurant) and Air Liner Number 4, and his designs of everyday goods, including Radio Corporation of America radios, Simmons beds, and Standard Gas Equipment (SGE) stoves.[4] By illustrating his book with lofty schemes and ordinary products, Bel Geddes lent an attractive allure to the mundane world of domestic design. The result was a public relations coup. At a time of economic depression, mass unemployment, and the apparent failure of capitalism, *Horizons*, which seemed to offer solutions to such machine-age problems, was widely reviewed by key cultural commentators in America's leading newspapers and magazines, including the *New York Times Book Review*, *The New Republic*, and the *Saturday Review of Literature*, launching Bel Geddes's ideas and designs into the public sphere.[5] Its 222 spectacular images of futuristic vehicles and unusual buildings enlivened the pages of America's Sunday color supplements, while effectively publicizing the Bel Geddes office.

Essentially a promotional exercise, *Horizons*'s emphasis on optimism, progress, and imagination harmonized with Christian Science beliefs and modernist design principles. It echoed contemporary pulp science fiction, machine-age punditry, and modernist ideals, all of which sought mechanistic solutions to social problems and proliferated before and after the Wall Street Crash. *Horizons*'s publicity described Bel Geddes as both prophetic and practical and presented his book as more plausible than science fiction. "*Horizons* is a glimpse of the future … written by… a man with the vision of a Jules Verne but combining the hardheaded practicalness [*sic*] of a successful business man to-day."[6] Science fiction, with its focus on technology and the future,

FIGURE 3.2 Model of Bel Geddes's Locomotive Number 1, 1931. Photograph by Maurice Goldberg. Harry Ransom Center, University of Texas, and the Edith Lutyens and Norman Bel Geddes Foundation, Inc. 2016.

offered another perspective on contemporary problem solving, an approach Bel Geddes knew from his reading of Jules Verne and H. G. Wells.[7] Hugo Gernsback, the pioneer of mass pulp science fiction, populated his stories with inventor heroes. In his publications, including the first science fiction magazine, *Amazing Stories* (1926), he promised to "publish only such stories that have their basis in scientific laws."[8] Likewise, *Horizons* cast Geddes as a real-life machine-age hero, and presented even his most extraordinary designs as technically feasible. He had previously developed imaginative and unrealized design proposals in *InWhich* and his book of the *Divine Comedy*, which helped to secure his most significant theatrical client, Reinhardt. Bel Geddes perhaps hoped *Horizons* would have a similar impact on his industrial design career. Just as Christian Science offered to renew and revive weak, passive individuals, he offered to transform weary, depression-plagued companies with his gospel of vision and success.

Shortly after its publication, George Nelson noted, "*Horizons* lies on many an important desk in Detroit and in Wall Street."[9] In fact, the appearance of *Horizons* coincided with invitations of employment from General Motors and Chrysler. The book's influence on streamlining as a design idiom has been widely recognized,[10] equally important was its introduction of modernist design to American businessmen—perhaps surpassing the influence of Le Corbusier, as Nelson suggested in 1934: "The book [*Horizons*] pictures the Parthenon cheek by jowl with grain elevators. In 1921 Corbusier, the architect, did the same in his book but not many industrialists have read Corbusier. It has been old stuff ever since" (Figure 3.3).[11] The tension between modernist rhetoric and commercial design found throughout the book underscored a significant contradiction of the practical visionary, the use of rationality to appeal to consumer desires.

ARCHITECTURE OR REVOLUTION   263

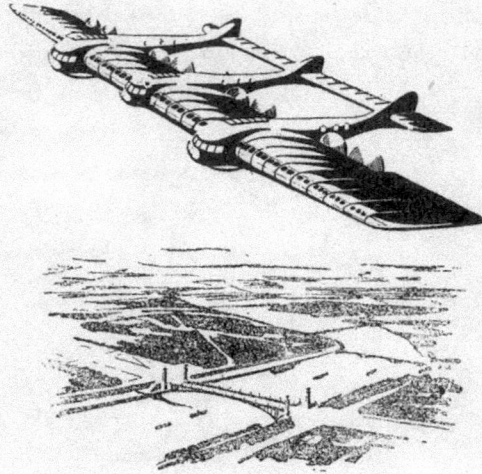

A FORECAST: THE AIRPLANE OF TO-MORROW

Industry has created its tools.

Business has modified its habits and customs.

Construction has found new means.

Architecture finds itself confronted with new laws.

Industry has created new tools : the illustrations in this book provide a telling proof of this. Such tools are capable of

A FACTORY (FREYSSINET & LIMOUSIN)

FIGURE 3.3 Page from Le Corbusier's *Towards a New Architecture* illustrating his forecast of the "airplane of tomorrow" and his celebration of industrial architecture. © FLC/ ADAGP, Paris and DACS, London 2017.

Promoting the artist in industry

The success of Fordism in the 1910s and 1920s led Bel Geddes and others to celebrate the ethos of the machine: its use as a tool to mass-produce affordable goods and reproduce well-paid worker-consumers, aiming to balance production and consumption in economic equilibrium.[12] As a technological romantic, Bel Geddes viewed the machine as *the* dominant symbol of the early twentieth century. In *Horizons*, he reduced the world to pure mechanics, proclaiming: "the person who would use a machine must be imbued with the spirit of the machine."[13] Such rhetoric echoed Le Corbusier, who called for a "mass-production spirit," a phrase Bel Geddes underlined in his copy of *Towards a New Architecture*, first published in English in 1927.[14] Mass production and the machine, however, were equally criticized: production lines displaced skilled workers; traffic chaos blighted cities; and the overproduction of poorly designed goods flooded the market. In the first decades of the twentieth century, it was widely thought that society had been outpaced by technology, and therefore, a material, spiritual, and psychological readjustment was needed.[15] Bel Geddes may have first encountered such machine-age musings in his 1913 copy of *Art for Life's Sake* by Charles Caffin, who wrote: "We must accept them [machines and factories] and discover the means to correct their crudeness and compel them into the service of Beauty; Beauty in the thing made and Beauty in the lives of workers."[16] In the intervening years, a chorus of critics questioned the success of industrial capitalism, chief among them being Stuart Chase, the outspoken consumer advocate. In 1929, Chase worried that mechanization diminished humanity's "psychic equilibrium."[17] By 1930, the prolific cultural commentator Lewis Mumford cataloged the environmental destruction and human misery wrought by recent industrialization and mechanized warfare. Yet, at the dawn of the machine age, he spoke optimistically of its cultural, social, and economic benefits, which, he asserted, have contributed a "new aesthetic" of "precision, calculation, flawlessness, economy and simplicity," and "obliterate[d] the distinctions of caste and financial status," adding, "Whatever the politics of a country ... the machine ... is a communist."[18] By 1930, Sheldon Cheney proclaimed the machine's inevitability: "We are past the possibility of challenging the machine, of curbing it... We must move by machinery, communicate by it—live by it."[19] "We must make it so easy, so efficient, so noiseless, that we rise beyond it to enjoy those serenities, those spiritual contacts ... into regions where we create new religions and more glorious arts" (76). This pervasive belief, that only a society in harmony with the machine could become more advanced, was at the heart of *Horizons*. Such a project, however, required not only the development of a machine spirit, but also the redesign of nearly every aspect of the material world.

The solutions to machine living were of great interest to American manufacturers. In 1930, America's premier business publication, the artistic and expensive *Fortune* magazine, welcomed Bel Geddes and industrial design with open arms, providing an advanced introduction to *Horizons'* key themes. In July 1930, a flattering profile entitled "Bel Geddes" appeared in the second issue of *Fortune* magazine and presented the designer as one of "the most gifted American interpreters" of industrial design, who "regards beauty, utility, and profit as mutually beneficial elements, as linked in a fundamental unity ... a nice conception which has ... made ... uncertain headway among esthetes and businessmen."[20] The article appealed for an American art-in-industry movement and offered Bel Geddes as its guiding light. Unlike the Arts and Crafts Movement, which rejected machine production, art-in-industry proponents embraced the machine as an improving force. Though numerous art-in-industry advocates were vocal throughout the 1910s and 1920s, especially museum professionals such as the irrepressible John Cotton Dana, director of the Newark Museum, New Jersey, and the associate in Industrial Art, Richard Bach, at the Metropolitan Museum, New York, it was only after the stock market crash that captains of industry began to listen seriously. However, a deep conservatism lingered among industrialists and engineers, the former fearing the radicalism of industrial designers, the latter resenting their authority.[21] *Fortune*'s readership of "tycoons," "vice-presidents," and corporate liberals—many of whom hoped art would provide a moral foundation for business—provided ideal clients for the emerging industrial designer.[22] *Fortune*'s embrace of modernism, art-in-industry, and a rationalized economy were consistent with Bel Geddes's concerns.[23] In fact, by 1931 Bel Geddes had joined the American Union of Decorative Artists and Craftsmen (AUDAC, founded in 1928), a group of designers, including Paul Frankl, Frederick Kiesler, William Lescaze, Kem Weber, and Frank Lloyd Wright, dedicated to developing an American modernism and art-in-industry movement, following the European models of the Deutscher Werkbund and the Bauhaus in Germany.[24] Distancing Bel Geddes from his pursuits of stage design and window display, *Fortune* fashioned him as a masculine modernist and man of tomorrow. Invoking Le Corbusier and denouncing art-for-art's-sake, the *Fortune* article noted that Bel Geddes has "long since left window-dressing commissions to his forty-odd assistants and is approaching the larger problems suggested by trains, automobiles, steamships, airplanes, theatres, restaurants, [and] factories."[25]

Four years later, George Nelson's *Fortune* article, "Both Fish and Fowl," offered a more balanced overview of the young profession. As a fledgling architect who later gravitated toward industrial design, Nelson had a vested interest in the new field. He described its faltering start, continued confusion, and future potential. In its early days, eager clients fell victim to design "fiascoes," including costly retooling and failed designs. "The first thing the new profession acquired was a black eye."[26] Van Doren later confirmed Nelson's view, describing the "unformed profession" as chaotic and undisciplined, indicating that the motley crew of "painters, architects, stage designers, sculptors, advertising artists, even typographers" were initially "ill prepared" for their entry into industry's "inner sanctum."[27] "From the client's point of view, industrial design was a gamble from start to finish" (19). Industrial designers "had almost everything to learn. Here in industry was a golden egg, and for lack of specific training, they almost killed the goose that laid it" (17). Nelson observed that the field was presently "filled with pretenders and visionaries,"[28] noting that industry viewed Bel Geddes, with his "visions of sugar plums," with some suspicion. Nelson, however, was eager to reassure *Fortune*'s readers and announced that the "depression-weaned vocation of Industrial Design," through its creativity and practicality, was a key weapon in the battle for economic recovery.[29] Commending the "serious new profession," Nelson encouraged industrial leaders to take the bold advice of designers like Bel Geddes (42). Nelson's salvage effort paralleled a similar one in the business world, which had acquired its own black eye after the 1929 stock market crash.[30] Reflecting this new situation in 1930, *Business Week* warned, "This depression ... is a crucial turning point in industrial civilization ... the philosophy of individual and organized initiative upon which our business system is founded ... is definitely on trial today, more decisively than it has ever been before."[31] The economic circumstances of the early 1930s required selling a progressive image of business "on an unprecedented scale, with staggering scope," a goal of Henry R. Luce's new magazine, a seemingly responsible and elegant publication that would guide business and industry into recovery.[32] The transition from past "fiascoes" to future successes demanded the improved image of both business and industrial design. As well as achieving clients' briefs, industrial designers had to repackage themselves as efficient and responsible. During the early 1930s, public relations narratives were essential in legitimating American corporations. As the historian of corporate America, Roland Marchand, has observed, the "fable of the efficient and benevolent giant, ever attentive to the welfare of the tiniest entity, was simply one of a myriad stories that pervaded corporate publicity during the first half of the twentieth century."[33] *Horizons*, which presented designers as the improving agents of big business, not only contributed to corporate public relations, but also cast industrial designers as ambassadors of efficiency, foresight, and democratization in a significant tale of twentieth-century progress.[34]

The public's appetite for Bel Geddes's visionary image allowed him to author several books and numerous articles, many requiring the aide of researchers, editors, and sometimes a "collaborator … to help on the actual writing," whose "job it was to present Mr. Geddes' ideas in [an] attractive literary style."[35] As with *InWhich*, edited by Belle Sneider, *Horizons* required additional guidance to contain Bel Geddes's immense imagination. Produced with the help of his key associates, Worthen Paxton and Frances Resor Waite, *Horizons* was primarily an argument for design as an improving force amid the tumult of twentieth-century modernity.[36] *Horizons* maintained that design would counter the problems of rapid industrialization and lead the country out of its spiritual and economic malaise. Uncontrolled modernization, the book proclaimed, had resulted in "noise, dirt, glitter, speed, mass production, traffic congestion," making us "victims rather than the masters of our ingenuity."[37] *Horizons* defined "design" as a combination of engineering, planning, and art, which in tandem with commerce, would improve the "social structure," "the organization of people, work, wealth and leisure," the "machines," "the arts," and "all objects of daily use" (4–5). Reorienting the mystical language of the stage design lectures, while maintaining a spiritual outlook, *Horizons* announced, "By the middle of the present century," design will allow for the "complete mastery of the machine… It will make for our greater peace and contentment and yield not only purely physical but aesthetic and spiritual satisfaction" (293). Illustrating the point, *Horizons* concluded with a double page spread depicting the Reims Cathedral (Notre Dame de Reims) rose window alongside the 1929 Lycoming radial airplane engine, suggesting an equivalence between spirit and matter and art and industry (Figure 3.4).[38]

According to Bel Geddes, the industrial designer balanced the roles of the artist and the engineer. In 1929, he claimed that the industrial designer thought, "in engineering terms as well as the aesthetic," a prominent theme of *Horizons*.[39] Describing the design of vehicles in *Horizons*, he wrote: "the problem … requir[es] the combined efforts of the engineer, the chemist, the designer; and only one of them, at least, must possess great imagination."[40] His competitors shared this perspective, including Van Doren, who called the profession "an uncharted sea [*sic*] half aesthetic and half technological."[41] In 1930, Mumford warned, "To conceive of engineering as the central art is to forget that the central fact of life is not mechanism but life."[42] During the late nineteenth and early twentieth centuries, engineers achieved significant cultural status. They promoted themselves as essential agents of progress,[43] engaged in impressive technical feats, including canal, bridge, and railway construction, and appeared as heroes in numerous popular novels.[44] Perhaps even more influential was the work of engineer Frederick W. Taylor, whose development of scientific management, the reorganization of workers' motions and equipment to increase productivity, blossomed into a hugely popular efficiency movement in the first decades of the twentieth century, encouraging a rationalistic approach to public and private spheres, helping to

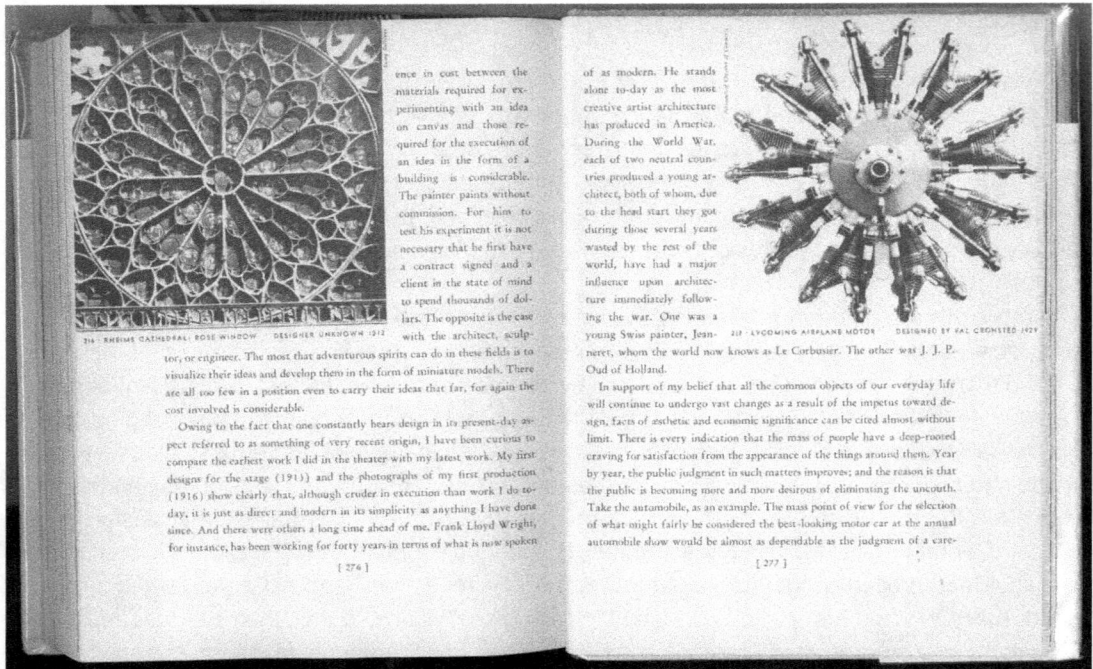

FIGURE 3.4 Reims Cathedral rose window and 1929 Lycoming airplane engine, *Horizons*, 1932. Photographer credits in *Horizons*: Ewing Galloway (left) Aeronautical Chamber of Commerce (right). Harry Ransom Center, University of Texas, and the Edith Lutyens and Norman Bel Geddes Foundation, Inc. 2016.

spawn the New Housekeeping, Christine Frederick's initiative to professionalize housework.[45] Bel Geddes came of age during this period and accessed the ethos of the engineer through the writing of Harrington Emerson (a popular "efficiency engineer"), the ideas of Thorstein Veblen (the influential sociologist who called for government by engineers), and Le Corbusier (who looked to the products of engineering for architectural inspiration).[46]

Anticipating the thesis of Museum of Modern Art's (MoMA) influential *Machine Art* exhibit of 1934, *Horizons* collapsed the distinctions between engineering and fine art and argued that products of engineering such as "a railway train, a suspension bridge, a grain elevator, a dynamo" have as much "aesthetic appeal" as a fine painting.[47] Invoking the logic of the engineer and the vision of the artist bolstered the image of the industrial design profession, concealed its roots in advertising and theater, and constructed a unique professional role. However, the image of the industrial designer as an artistic dreamer threatened the young profession. As late as 1932, it was not unusual to hear the complaint that "the word 'artistic' either brings out the Bronx cheer or a wry smile from the Gods of Industry."[48] Despite such views, industrial designers hoped to convince their clients of their unique knowledge, a combined understanding of engineering and art, something neither company salesmen nor factory engineers could supposedly lay claim to.

Bel Geddes's love of the machine guided *Horizons*' bold predictions. Technological forecasting found in popular science magazines and science fiction provided him with important examples for his flights of prophecy in *Horizons* and his 1931 *Ladies' Home Journal* article, "Ten Years from Now."[49] In the 1930s, such writing was essential in associating industrial design with prophetic practice. During this period, Bel Geddes's futuristic models of his streamlined Ocean Liner and Aerial Restaurant appeared on the covers of the sensational and colorful science and technology magazines, *Popular Science* and *Popular Mechanics*, respectively (Plates 15 and 16).[50]

While the presentation of the industrial designer as a practical visionary did help to publicize the profession and attract new clients, fanciful prophecies were not always welcomed by colleagues. Many industrial designers abstained from futuristic speculation: Teague and Dreyfuss rejected the ostentatious image of industrial design, presenting themselves instead as sensible realists.[51] In 1932, Teague was highly critical of the "merely visionary [who] plays no part in either the work or conversation" of the industrial designer.[52]

Horizons placed the industrial designer in the central position between the worlds of machines and individuals, between production and consumption, catering to the needs of manufacturers on the one hand and the desires of consumers on the other.[53] In *Horizons*, the consuming public was characterized as a fickle and inarticulate mob whose aesthetic choices could ruin a manufacturer. Industrialists were portrayed as aesthetically ignorant and vulnerable to consumer rebellion, while the industrial designer was offered up as an expert interpreter of consumer longing. The industrial "artist," Bel Geddes wrote, was "somewhat ahead of the consumer, while the average manufacturer is farther behind."[54] While critics of industrial capitalism blamed the depression on overproduction, industrialists accused a thrifty public of underconsumption. Bel Geddes pointed his finger at poor product aesthetics and lack of forward planning by manufacturers. For him, the consumer reaction to the uniformity and ubiquity of the Ford Model T, which dominated the automobile market in the early 1920s and lost ground to the more stylish cars after the mid-1920s, evidenced an "inarticulate demand" by consumers for "quality of appearance" (15, 16). An art and industry partnership guided by a forward-looking industrial designer would solve the problems of aesthetics and demand. "To-morrow's merchandising policy," Bel Geddes wrote in *Horizons*, "must … anticipate public demand and supply it. Since public demand now is for quality in appearance as well as for quality in service, artists and industry will still further unite their efforts to win the confidence of the public" (15, 16). For him, the industrial designer, a practical visionary who combined beauty, utility, and vision, would provide the needed social, economic, and spiritual solutions to the problems of the depression decade.

The Aerial Restaurant, Air Liner Number 4, and the Standard Gas Equipment stove

Horizons' presentation of the Aerial Restaurant, Air Liner Number 4, and the Oriole stove for SGE emphasized Bel Geddes's practical and visionary image. The Aerial Restaurant was one of his nine designs for the 1933–1934 Chicago World's Fair of novel restaurants and theaters, which ranged from the intimate to the monumental. A member of Bragdon's group of Prometheans, Harry Barnhardt suggested that Bel Geddes "Make one of the … theatres 'The Temple of Song.'" Barnhardt promoted "song" as an important spiritual act which united "forces and release[d] creative energy." Such a theater, he believed, would have "a revolutionizing effect": it would direct actors' minds to a "fundamental need," dramatize "universal and world embracing ideas," and "engage mass spirit." In fact, Bel Geddes did develop a Temple of Music for the fair, perhaps in response to Barnhardt's suggestion.[55] While revolving architecture was not a new concept, perhaps more than any of his engineering or architectural plans, the Aerial Restaurant established Bel Geddes's reputation as an ambitious designer of novel structures. The plan of the Aerial Restaurant illustrated his flair for infusing architecture with drama (Figure 3.5 and Plate 17). The design required a 278-foot-tall structure with a steel shaft supporting a three-level, cantilevered platform, which made a complete rotation every thirty minutes. The revolving three levels for dining and dancing held up to 1,200 people. The restaurants had floor-to-ceiling glass windows, surrounded by open-air terraces. Like a theatrical auditorium the interior floors and exterior terraces were stepped to accommodate viewing of a dizzying fairground panorama and the Chicago skyline. The thin towering shaft of twenty-eight feet in diameter, in comparison to the cantilevered horizontal platforms, created the illusion of architecture in flight.[56] Bel Geddes may have developed the idea of the floating building from the Russian Constructivist, El Lissitzky's "Wolkenbügel" (1924), which balanced administration buildings atop towering structural shafts and was pictured in Bel Geddes's copy of *Russland: die Rekonstruktion der Architektur in der Sowjetunion* (Figure 3.6).[57]

The design of the Aerial Restaurant was dynamic, commercial, and technological—a spectacular synthesis of Bel Geddes's knowledge of drama, advertising, and modernist architecture. Like the engineering feats of previous fairs, such as the Eiffel Tower of the Paris Exposition Universelle of 1889, the Aerial Restaurant was a technological spectacle designed to elicit both wonder and awe.[58] While one commentator considered the Aerial Restaurant "a little mad,"[59] the boldness of its design was seen as a product of Bel Geddes's theater background. Its theatricality was considered its most significant contribution to contemporary architecture: "at least we have here experiments untrammeled by reverence for that tradition of the theater which has been too powerful so far for even our most courageous architects."[60] A Chicago writer was less flattering, considering the building a "trivial" and impractical novelty, and describing Bel Geddes as "well-known for unique and bizarre designs." He dismissed the restaurant as a grotesque confection and a product of a "wild man's dream": "[it] looks like a huge layer cake, with a piece cut from each layer, held high in the air by a long-stemmed cake platter … but Mr. Geddes, insists it is perfectly feasible." Bel Geddes, however, asserted that the "practicable" design "should become a permanent part of the city." Accompanied by an image of a wild-haired Bel Geddes, the scornful article may have encouraged resentful, unemployed Chicago architects to turn against the New York stage designer. Bel Geddes would later blame the failure of his world's fair plans on pressure from registered architects along with the stock market crash.[61] Undaunted, Bel Geddes widely published and exhibited his unrealized buildings. Spurred perhaps by his failure in Chicago and his keen desire for increased artistic control, he soon sought an architect's license. Historian of revolving architecture Chad Randl suggests that the mechanism for rotating the Aerial Restaurant was "perhaps not fully considered" and may not have been physically feasible, while suggesting that the Aerial Restaurant "foreshadowed the era of the revolving restaurant three decades in the future."[62]

While the Aerial Restaurant simulated architecture in flight, Air Liner Number 4 was essentially flying architecture. One of Bel Geddes's most ambitious designs, Air Liner Number 4 illustrates the vast reach of his imagination. Designed in 1929, the plane was a huge flying wing with streamlined pontoons for water takeoff and landing. A prediction of

FIGURE 3.5 Bel Geddes's model of the Aerial Restaurant, *c.* 1929. Photograph by Maurice Goldberg. Harry Ransom Center, University of Texas, and the Edith Lutyens and Norman Bel Geddes Foundation, Inc. 2016.

FIGURE 3.6 El Lissitzky, Skyscraper (Wolkenbügel) on Strastnoy Boulevard in Moscow, 1925. Found in the collection of the Van Abbemuseum, Eindhoven. © 2017. Photo Fine Art Images/Heritage Images/ Scala, Florence.

"the intercontinental air liner of 1940," with its immense wingspan and a crew of 155, the plane would provide sleeping, recreational, and leisure facilities for 606 persons.[63] While its monumental scale and novel form made it an ideal publicity image and promoted Bel Geddes as a visionary designer, its presentation as a viable commercial venture presented him as a sensible entrepreneur (Figure 3.7). Though streamlining was more often associated with speed, Bel Geddes's mammoth flying wing emphasized comfort, an increasingly important factor in his design projects and an important element in airplane design as airlines competed with railroads for long-distance passengers. Air Liner Number 4 was inspired more by slow-moving ocean liners than high-speed planes. Designed with safety as its first priority and

FIGURE 3.7 Bel Geddes rendering of Air Liner Number 4 (aerial front view), *c*. 1929–1932. Pencil on paper. Harry Ransom Center, University of Texas, and the Edith Lutyens and Norman Bel Geddes Foundation, Inc. 2016.

comfort as its second, it would travel at 100 miles per hour, and be as commodious and well equipped as a large cruise ship.[64] Despite its expected gross weight of 1,275,000 pounds, Bel Geddes insisted that his plane would take off: "As a premise, one must accept the fact that the air liner I am going to describe will fly" (112, 111). Bel Geddes's tendency to develop attention-grabbing designs that remained untested contributed to his public persona as a primarily visionary designer. The idea for such a plane was not original. Le Corbusier "forecast" "the airplane of to-morrow," a large flying wing, in *Towards a New Architecture*, illustrating the convergence of modernist design and technological prophecy (Figure 3.3).[65] Le Corbusier's plane borrowed from the Junkers 1926 boat plane, while Bel Geddes's Air Liner Number 4 looked to Claude Dornier's DO-X (1928), illustrated in *Horizons*, a flying boat of three levels with a wingspan of 157 feet, 10 engines, a weight of 48 tons, and a 170-passenger capacity.[66] However, he claimed that his plane was a product of recent advances in aerodynamic science and provided more comfort.[67]

Bel Geddes presented his project as a practical, profitable, and luxurious alternative to ocean travel. The plane would complete three transcontinental crossings per week from Chicago to London. It was to have nine decks, with four of these in the spacious pontoons (116). The "main lounge" was to be 175 feet long and three stories high (117). Other amenities included a library, writing rooms, a doctor's consulting room, barber's and hairdresser's shops, a children's playroom, two solariums, recreation decks, and six shuffle-board courts. The glass-fronted promenade deck along the length of the front wing provided passengers "with the same view and conditions as on the finest ocean liner" (117–119). Concerned to emphasize the feasibility of his ambitious plane, Bel Geddes asserted, "this is in no sense a mad or foolish idea but sound in every particular" (110). He wrote that it was "not 'big' for the sake of being big," but for reasons of comfort in both spaciousness and smoothness of ride (109, 111). Otto A. Koller, one of Germany's chief aeronautics engineers, was responsible for the completion of the model, drawings, and aerodynamic computations of Air Liner Number 4.[68] Due to Koller's inability to meet Bel Geddes's deadline, the industrial designer informed the German that he would publish the material "regardless of whatever error may be apparent in its aerodynamical [sic] aspects." Despite the unproven aerodynamics of the plane, the illustrations of Air Liner Number 4 in Horizons and the nation's newspapers and magazines boldly announced the emerging streamlined style.[69]

While the Aerial Restaurant and Air Liner Number 4 presented Bel Geddes as a designer of unbridled vision, his designs of domestic goods, including the SGE stove, demonstrated to potential clients his practical abilities, and his understanding of both production and consumption. In his Horizons chapter on product design, Bel Geddes proclaimed:

> The artist's interest in machines has laid the foundation for a new department in industry, in which the relations of product manufacturers and of consumers reach a new level of understanding and congeniality. The artist's contribution touches upon that most important of all phases entering into selling—the psychological. He appeals to the consumer's vanity and plays upon his imagination, and gives him something he does not tire of.[70]

Bel Geddes's SGE stove designs were guided by his faith in the machine, modernism, and his understanding of consumer psychology.

A significant impetus to the creation of the stoves was the recent threat to the gas industry by electrical appliance manufacturers. In late 1932, SGE president W. Frank Roberts warned the gas appliance industry that "electricity walked boldly into the kitchen" and challenged the dominance of the gas industry. He considered this sea change a "blessing in disguise… It waked [sic] us up." Roberts believed that "a new conception of gas cooking must be sold to the American public; a modern, up-to-date, attractive conception." His strategy to compete with electricity went beyond styling. Invoking the fundamental tenets of Fordism and Sloanism, the production of worker-consumers, and the promotion of stylistic obsolescence, he proclaimed, "[O]ur new responsibility is that of manufacturing customers, not products. Then let us design our products to make the public dissatisfied with those they now own."[71]

Designed by Bel Geddes, Roberts's stove appeared in showrooms in early 1933 and quickly achieved an almost iconic status through a combination of sleek design, strong sales, and a flood of publicity. From 1932 to 1934, the image of the Oriole was widely disseminated via Horizons, an intensive brochure mailing campaign, hundreds of model kitchens, and through advertisements and articles in business, trade, and home decorating magazines.[72] The sheer volume of publicity provoked the SGE advertising manager to declare: "I doubt very much if there have been five ranges manufactured in the last twenty five years that have received as much free advertising combined as this Geddes model."[73] The publicity emphasized the harmonious partnership of design and industry and linked the stove with modern architecture—with both the whiteness of modernist buildings and technical innovations of skyscraper construction. An article in the Philadelphia Record of March 1933 described the stove as a "streamline range" with "the smooth, sweeping lines of a skyscraper, divested of all gadgets, sharp corners and superfluous appendages."[74] Promoted as hygienic, visually harmonious, and technologically advanced, the SGE appliance initiated a trend for white finishes within the American stove industry, and, according to Bel Geddes, was the first all-white range.[75] *Fortune*'s 1934 "Story of a Stove," a one-page case study, underscored the rational and bold way Bel Geddes designed a profitable appliance, countering the image of the chaotic "unformed profession."

Horizons's publication in 1932 provided advanced publicity for the stove months before its release. Such carefully timed promotion became common practice at the Bel Geddes office and was later described in the office's *Standard Practice* manual: prior to approaching a client "an industrial design group is determined," "four or five stories are outlined … one [aimed] at a national periodical for popular consumer appeal, another for the leading trade journal written from the view point of the prospective client, another at a literary or high-brow periodical," as well as a "feature newspaper article, a news story, radio and newsreels."[76] These allowed Bel Geddes to speak to a range of audiences, including industrial clients, consumers, and cultural elites, confirming his desire for continued business and artistic recognition.

In an effort to appeal to the business readership of *Fortune*, the "Story of a Stove" was written from the perspective of a potential client and outlined the benefits of a progressive art and industry partnership. Populating the story was a bold and visionary industrial designer, Bel Geddes, and a wary industrialist, W. Frank Roberts, president of SGE. Roberts was presented as a cautious businessman who considered the industrial designer a mere stylist, expecting to pay $1,500 and "have his drawings in a week or two."[77] However, Bel Geddes had other plans. Covering his office floor with a chaotic heap of "hundreds and hundreds" of tiny blocks, each representing a component of SGE's present stoves, Geddes depicted the company's inefficient production methods (Figure 3.8). After showing these to an alarmed Roberts, Bel Geddes revealed his own models, of which there were only sixteen elements, dramatically illustrating the impact of standardization on SGE's production line.[78] Based on the block unit concept developed for his Franklin Simon window displays, the new stoves would be built from basic components of compatible dimensions—a standard tabletop stove, a three-quarter tabletop, a single oven type, and a console type—which could be stacked together, resulting in a "de luxe stove."[79] Impressed by the economy of Bel Geddes's plan, the president of the company had "the courage" to sign him to a $25,000-a-year contract, "shocked though he may have been by his first encounter with the serious new profession of industrial design."[80]

In *Horizons*, Bel Geddes provided his own story of a stove: a brief history of outmoded stoves that underscored his innovative design. The story created a progressive image for him and provided functional reasons for adopting modernist design principles. He was, however, careful to avoid the term "modernism," anticipating his clients' and readers' suspicion of avant-garde aesthetics. The historian Mark Wigley has observed that by 1927 whiteness had become firmly associated with modernist architecture. That year in Stuttgart, Germany, the influential Weissenhofsiedlung exhibition of modernist homes presented the work of seventeen European architects, including Le Corbusier, J. J. P. Oud, and Bruno Taut, whose buildings were unified by white exterior walls and flat roofs. The exhibit received the attention of both the popular and architectural press and helped to publicize the notion that modern architecture was white.[81] The association of whiteness with modernist architecture was further reinforced through its depiction in black-and-white photography, despite the use of color by many avant-garde architects. By 1932, the MoMA's exhibit *Modern Architecture: International Exhibition* helped to establish the International Style in architecture and link whiteness and modernist design. Prior to these exhibitions, Le Corbusier and the Viennese architect Adolph Loos achieved notoriety in their

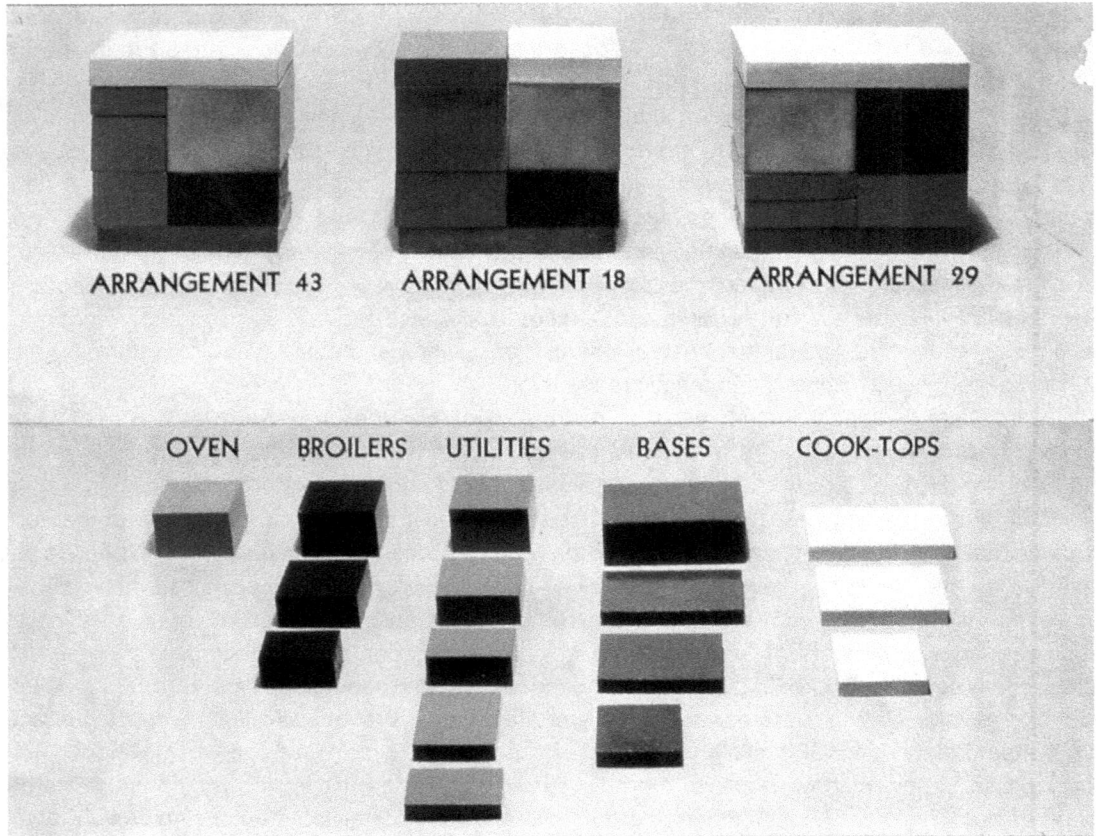

FIGURE 3.8 "Block Units" study for Oriole stove for the Standard Gas Equipment Corporation, *c.* 1932. Photograph by Norman Bel Geddes and Co. Harry Ransom Center, University of Texas, and the Edith Lutyens and Norman Bel Geddes Foundation, Inc. 2016.

rejection of ornamented surfaces and preference for white ones. Le Corbusier republished Loos's canonic essay "Ornament und Verbrechen" (Ornament and Crime) of 1908 in the second issue of *L'Esprit Nouveau* in 1920, a journal he edited with Amédée Ozenfant, the Purist painter. In the essay Loos linked ornament with criminality and the so-called primitive societies, associated blank surfaces with progress, and wrote that the removal of ornament would result in a purified environment of white walls.[82] In *Towards a New Architecture*, Le Corbusier wrote: "Decoration is of a sensorial and elementary order ... and is suited to simple races, peasant and savages... The peasant loves ornament and decorates his walls."[83] Bel Geddes's awareness of Loos and Le Corbusier's theories on ornament and whiteness was apparent in his unpublished 1931 interior design article for the *Ladies' Home Journal*, in which he wrote that if you gave a man a pencil and a white wall, he would demonstrate "the most primitive instincts of man—the desire to decorate his possessions."[84]

Horizons echoed the pioneer modernist architects, transposing their architectural theories to the world of consumer goods. The description of the Oriole stove reached toward both the white walls of modernist architecture and the smooth surfaces of streamlined products. Arguing for hygiene and visual harmony in the kitchen, the book asked rhetorically, "should a stove fit, in appearance, with the refrigerator, cabinets, sinks, and the other dominant kitchen features?"[85] *Horizons* proclaimed: "White is universally accepted as the most sanitary color;" and that the "style" of the SGE stove was "due entirely to its proportion and [white] color" (Figure 3.9).[86] The book explained that the stove's smooth form was a result of functional requirements: "The stove has no projections, dirt–catching corners, the fewest possible cracks or joints where dirt can accumulate."[87] Bel Geddes was not, however, a strict functionalist, insisting, "While function once arrived at, is fixed, its expression in form may vary endlessly under individual inflection."[88] This rejection of the type-object, the anonymously created product whose perfect form was the result of evolution and function, a notion promoted by Le Corbusier in 1925, allowed Bel Geddes an important role as a celebrity shaper of goods and sponsor of stylistic obsolescence.[89] Asserting that new industrial products must be released from their dependence on traditional forms, *Horizons* disparaged cars modeled on the horse and buggy and radios based on the Victrola.[90] However, the book trumpeted the fact that the Oriole looked unlike any contemporary or traditional stove: "A housewife would be surprised to see no evidence whatever that this enameled cabinet is a stove."[91] Apparently sharing this view, a journalist commented: "It [the SGE stove] looks like a chest of drawers."[92] Emphasizing white, continuous surfaces and hinged panels that covered burners and knobs, the Bel Geddes design, ironically, disguised the appliance's use, countering the modernist principle of "form follows function," thus undermining Bel Geddes's modernist identity.[93]

According to a *Sales Management* article c. 1933, the form of the SGE stove was determined less by function than by finance: changes in appliance selling. Gas stove sales were threatened by electric competitors; consumers increasingly demanded attractive styling; and, with the threat of recent anti-utility merchandising legislation, many gas companies were being barred from appliance selling.[94] Retailers therefore needed eye-catching products that would stimulate floor traffic and turnover. To face this new merchandizing situation, SGE opened new outlets, made use of a direct mail campaign to dealers, and emphasized "modern design" as a significant sales tool. Clearly spelling out the new sales strategy, one SGE pamphlet was entitled "This Modern Style Will Sell This Modern Product in This Modern Market," thus moving dealers away from the "price angle" "toward quality merchandise and style."[95] The mailings were a huge success, opening untapped markets for the stove company.[96]

Although Bel Geddes had emphasized the block unit idea in *Horizons*, W. Frank Roberts rejected his modular design as too expensive, producing instead a Bel Geddes-designed stove with a "single-piece stamped steel front." Roberts pointed out that Bel Geddes's plan would have required "separate front frames for every" stove unit, leading to excessively high die costs.[97] Despite Bel Geddes's accusation that Roberts "missed the boat" on "standardization," "Sales [of Geddes's SGE stove] rose, doubled, [and] held their gains."[98] In this instance, both Bel Geddes's modular design and his self-promotion in *Fortune* magazine and *Horizons* failed to convince his client of the unit block idea. The product's success, Roberts suggested, was as much a result of the "improvement in general business conditions" as the new design.[99] While Roberts was privately unimpressed with Bel Geddes, the purchasing public was introduced to the Bel Geddes

FIGURE 3.9 Bel Geddes-designed Acorn stove for Standard Gas Equipment Corporation, 1932. Photograph by Richard Garrison. Harry Ransom Center, University of Texas, and the Edith Lutyens and Norman Bel Geddes Foundation, Inc. 2016.

signature, thus initiating an important design device. As agreed in late 1930, the stove displayed the designer's monogram and the phrase, "This product designed by Norman Bel Geddes." The "signed" appliance presented the designer as akin to a named artist, and the industrialist as his patron. This image of an enlightened art and design partnership benefited the designer and the manufacturer, and the trend of "signing" mass-produced goods became common practice among industrial designers.[100]

Promoting the Bel Geddes name was essential to the design office. Despite a dependence on a large number of highly trained staff, Bel Geddes underlined the importance of maintaining his name above those of other office members, explaining, "it is necessary and advisable to handle most of our publicity through the channel of Norman Bel Geddes." He believed that "Other partners and associates, on occasion, should be developed, and built up." However, he reminded his staff that "establish[ing] a name requires so many years and such a series of outstanding performances that the bulk of our publicity will be more profitably placed through the Norman Bel Geddes name." Such promotion was "not a job of getting personal publicity for Mr. Geddes," but "only of value when it enhances the status and stature of our business as a whole."[101] Bel Geddes's publicity, whether it was advertising for a stove or a publication on visionary design, continued the personality-driven approach first established with *InWhich*. While this may have led to accusations of egotism, in 1958 *Industrial Design* magazine defended his self-centered promotion: "Geddes was absorbed not in himself, but in any work he was doing at that moment. Yet, he had a tremendous respect for other people's talent and ideas; he only demanded of them the same high standards which he imposed upon himself."[102]

Horizons and *Towards a New Architecture*

Despite Bel Geddes's self-presentation as an original designer, his understanding of modernism was derived from a range of contemporary avant-garde designs and ideas. In *Horizons*, he employed functionalist rhetoric to present himself as a modernist, explaining "when an object is in keeping with the purpose it serves, it appeals to us as having a distinctive kind of beauty" (20). Prior to its publication, he wrote that *Horizons* would be a "book of plans and designs by an architectural designer" that was "workmanlike" in appearance, "inclined toward the modernistic" without being "freakish."[103] His appropriation of modernism may have been an attempt to legitimate the emerging field of design consultancy, but it was also an important strategy in selling goods. In 1930, Earnest Elmo Calkins, an advertising man at the Calkins and Holden advertising agency and long-time advocate of the cash value of art in design, championed what he termed "styling the goods," offering "modernism" as a key tool in "merchandising." He suggested that the redesign of goods in the "modern spirit" could generate "consumer dissatisfaction" and encourage the "displace[ment]" of "outdated, old-fashioned, obsolete," but "still useful" things.[104] His approach seemed to turn modernism against itself, advocating modernist design to achieve obsolescence and nonfunction. Keenly aware of the expressive power of modernism in design and advertising, he wrote, "modernism offered the opportunity of expressing the inexpressible, of suggesting not so much a motor car as speed, not so much a gown as style, not so much a compact as beauty" (497). Likewise, as a stage designer Bel Geddes knew the importance of distilling the essence of a play in order to interpret its mood.

Although Bel Geddes's initial understanding of modernism was through avant-garde stage design, Le Corbusier's architectural manifesto, *Towards a New Architecture*, provided a significant tutorial in modernist architectural design and an essential blueprint for *Horizons*. *Horizons*'s content and philosophy closely follow *Towards a New Architecture*: both are littered with industrial imagery and modernist rhetoric. Both celebrate airplanes, steamships, automobiles, engineering, and architecture. While *Towards a New Architecture* contained the sections, "Airplanes," "Automobiles," and "Mass-Production Houses," *Horizons* included the chapters, "By Air To-morrow," "Motor Cars and Buses," and "New Houses for Old." *Horizons*, however, exceeded *Towards a New Architecture* in its sensational tone, expressive imagery, and its focus on design for mass consumption and entertainment, including lengthy discussions of stage design, world's fair exhibits, and window display.[105] Unlike Le Corbusier, Bel Geddes found a balance between rational modernism—which valued the "functional" and the "scientific" and was "divorced from stylistic considerations"—and more expressive forms of modernism, which harmonized with his interests in showmanship, drama, and commerce.[106]

Both Le Corbusier and Bel Geddes privileged the engineer's practicality and logic, and embraced the artist or architect's spiritual contributions, arguing for the tempering of utilitarian design with an emotional sensibility.[107] Le Corbusier proclaimed, "[t]he Engineer, inspired by the law of Economy and governed by mathematical calculation, puts us in accord with universal laws" (11). Bel Geddes highlighted these words in his copy of *Towards a New Architecture*, and parroted the Swiss architect in *Horizons*: "These engineers, inspired by economy and mathematics ... accepted the machine as the proper inspiration."[108] Both authors heralded the machine as design's guiding light and called for a break with outmoded forms. Le Corbusier wrote, "Let us look at things from the point of view of architecture, but in the state of mind of the inventor of airplanes" (109–110). Bel Geddes proclaimed that both "the airplane' and "the finest architecture" elicit an "emotional response."[109] Both designers juxtaposed images of classical architecture with structures of mass production, power, and flight, including the Parthenon, cylindrical grain silos, and the arcing, concrete Freysinnet dirigible hangar, illustrating a shared appreciation for both the geometric-based forms of classical modernism and the parabolic curve found in streamlined design.[110] Bel Geddes may have also seen Francis S. Oderdonk's *The Ferro-Concrete Style: Reinforced Concrete in Modern Architecture* (1928), which depicted the French hangar and rhapsodized about the parabola as a symbol of the infinite and the divine.[111]

While the photographs in Le Corbusier's book represented such objects and structures in a documentary fashion, Bel Geddes illustrated almost identical subjects, photographed in an expressive manner, using abstraction, dramatic lighting, and extreme perspectives. Such heightened modes of representation are consistent with his background in the New Stagecraft, his awareness of Expressionism and his interest in alternate forms of belief such as Theosophy, which encouraged envisioning an alternate world beyond everyday reality (Figure 3.10). *Horizons*'s emphasis on photography is consistent with Bel Geddes's appreciation of machine art. In his book, he predicted, "Art will be achieved by the machine... Artists are fast mastering the camera, which is purely a machine."[112] *Horizons* displayed the work of America's leading avant-garde photographers, including Imogen Cunningham,

THREE REMINDERS TO ARCHITECTS 29

CANADIAN GRAIN STORES AND ELEVATORS

FIGURE 3.10 Le Corbusier, Canadian Grain Store, and Elevators, in *Towards a New Architecture*, 1927. © FLC/ ADAGP, Paris and DACS, London 2017.

Ralph Steiner, Margaret Bourke-White, and Edward Steichen, a pioneer of advertising photography. Bel Geddes reprinted Steichen's "Spectacles," a cubistic grid of dramatically lit eyeglasses, whose shadows and refracted light produced a repeating, two-dimensional abstraction. Steichen, who became the "most successful commercial photographer of the 1920s and 1930s—both artistically and financially,"[113] produced "Spectacles," as well as photographic abstractions of matches, sugar cubes, and mothballs, for the Stehli Silk Corporation's pioneering Americana Print series (1925–1927), a group of modernist textile patterns by well-known American artists—an early example of modernism in American design.[114] *Horizons*'s inclusion of Steichen and the photograph produced for the Americana Series suggests Bel Geddes's awareness of the historical link between industrial design, which was understood as an outgrowth of advertising, and commercial art, where many industrial designers got their start. Bourke-White's expressionistic photographs employed the visual vocabulary of modernist image-makers, using repetition to mimic machine rhythms and extreme perspectives to add visual dynamism. Bel Geddes included Bourke-White's dramatic images of foreboding dynamos and looming grain silos in *Horizons*. The prolific Bourke-White, whose work appeared in *Fortune* and the widely read picture magazine *Life*, "arguably, set the visual style for industrial America."[115] Her image of plow blades appeared in *Fortune,* March 1930, and in *Horizons* two years later, demonstrating a kinship between the publications (Figure 3.11).

The final image of both *Horizons* and *Towards a New Architecture* reveal key differences between Le Corbusier and Bel Geddes. *Horizons* closed with a photograph by the American experimental photographer Bruguière, a mysterious nonrepresentational composition of light bursting through a series of cuts in a two-dimensional plane (Figure 3.12). Bruguière became known for his psychologically expressive photographic abstractions, using multiple exposures and forms modulated by light. Bruguière had photographed the light compositions of the Clavilux; and Bel Geddes may have met him through the Theater Guild, where he was the official photographer (1919–1927) and had contributed to a theater design.[116] *Towards a New Architecture*, on the other hand, concluded with a photo-realistic illustration of a briar pipe isolated on a white background. While Le Corbusier presented an ideal type-object and tool for contemplation, Bel Geddes's expressive image, by the follower of Theosophy photographer Bruguière, suggested the evolution of visionary thought. Despite these differing images, the final remarks of each tract outline a shared belief in the progressive power of design. Continuing his effort to expand the mental horizons of his readers and encourage a wider acceptance of modern design among industrialists and the public, Bel Geddes concludes: "It takes more even than imagination to be progressive. It takes vision and courage."[117] Likewise, Le Corbusier called for the rejection of conventional habits, warning "Architecture or Revolution. Revolution can be avoided."[118] *Towards a New Architecture*'s rational tone contrasted starkly with *Horizons*'s visionary outlook. While Le Corbusier applied the engineer's aesthetic to modernist architectural design, Bel Geddes hoped to engineer consumption through modern design and expressive imagery. Le Corbusier addressed architects who he wished to reform, while Bel Geddes spoke to industrialists who he desired as clients and consumers he hoped to transform. Bel Geddes looked to Le Corbusier to present industrial design as a serious profession, which was as logical as engineering, as avant-garde as modernist architecture, and more effective than both in selling goods.

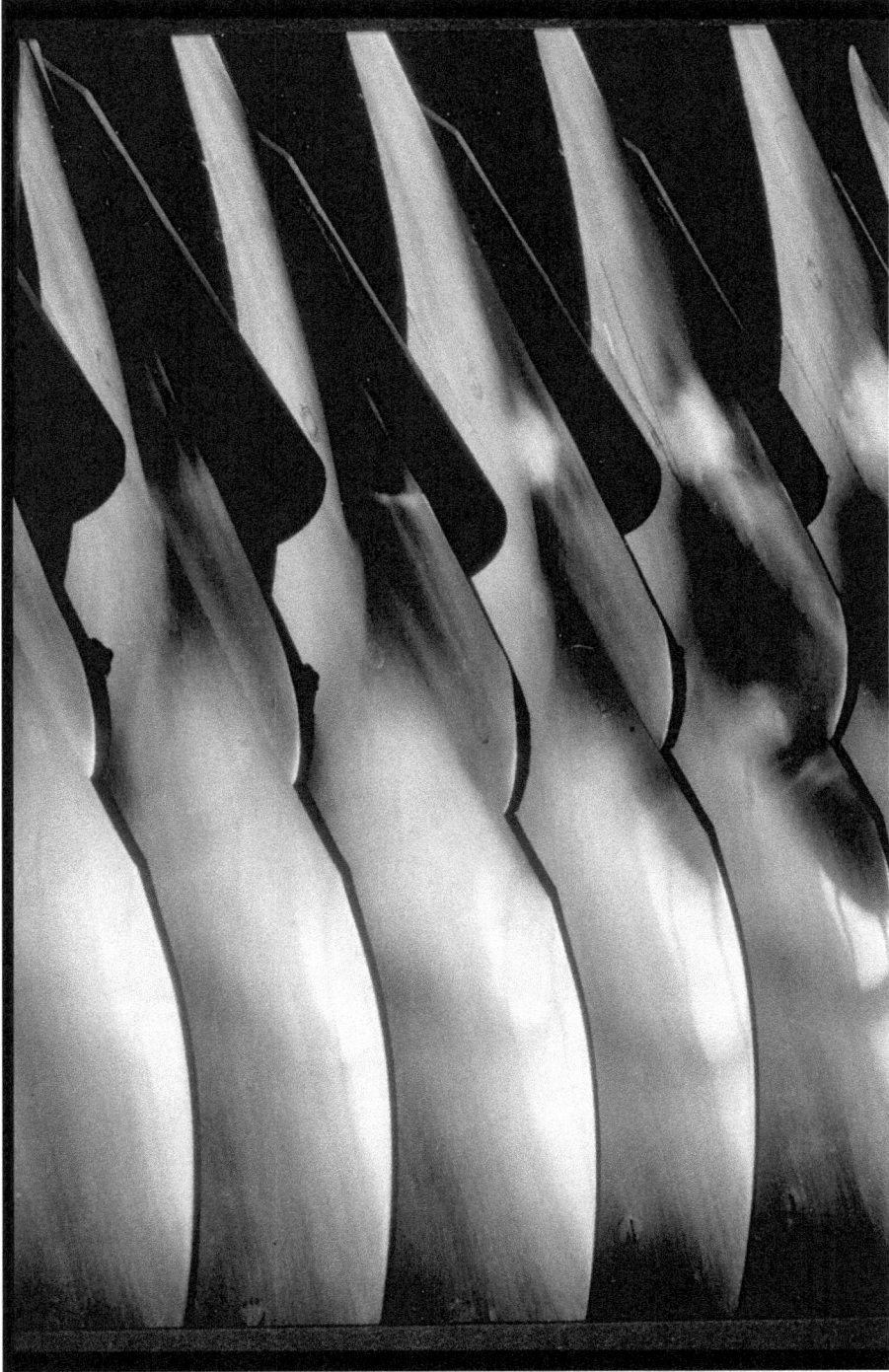

FIGURE 3.11 Margaret Bourke-White, "Plow Blades, Oliver Chilled Plow Co.," 1929, illustrated in *Horizons*, 1932. © Getty.

222 · STILL LIFE   PHOTOGRAPH BY FRANCIS BRUGIERE 1927

FIGURE 3.12 An abstract study based on a skull by Francis Bruguière, *c.* 1930, appeared as "Still Life" and was the final image in *Horizons*, 1932. Kenneth Hamilton (Sather) Bruguière 2016.

Influences of technocracy and scientific management

Horizons included a detailed critique of America's productive system. The book called for the commercial competition of "rampant individualists" to be exchanged for "rational cooperation" between manufacturers.[119] Again, Bel Geddes returned to the machine metaphor that suffused the book. His "plan" would provide a "self-adjusting, economic mechanism" where "output would be controlled, the cost of competition would be eliminated, and the evils of fluctuation in industrial activity would be greatly reduced" (289). In keeping with the social Darwinism of engineering ideology, Bel Geddes outlined his solution—the inevitable evolutionary change in business toward the rule of experts and cooperation in the marketplace. "Industrial organization is gradually changing from the free competition ... toward a unification of these independent companies cooperating with each other towards a common purpose ... progress and combination are synonymous" (289). Bel Geddes's concepts were not unique. His recommendations were derived from the Russian five-year plan (1928–1932) and recent technocratic theory, especially its promotion of governance by technical experts. In the "future," he wrote, the "most capable people in the municipality will run it in the same way that the best brains in a business manage it" (284). While he was skeptical of Russia's revolutionary project, he believed American business had much to learn from the soviet experiment (289–291).

Bel Geddes's belief in machine solutions to social and economic problems echoed efficiency movement theorists and technocratic leaders, who promoted a rational approach to mastering machine-age modernity. Published in the year of the Bolshevik Revolution, Bel Geddes's copy of *The Twelve Principles of Efficiency* (1917), by Harrington Emerson, a significant popularizer of scientific management, equated efficiency with civilization and higher morals, and saw the machine as the primary engine of progress.[120] Likewise, Veblen felt that America's productive system was dangerously mismanaged and believed the engineer, rather than the financier or businessman, should regulate industrial output. Many of the strategies outlined in Bel Geddes's critique of capitalism recall those of Veblen's influential tract *The Engineers and the Price System* (1921).[121] After the stock market crash, Veblen's economic philosophy was revived through the sudden vogue for technocracy, a political and economic movement that advocated technical expertise to promote human welfare by balancing production and consumption capacities.[122] While *Horizons* may have attracted interest as Technocracy gained momentum, it may equally have suffered from its association with the extreme views of the movement and the dubious status of its founder, the bogus engineer Howard Scott (1890–1970).[123]

Like Veblen, Bel Geddes called for centralized planning, price controls, commercial cooperation, and controlled productive output.[124] Bel Geddes, however, never went as far as Veblen who had called for a "soviet of engineers," a new ruling class of technicians. Nor did Bel Geddes call for an end to "salesmanship," which Veblen viewed as an unnecessary accompaniment to competition and a substitute for price reduction.[125] Bel Geddes wrote that his plan would put an end to commercial competition and employ "good design" "to gain the confidence of the public for particular products."[126] The economic theories expressed in *Horizons* seem at odds with the very aims of the American industrial design profession and its origins within competitive capitalism. Was Bel Geddes advocating a dead-end strategy for industrial design? Or was he searching for the ultimate environment for nurturing design practice? Was Bel Geddes an idealist who urged the reform of industrial capitalism, or was he merely aping the rhetoric of liberal intellectuals? One thing is certain: Bel Geddes's foray into economic theory and social planning lifted *Horizons* from mere popular mechanics to the realm of economics and politics. *Horizons*'s machine-age punditry and visionary designs effectively presented Bel Geddes as a technological prophet, delighting some and infuriating others.

Horizons' press reception

When it was first published in 1932, *Horizons* appealed to a popular interest in optimistic visions of the future. It was widely reviewed in many local and national newspapers, as well as specialist magazines dealing with transportation and engineering.[127] As cultural historian Jeffrey L. Meikle has written, "*Horizons* (1932) cornered the market on Sunday supplement views of 'the world of tomorrow.'"[128] Some reviewers saw the book as logical and serious—evidence of the triumph of machine-age mentality, while others thought it merely promoted change for its own sake. Despite its prolonged investigations of architecture—five of its fourteen chapters dealt with the subject—and its embrace of modernist design, Bel Geddes's book was dismissed as mere advertising and spectacle by numerous architectural commentators.[129] Architectural critics who panned the book included Lewis Mumford, who considered it derivative, and Douglas Haskell, who thought it wedded "the ingenuities of popular mechanics to those of advertising psychology."[130] Mumford included *Horizons* in the bibliography of *Technics and Civilization*, 1934, his influential cultural history of technology. However, he was cautious in his judgment, writing that it provided "suggestions of new forms for machines and utilities... While it owes more to publicity than scholarship."[131] Frank Lloyd Wright, on the other hand, was scathing, in his review of the book for the *The Saturday Review of Literature* (1932) warning the theatrical designer, "lip-service to the results of scientific research ... has little of value to offer either art or industry except as it becomes a sort of stage scenery continued for sensational effect."[132] These criticisms suggest that the architectural profession had yet to fully embrace the commercial impulse that underpinned the growing advertising and marketing industries.

A *New York Times* critic, R. L. Duffus provided a detailed commentary of *Horizons* in 1932. Duffus viewed Bel Geddes's work as derivative, particularly of the architectural ideas of Louis Sullivan and Wright, but felt that the importance of the book lay in its unbounded vision, "the imagination, the energy and the daring—one might almost say the recklessness... He has swallowed the machine, cogs and all, and has shown how it can be assimilated into a thing of beauty,"[133] a view shared by Nelson in 1934, who considered Bel Geddes's "H.G. Wells type" "artistic criticism" "effective and forceful."[134] Despite his qualified approval, Duffus resented Bel Geddes's assumption that the machine had come to dominate life. "Mr. Geddes takes a heavy burden upon his shoulders when he assumes, as he does, that machinery must remain an integral part of our lives because we use it to produce goods and services. It would be just as easy to make an opposite deduction."[135] Duffus countered Bel Geddes's assertion that the depression was the result of a consumer rebellion against poor design, suggesting instead that it was caused by a revolt against the "gadget civilization—against the assumption that industry is a way of life rather than a means of living."[136] Ironically, the *Christian Science Monitor* sought to rein in Bel Geddes's visionary tendencies, revealing perhaps the greatest anxiety toward the emerging industrial design profession, "we are more than a little fearful of the work of that small group of extraordinary artists known as product designers ... we fear the product designer because his commodity is change."[137]

While some reviewers saw the industrial designer as the source of disruptive modernization, others celebrated Bel Geddes's attempt to engineer a Depression recovery, whether through consumption or monumental planning. Those who applauded the book viewed it as evidence of the triumph of the machine-age mindset and the mentality of the engineer. In a publication aimed at engineers it was proclaimed that "the public imagination is to-day as active as the creative minds of the engineers."[138] The engineering magazine the *Power Specialist* recommended the book for "every industrial and business executive, every engineer and every man." The author presented Bel Geddes's ideas as logical and farseeing and *Horizons*'s large-scale projects as "practical" solutions to the present economic crisis.[139]

Though Bel Geddes hoped that his book wouldn't be seen as "freakish," many commentators recognized the fantastic and the dreamlike in its illustrations and text.[140] "'Horizons,' [*sic*] is, as its name implies, a far off state, a dream hidden deep in the subconscious of most men. This dream will eventually become a reality," wrote one Cincinnati reviewer.[141] Duffus considered Bel Geddes's world of tomorrow bizarre and offered a surreal interpretation of *Horizons* that wedded mechanical and organic imagery: "motor cars looking like beetles progressing backward; theatres with contours suggesting puddings or poached eggs; aerial restaurants set on stalks like mushrooms—these are the impressions to be derived by the habit-bound reader from Mr. Geddes's book, and they may be painful" (Plate 18).[142] Despite the critics' opinions, *Horizons* helped construct the image of the industrial designer as a visionary and depression-era savior. As a servant and savant of industry, the new industrial designer as outlined in Bel Geddes's book epitomized efficiency and foresight, allowing clients to see beyond technological, stylistic, and economic horizons.[143]

Technological forecasting in *Horizons*

In the 1930s, industrial design became closely associated with prophesying, especially through the forecast of technological and stylistic trends. *Horizons* played a key role in this development. While the book's fantastic imagery of streamlined vehicles helped to visualize the future, its predictions of new inventions, materials, and technologies provided specific details about the shape of things to come. The business magazine *Forbes* noted "most" of Bel Geddes's "seemingly fantastic" predictions "are on the way," and presented Bel Geddes as a "sort of Jules Verne hero to millions of readers of the Sunday magazine sections." Adding, "The boldness of his ideas, plus his talent for capturing the spotlight, started a tidal wave of publicity."[144] Though Bel Geddes claimed his forecasts were logical and plausible, critics often dismissed them as pure fantasy. In *Horizons*, they included: the use of science to dissipate fog and high winds,[145] all-metal dirigibles,[146] art produced by the machine,[147] and the mass production of personal airplanes.[148] In 1931, Bel Geddes published a torrent of forecasts in "Ten Years from Now" in the *Ladies' Home Journal*.[149] As in *Horizons*, the article presented technology and science as improving and rationalizing forces. Whereas *Horizons* was aimed at America's industrialists, his *Ladies' Home Journal* articles introduced Bel Geddes to a primarily female readership as "one of the most daring yet practical originators of new ideas." Illustrated with a zeppelin moored above a futuristic city, the article predicted that in ten years, "all of the following prophecies will be old fashioned": double-deck streets, airplanes that take off vertically, inner-city airplane hangars, landing field roads, neon tube lighting, three-dimensional movies, and rear-engine, streamlined cars; all diseases will be eradicated; "Artists will be thinking in terms of the industrial problems of our age"; not forgetting his fellow Promethean Thomas Wilfred, the "Color Organ" will become a "recognized medium of expression"; weather and agriculture will be scientifically controlled; and crime will be diminished through medical and surgical treatment.[150] As in *Horizons*, Bel Geddes offered a rational solution to the economic instability of capitalism. In the future, he suggested, a "Commercial League of Nations will regulate international commerce. So, there will be no slumps [and] no booms." Perhaps revealing pessimism in the pace of technological change, by the late 1930s Bel Geddes's prophecies would look twenty, rather than ten, years into the future.

Despite the predicted flood of beneficial change, the article concluded with a sobering, yet accommodating, message. Bel Geddes wrote that ten years from now "There will still be cruelty and intolerance. There will still be generosity and unselfishness. There will still be workers and drones. In other words there will still be—men and women."[151] Perhaps meant to ease any fears of radical rupture brought on by technological change, the quote suggests that the future will be based upon the past, and reminded readers that people won't change, but the material world will.

Bel Geddes was not alone in prophetic writing, which proliferated during the period in both the general press and popular science journals. Technological forecasting had been common in nineteenth-century utopian novels, as well as late-nineteenth and early-twentieth-century science fiction, often populated by towering ziggurats, streamlined vehicles, and sleek zeppelins. Much of the science fiction of the 1930s had its roots in progressive thought of the first decades of the twentieth century.[152] The fashion for science fiction writing was accompanied by a similar vogue for futurology. Bel Geddes owned many books by the leading forecaster and author H. G. Wells, including *A Year of Prophesying* (1925), *The Way the World Is Going: Guesses and Forecasts of the Year-Ahead* (1929), and *The Shape of Things to Come* (1933), which Bel Geddes filled with pencil markings. He also collected prophetic newspaper articles, including Thomas Edison's opinions on the future.[153] Bel Geddes's appreciation of H. G. Wells illustrates the designer's view that futurology was an essential part of industrial design. "Though I have never met H. G. Wells, if I do I have a speech prepared in which I will ask him to deed the title of one of his finest works 'The Shape of Things to Come' for use by the industrial designer."[154] Wells's writing was in many cases about the fourth dimension: time—whether time travel or predicting the future. In that sense, Bel Geddes's interest in his writing is consistent with his wider fascination with Ouspensky and Bragdon's more spiritual notion of the fourth dimension.

Why was there such an abundance of prognosticating, especially in the early 1930s? Why was Bel Geddes eager to participate? Perhaps there was a public desire for fantasy and escape during the period of economic stagnation and uncertainty. Was the creation of utopian technological fantasies a contemporary response to cultural lag—the sense of imbalance between technology and society?[155] Arthur Pulos suggests that industrial designers who produced radical futuristic conceptions did so because they were "often impatient with industry's cautious movement."[156] Pulos also offers that "blue-sky" design, houses of tomorrow and dream products "generated a public restlessness and a desire to move forward more quickly in the future."[157]

Technological forecasts by industrial designers were usually predictions of future consumer activity. Though forecasting was a consistent practice of Bel Geddes throughout most of his career, it tended to be most prolific during periods of decreased consumption, such as the 1930s depression and the Second World War.[158] Therefore, technological prophecy, though ostensibly about invention and production, should be viewed as an effort to stimulate consumer desire. Bel Geddes's forecasts helped him attract industrial clients who hoped to cash in on his celebrity as a practical prophet. In addition, his technological forecasts helped to promote an image of control and foresight for the fledgling industrial design profession.

Bel Geddes was aware that prophecy might provide comfort in hard times, especially during periods of decreased consumption and material scarcity. A transcript collected by the Geddes office of a 1932 *San Francisco Chronicle* article made just that point. "Depressions, oddly enough, are always high old times for prophets. Perhaps this is because during days of economic stress prophesying is about all there is from [which] common man may take comfort; or perhaps people simply get into the habit of listening to their prophets in bad times."[159] The author expressed a suspicion of technological prophets and an awareness of the public's vulnerability under economic duress. Such an expression of despair and cynicism remained unspoken in Bel Geddes's writing.

The industrial designer Harold Van Doren in his textbook *Industrial Design*, 1940, echoed a negative view of prophesying. Van Doren was, however, more concerned with the detrimental effect of associating prophetic fantasies with the increasingly professional practice of industrial design. The more outrageous technological forecasts, especially those of flying cars and push-button living, linked industrial design more with science fiction than the seriousness of an emerging profession. Bel Geddes's book *Magic Motorways*, 1940, was equally promotional and prophetic and outlined his plans for a national highway system. In the spirit of the practical visionary, it claimed, "This book is not merely a prophecy—it is a warning especially to planners, that their plans will soon be outdated unless they are truly forward thinking."[160] Pulos has written that the "glamour" of design forecasting within the profession attracted "less qualified opportunists," and the profession's "glittering reputation began to tarnish."[161] Designers, like Dreyfuss, emphasized that spectacle and sensationalism didn't belong in industrial design (402). This raised consciousness encouraged more experienced designers to "monitor their own behavior and set themselves apart from less responsible usurpers of the unprotected title of industrial designer" (402). Pulos suggests that the eventual outcome of this situation was the establishment of the Society of Industrial Designers (SID) in 1944 in New York (402).

In a chapter entitled "Ethics and Practice," Van Doren reprinted the Code of Practice adopted by the SID, which included both Van Doren and Bel Geddes among its founding members.[162] Like the ideology of the engineer, the code emphasized moral responsibility to the client and the public. It also sought to protect the image of the industrial design profession.[163] This was done, in part, by prohibiting general and unfounded forecasts. Van Doren wrote: "He [the industrial designer] shall refrain from making forecasts or prophecies for publication or publicity, graphic or written, unless they are the result of thorough research and analysis of a specific design problem" (31). If the SID was founded to protect the professional status of industrial designers, to purge it of the "less responsible usurpers," how can we explain Bel Geddes's inclusion as a founding member? He was arguably the most sensational and prophetic of the society's founders. Perhaps his celebrity status as well as his design achievements made it impossible to exclude him.

To sell his services to new clients, Bel Geddes developed an image for himself as a practical visionary. He fused the rational rhetoric of the engineer with that of the visionary artist. He did so by mimicking modernist designers like Le Corbusier, borrowing philosophies from technocratic idealists like Veblen and Emerson, and engaging in technological forecasting. This approach, developed and articulated in *Horizons* and publicized in both the popular and trade press, significantly contributed to the image of industrial design in the early 1930s and played an important role in legitimating industrial design during its early years. As with *Horizons*, Bel Geddes's architectural designs would be guided by the understanding of the machine as the dominant symbol of the era.

4

A Machine-Age Architecturalist: Planning the Factory, Service Station, and the Mass-Produced Home

The capacity of Bel Geddes's imagination was matched perhaps only by his professional ambitions. The inescapable fact that he lacked architectural training seemed only to spur his career-long engagement in architectural design, whether he planned a progressive factory, novel restaurants, modern gas stations, or prefabricated houses. As with much of Bel Geddes's work, these projects were guided by a desire for publicity and increased income for himself and his clients. His numerous architectural plans expressed machine-age values, helped to sell goods, and enhanced the image of Bel Geddes and his clients as logical and farsighted. Bel Geddes ensured that his building designs had at least one attention-grabbing, publicity-generating feature, whether prefabrication, speed of assembly, or modern styling.

Between 1929 and 1945, Bel Geddes's designs included an innovative factory development for the Toledo Scale Company (1929), a modern service station for the Socony-Vacuum Company (1934), a cooperative residential development for the Housing Corporation of America (1939–1940), and a futuristic factory-built home for Revere Copper and Brass (1941–1945). Though these projects were not fully realized, Bel Geddes's designs addressed issues that concerned many modernist architects: new technologies, mass production, affordable housing, and worker welfare. These plans, with their emphasis on modernist design, social reform, and new technology, linked Bel Geddes with the architectural avant-garde, as well as the popular utopianism of science fiction. Having largely created the role of industrial designer, Bel Geddes's new profession effectively challenged the position of architects, and "in a number of key instances, set the pace."[1] However, designing buildings without proper qualifications attracted scorn and jeopardized his schemes, spurring the self-proclaimed "architecturalist" to seek an architectural license during the 1930s. The reasons his application was declined are explored below.[2]

In the first decades of the twentieth century, numerous progressive manufacturers, designers, and architects trumpeted the machine as a utopian symbol and, accordingly, the factory as the "master machine."[3] In 1901, Frank Lloyd Wright argued that the intelligent use of the machine as a tool of abstraction and purification could redeem architecture.[4] Three years later he wrote that the "machine" as an artistic tool had become a "truism" throughout the world, a passage Bel Geddes underlined in his copy of Wright's book, *Modern Architecture* (1931).[5] In *Towards a New Architecture*, Bel Geddes highlighted a section where Le Corbusier presented the Fordist ethos as the salvation of architecture:

We must create the mass-production spirit.
The spirit of constructing mass-production houses.
The spirit of living in mass-production houses.
The spirit of conceiving mass-production houses.[6]

Le Corbusier's marriage of industrial and spiritual rhetoric would have appealed to Bel Geddes, who sought a metaphysical foundation for the machine age.

Toledo Scale factory

Since the beginning of Western industrialization, the factory has been a potent and multivalent symbol of modernity, equally romanticized and criticized as a revolutionary site of change. In the nineteenth century, it was alternately blamed for the degradation of labor and praised as a harbinger of social reform.[7] In the twentieth century, with the advert of Ford's Five Dollar Day, the factory promised both social and technical innovation, heralding an era of affordable goods and well-paid worker/consumers. During the first decades of the twentieth century, engineers described ways to build better factories following the principles of scientific management. Through the application of Taylorism and progressive design, they sought to reduce wasted time, energy, and materials, while improving productivity.[8] In addition, architects increasingly included in their factory designs social and recreational facilities, reflecting a wider concern for corporate welfare and the image of service, thus countering critics of rampant capitalism.

Many modernist architects understood the factory as the ultimate machine-age icon. In the 1910s, Antonio Sant'Elia, the Italian futurist architect, and Erich Mendelsohn independently completed expressive sketches of imaginary factory projects. The Faguswerk, designed in 1911 by Walter Gropius and Hannes Meyer, is often considered the "first building of the Modern Movement."[9] Le Corbusier would later declare, "Such are the factories, the reassuring first fruits of the new age."[10] In 1928, Harvard's dean of architecture G. H. Edgell wrote, the "scale" and "impressive structure" of a "power-plant has a certain romance ... It suggests the titanic forces of nature controlled by the genius of man and ... on a large scale, it can hardly lack a certain grandeur."[11] By 1930, Cheney joined the chorus, considering the factory the moral symbol of the age and the guiding metaphor in domestic design.[12] Echoing Le Corbusier, he wrote, "[j]ust as the inefficient house, the unmechanised house, is immoral, so is the dirty, ill-lighted, badly planned factory immoral."[13] Bel Geddes would also conflate the factory and the home: "In all its essentials, a house should be organized as a factory is. For it *is* a factory of a kind."[14] Despite such unswerving machine-age optimism, during the economic depression of the 1930s overproduction and technological unemployment shook the economy and society, leading many to blame American industry and question the ideology of progress.[15] Bel Geddes's designs of gleaming industrial architecture, however, aimed to stem this tide of discontent by contributing to the iconography of modernity and encouraging a renewed faith in industrial capitalism.[16]

By hiring Bel Geddes, the Toledo Scale Company aimed to produce improved products, better workers, and a progressive corporate image. Although the Toledo Scale Company was a J. Walter Thompson client, Bel Geddes had links with the firm through his uncle Fred Geddes, a member of the Toledo Scale Board of Trustees. Despite being invited to plan a vast but unrealized factory development for Toledo Scale in April 1929, Geddes's first assignment for the company was to conceive a group of innovative weighing scales.[17] His designs of scales for the Ohio manufacturer reflected his Taylorist approach to factory design. His island scale, which integrated a counter, scale, and storage, consolidated equipment and worker motions, "thus a package can be weighed and wrapped without leaving the counter, saving innumerable steps." Mechanized components were "concealed" in the base, and an "illuminated weight dial" at eye level provided the consumer with a promise of accuracy. During a period of economic belt-tightening and an increased concern regarding the precision of weighing scales, the consumers' trust could make or break a new product.[18] The architectural porcelain cylinders contained wrapping paper, while the rack below held paper bags and sundries and was made of Monel metal.[19] At the time, the nickel and copper alloy became strongly associated with both industry and modernist design. A predecessor to stainless steel, the noncorroding white metal was widely used in industrial and architectural applications in the first decades of the twentieth century. It would later be embraced by modernist designers such as George Sakier, whose Monel metal sink featured prominently in MoMA's *Machine Art* exhibition of 1934. The sleek design of the Bel Geddes island scale created a weighing surface that was flush with the black, glass countertop. The overall effect was one of honesty and efficiency. Referencing avant-garde art and American industry, it echoed cubist lines in its angular base and the modernist iconography of grain silos in its porcelain cylinders (Figure 4.1). Harold Van Doren later took up the weighing scale job, capitalizing on recent innovations in plastic.[20] Bel Geddes's scale designs never made it off the drawing board, perhaps due to the company delays in plastics research, a development initiated by Bel Geddes. However, the impressive architectonic forms were visualized in watercolor and graphite by Alexander Leydenfrost and seen in *Fortune*, *Horizons*, and the trade press.[21]

Bel Geddes's next job for Toledo was designed to appeal to industrialists, workers, and consumers—an eighty-acre factory development, which included an administrative building, a factory, a testing laboratory, recreational facilities, and an airport. A poplar-lined avenue led to a 120-foot-wide reflecting pool fronting the eleven-story administrative building (Figure 4.2).[22] Bel Geddes considered the project a significant example of impression management that used functionalist design to provide an image of beauty, efficiency, and industrial welfare. He described the development's main avenue as the company's "front door," contrasting it with the "unsightly backyard ... that distinguishes the approach to our industrial cities."[23] The design of the various buildings emphasized cleanliness (the removal of dust-catching surfaces), improved ventilation

FIGURE 4.1 Rendering of Toledo Scale Company, Island Scale, probably Alexander Leydenfrost, undated, *c.* 1929. Harry Ransom Center, University of Texas, and the Edith Lutyens and Norman Bel Geddes Foundation, Inc. 2016.

and lighting (larger windows, glass walls, and uniform illumination), flexibility (moveable partitions and structures designed for future expansion), and efficiency (spatial considerations for line production). Parroting the language of functionalist design, Bel Geddes asserted that the buildings

FIGURE 4.2 Rendering of Bel Geddes-designed Toledo Scale administrative building showing tree-lined avenue and reflecting pool, *c.* 1929. Harry Ransom Center, University of Texas, and the Edith Lutyens and Norman Bel Geddes Foundation, Inc. 2016.

were designed as a "direct expression of the[ir] purpose," employing steel, glass, concrete, cantilever construction, and no ornamentation.[24] Consistent with contemporary industrial reform, the factory development provided workers with recreational facilities, including tennis courts, a baseball field, and a picnic ground.

Fortune's 1930 article on Bel Geddes praised the Toledo development: "there are many who feel that the industrial civilization is capable of producing a vibrant, distinctive art, and that Toledo's plant, now under construction, is an example and a harbinger."[25] Emphasizing industry as an artistic patron, *Fortune*'s celebration of factory architecture benefited Toledo Scale, Bel Geddes, and corporate capitalism. Reaching a significant segment of American business, *Fortune* presented the Toledo Scale plan as a symbol of progressive commercial enterprise and cast Bel Geddes as an art-in-industry leader.

The magazine assured its readers of the benefit of art-in-industry, while sympathizing with the corporate leader who may view artists with suspicion. *Fortune* noted the initial skepticism with which industrialists regarded Bel Geddes (55). H. D. Bennett, the president of Toledo Scale, thought Bel Geddes "inexperienced and suspiciously esthetic." As if to soothe the worries of the business magazine's readers, the Toledo scheme was called "heroic in scale" and "planned" for "present and future utility" (56). Attempting to sell modernism to American captains of industry, the article linked Bel Geddes with European avant-garde architects, including Le Corbusier and J. J. P. Oud, the Dutch rationalist (51). Quoting Oud, the author appealed to the matter-of-fact sensibility of American business, describing "new architecture" as "[d]isengaged from all impressionistic sentimentality; dependent on clear proportions, frank colors, plainly organic forms; [and] divested of all that is superfluous."[26] By associating modern architecture with American industry, the author sought to redefine corporate capitalism as pragmatic, honest, and straightforward.

In *Horizons*, Bel Geddes devoted an entire chapter to factory design as a tool to improve employee welfare, productivity, and public relations, using his Toledo Scale plan as a shining example. The chapter's discussion of early developments in American factory planning and its embrace by European designers gave the Toledo Scale project a modernist pedigree.[27] Essentially a pitch for Bel Geddes's services as a factory planner, the section echoed the Arts and Crafts Movement's critique of industry's dark past, criticizing "the beginnings of the industrial age— exploitation of the workers, oppressive hours, inhumane conditions, dirt, poorly organized buildings."[28] Insisting that a "first-rate product" cannot be made in a "third-rate plant," Bel Geddes argued for the industrial designer as the ideal factory architect, one who knew the merchandize and its method of manufacture, thus usurping the roles of both engineer and architect.[29] Offering a solution compatible with big business and consistent with enlightened factory design, he insisted that success in industry relied on the "human factor"—the relationship between employer and employee: "light, cleanliness, ventilation, and even agreeable surroundings were advantageous not only to the employees but to the profits and peace of mind of the employers."[30] Bel Geddes's progressive factory countered past associations with William Blake's "dark satanic mills," while providing an image of industrial reform.[31]

In the years following the Bolshevik Revolution, the view that architecture could ideologically and socially shape its inhabitants was not uncommon. Bel Geddes was aware of European design theories regarding the influence of architecture on its users. In his copy of Bruno Taut's *Modern Architecture* (*c.* 1929), he underlined numerous sections on architecture's effects on human behavior. Like Bel Geddes, Taut had cast off an earlier fascination with the spiritual in design, turning instead to an emerging functionalism, exemplifying a wider transformation among German expressionist architects after the First World War.[32] In 1927, Taut wrote: "To speak of spiritualization is also impossible today."[33] By 1929, he described architecture as a tool of social engineering, writing that a building of functional and unified design

> will not only fulfil our needs, but organise them into a superior and better order than previously experienced. The architect who achieves this task becomes a creator of an ethical and social character ... Thus architecture becomes the creator of new social observances.[34]

In *New World Architecture*, a 1930 survey of modernist architecture, Cheney extolled the contributions of Le Corbusier, Mendelsohn, and Taut. Like Taut, Cheney viewed architecture as a catalyst of a new social order.

> If the workmen are to rule the world ... then let us hope that there is a symbol in the lightness and openness here; let us even believe that the new architecture here again reflects a world drift to open minds, light let in, the life of unconcealment [*sic*] – darkness conquers.[35]

For Cheney the increased openness and illumination of the progressive factory, available through the generous use of glass, steel, cantilevering, and electric lighting, symbolized political transparency and social enlightenment—the empowerment of laborers and the hopes for a worker-run society. Despite his friendship with Cheney and his dabbling in Taut's socialistic theories, Bel Geddes was essentially interested in the balance between worker welfare and commercial culture, noting "the factory may be regarded as of real inspirational value to the workers and of advertising value to the manufacturer by virtue of its effect upon the passerby, who is also the consumer."[36]

Cheney observed that the machine aesthetic in architecture had derived from European architects' interpretation of American factories. He noted that Europeans, especially Le Corbusier and Mendelsohn, had urged their contemporaries to look to American factory architecture.[37] Cheney included Gropius, Poelzig, Taut, and Peter Behrens among the pioneers of factory design.[38] An important trailblazer of unified corporate identity, Behrens designed graphics, appliances, and factory buildings at the Allgemeine Elektrizitäts-Gesellschaft (AEG) after 1907.[39] Cheney was most impressed by Mendelsohn, who "rationally and most intensively" created images of factories, hangars, and train stations "expressive of the feel of the machine" (76, 97). Significantly, Cheney's book positioned Bel Geddes as a major designer of expressive buildings and included Alexander Leydenfrost's luminous renderings of the Toledo Scale factory, offering the project as the glowing future of America's "new world architecture."[40]

Despite their futuristic aura, perhaps inspired by the luminous architectural renderings of Hugh Ferriss, the images of the Toledo Scale factory show the influence of past designs by Mendelsohn

FIGURE 4.3 "Industrial Arts," Hugh Ferriss, from *The Metropolis of Tomorrow*, 1929. © Christopher M. Leich 2016.

and Wright, in their emphasis on horizontality, rounded corners, and overhanging roofs.[41] Bel Geddes's luminous nighttime image of the Toledo Scale factory employed a similar visual language as architectural renderer Hugh Ferris, whose depictions of often-imagined buildings based on modernist design principles seemed to harbor an urban utopia (Figures 4.3–4.5). Mendelsohn, who injected vitality and movement into his commercial architecture, had perhaps the greatest influence on Bel Geddes's architectural style.[42] Both designers had an interest in the metaphysical and the scientific, and shared a penchant for "dramatizing industry."[43] Mendelsohn may have introduced Bel Geddes to the idea that new architecture would be derived from the look of engineered products, such as engines and transport machinery.[44] Bel Geddes knew of Mendelsohn's factory design from his copy of *Structures and Sketches*, a gift from the author in November 1924. The streamlined forms of Bel Geddes's architectural designs, particularly the sweeping curves of the 1939 General Motors building and the corner facades of its life-size intersection, may owe much to those developed by Mendelsohn and depicted in his book.[45] The two designers' friendship continued after the Second World War.

Bel Geddes's ability to realize his visualizations as actual buildings was hampered by the economy's collapse after 1929. Despite this and other setbacks, including county and state clashes over road development near the site, which delayed the project as the depression worsened, Bel Geddes's factory design attracted significant publicity through the business and trade press, helping to fashion a corporate identity for the Toledo Scale Company that reflected social improvement and forward planning.[46] Much of Bel Geddes's architectural work would exist only on paper, thus lending it an impressive and utopian aura. During the 1930s, such architectural imagery helped to refashion Bel Geddes from a bohemian artist to a pragmatic planner. However, upon the economy's recovery in 1939, Bennett hired the country's premier factory designer, Albert Kahn, having rejected Bel Geddes's ambitious plan.[47]

FIGURE 4.4 A night view of Bel Geddes's Toledo Scale factory development: Laboratory in foreground and machine shop in background, *c.* 1929. Harry Ransom Center, University of Texas, and the Edith Lutyens and Norman Bel Geddes Foundation, Inc. 2016.

FIGURE 4.5 Toledo Scale factory development model of machine shop, assembly shed, and laboratory. Photograph by Richard Garrison *c.* 1929. Harry Ransom Center, University of Texas, and the Edith Lutyens and Norman Bel Geddes Foundation, Inc. 2016.

The House of Tomorrow, 1931

Bel Geddes's residential schemes reflected his continued interest in modernist design as well as his entrepreneurial ambitions. Spanning 1931–1945, they highlight his desire for mass-produced housing, his sympathies with socialistic planning, and his efforts to take advantage of the anticipated construction boom, during a period of increased government housing programs designed to benefit the economy while assisting house builders, lenders, and homeowners.[48] Bel Geddes's residential plans illustrate his success in marshaling modern design and rhetoric to construct a progressive image for himself and his clients, as in the *Ladies' Home Journal* "House of Tomorrow," a luxurious International Style home presented in the popular women's magazine in 1931 and later published in *Horizons* as "House Number 3." This was his first major effort to present himself as a knowledgeable designer of modern homes, explaining that to achieve "universal architecture" we must start from the "purely utilitarian basis to create a type of architectural beauty which reflects the spirit of the age."[49] The accompanying house design was consistent with much contemporary modernist design. It sported a flat roof and reinforced concrete and steel beams to accommodate generous fenestration, including horizontal strip windows, and an open plan interior (Plate 19).

Despite the fact that Bel Geddes referred to it as a small house, it contained two floors, five baths, five bedrooms (including one for a live-in maid), two roof gardens, and a garage. It was created in the spirit of the Corbusian villa of the mid- to late-1920s. Le Corbusier's often-luxurious villas illustrated his "five points" of architecture, which included the elevation of the mass from the ground through the use of pilotis; a free interior plan; a free façade; the long, horizontal strip window; and the roof garden.[50] Bel Geddes may have learned of Le Corbusier's domestic architecture as early as 1925 while in Paris staging *Jeanne d'Arc*. That year the Swiss architect had presented his Pavillon de L'Esprit Nouveau at the Exposition des Arts Décoratifs.[51] Like Le Corbusier, Bel Geddes employed functionalist rhetoric, yet produced designs of lavish residential architecture. While the *Ladies' Home Journal* "House of Tomorrow" made no attempt to heed Le Corbusier's call for a mass production spirit, three years later Bel Geddes's design of a gas station for Socony-Vacuum Oil Company did. In so doing, he continued his effort to wed the utopian and utilitarian ideals of modernism with American industry.

A modern, mass-produced service station: Socony-Vacuum, 1934

In the late 1920s, in the United States an increased need for service stations accompanied a rise in automobile ownership, paving the way for designers to redefine the American road as a landscape of speed and efficiency. In 1934, Bel Geddes showed how dramatic design and mass production architecture could benefit American service stations: how merchandising and modernism could be successfully applied to commercial roadside buildings in a job for Socony-Vacuum Oil Company, one of America's largest oil refining firms of the period.[52] Bel Geddes introduced his forward-looking designs at a time when many service stations inspired by domestic architecture ranged in style from Arts and Crafts to Tudor Revival, some even sporting Chinese pagodas, appealing to a notion of road travel as an exotic adventure. Indicating a shift from the house to the box as the dominant design paradigm, Bel Geddes and others, including Walter Dorwin Teague, began to introduce International Style modernism to service station design in the early 1930s. From 1934 to 1937, Teague began a successful association with Texaco, producing thousands of low-slung stations with rounded corners, sporting three continuous green horizontal stripes below the roofline, communicating an image of speed and efficiency.[53] Teague and Bel Geddes entered the field of gas station design during a slump in automobile registration from a peak in 1929 of just over 26.5 million to 24 million in 1933, suggesting a possible impetus to the hiring of two of America's leading industrial designers.[54]

Bel Geddes's thorough report prepared for Socony-Vacuum Oil Company, while also seeking an image of efficiency, explicitly emphasized theatricality and modernity. It called for the use of "psychological factors" and "dramatic appearance" to increase sales of lubrication services, motor oils, and other merchandize while also advising "greater attractiveness, distinctiveness, customer comfort and merchandising force."[55] A greater emphasis on sales of service and merchandize occurred during the economic depression as gas revenues fell, thus requiring buildings that accommodated this changed approach to income generation.[56] Reflecting a wider public concern with the chaotic, visual brashness of roadside advertising, Bel Geddes advised a simple and modern structure.[57] Aware that his client might be shocked by the modern look of his design, Bel Geddes argued that modernism was already established across a wide range of building types. The "new architectural approach," he explained, had "stimulated and attracted" "the great proportion of the American public" at the Chicago World's Fair and Rockefeller Center and had been successfully applied to "commercial buildings, schools, churches, apartment houses and private houses."[58] Suggesting that the service station was quintessentially of its time, Bel Geddes considered it "essential that the modern tempo be caught in the appearance" of the "service station [which] should create the impression of ... efficient service."[59] Preempting any interpretation of his design as "modernistic," a disparaging term used to describe a visually jarring strain of modern design of the late 1920s, Bel Geddes insisted his design "does not rely for its effect on fantastic forms and shape, but is ... based on utility and economy" and "reflects the trend of modern architecture," which is "simple," "proportioned," and "does not require applied ornamentation."[60]

At the time when Bel Geddes proclaimed, the "appearance of the station should be so distinctive" it would remove the need for signage: the building "will be in effect a Socony trademark." Bel Geddes proved his modernist allegiance, employing architectural formalism, where the building's shape, rather than its signage, was emphasized.[61] The Bel Geddes report suggested that the main elements of the building—its façade, large central lubrication bay, and two curved exterior corners—would be its most recognizable features.[62] "The unbridled use of signs," Bel Geddes claimed, "has undoubtedly been a major factor in the unfavorable attitude of communities towards service stations." Communities that were once attractive now "approximated traveling carnivals."[63] Only a year earlier concern with the "indiscriminate" placement of road signage that threatened "public safety and scenic beauty" prompted the Outdoor Advertising Association of America to propose regulatory legislation for the industry.[64] The turn against visual pollution (the cacophony of varied signage and the lack of regulations of roadside advertising) on American roads created an opportunity for designers such as Bel Geddes and Teague to apply the more minimal modernist styling to American gas station architecture. While Bel Geddes's design rationale focused on its modernist origins, the actual design employed the attention-grabbing techniques of advertising and illumination engineering. At night the interior of the service bay was to be lit in red in order to create a dramatic spectacle visible to passing motorists. In 1939, Bel Geddes would use the same technique, the glowing crimson entrance, to draw throngs of visitors through the entry of his General Motor's building.[65] Ultimately, Bel Geddes's ideal, the modernist emphasis on form over content, did not prove practical. He eventually recommended that the Socony-Vacuum name and Pegasus figure should be prominently featured in the design (Figure 4.6).[66]

In the first decades of the twentieth century, modernist architects from Walter Gropius to Buckminster Fuller dreamt of mass production architecture.[67] Not surprisingly, Bel Geddes's service station design recommended prefabricated construction, claiming it would provide variation in form and ease of disassembly and reuse.[68] While prefabrication systems were used

FIGURE 4.6 Night view of model of Bel Geddes service station design for Socony, *c.* 1934. Photograph by Richard Garrison. Harry Ransom Center, University of Texas, and the Edith Lutyens and Norman Bel Geddes Foundation, Inc. 2016.

in service stations prior to 1934, and prominently featured in the designs of exhibition homes at the Chicago World's Fair, Bel Geddes noted that no such system, as yet, was affordable or attractive.[69] The system he recommended used load-bearing wall panels with galvanized metal and fireproof insulation, which, he insisted, could be erected in fifteen days.[70] Despite his in-depth research and design, Bel Geddes's goal of mass production architecture would not be achieved in 1934. Nor would his station design be rolled out by Socony-Vacuum: only one of his prototype stations was built.[71] Socony worried that the design was too radical, diverging too much from its existing stations which employed classical pediments, later hiring Frederick Frost, a consulting architect who produced a more conservative design, a boxlike service area with drumlike office.[72] Despite this setback, Bel Geddes did use images of his Socony-Vacuum station for self-promotional purposes. A 1937 article in *Pencil Points* profiled Bel Geddes's design and theater work and included six images and a lengthy description of the Socony-Vacuum station.[73] Bel Geddes would soon apply this knowledge of mass production architecture to domestic design, including the Housing Corporation of America's cooperative housing development (1939–1941); and Revere Copper and Brass's industrial-built house, used for promotional purposes (1941–1945).

Hopes for the factory-built house, 1939–1945

As early as 1939, Bel Geddes planned to take advantage of government funding and developed his ideas for prefabricated housing in his Housing Corporation of America cooperative development, a name that echoed the numerous New Deal initiatives of the 1930s. Like his SGE stove, his mass-produced homes would be made up of a limited number of modules to create a variety of structures. The low-cost houses would sport flat roofs, a central utility unit, and sliding screen walls, and could be delivered and built in less than twenty-four hours. To advertise his venture, the project was promoted in *Business Week* in January 1940, where it was proclaimed that Norman Bel Geddes "has entered the housing sweepstakes."[74] A socially progressive plan, the scheme would allow Works Progress Administration laborers to form cooperatives, build the houses, own all the stock, and earn yearly dividends. Surplus money would be set aside for accident and health insurance, and workers would move into the first 1,000 houses they built. This plan, however, was never realized. In August 1941, Bel Geddes's partners in the scheme went bankrupt and withdrew.[75]

Bel Geddes seeks an architectural license

Bel Geddes's attempt to petition for an architectural license was consistent with his unflagging self-belief, his facility for self-invention, and his unswerving desire for status as a modernist designer. His previous guises ranged from vaudevillian to stage designer: Why would architecture be off limits? In addition to providing increased financial opportunities, an architectural license would improve Bel Geddes's professional standing and significantly aid the completion of his ambitious projects. Bel Geddes had engaged in architectural design as early as 1914 with his plans of what he later called Theater Number 6. By 1923, he fought for the designation of "Associate Architect" for his consultation work on the design for the Guild Theater, New York.[76] The organization's executive director, Theresa Helburn, informed Bel Geddes, "'Associate Architect' is a name that can't be used for anyone who is not really an architect."[77] Helburn was equally critical of Bel Geddes's theater design, which was rejected as too impractical and included a costly plan for a hydraulic stage.[78] Helburn accused Bel Geddes of neglecting "one of the basic requisites of architectural planning," providing an affordable design.[79] Bel Geddes's insistence on ideal design solutions created problems throughout his career. While this utopian approach contributed to his visionary reputation, it curtailed the realization of many of his projects.

In August 1930, just months after producing his design for the Toledo Scale factory, Bel Geddes applied for an architectural license in the state of New York. His appeal for registration was based on his self-taught knowledge of design and his six-year experience of restaurant and theater design, including the Olive Hill Theater, Los Angeles, which Bel Geddes claimed to have designed "on a fifty-fifty basis" with Frank Lloyd Wright, and the Guild Theater, New York.[80] As Bel Geddes was not credited as the sole designer of any of his theater designs, he could not declare them his own.[81] His initial application was rejected in August 1930 due to his lack of technical education.[82] A subsequent petition to waive the technical requirement was accompanied by glowing letters from prominent New York architects, including Harvey Wiley Corbett, Raymond Hood, and

Ralph T. Walker, depicting Bel Geddes as a creative and original designer.[83] Walker praised Bel Geddes's "architectural work" as "highly interesting and unusual ... not so much architecture as the beginnings of a new architecture."[84] The petition to gain an architectural license in New York passed on aesthetic grounds. However, it failed to convincingly prove Bel Geddes's technical understanding of architecture and was rejected in January 1931.[85]

Despite this setback, Bel Geddes became even more aggressive in presenting himself as an architectural designer. In August 1931, he gave *Horizons* the working title *My Theories on the Future of Architecture*.[86] With its focus on architectural projects and its reliance on Le Corbusier, *Horizons* was a bold attempt to cast Bel Geddes as a courageous modernist architect. Bel Geddes knew that industrial artists were vulnerable to accusations of aestheticism. In a 1932 staff memorandum, he described himself as an "architectural designer" and warned that *Horizons* "must not be subject to criticism as 'arty.'"[87] The use of such phrases as "architectural designer" and "architecturalist" allowed Bel Geddes to fashion himself as an architect without actually becoming one. In the April 1931 issue of *Ladies' Home Journal*, Bel Geddes proclaimed himself an "architect" and presented his "House of Tomorrow."[88] By unveiling his house plans in the *Ladies' Home Journal*, Bel Geddes participated in a wider project of architectural reform begun by the *Journal*'s editor, Edward Bok. From 1895 to 1919, Bok had published house plans by Frank Lloyd Wright, Stanford White, and others, aimed at improving the aesthetics, technology, hygiene, and planning of the American home. Bel Geddes thus joined an illustrious group of American architects and further aligned himself with progressive architectural design.[89]

At a time when industrial design provided a real threat to architectural practice, unemployed architects forced the withdrawal of Bel Geddes's Chicago World's Fair designs and ousted him from the fair's Architectural Commission due to his lack of registration.[90] In early 1935, afraid of further hostility Bel Geddes warned those around him not to refer to him publicly as an architect. In response to a recent *New York Times* article that described him as such, Bel Geddes sternly informed the author that he was not a member of the profession nor could he join:

> Although I have done considerable work in the field of Architecture, I am not an "architect" ...
> I am not licensed and cannot be so licensed. It is of great importance for the success of what
> we all hope to accomplish in this undertaking that we do not incur the animosity of registered
> architects by associating the word "architect" with my name.[91]

Though this passage implies an accepted defeat, it also suggests a continued effort to develop an architectural practice.

Reflecting his larger ambitions, Bel Geddes filled his office with experienced architects and engineers. By 1934, the Bel Geddes office maintained thirty employees.[92] Key staff included: Worthen Paxton, who was educated in engineering and architecture from Yale and became Bel Geddes's assistant designer around 1934; Roger Nowland, a 1927 graduate of MIT in aeronautical engineering; Peter Schladermundt, another Yale architecture graduate and prior employee of Raymond Hood; and Garth Huxtable, a 1933 graduate in design from the Massachusetts School of Art.[93]

In 1935, Bel Geddes sought to consolidate his professional ambitions through a partnership with the architect George Howe: the new office was announced in the *New York Times*. Bel

Geddes viewed the Howe partnership as a logical step after the architectural license debacle and his Chicago fair failures.[94] In 1935, Howe was perhaps best known for the pioneering 1932 Philadelphia Savings Fund Society building designed with the innovative Swiss émigré William Lescaze. The monumental office building combined an international-style tower with a streamlined façade, a marriage of rational and expressive design that would have appealed to Bel Geddes. With an anticipated staff of fifty persons, Bel Geddes and Howe hoped to cash in on an expected housing boom and began to publicize their plans for modern community housing and prefabricated homes. In "Old Friends Plan to Soar on Building Boom," a *New York Times* article of May 1935, Bel Geddes proclaimed, "The world is going to have its face lifted."[95] A brochure promoting the partnership presented Bel Geddes's move to architecture as part of a carefully calculated scheme, "another step in his plan, inaugurated eight years ago, of extending his creative activities in design to industry." The brochure was aimed at leaders of industry and "prospective building owners" who sensed the new trend in taste and utility.[96] The Bel Geddes-Howe partnership, however, was doomed from the start. They were immediately given a summons to dissolve it.[97] "We did not know it," Bel Geddes later wrote, "but there was a law against a partnership between a registered architect and one who was not registered."[98] Despite this setback Bel Geddes continued to seek a license. By 1940, he had hired an expert on architectural contracts to help him achieve his goal, writing that it would only be a matter of time.[99] Bel Geddes's dogged determination seemed to reflect a belief that he was, in fact, an architect and that it was just a matter of convincing the authorities. Despite his embrace of modernist design and the completion of numerous architectural projects, by 1935 Bel Geddes had "no standing among the utilitarians." Within architectural circles his work was considered a mere novelty, "a good deal like a cocktail before dinner: there may not be much food value in it ... but it is stimulating and opens the pores of the mind."[100] While *Fortune* magazine heaped praise on Bel Geddes, architects were more ambivalent, illustrating a gulf between big business and the architectural profession.

During the Second World War, American government agencies and private companies built around 200,000 prefabricated housing units. Toward the end of the war prefabrication was considered the answer to the immense housing shortage.[101] Around this time Bel Geddes continued his goal of mass-produced housing with Revere Copper and Brass. Like the block unit plan for the SGE stove, the Revere house required basic modular components that could be arranged to create eleven different models. Its walls were made of prefabricated wood panels mounted on a core of expanded sheet metal. The house, Bel Geddes claimed, could be built in eight hours and cost less than $2,000. The emphasis on speedy construction anticipated a public eager for postwar prosperity. "Your house could be ready for you by dinner time," Revere's advertising claimed.[102] In 1943, George Nelson contributed to Revere's campaign with the pamphlet "Grass on Main Street," which emphasized pedestrianized urban development.[103] Bel Geddes's Revere pamphlet, on the other hand, was more futuristic, picturing a real estate agent in pilot's garb and goggles introducing a young couple to their new home. The ad copy appealed to consumers who believed in progress and longed for postwar plenty.

No matter what else results from the all–out effort our country is making, one thing seems certain. When it is over, real enjoyment of life in our homes can be greater, can be available to millions more. For in this great emergency, new standards are being created. Industry is experimenting with new processes. Revere is working out new things in copper. Architects are inventing new methods of building.

Here is one conception by the famous designer, Norman Bel Geddes. It shows the deep comfort, the complete convenience, the dignity of living which American production methods could easily provide.[104]

The pamphlets used the promise of technology to nurture consumer desires, associated prefabricated homes with modern living, and thus provided Bel Geddes and Revere with a forward-looking image. The emphasis on "comfort" and "dignity" was perhaps intended to allay fears of modernist house design as cold and inhuman. While Bel Geddes's Revere houses were never built, the copper and brass company's glossy pamphlets, 800,000 of which were distributed, helped to present the metals manufacturer as a cutting-edge firm.[105] Prefabricated homes never managed to usurp the popularity of traditionally built ones. In 1942, prefabricated housing peaked to nearly 16 percent of the single-family housing market in the United States. Production fell to 7 percent by 1946 and 4.8 percent by 1950. During the 1950s and 1960s, interest in industrialized housing continued to wane.[106] Had Bel Geddes mistakenly tried to sell modern design to consumers who longed for the past? Factors contributing to the failure of mass production housing during the postwar period included conflict with local building codes, the collapse of government funding, and difficulty in establishing a distribution system.[107]

Throughout his career Bel Geddes engaged in a range of architectural projects in pursuit of his financial and professional goals. His use of the machine as a dominant symbol and rhetorical trope was consistent with his interest in rational modernism and its emphasis on machine values, as well as his appreciation of Expressionist stage design, which used symbols to reveal the "soul" beyond ordinary experience. Bel Geddes's designs for the Toledo Scale factory plan, the Socony-Vacuum service station, the "House of Tomorrow," and prefabricated houses helped to develop his image as a visionary modernist, while promoting his clients as enlightened capitalists. Bel Geddes's continuing interest in the symbol of the machine guided his designs of streamlined trains, planes, and cars.

5

Streamlining: From Imagined Ideal to Commercial Reality

In the 1930s, streamlining symbolized movement and power, referencing speed and force in both mobile and static objects. In Bel Geddes's stage design lectures, he presented movement, especially of masses of people, as an essential dramatic element. Offering a metaphysical concept of movement, Bel Geddes associated dynamism with vitality, writing in 1929 that the "static" realist overlooks the "great truth" that "life is not matter but movement. The bud opening into a flower is not life, but the action is. And this action is a continuous one."[1] Perhaps this understanding of motion was inspired by Theosophy which understood the growth of the individual in evolutionary terms: the more highly developed self was in constant transformation, allowing increasing access to the spirit world through an evolutionary movement from one dimension to another. Like his earlier views of dramatic design, Bel Geddes's discussions of streamlining linked the style to nature, evolution, and visionary thought. Just as modernism influenced his practice of stage design, it would also inform his understanding of aerodynamic form. While proponents of modernist design would later condemn the decorative use of streamlining, in its early days, streamlining, with its emphasis on function and science, corresponded with the rational ethos of modernism.

During the early 1920s, Le Corbusier, arguably the era's leading proponent of modernism, proved a significant advocate of streamlining concerned with the ideal form of the automobile and its inevitable evolution.[2] Illustrating the streamlined shapes of racing cars in *Towards a New Architecture*, Le Corbusier asserted that the "cone which gives the best penetration is the result of experiment and calculation, and this is confimed by natural creations such as fishes, birds, etc."[3] In 1930, Cheney parroted the architect's functionalist hyperbole to promote streamlined cars, describing recent models as "organic," "honest," and "athletic," whose "beauty" was "due to the honest decorativeness ... efficient disposal of parts, massing, [and] stream lines."[4] In 1929, Bel Geddes published his views on streamlining in his article "Modern Theory of Design" for the *Encyclopaedia Britannica*. The entry heralded the airplane as *the* functionalist design icon of the era, whose streamlined form was a response to aerodynamic principles: "As the automobile and the train achieve greater efficiency and comfort, their contours become unbroken and each becomes a better expression of fundamental purposes."[5]

Bel Geddes was certainly not the first to apply streamlining to vehicles and other goods.[6] However, the persistent and canny promotion of his streamlined visualizations of planes, trains, cars, and boats guaranteed his notoriety as a streamlining pioneer. During the 1930s and 1940s, in the trade and national press, Bel Geddes was often presented as *the* leader of both aesthetic and scientific streamlining, styling which borrowed from the smooth surfaces of airplane design on the one hand and the scientific application of aerodynamic principles on the other. After 1932, Bel Geddes's futuristic tapered vehicles, first pictured in *Horizons*, were reprinted in newspapers across the country, helping to popularize the style. Such "development work" produced by the Bel Geddes office scheduled during "slack time" resulted in the designs of "ovoid ships, cars, and trains, nine-deck airliners, [and] multicellular houses," which, Nelson noted in 1934, "put Norman Bel Geddes in the small company of Sunday Supplement subjects along with his admirer Stratosphere Piccard, Hugh (City-of-the-Future) Ferriss, and the rocket trip to Mars. These drawings have all built the Geddes myth."[7] The influence of the "Geddes myth" would soon be felt in the design studios of America's leading carmakers. *Horizons* proved an inspiration to many automotive engineers, and Bel Geddes was quickly hired by America's leading manufacturers to aid their publicity and design. In 1933, Chrysler employed Bel Geddes to publicize the Airflow, America's first production car shaped according to aerodynamic principles.[8] The same year General Motors hired Bel Geddes to design its twenty-fifth anniversary commemorative medal. In 1934, Bel Geddes hoped to secure his reputation as a streamlining expert with the publication of his technical article "Streamlining" for the *Atlantic Monthly*.[9] By 1934, General Electric's Institute of Aerodynamic Research proclaimed, "overnight Norman Bel Geddes has become the father of a new type of aero-dynamic engineering."[10] In 1940, Van Doren admitted, "what Geddes did was to dramatize it [streamlining], well before it had really arrived, and so convincingly as to crystallize the scattered forces already tending in that direction."[11]

An early theorist of "horizontality," the Austrian émigré Paul Frankl noted in 1930, "the horizontal line is expressive of the style of today,"[12] linking the low-slung silhouettes of streamlined products with twentieth-century modernity. In their 1936 book *Art and the Machine*, Sheldon and Martha Cheney viewed streamlining as *the* style of the age and presented Bel Geddes as its trailblazer. Emphasizing his expressive, rather than scientific, use of the style, the Cheneys "credited [Geddes] as having contributed the word 'streamline' to the everyday vocabulary, and with making explicit the streamline as an appearance value, and as a symbol of machine-age style in objects far outside the legitimate field of its scientific application."[13] As a representation of progress and dynamism, they saw even the most ordinary streamlined product as "conspicuous a symbol ... of the age" as the "symbol of the cross" was to the "medieval mind."[14] Bel Geddes is said to have been "embarrassed" to be called the father of streamlining.[15] However, writing after the Second World War, he characterized himself "as the father of 'Industrial Design' who put 'streamline' in the dictionary."[16]

Bel Geddes's reputation as the originator of streamlining was secured early on in his industrial design career through a series of well-publicized designs: including the Graham-Paige motor car (*c.* 1928), Bel Geddes's first streamlined car design; Air Liner Number 4 (1929); and Car Number

8 (1931), a rear-engine car based on the "ultimate" streamlined form—the egg or teardrop. The notoriety of such projects attracted clients eager to be associated with the streamlining pioneer, leading to promotional work for the Chrysler Airflow, interior and exterior designs for the De Soto and Airflow (1933–1935); the General Motors Silver Anniversary Medal (1933); the styling of an Electrolux vacuum cleaner (1934); a redesign of the Globe Slicing Machine (1940–1943); packaging for Loose-Wiles Biscuits (1941–1942); and work on Rice Weiner's "flow motion" jewelry (1949–1950). Many of these designs suggest that Bel Geddes had no qualms applying streamlining to stationary products. His designs of the 1940s illustrate how streamlining changed in meaning over two decades, from a concern with aerodynamics and forward thrust in vehicle design to the gentle motion of the human body in jewelry design, mirroring the changing emphasis from machine aesthetics to organic design.

Streamlined styling grew out of the study of aerodynamics and hydrodynamics, which were established long before "streamline" first appeared in print in 1873. By 1909, the term was used by car manufacturers to describe the "sweeping lines" of their products.[17] In the 1920s the word was applied to the gentle curves of crafted luxury cars. Its application to domestic goods and transportation design helped to introduce the style in both the private and public spheres. By the early 1930s, America's railroads saw a reduction in passengers due to the economic depression and competition from airplanes, buses, and automobiles. In response, rail companies produced eye-catching streamlined trains, including the Union Pacific's *M-10,000* and the Burlington *Zephyr*, infusing glamor and modernity into rail travel. In 1934, millions of Americans caught their first glimpse of streamlined trains, which were displayed at the Chicago World's Fair and traveled to towns across the country where millions rushed to view them, aiding in the popularization of the style.[18] At the 1934 annual meeting of the Society of Automotive Engineers, the enthusiasm for streamlining was considerable, where it was embraced as a major conference theme. Hoping to cash in on the growing excitement, Chrysler released its pioneering car, Airflow, the same year.[19] However, it was at the Graham-Paige Motor Company that Bel Geddes would get his initial opportunity to combine streamlining and modernist design in his first plans for automobiles.

Graham-Paige Motor Cars, *c.* 1928–1933

As with many of his earliest industrial design assignments, Bel Geddes acquired the Graham-Paige job through family contacts, having met Ray Graham in the late 1920s through his uncle Fred Geddes.[20] While Bel Geddes's earliest Graham-Paige contract is from 1929, and *Horizons* dates the designs of the cars as 1928, Bel Geddes placed the origin of the designs to 1927, when he was first asked to design cars during a weekend with Graham, thus initiating his industrial design career.[21] On January of 1929, Bel Geddes informed Graham that his competitors' models were not of a "progressive nature," that car manufacturing was a "wide open field," and the time was ripe to apply the "principles of design" to the automotive industry.[22] By the middle of that year, excited by Bel Geddes's ideas, Ray Graham invited his friend to develop "new designs" in "motor car bodies."[23]

The Graham-Paige Motor Car Company originated from the purchase of the Paige-Detroit Motor Car Corporation by the three Graham brothers in 1927.[24] Graham-Paige is perhaps best known for pioneering automatic production in American automobile manufacture after 1929 with the use of the transfer machine, which relied on machining stations using "work feeding devices."[25] In 1932, the company would produce one of the first mass-manufactured cars to employ the streamlined aesthetic, the Graham Blue Streak designed by Amos Northrup.[26] The use of styling to increase sales and promote obsolescence had become a mainstay of the automotive industry after the late 1920s, epitomized by General Motor's La Salle of 1927, the first mass-produced car to be completely styled by one individual, Harley Earl, who would soon be made the head of General Motors's influential Art and Color Section.[27]

Compared to his later designs, Bel Geddes's initial plans for Graham were tame, emphasizing innovations such as graduated paint jobs and detailed upholstery.[28] But soon Graham and Bel Geddes would adopt a five-year plan to the Graham-Paige Motor Company: the launch of five streamlined cars over a five-year period, each one more radically styled than the previous and all leading to an ideal vehicle—the "Ultimate Car."[29] Although Bel Geddes presented his Graham-Paige design as the "first streamlined car," he did not originate streamlined automobile design.[30] As with much of his design work it was derivative, yet skillfully marketed and novel enough to attract ample publicity. His car designs for Graham-Paige contributed significantly to his reputation as a leader of streamlined design, and were fundamental to his industrial design career. He would later credit "Ray Graham's encouragement, faith and inspiration" for his success in the automobile industry.[31]

For a 1929 *Automobile Topics* article written in collaboration with Munroe Innes, Bel Geddes described how Graham had asked him to design the "perfect," "Ultimate Car":

"Set a style," said Graham, "that is perfection in its own type of treatment. When that design is finished, we will call it *the car of five years from now*. Then we will work backwards, step by step, year by year, over the five-year period, introducing certain details of the design into our yearly models until in the fifth year we will be in production of the Ultimate Car. By that means we will educate the public gradually to our design...." A taste of novelty every year will whet the appetite of the public and lead it on to the ultimate discovery of the perfected design.[32] (Figure 5.1 and Plate 20)

Bel Geddes's Motorcar Number 1 was meant to be the first car in the series leading to the ultimate car. His approach illustrated his distaste for faddish styling and preference for design that progressed toward an ideal form. "Each of the five models represents a twenty percent change over the previous one as each is advanced by degrees toward a definite ideal standard—not in terms of transient modes."[33] Such utopian language may have disguised a deeper concern: fear of consumer resistance to radical styling.[34] It also echoed Le Corbusier, who considered "perfection" in design, including the ovoid shape of racing cars, to be the result of evolutionary principles, the "product of selection applied to an established standard."[35] While Bel Geddes referred to his ideal car as the ultimate, Le Corbusier called his the "Essential," a result of "rejection, pruning, cleansing," in order to reach a generic object type.[36] Revealing his desire for the ideal automobile, Bel Geddes criticized the automobile industry's seasonal model change and called instead for the "ultimate motor car."[37] In the end, Bel Geddes's Ultimate Car, however, was neither perfect nor extreme. Like General Motor's La Salle of 1927, Bel Geddes's car was long, low slung, with a gently curving body and fenders. Unlike the La Salle, the Graham-Paige car sported a tapered front end and was devoid of molding, giving the car a sleek, dynamic look.

FIGURE 5.1 Clay model of Motorcar Number 1 (convertible) designed by Bel Geddes for Graham-Paige, 1928. Photograph by Maurice Goldberg. Harry Ransom Center, University of Texas, and the Edith Lutyens and Norman Bel Geddes Foundation, Inc. 2016.

The *Automobile Topics* article presented Bel Geddes as an industrial Michelangelo, echoed modernist design principles, and was consistent with his self-promotion as a visionary and pragmatic artist.[38] The process of designing a car body, he claimed, was the same

> to the artist as designing a statue, a building, or a bed... He must close his eyes and visualize a cube of certain dimensions in space. Then with the two-fold purpose of fitting the article to its purpose, and of making it beautiful, he must whittle into the cube and reduce it to a thing of lines and proportion.[39]

This method seemed to harmonize with both modernist design and streamlining, both of which emphasized simplification and the reduction of form. However, contradicting the technique of sculpting stone, the article described Bel Geddes's Ultimate Car as "organically designed" "from the motor outwards,"[40] an approach shared by Le Corbusier, who in 1923 wrote, "The Plan proceeds from within to without, the exterior is the result of an interior."[41] Bel Geddes's ideal car would be devoid of "whatnots" and its "accessories, such as lamps and license plates, [would] fit into the organic whole of the body. Thereby the body becomes a single unit of uninterrupted, flowing lines." Attempting to reassure the automobile manufacturers of the public's ultimate acceptance of streamlining, Bel Geddes described the recent appreciation of "modernistic" furniture, which was initially rejected, but "now ... [people] are becoming accustomed to [its] lines ... buying it and using it."[42]

According to Bel Geddes, the Graham-Paige car was ultimately considered "too radical" by both Ray Graham and his "factory men."[43] Another victim of the depression, the Graham-Paige car never went into production.[44] Bel Geddes's desire for the ideal streamlined automobile was motivated by a profound contradiction, the desire to achieve the perfect form in an industry dependent on stylistic change. Incremental styling relied on the public's appetite for novelty. Would the public have been satisfied with the "perfect" and unchanging aesthetic of the Ultimate Car? In 1945, Bel Geddes claimed that the proof of his "practical vision is the fact that it [the Graham-Paige car] could be put on the road today and be entirely in keeping with the latest car manufactured."[45] In 1929, however, Bel Geddes assured his public he was "not interested in designing a car that looks like a cigar or an aeroplane, or anything of the sort... All I want to do is build something beautiful that looks like an automobile."[46] Despite such promises, as Bel Geddes's streamlining advanced beyond the Ultimate Car, he increasingly employed the ovoid form in his automobile designs, developing his teardrop-shaped Motor Car Number 8 in 1931.

Horizons and ideal streamlining: Car number 8 and Pan American Airways

While the Wall Street Crash may have frightened automobile manufacturers from streamlined design, it fired Bel Geddes's enthusiasm for aerodynamic forms. He was soon developing even more ambitious streamlined vehicles that he would later publish in *Horizons*, including his designs for Motor Car Number 8 and Air Liner Number 4. He explained, "When a depression hit, instead of letting my people go... I put them to work on the stream-line subject."[47] *Horizons* secured Bel Geddes's reputation as a streamlining pioneer and presented the industrial designer as a knowledgeable and imaginative artist-engineer, a modern professional with a combined understanding of aesthetics and function. In his ongoing effort to usurp the role of the product engineer, he wrote, one shouldn't assume "that if the engineer does his job well the result will be beautiful ... the artist is essential, for he knows how to make a thing of beauty with the minimum of means."[48] Offering an argument for both scientific and symbolic streamlining, he argued that the "motor car of to-day" must be "designed in accord with the same functional principles" as "the projectile-like racing car," but they must also be "expressive of their function" (49–50, 51).

In *Horizons*, Bel Geddes proclaimed the teardrop as the ultimate streamlined form. "It is well known that a drop of water falling in still air assumes an almost perfect streamline form. This form is approximately that of an egg" (45).[49] He had experimented with streamlining in the late 1920s while sailing, testing the water resistance of a variety of wooden blocks, including those of "rectangular" and "teardrop form." He also built a "crude wind tunnel" on the roof of his house, assessing the air resistance of the same blocks, "both in suspension, and on the ground."[50] In *Horizons*, Bel Geddes printed a diagram of air currents acting upon a square, a circle, and teardrop, the latter proving to be the most efficient. The image mimicked a similar chart in Le Corbusier's *Towards a New Architecture* (Figures 5.2 and 5.3).

Presented in *Horizons*, Car Number 8 most closely represented the application of Bel Geddes's theories of streamlining. It relied on the teardrop form; had a truncated front end; used a rear engine; and sported rear fins to improve stability[51] (Figure 5.4). With the exception of the ground

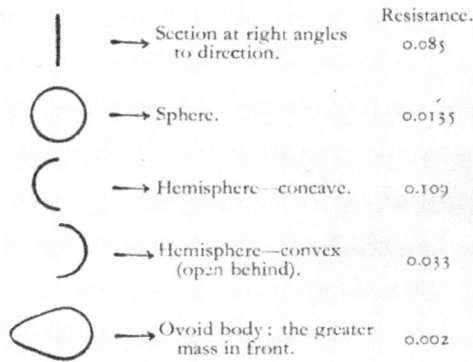

FIGURE 5.2 Air resistance diagram with the ovoid shape showing the highest resistance rating in *Towards a New Architecture*, 1927. © FLC/ ADAGP, Paris and DACS, London 2017.

its exterior surface is so designed that upon being projected through air, a useful dynamic reaction is imparted to the object by the action of the air. The lift of an airplane wing is an excellent example of a useful dynamic reaction. An object is *streamlined* when its exterior surface is so designed that upon passing through a fluid such as water or air the object creates the least disturbance in the fluid in the form of eddies or partial vacua tending to produce resistance. In other words, an object is airfoiled in order to *create* a

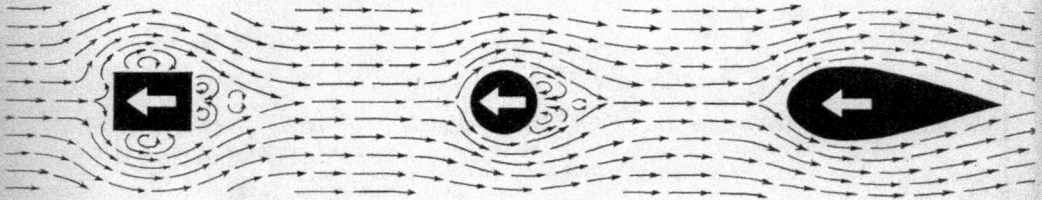

33 · DIAGRAM ILLUSTRATING THE PRINCIPLE OF STREAMLINING

disturbance and an object is streamlined in order to *eliminate* disturbances in the media through which they pass.

It is well known that a drop of water falling in still air assumes an almost perfect streamline form. This form is approximately that of an egg, though the small end of the drop tapers more sharply to a conical point. In falling, the larger and blunt end of the drop is foremost. This is the shape that creates the least turbulence in the form of eddies and partial vacua which increase wind resistance.[33] A stationary sand bar or sheet of ice in a fast-moving stream takes on a streamline form due to the water's action in passing.[34] A strut or wire, as on an airplane, has twenty times the resistance of a streamlined form having the same thickness as the diameter of

34 · SHEET OF ICE IN FLOWING STREAM DEMONSTRATING NATURE'S STREAMLINING

[45]

FIGURE 5.3 "Diagram Illustrating the Principle of Streamlining," in *Horizons*, 1932. Harry Ransom Center, University of Texas, and the Edith Lutyens and Norman Bel Geddes Foundation, Inc. 2016.

FIGURE 5.4 Drawing of Motor Car Number 8, rear view, 1931, as it appeared in *Horizons*. Pencil on paper. Harry Ransom Center, University of Texas, and the Edith Lutyens and Norman Bel Geddes Foundation, Inc. 2016.

side, the exterior shell was "streamlined," Bel Geddes wrote, "to as near the drop form as is practicable" (55) and insisted that the design was an extreme but "logical" example of visionary design. "At first sight, you may not think this design looks pleasing... You may think it odd... To myself and my staff the novelty of this Car Number 8 has worn off, and it appears more logical and attractive than present-day designs"[52] (57). Le Corbusier offered a similar view, conceding that his own "Essential" and "rational" automobile "may have a strange look at first sight."[53] Not all designers of streamlined cars accepted the effectiveness of the teardrop form. In 1924,

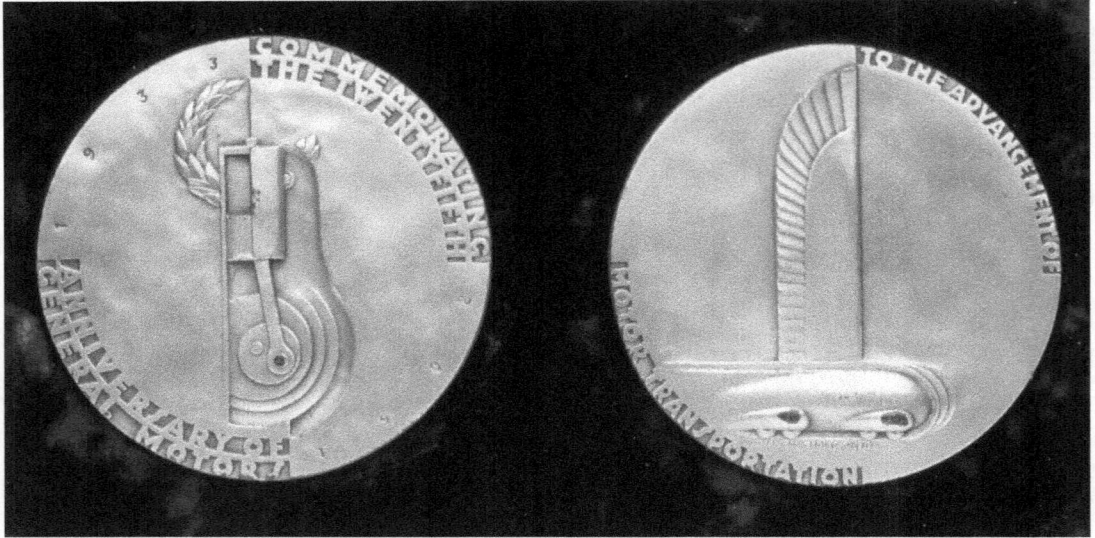

FIGURE 5.5 Bel Geddes–designed General Motors Silver Anniversary Medal, front and back, 1933. Harry Ransom Center, University of Texas, and the Edith Lutyens and Norman Bel Geddes Foundation, Inc. 2016.

the Hungarian engineer and pioneer of streamlined automotive design, Paul Jaray, noted that "comparisons of aerodynamically efficient bodies with a falling drop of water" are "a fallacy"; "in fact the falling drop is essentially spherical … unstable … rocking or swirling in motion."[54]

Bel Geddes combined his interests in the romance of flight, the automobile, and streamlining in his design of the General Motors Silver Anniversary medal of 1933. In accord with the visual language of streamlining, the medal fused the plane and the automobile into an organic whole, depicting an abstract teardrop-shaped car with a feathered wing on one side and an equally stylized engine on the reverse, which was described as the "heart of the motor"[55] (Figure 5.5). In 1940, the General Motors medal was selected for exhibition at the Whitney Museum of American Art and entered the permanent collection of the Metropolitan Museum of Art, New York, the same year.[56] While Bel Geddes described the medal's streamlined car as "abstract," he would soon have a chance to make his ideal a concrete reality.[57]

Critics of streamlining

During the 1930s, both stylistic streamlining (derived from the ellipse) and classical modernist design (based on the circle, square, and triangle) gained prominence as significant design idioms. By the mid-1930s, both were promoted as *the* machine style within America's diverse design communities. In 1934, as streamlining blossomed into a full-blown craze, the Museum of Modern Art's (MoMA's) *Machine Art* exhibition, a reverential display of tools, mechanical components, and machine-inspired industrial design, including furniture by Marcel Breuer and Le Corbusier, officially sanctioned a neo-Platonic machine style based on geometric forms and classical modernism (Figure 5.6). The organizers of the exhibit, Alfred H. Barr, Jr., MoMA's director, and Philip Johnson, who grew to fame as an outspoken architect, constructed an aesthetic inspired by the geometric simplicity of certain European modernist design and the vernacular of American machine tool manufacture. This emphasis on an industrial folk heritage in American design was symptomatic of a wider search for an authentic American aesthetic during the 1930s.[58] In his catalog essay, "History of Machine Art," Johnson rejected Art Deco and aerodynamic styling: the machine styles of the "'modernistic' French machine-age aesthetic" and American "principles such as 'streamlining.'"[59] While he praised the Bauhaus for what he considered their partial attainment of his design ideal, he pinned his greatest hopes on anonymous American industrial art, because of its supposed lack of Arts and Crafts Movement influence and its dependence on the "purer and stronger" "tradition of machine construction."[60]

Johnson reviled the commercial aesthetic of streamlining, noting that in the 1920s Americans developed a "desire for 'styling' objects for advertising" to give them "'eye-appeal' and therefore help sales." He deplored styling, and concluded that, "Principles such as 'streamlining' often receive homage out of all proportion to their applicability."[61] Rather than a style employing gently sloping curves based on the forms of airfoils, eggs, or teardrops, MoMA's curators promoted a classical one based on geometric shapes of the sphere, cube, and cone, quoting Plato to underline their point: "By beauty of shapes... I mean straight lines and circles, and shapes, plane and solid, made from them by lathe, ruler and square. These are not, like other things, beautiful relatively, but always and absolutely."[62] At a time when American intellectuals worried that American culture lagged behind Europe, the invocation of Plato identified America's industrial culture with that of Classical Greece.

Like Geddes, MoMA's curators found inspiration in *Towards a New Architecture*. In his book, Le Corbusier gave special attention to the "pure forms" of classical design and praised the "The Pantheon, the Colosseum, the Aqueducts, the Pyramid of Cestius, the Triumphal Arches, the Basilica of Constantine, the Baths of Caracalla."[63] He offered the cylinder, pyramid, cube, and sphere as fundamental "elementary shapes," whose unified arrangement provided a "sane morality."[64] Van Doren, on the other hand, viewed the circle as "static" and the teardrop as a "dynamic" and significant symbol of progress.[65] He defended streamlining as a natural evolution of production technology, arguing that what was often dismissed as a "faddish style" was the "technological result of high-speed mass production," explaining that plastic molding and pressed sheet-steel production worked more effectively with streamlined products than those with sharp corners.[66] In 1936, on the other hand, Bel Geddes combined the ovoid form with elementary geometry, including the circle and triangle in his streamlined soda siphon for Walter Kidde Sales Company, which incorporated a teardrop-shaped body, pyramidal spout, and cylindrical release button (see Figure 1.4).

Despite his love of elementary geometry, Barr's position on streamlining in 1934 was not unswerving: he admitted, "Even the streamlined object is more frequently admired when at rest than when in motion."[67] By 1938, however, John McAndrew, MoMA's curator of Architecture and Industrial Art, took a more strident position. McAndrew continued to promote Bauhaus modernism, yet found nothing admirable in streamlined goods, whether at rest or in motion, ridiculing such "re-styling" as a form of stylistic obsolescence.[68] While MoMA's curators understood Platonic design as the ultimate aesthetic, Bel Geddes viewed the streamlined object as the ultimate form. At Chrysler, Geddes would have the opportunity to design the "ultimate" streamlined car.

FIGURE 5.6 Albers, Joseph (1888–1976): Cover of the exhibition catalog "Machine Art," 1934. New York, MoMA. Offset lithograph, printed in black, page size: 10 × 7.5 in. (25.4 × 19.1 cm) © 2017. Digital image, The Museum of Modern Art, New York/Scala, Florence.

Chrysler job: Publicizing and designing the ideal car, 1934

With the success of *Horizons*, Bel Geddes became a streamlining prophet overnight. By September 1933, he was hired by the Chrysler Corporation to publicize its Airflow cars, the first production automobiles to integrate visual, aerodynamic, and structural streamlining. Visual streamlining integrates the separate visible automotive components into a larger, flowing whole; aerodynamic streamlining directs air currents acting upon the car's exterior into more unified and less turbulent ones; while structural streamlining combines the chassis and body to add structural integrity.[69] The publicity leading up to the release of the Airflow at the annual auto show in January 1934 cast Bel Geddes as a streamlining visionary who employed the values of function, science, and simplicity. Chrysler hoped the wave of publicity created by *Horizons* would ensure the success of their new streamlined car. *Horizons* had already made an impression within the design studios of Chrysler. In October 1933, Fred M. Zeder, the head of the engineering department at Chrysler, told Bel Geddes that *Horizons* had been like a bible to him and his associates, having received copies from Walter Chrysler.[70] Zeder said that the book gave him the courage to replace their conventional cars with the Airflow type in the Chrysler and De Soto lines, and that he made all his engineering staff read it.[71] The appreciation of *Horizons*, as well as Bel Geddes's publicity as a streamlining pioneer, was undoubtedly crucial in his hiring by Chrysler. While at Chrysler Geddes was invited to design automobile interiors and exteriors: an ideal opportunity, Bel Geddes thought, to promote his ideal car.[72] However, not all of Chrysler's staff were so uncritical. After receiving a copy of the book from Bel Geddes in 1933, Charles F. Kettering (Director of Research and Development at General Motors in 1935) informed Bel Geddes that he greatly overestimated the speed "gain" in a "streamlined motor car" of 60 percent at forty miles per hour, which his team put at around 5 percent.[73]

The publicity for Chrysler's new cars quoted *Horizons* and used Bel Geddes's image as a symbol of progress and innovation. A 1933 pamphlet, "Airflow: A New Kind of Motor Car," concluded with text from Bel Geddes's visionary book, predicting the success of the corporation that produced the first streamlined production car.[74] He wrote that such a "farseeing" manufacturer "will start afresh and his objective will be the ultimate form of the future motor car."[75] As if to confirm his prophecy, a Chrysler advertisement in the December 1933 issue of the *Saturday Evening Post* pictured Bel Geddes stepping from the new streamlined Airflow, holding an open copy of his prophetic tome and with the tagline, "Norman Bel Geddes [with] famous book 'Horizons,' in which he forecast Airflow motor cars."[76] Continuing their association of the Airflow with the visionary designer, the 1934 automobile show exhibited the Airflow alongside a model of Bel Geddes's mammoth Air Liner Number 4. Seeming to follow the Chrysler–Geddes public relations script, a reviewer of the show wondered, "Will this 1934 design of motor transportation give way to this air leviathan of the future?"[77]

As with Graham-Paige and consistent with Bel Geddes's desire for modernist status, publicity for the Airflow linked streamlining with the principles of modern design, promoting the style as functional, honest, and unornamented. In the *Saturday Evening Post* Bel Geddes proclaimed, "I want to salute Mr. Chrysler and Fred Zeder for building the first sincere and authentic streamlined car ... the first *real* motor car."[78] "Design ... style ... art ... all must be bound up with usefulness." Such fitness to purpose, Bel Geddes asserted, was a hallmark of good design. "It is the beginning of a new style ... a style that is great because it is right." "Gingerbread carving stuck on a building is not great architecture. Meaningless surface design on a motor car is not great style."[79] Whereas

FIGURE 5.7 Comparative photograph of clay models of the Chrysler Airflow (left) and Bel Geddes's redesign (right). Photograph by Richard Garrison, no date, *c.* 1933–1934. Harry Ransom Center, University of Texas, and the Edith Lutyens and Norman Bel Geddes Foundation, Inc. 2016.

Le Corbusier looked to the undecorated car for architectural inspiration, Bel Geddes turned to clean modernist architecture to validate streamlined car design. Bel Geddes's advertisement attempted to give product design the same cultural aura as avant-garde architecture.

An article published in the *Chrysler News*, an industry-produced newsletter, on the other hand promoted the Airflow not as a product of modernity, but as a thing of natural beauty, an attractive form that was natural rather than revolutionary. The article penned by a leading stylist for *Harper's Bazaar* highlighted the stylishness of the new car.[80] "The new Airflow Chrysler is not a radical design but a natural design... Its beauty is the beauty of nature herself." Walter Chrysler had informed Bel Geddes that he wanted his car to appeal to women. Perhaps the use of a fashion journalist to promote the Airflow was an attempt to attract female consumers, while Bel Geddes's emphasis on function was meant to appeal to men.[81]

Around 1934 Chrysler's engineer Carl Breer extended the analogy between streamlining and nature.[82] Rather than crediting Bel Geddes as a pioneer of automotive streamlining, Breer claimed that he conceived it in 1927: "In the summer of 1927... I was forcibly struck with the thought that the success of the airplane had been due to a close application of the laws of nature, as exemplified by the bird in flight."[83] Publicity writing for Chrysler, by "aerodynamic expert" Professor Alexander Klemin, proclaimed that the Airflow was "truly streamlined" and "has true natural beauty ... that is accepted because it is sound."[84] Presenting streamlining as a natural aesthetic made the unfamiliar familiar and literally naturalized a manufactured style, and was perhaps symptomatic of a deeper concern regarding consumer resistance to aerodynamic styling.

Numerous streamlined automobiles were developed prior to the Airflow and Bel Geddes's cars, including: Count Ricotti's, Alfa Romeo, 1914; Paul Jaray's, Zeppelin-built car of 1922; and the British aviation designer Charles Burney's Streamliner of 1930.[85] Mass-produced American cars that incorporated streamlining and paved the way for the Airflow included the popular Reo Royale Eight, 1931, the first mass-produced car to sport the streamlined style. Designed by Northrup, the car maintained the general form of contemporary automobiles, while rounding and integrating the body. The success of this and the more conspicuously streamlined Graham Blue Streak, designed by Northrup in 1932, encouraged the industry to take a more serious look at the new aesthetic.[86]

Bel Geddes designs for Chrysler

With the automotive industry's door now open to streamlined design, in September 1933 Norman Bel Geddes and Company were contracted for one year to assist in the designing and styling of Chrysler's passenger cars. This project eventually included work on the Chrysler and De Soto Airflows for 1934. By the end of the job the Bel Geddes firm had completed designs of interiors, exteriors, details, and bodies, including a restyling of the front end of the Airflow (Figure 5.7). For the Airflow job, Bel Geddes brought in Carl Otto, whose previous experience included work in General Motors's Art and Color Section.[87] Bel Geddes saw this job as an opportunity to put his "ultimate" car into production, informing his staff that he hoped to have a "completely streamlined" car on the road in approximately one year.[88]

By the time Bel Geddes became involved in the Airflow project, the basic structure and engineering of the car had been decided. Developed primarily by the engineers, Fred Zeder, Owen Skelton, and Carl Breer, it was the first mass-produced car to emphasize functional streamlining. Additionally, it pioneered the structural integration of the body and frame, resulting in rigidity and lightness. The use of such unitary construction became standard in the automotive industry after the Second World War.[89] The Airflow was originally intended to have a teardrop shape and rear engine. But this was rejected because it made the car "tail heavy."[90] Its 1934 incarnation sported a parabolic curved roofline, teardrop fenders, integrated headlights, and a sloping flat front end, which was eventually blamed for its poor sales.

Despite considering the Airflow insufficiently streamlined, in October 1933 Bel Geddes gave his reserved approval to the car, proclaiming that it is "all that Mr. Q [Walter Chrysler] had claimed for it." Bel Geddes believed it drove more easily and was "more comfortable than any motor car that [he'd] ever ridden in." However, he warned, it was a "compromise" between present car body styling and the "completely streamlined job of ultimate use."[91] Not disagreeing with Bel Geddes, Walter Chrysler explained that the car's comfort was derived from balanced weight rather than streamlining.[92] In October, Bel Geddes presented Walter Chrysler with four car designs, including two teardrops and one with a gas tank in its fin.[93] Chrysler rejected these designs, insisting that radical streamlining wouldn't be seen for another five years, as "the public is not yet educated."[94] In the meantime, "perfect streamlining," Chrysler believed, would have to be sacrificed to achieve consumer comfort—width at the rear, for example, was required for extra headroom.[95]

By November 1933, the Bel Geddes team felt that the Chrysler engineer's explanations of the Airflow "did not concur with fundamental engineering principles."[96] The design office criticized the "balance" of the Airflow and its "resulting riding qualities," which they believed "were as much accidental as they were the result of applied engineering principles." Bel Geddes and his staff were particularly critical of what they considered the lack of aerodynamic research on the car, having earlier pressed Chrysler for a large wind tunnel to measure front and side wind and ground action, which Bel Geddes considered "absolutely essential in determining the ultimate form towards which the motor car should tend."[97] This latter claim, however, did not take into account wind-tunnel research assisted by aviation pioneer Orville Wright and others that had fired Breer's enthusiasm for a scientifically streamlined automobile.[98]

Ideal streamlining and the rear-engine debate

In a series of meetings with the Chrysler team in late 1933, Bel Geddes and his staff pressed hard for what they considered the ideal placement of the car's engine. They believed that the rear engine would reduce the tendency of the Airflow to skid on corners and pitch when braking.[99] The Chrysler team disregarded the criticism of "balanced weight," a problem they thought their design tackled. Though Chrysler's engineers unanimously considered the rear engine the "ultimate solution to ideal streamlin[ing]," they worried about production difficulties, poor center of gravity, rear gas tank explosions, and consumer acceptance of the teardrop form.[100] Breer and Zeder believed that further tests were needed to achieve a satisfactory rear-engine car, thus requiring a lengthy period of research.[101] Dissatisfied with Chrysler's engineers, Bel Geddes raised the rear engine issue with Edward G. Budd, a pioneer in the development of all-steel car bodies, who had been working on the Chrysler job. Budd echoed Zeder and Breer, agreeing that a rear-engine car should eventually be produced, but that die costs were too great and they needed a car in production right away. There just wasn't enough time to solve the engineering problems. Taking his usual long view, Bel Geddes replied, "it was to save that expense … [that] rear engine drive [should be] established at the very beginning of streamline design."[102]

At a subsequent meeting with Walter Chrysler, a more emphatic argument ensued over the merits of the rear engine. Bel Geddes told Walter Chrysler that they had a "two years' jump" on any competition, which could only be maintained by means of "continuing the study of streamlining in all its aspects for its most ideal conditions." Bel Geddes explained that the Airflow would educate the public to streamlining. Then in two or three years the public would demand a streamlined car "which is not a compromise … and will live for several years without substantial change."[103] This approach, where the design was altered every few years, stood in contrast to that of the Graham-Paige car, which incrementally achieved an ideal form over a five-year period.

Despite Bel Geddes's arguments, the Chrysler team rejected the rear engine for a variety of reasons: including tail sway, "tear away" of the motor during collision, lack of protection during head-on crashes, and a rougher ride. Roger Nowland of the Bel Geddes office deftly tackled these criticisms. He argued that it was more dangerous to have the engine in the front. Deaths from head on collisions, he argued, were the result of the rigidity of the front end, which threw passengers forward. A rear-engine car would provide a more resilient front structure that would "crumple" and absorb the impact, thus protecting the passenger. Tail sway, Nowland claimed, was not the result of motor placement, but poor center of gravity. A good center of gravity could be achieved just as easily in a rear engine car as in a front engine one. Engine tear away, he asserted, was a concern of airplane pilots and could not be transposed to the automobile. Finally, he reminded the Chrysler team that a rear engine car had never been tested in a wind tunnel, and therefore its outright rejection would be a folly.

Nowland convinced Breer that the rear engine car was "too sound an idea not to be fully developed." The Bel Geddes team had won the debate. In mid-November 1933, Bel Geddes was told to begin work on streamlined front- and rear-engine cars.[104] However, two months later Breer asked Bel Geddes's staff to forget engine placement and focus on streamlining the body toward a "perfect aerodynamic form." The assignment was to develop a series of body designs and interiors for the De Sotos and Chryslers based on the results of aerodynamic study for 1935, an aerodynamic study of the De Soto and Chryslers for 1935; and restyling of exteriors and interiors of all De Soto and Chrysler Airflows for 1934 1/2.[105] By January, Bel Geddes had convinced Walter Chrysler to let him put up to four men "on the design of what we considered the ultimate streamline shape."[106] Days later, however, Chrysler asked Bel Geddes to back away from the project. Bel Geddes's design made it to the quarter-size model stage, but no further.[107] While the Chrysler job helped transform Bel Geddes's image from that of a dreamy stage designer to a serious design consultant, Bel Geddes failed to achieve his ultimate goal: the production of the ideal streamlined car. It was perhaps this attachment to the teardrop ideal that led to his failure at Chrysler. The Chrysler team's concerns regarding the rear-engine automobile would prove prescient. In the early 1960s, the rear-engine Chevrolet Corvair's tendency to oversteer when cornering resulted in numerous deaths. The car became a target of the consumer advocate Ralph Nader in his book *Unsafe at Any Speed*, leading to poor sales and its withdrawal from production in 1969.[108]

Publicizing streamlined design

It was standard practice for the Bel Geddes office to publish articles as a form of publicity, to either gain new clients or maintain existing ones. The November 1934 article "Streamlining" for *Atlantic Monthly* may have been intended to coincide with the streamlined design work for Chrysler. "Streamlining" was most likely ghostwritten for Bel Geddes,[109] and summarized his thoughts on aerodynamic car design.[110] Detailed and scientific-sounding, the treatise positioned Bel Geddes as a streamlining expert and may have deflected post-*Horizons* criticism of him as an impractical visionary. The article provided a brief history of aerodynamic study, from Leonardo da Vinci to the present and aimed to rectify the lazy use of the term, especially by "advertising copywriters" who have "seized upon it as a handy synonym for the word 'new' ... using it indiscriminately and often inexactly to describe automobiles and women's dresses, railroad trains and men's shoes" (553). While Bel Geddes was openly critical of this view of streamlining, he would increasingly accept jobs from clients who did not share this perspective, especially in the 1940s.

Bel Geddes's notion of automotive streamlining emphasized efficiency and comfort rather than speed. In his *Atlantic Monthly* article he wrote, "greater speed is not the goal of the car as it is of the airplane" (559). The goal of reduced air resistance, wrote Geddes, was "to increase efficiency and economy of operation" (559). Bel Geddes estimated that streamlined cars would save a billion dollars a year for automobile owners (560). He wrote that the influence of drag resistance on the new De Soto and Chrysler cars was questionable. What was important about these new cars was that they departed from traditional appearance, therefore ushering in the public acceptance of real streamlining. Bel Geddes explained that because automobiles experienced different resistance than planes, including "ground effect," the car must not take the form of the airplane (556–558). Bel Geddes recommended the elimination of protuberances, "clean, continuous lines from front to rear," the change of body form based on better air tunnel tests, "roominess and comfort that are enjoyed in a small room of a home," "broad visibility and ease of riding, driving, and parking" (558).

After its publication, the Bel Geddes office sent copies of "Streamlining" to 1,200 individuals. A letter from Bel Geddes was included that cast the designer as a guardian of the scientific streamlining, stating, "Industrial applications [of streamlining] have in some cases been made willy-nilly without apparent basis or benefit." The letter was received by captains of industry, industrial designers, heads of museums, the industrial press, advertising agencies, and government officials, including Alfred Barr Jr. (MoMA), George Howe, Frank Lloyd Wright, Erich Mendelsohn, Richard F. Bach (Metropolitan Museum of Art, New York), Ernst Wasmuth (Wendigen), Charles Kettering (vice president, General Motors Corporation), Fred Zeder (head engineer, Chrysler Motors Corporation), Henry Ford (Henry Ford Motors), Harvey Firestone (Firestone Tire and Rubber Company), as well as Continental Bakery, Socony-Vacuum Oil Company, and Chase Copper and Brass Company. At General Motors, an additional 100 copies were requested for circulation.[111] The goals of the letter campaign were to gain clients, publicize the office, and inform colleagues. During this effort, Bel Geddes sent staff to prospective clients to discuss the article and offer the services of the office. This follow-up was a common practice at the office, and was intended to nurture a strong client base.

Significantly, most respondents complimented Bel Geddes's succinct presentation of aerodynamics and his attempt to guard against its misuse, while a handful congratulated the firm for its canny publicity campaign. Alfred Barr's sympathetic reply was typical of many letters. "It seems to me that streamlining has been an absurdity in much contemporary design." Referring to a Raymond Loewy design, Barr noted, "I have even seen a streamline pencil sharpener by one of the highest paid industrial designers." Perhaps revealing his desire to be linked with scientific rather than stylistic streamlining, Bel Geddes underlined Barr's final sentence: "This blind concern with fashion is one of the things which makes it difficult to take the ordinary industrial designers seriously."[112] The architect Ely Jacques Kahn echoed Barr and wrote, "As you so aptly put it, streamlining has, unfortunately, become as much of a fetish as functionalism, and we have streamlined ash cans and breakfast food. Perhaps if we know more of the scientific angle, we may be less inclined to do stupid things with design."[113]

However, another recipient was less concerned with the debates regarding style and science and more intrigued by the effort to erase Bel Geddes's image as the P. T. Barnum of design.

I was impressed by its [the article's] sobriety and believe that for this reason it was an extremely wise step for you to take. I believe that a great many people who read it are going to have a new conception of Norman Bel Geddes & Company. You are of course not blind to the fact that your spectacular history has led people to believe that you are essentially a show man [sic].

The writer revealed he had "discussed the article with Earl [Newsom] in advance … [and] knew what its real objective was."[114] As a skilled public relations man, Newsom's objective had long been to strategically develop the Bel Geddes persona.

This and similar publicity was essential in maintaining the Bel Geddes image and was guided by the office's press relations representative, who, with "many contacts in the newspaper, magazine, book, radio and trade journal field," was "responsible for creating the best possible impression of Norman Bel Geddes and Company ... through the subtle and expert guidance of public opinion through proper publicity, expertly prepared."[115] By the early 1940s, the study and practice of shaping public opinion was well established in America, having been famously scrutinized in Walter Lippmann's *Public Opinion*, 1922. And by 1935 opinion polling had become commonplace through George Gallup's American Institute of Public Opinion.[116] The Bel Geddes office recognized that a carefully managed public image could determine the response of both prospective clients and consumers. "He [the press relations representative] must also be constantly aware of all our activities that would tend to excite prospective customers and fill them with admiration for our work ... he is constantly striving to stimulate new accounts under various disguises."[117] Such "disguises" might include publicity gained through an article on scientific streamlining or activities seemingly unrelated to industrial design. Articles on Bel Geddes's hobbies and interests, whether elaborate war games or prophecies of the future, found their way into numerous celebrity newspaper columns and were consumed by a public hungry for manufactured personality and tales of tomorrow. In addition to such publicity, Bel Geddes maintained his office through the sheer strength of his personality. His jovial company as a nightclub companion and regular host of dinner parties helped him to maintain a devoted group of businessmen as financial investors.[118]

While Bel Geddes's *Atlantic Monthly* article may have helped to sell his image, it had little effect on the fortune of the Chrysler Airflow. Although the Airflow was appreciated for its role in educating the public to the idea of streamlining, it was ultimately a commercial failure—its visual styling was considered too extreme for the average consumer. Due to weak sales, Chrysler withdrew the car from production in 1937, leading to a long hiatus in innovative styling at the company. However, other streamlined cars, such as the 1938 Cadillac 60 Special, soon found an eager market. In the following decade, the essential aspects of the Airflow, including the lower silhouette, the all-steel frame and body, and the unified exterior shell, would become standard components in most production automobiles. During the postwar years, aerodynamic automotive design would continue to progress, resulting in a glut of nonfunctional styling. The first postwar car to display tailfins was the 1948 Cadillac Coupé, designed by Harley Earl's General Motors team. A profusion of American automotive manufacturers quickly followed suit.

Cleanlining and novel uses of streamlining, c. 1932–1950

Despite Bel Geddes's rational arguments for streamlining at Chrysler, he clearly understood the style's symbolic appeal. At the same time, he argued for scientific streamlining in the field of transportation; he applied aesthetic streamlining to household goods (Figure 5.8). In 1934, while critics of streamlining derided its application to inanimate objects as "quackery,"[119] Bel Geddes applied the imagery of speed to a domestic appliance, the Electrolux vacuum cleaner, associating the romance of technology with mundane housework. Bel Geddes's vacuum cleaner was a low, rectilinear form with rounded corners, echoing the look of his proposed streamlined train of 1932. Its "runners stamped into the bottom of the casing" echoed the look of train tracks and allowed the machine to travel along the floor, anticipating Lurelle Guild's streamlined Model 30 vacuum cleaner for Electrolux of 1937. The Bel Geddes team sought to eliminate "projections" to achieve "clean," "unbroken lines and surfaces." Designed for "practicality" to "appeal to women," the intended

FIGURE 5.8 Bel Geddes's Electrolux vacuum cleaner, *c.* 1934–1935. Photograph by Richard Garrison. Harry Ransom Center, University of Texas, and the Edith Lutyens and Norman Bel Geddes Foundation, Inc. 2016.

"total effect" of the Electrolux was of "modern simplified efficiency."[120] The design sported three parallel "louvers," like those found on automobiles and trains, which were not "merely … a mechanical element of the machine," but were "enlarged" "to add interest to the design." The motif of three parallel lines was a decorative device widely used by industrial designers in the 1930s. Walter Dorwin Teague helped to popularize it through his Texaco service station designs after 1934, which employed three thin green horizontal stripes along the top perimeter of the canopy and building. By 1940, 400 such stations had been built.[121] Discussing the Teague stations in late 1945, Frederic Pawley, a design director at the Bel Geddes firm, criticized the "three stripes" as "dated" and "a fetish for certain industrial designers" in the mid-1930s, suggesting that the aesthetic of speed and efficiency had lost its appeal by the end of the Second World War.[122]

In the early 1940s, however, streamlining remained a popular style, and manufacturers eagerly sought Bel Geddes, the streamlining pioneer. During and after the Second World War, Bel Geddes was asked to apply the aesthetics of streamlining to a variety of products, including a meat slicer, packaging, and jewelry: for the Globe Slicing Company (*c.* 1940–1943), the Loose-Wiles Biscuit Company (*c.* 1941–1942), and the Rice-Weiner and Company (1949–1950), respectively. The step from car design to package and product design was not huge, each requiring the design of unified exterior shells. In these new jobs any lingering scientific definitions of streamlining disappeared almost entirely. Despite his criticisms of the "indiscriminate" use of the term "streamlining" by advertising copywriters, during this next phase Bel Geddes used the word as a synonym for "styling" and "novelty," while his designs became increasingly linked to bodily movement, rather than the mechanical thrust of the plane or train. However, it was this ability to adapt the notion of streamlining to a variety of design jobs during the 1940s that stands in stark contrast to Bel Geddes's more rigid association of streamlining with ideal form during the 1930s. Bel Geddes's ability to accommodate the multiple meanings of the style led to successes with his new clients, even while distorting streamlining's original meaning.

At the end of 1930s, the Bel Geddes firm capitalized on its reputation for streamlining expertise through their work for the Chrysler Corporation and the General Motors Futurama exhibit. In November 1940, the office was asked to visually restyle a food-slicing machine used in delicatessens and butcher shops.[123] The Globe Slicing Machine Company's gravity feed patent was soon to expire and the company was concerned about expected competition. Bel Geddes and Company was asked to make it "streamlined," but not to simply "pretty it up."[124] In this job, the client understood streamlining to mean the reduction of angular elements to improve the product's visual appeal. In contrast to Bel Geddes's view of automobile streamlining, consumer appeal rather than ideal form was the primary goal. Bel Geddes and his staff were asked to "eliminate the many "bumps" caused by the motor housing sticking out; the many exposed levers and handles."[125] The Bel Geddes office was informed that consumers of the slicer had the following prejudices: "The mechanical look" and "too many exposed machine parts" (Figure 5.9).[126] While the symbolism of speed and power may have appealed in automotive design, such references in food service equipment were not always welcome.

In the 1940s, MoMA's curators condemned the streamlining of any inanimate object. In its bulletin of November 1940, streamlining was ridiculed as a "fad" which had "seriously perverted American design."[127] Three years later MoMA compared a rectangular, undecorated toaster shown at the Machine Art exhibit of 1934 to a streamlined one. While it considered the toaster of 1934 "forthright, clean and simple," the toaster of 1940, "which is streamlined as if it were intended to hurtle through the air at 200 miles an hour" and "ornamented with trivial loops," was derided as absurd.[128] The architecture and design historian Siegfried Giedion later joined in the lampooning of streamlining in his book Mechanization Takes Command (1948). Giedion argued that there were two kinds of streamlining—the scientific, which reduced the form; and the aesthetic, which "bloated" it. "Streamline form in the scientific sense aims at the utmost economy of form, at a minimum volume. The exploitation of the streamline form in the daily objects of use aims to produce an artificial swelling of volumes."[129] MoMA and Giedion shared a preference for a modernist machine aesthetic that allowed little room for the organic forms of streamlining, connotations that were often implicit in 1930s streamlining and became more pronounced in the 1940s. By the 1940s, Bel Geddes's notion of streamlining had drastically changed. He no longer called for the ideal or ultimate streamlined form, but accepted its rhetorical and stylistic use as a novelty to sell goods of all kinds.

A cartoon published in Fortune magazine in February 1934 presaged Bel Geddes's design work for the Loose-Wiles Biscuit Company between 1941 and 1942 (Figure 5.10). The cartoon showed a group of businessmen gathered in a boardroom. Several framed pictures were hung in the

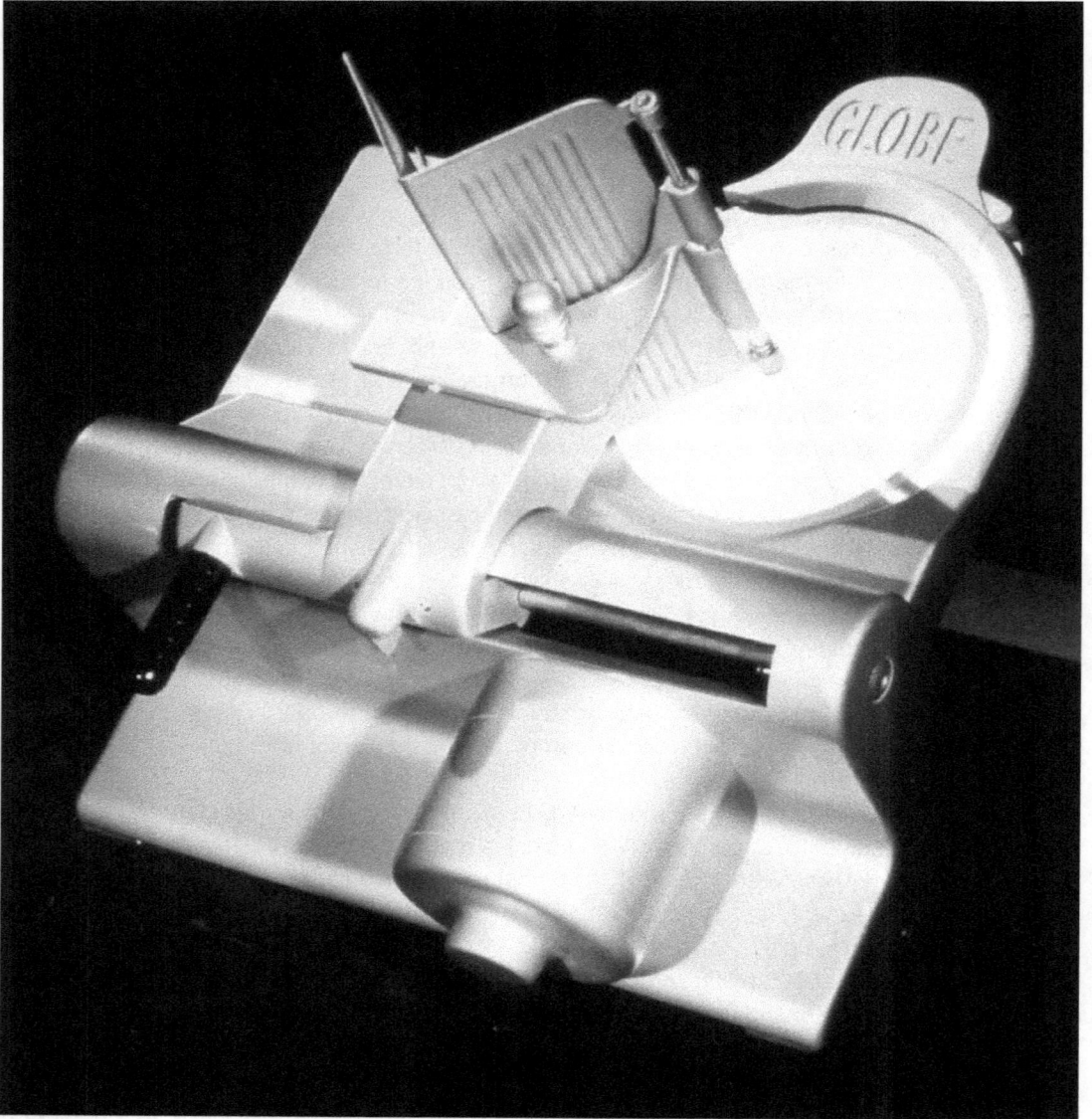

FIGURE 5.9 Globe slicing machine after Bel Geddes redesign, *c.* 1940. Photograph by unidentified photographer. Harry Ransom Center, University of Texas, and the Edith Lutyens and Norman Bel Geddes Foundation, Inc. 2016.

background: one of a factory building, and the other depicted a variety of biscuits. A standing man holding a cigar announced to the others, "Gentlemen—I am convinced that our next new biscuit must be styled by Norman Bel Geddes."[130] The cartoon evidenced Bel Geddes's notoriety, while reflecting anxieties regarding the increased role of styling in everyday life. While Bel Geddes did not redesign the actual biscuits for the Loose-Wiles, in 1941 he was asked to create packaging

"Gentlemen—I Am Convinced That Our Next New Biscuit Must Be Styled by Norman Bel Geddes"

FIGURE 5.10 Kemp Starrett, *New Yorker* cartoon, 1934. © Kemp Starrett, The *New Yorker* Collection, www.cartoonbank.com.

that was "modern, streamlined and arresting in composition and color" for Hydrox, Cheez-Its, and Chocolate Mallomars, among others.[131] As with the publicity for Graham-Paige and Chrysler, streamlining and the "modern" were again linked, suggesting equivalence between popular goods and avant-garde aesthetics. The Bel Geddes staff were asked to produce packaging designs which were "extreme" and "novel," yet still retained the familiarity of the brand image, which was associated with the "inimitable 'Sunshine Bakers' … these rotund and merry men."[132] For Loose-Wiles, streamlining meant novel designs with eye appeal that included the brand's traditional image.

In the late 1940s, Bel Geddes began designing "Flow-Motion" costume jewelry for Rice-Weiner and Company, coinciding with the wider emergence of the organic aesthetic in design, a style nascent in many of his earliest streamlined designs. The client hoped to take advantage of Bel Geddes's reputation as the father of streamlining. However, it was the gentle, sinuous shapes of aerodynamic forms, rather than any association with speed and technology, that appealed to Rice-Weiner. Bel Geddes's initial designs for Rice-Weiner were not avant-garde, but whimsical, some borrowing from popular surrealist imagery. Salvador Dali's influence can be noted in the two designs of brooches, one in the shape of a long-lashed eye and another of a pair of disembodied lips. Many of the pieces were simply novelty items, for example a necklace with a pair of dangling dancing figures; and pieces depicting large-eyed, cartoonish, cats and monkeys.

Company president Howard Weiner initially found Bel Geddes's designs too "conventional and conservative."[133] He suggested that Bel Geddes look to his streamlined designs in order to capture "the feeling in the lines and the flow of motion which you … practically developed in the design field." Adding that, Bel Geddes's jewelry "designs do not seem to have the depth, body and rhythm contained, for example, in your 'Futurama.'"[134] Bel Geddes's hook-shaped General Motors building, designed in association with Eero Saarinen, the pioneering architect of organic structures, was inspired by the curves of streamlined automobiles, while the Futurama ride depended on smooth and seamless motion.

Weiner eventually rejected the surreal designs, preferring those of novelty and nature. Ironically, he chose the whimsical and conservative designs Bel Geddes had initially offered, including a necklace of meandering floral tendrils, as well as stylized pendants depicting women of various ethnicities (Plate 21). Clearly these designs had little to do with the conventional view of streamlining—of speed, technology, and the world of tomorrow. Highlighting this disparity, a reviewer wrote with surprise that the designs did "not resemble something from Mars, as might be expected by persons familiar with Geddes' [sic] futuristic thinking."[135]

The "Flow-Motion" catalog highlighted Bel Geddes's role as a streamlining pioneer, yet emphasized the product's harmony with nature and bodily movement. The catalog noted Bel Geddes's streamlined transport "firsts," yet the cover illustrated a series of flowing, biomorphic lines,[136] contrasting sharply with the horizontal piercing movement associated with streamlining. In comparison to machine-inspired design of the 1930s, "Flow-Motion" evidenced the contemporary turn toward organic design—a less-severe aesthetic, which looked to nature, rather than the machine. Even the name, ostensibly a reference to streamlining, was more suggestive of slow motion than high speeds.

Bel Geddes would have been very familiar with the trend in organic design through his copy of *Organic Design in Home Furnishings* (1941), a competition and exhibition organized by Eliot Noyes in 1940 as the first curator of industrial design at MoMA. After leaving MoMA, Noyes became design director in the Bel Geddes office, where he redesigned the IBM 562 typewriter, developing it into the influential, ergonomic "Executive."[137] After the closure of Bel Geddes's Rockefeller Center office in 1946, Noyes set up his own architectural and industrial design office with Marcel Breuer in New York.[138] While the ideological meanings of aesthetic streamlining and organic design may have seemed miles apart (the former associated with machine-age values and the latter with their critique), the seeds of organic design are found in the contemporaneous view of streamlining as a natural and evolutionary phenomenon. During the postwar years, the natural, flowing qualities of streamlining were not necessarily at odds with organic design, and were particularly applicable to jewelry. The shift in the meaning of streamlining may have reflected a society less enamored of technology after witnessing its devastating wartime applications.

During a period in which design critics derided streamlining as a commercial vulgarity, Bel Geddes presented the style as both modern and commercial, appealing to industrialists, tastemakers, and consumers. Bel Geddes's high-profile promotion of streamlining, whether stylistic or scientific, aided its acceptance in the boardrooms of America's automotive industry and beyond. Bel Geddes's diverse designs show how streamlining accommodated a range of meanings from the mechanical to the organic—from the horizontal thrust of motorcars to the flow of the body. Sometimes these meanings were balanced within a single design, such as the Chrysler Airflow, the marketing of which referenced the aerodynamic forms of airplanes and fish. At other times, the natural, rather than the mechanical, was brought to the fore, as in the "Flow-Motion" jewelry. Through such work Bel Geddes constructed his image as a streamlining pioneer, while continuing to balance the seeming oppositions of the practical visionary. Bel Geddes's wish to produce the ultimate streamlined product reflected his own beliefs, rather than the desires of the average consumer. This personal and utopian approach was often out of step with market demands, which required expert knowledge of consumer wants. This tension between Bel Geddes's aesthetic and the material longings of the buying public are explored in the following chapter.

6

Consumer Research: Imagining the Ideal Consumer, Developing a Popular, Modern Aesthetic

Those who blamed the economic crash of 1929 on underconsumption, including advertisers, engineers, and designers, called for the intensive study of consumer behavior. Just as new technologies had rationalized production, it was believed that a new science of consumer engineering would rationalize consumption and stabilize the economy. In their 1932 book *Consumer Engineering*, Arens and Sheldon called for sociologists, psychologists, and behaviorists, not merely to create demand, but to respond to it and to discover what people wanted through consumer surveys and scientific theory, and thereby promote consumption while avoiding another economic depression.[1] Supporting this project, American industrial designers offered their services as essential intermediaries between supposedly fickle consumers and vulnerable producers. In 1930, the industrial designer Ben Nash urged manufacturers to hire consultants to interpret the "dangerously inarticulate" consumer in order to avoid "overproduction, dealer complaints, distress prices and returned goods."[2] Likewise, Bel Geddes presented the consumer as an increasingly powerful and potentially ruinous force whose desires required expert mediation. Historians have referred to such professionals as consumer "translators," ranging from designers to department store buyers and manufacturing personnel, who "facilitated communication between consumers and producers," and attempted to "understand, appropriate, and alter popular conceptions of leisure, pleasure, and utility."[3] Bel Geddes's representation of the designer as consumer expert was an effective strategy, helping the emerging design profession to attract clients enthralled by consumer expertise. After 1930, Bel Geddes's staff energetically engaged in consumer research and believed that consumer wishes should not be blindly obeyed, but monitored and interpreted by design consultants through surveys and interviews. This approach put designers in an enviable position. As the primary translators of consumer desires, clients regarded designers as having scientific authority and economic influence. Such analysis allowed Bel Geddes, his competitors, and consumer experts to speak for "inarticulate" consumers, who, Bel Geddes claimed, "do not know exactly what they want, but they do know that they want it. They want something new but they are going to be timid about accepting it."[4] As late as 1943 Bel Geddes and company maintained, "In our work we have found that due to lack of imagination of the dealer or consumer, it is impossible to obtain from him any valid improvements or suggestions."[5] In 1946, Bel Geddes asserted "The successful designer is a leader, otherwise the results of his thinking are obsolete by the time they are on the market."[6] This approach filtered, transformed, and sometimes ignored consumer preferences, allowing Bel Geddes to promote a progressive aesthetic, both modern and popular, aimed at consumers of average taste and income.

As the Bel Geddes office developed, its consumer research became increasingly sophisticated. In the early 1930s, the Bel Geddes firm merely surveyed the product preferences of consumers and dealers through interviews and questionnaires. This approach was employed in the designs of stoves for the Standard Gas Equipment Company (1930) and radios for the Philadelphia Storage Battery Company or Philco (1930). By the mid-1930s, however, the office had produced extensive sociological and demographic reports that optimistically forecast positive trends in consumer desire, education, and income, and offered designs intended to appeal to a range of middle-class tastes. The earliest such study was for John D. Rockefeller, Jr.'s Abeyton Realty Corporation (1934), investigating a plan for a residential development in Cleveland, Ohio. The method was also used for Rittenhouse Chimes (1943), and became more advanced in subsequent jobs for Shell Oil and the Radio Corporation of America, RCA (1942–1945). In his consumer surveys, Bel Geddes intentionally sought participants who combined "average" outlooks with strong purchasing power. "The important factor in conducting a survey of this kind," he explained in *Horizons*, "is to pick the right individuals from whom to get information. The survey should represent the average mass viewpoint, the viewpoint of the greatest buying power."[7] Despite his appreciation of modernism and the ultimate streamlined form, Bel Geddes warned designers against avant-garde experimentation: "If he does something tricky, a few people will be enthusiastic about it, but the majority will not."[8] Throughout his creative life Bel Geddes had been fascinated by the masses, including mass production, mass taste, and mass politics, whether socialist or capitalist. The industrial design profession associated the mass market with the notion of "average taste" and pitched its products accordingly at "all but the poorest and the wealthiest households."[9] In 1932, the trade journal *Product Engineering* proclaimed that good design should "hit the average taste" and "aim generally at producing a quiet, unobtrusive effect."[10] In 1940, Harold Van Doren suggested that designers should take a "middle course," and provide "the very best it [the public] will absorb, and not one bit more."[11] Raymond Loewy would later develop an acronym for this tendency, the MAYA principle, the "Most Advanced Yet Acceptable," a design aesthetic that sought a balance between novel styling and the reassuringly familiar.[12]

Bel Geddes was aware of the diminishing influence of Fordism, named after Henry Ford's sales strategy used at the Ford Motor Company after the introduction of the 1908 Model T, which provided a single, "universal" design at the lowest possible price. This marketing approach was superseded by Alfred Sloan's more successful annual model changes at General Motors in the 1920s, which used a "price pyramid" to aim a variety of models at a broad range of customer groups.[13] Increased commercial competition during the 1930s intensified market segmentation and consumer research, including the study of demographics—age, income, and education—and psychographics—the quantitative investigation of consumer attitudes. This information was used to divide markets into segments large enough for scale economies.[14] General Motors, a leader in consumer research during the 1930s, aggressively surveyed its consumers in order to maintain both its profitability and its socially responsible image.[15] Following the increasingly sophisticated consumer research within the motor industry, manufacturers in other sectors consulted outside experts who presented their knowledge of consumers as a kind of "business science."[16] Bel Geddes's consultancy services relied on his self-presentation as an expert in consumer research. Rather than seeking a uniform mass market, as Ford had done with the Model T, Bel Geddes sought to divide the remaining middle market into several segments. Bel Geddes's embrace of market segmentation reflected his need to satisfy clients just as it coexisted with his utopian desire for achieving his idea of the ultimate design.

Early consumer surveys: Philco and Abeyton Realty

In *Horizons*, Bel Geddes outlined the multiple stages involved in a design job, including extensive research, an activity that Bel Geddes considered essential. At the beginning of the job all relevant staff, including designers, engineers, merchandizers, and researchers, gathered in Bel Geddes's office to discuss the design problem (Figure 6.1). Design objectives and means of achieving them, along with a schedule, were agreed. Bel Geddes considered scheduling of "utmost importance" and planned jobs six months ahead in general and three months ahead in detail. In 1946, Bel Geddes wrote "Visualize an office with twenty jobs being worked on at once all having to meet different dates at different period [*sic*] of the work, all interchanging personnel because of specialized abilities, all involving people traveling around the country or on vacation, and allowing for contingencies such as illnesses."[17] Next came a lengthy period of research, which included familiarization with the client's product: its present function, its ultimate function, and its manufacture, sales, and servicing. Bel Geddes's team visited the client's factory to match the final design with the available manufacturing technology. Equivalent information was then gathered on the competitors' models, materials, production, merchandising, and servicing. At this point comments from consumers and retailers were solicited. Bel Geddes considered this the most important phase of the design job.[18]

Only following this initial research, "and having established clearly in his own mind and that of his client what purpose and conditions the product must meet," should the designer apply "himself to the problem of redesign."[19] The job would be organized using a card index system, "consisting of several hundred printed forms—covering every phase of every type of work" (231). Bel Geddes warned that design is more a matter of "*thinking*" than drawing (232): only after the "objective" and "facts" were "clearly visualized" may preliminary sketches be completed (231). Just as he had taught his stage design students to visualize their ideas before drawing them, he recommended that "There is no use putting hand to paper until you can close your eyes and see with *complete* clarity all details of what it is you wish to draw" (231). Following client approval, finished sketches were developed into larger and more detailed working drawings, and, finally, full-sized models (233). Although Bel Geddes made very few sketches, he maintained great control over the design process, insisting, "Every drawing, at every stage of the work, from the preliminary sketches up to the final shop drawings, passes across my desk" (232).

FIGURE 6.1 Bel Geddes and staff with radios, *c.* 1940s. Photograph by Richard Garrison. Harry Ransom Center, University of Texas, and the Edith Lutyens and Norman Bel Geddes Foundation, Inc. 2016.

Bel Geddes described how he avoided any reliance on his client's knowledge, using product surveys instead to achieve an independent perspective.[20] Bel Geddes's office highlighted the almost scientific nature of their consumer research: they "assigned various individuals with proper qualifications to ... carefully selected parts of the country to make numerous specific inquiries" (227). "Among these investigators were designers, merchandising specialists, salesmen, [and] engineers: men to get the men's point of view, women to get the reaction of women .... from the metropolis to the scantily populated rural community" (227–228). Bel Geddes's "investigators" "mailed in daily" reports which the office "sorted and compiled in statistical form" (228). Appearing in the pages of *Horizons*, such descriptions of highly systematized and rigorous research presented Bel Geddes's design consultancy as essential to any ambitious client.

In 1930, Philco spent nearly $10,000 to fund Bel Geddes's consumer research, indicating the radio industry's commitment to consumer study following the stock market crash.[21]

While nearly ten million families owned radios in 1929, this figure had jumped to an estimated twelve million the following year. Revealing the cultural importance of the radio in public life in 1930 the US census included the question "Do you own a radio?"[22] Philco had entered the field in the late 1920s, shifting its emphasis from battery production to the manufacture of electric radios. The company made an impressive start in 1929[23] through its introduction of smaller radios, aggressive marketing, and expensive advertising, Philco substantially increased its sales.[24] By the end of 1931, it had captured 40 percent of the radio market.[25] The ambitious company's propensity for investment benefited Bel Geddes, whose 1930 contract to design Philco radio cabinets promised $25,000 per year plus royalties over five years.[26]

Bel Geddes's Philco survey questioned 100 radio dealers and 288 consumers.[27] In addition to the surveys, informal conversations were conducted with "various people concerning [the] radio," including Helen Lansdowne Resor, a central figure at the J. Walter Thompson advertising agency, and Lee Simonson, the influential stage designer and author.[28] During an era when period styles dominated furniture sales those questioned overwhelmingly rejected simple, unornamented radios, preferring those that "would harmonize" with existing "furnishing." Of the top four characteristics radio users desired, tone came first, followed by price, reception, and style, "modernity" appearing fourteenth.[29] The emphasis on function and price seemed to leave little room for modern styling. In *Horizons*, on the other hand, Bel Geddes attempted to strike a balance between avant-garde and widespread allure, presenting a radio aesthetic that rejected period styles, embraced "simplicity," and "appeal[ed] to popular taste." Aware of the public's desire for visual harmony, yet keen to sweep away the trappings of the past, Bel Geddes wrote that a radio cabinet need not be "of a definite period, that is, Tudor, or Louis XIV, or Jacobean," but should "have a form that would be appropriate anywhere."[30] Despite the Philco respondents' rejection of "modernity," in *Horizons* Bel Geddes asserted that good radio design should conform to a modern, machine-age style: "Essentially the radio is one of the most representative products of the modern era, an era in which the mechanistic and the aesthetic are related. Its future design will proceed upon this basis."[31]

While Bel Geddes longed to introduce modernism to the American public, the home furnishing trade proved conservative, either rejecting novel styling or calling for its gradual introduction. During the late 1920s and early 1930s, a small number of American designers encouraged a restrained form of modern design, characterized by horizontal lines and pure geometric forms, as opposed to the "modernistic," often angular, styling often associated with the Paris Arts Décoratifs exhibition of 1925. "Modernistic" styling was thought by many American designers and commentators to have turned the public against modernism altogether. In the early 1930s, it was rejected as an "insane and bizarre" foreign idiom, while "frank" and simple design, based upon the supposedly American trait of "practicality," was met with approval.[32] In the pages of *Product Engineering* in 1931, Bel Geddes joined the debate:

> For the majority of people, to describe a room as being decorated in the modern style instantly calls up a lurid picture of angular gadgets on box-like furniture in nursery colors. Such work is simply bad work, which can occur in any age in history, and it is sheer ignorance to believe that it represents good modern design. Freaks are inevitable in any era, but it is not the freaks which live, but the honest creations grounded in the essentials of proportion, color and texture.[33]

Despite the conservative preferences of the Philco respondents, Bel Geddes illustrated the most progressive of his Philco designs in *Horizons* and called for the application of modern design to radio cabinets, proclaiming, "Radios are still in their horseless carriage days."[34] To illustrate his point, he compared a full-blown period-style Philco radio of 1930, with his simply designed Philco Lazyboy of 1931—a low-cabinet radio with tabletop controls, dark grained wood, and beaded molding (Figure 6.2 and Plate 22).[35] The manageable size of the Lazyboy capitalized on the recent craze for smaller "midget" sets, which by 1930 represented 50 percent of radio sales in the United States.[36] Far from modern, Bel Geddes's other designs for Philco also included simplified period features, dark woods, and carved moldings. The Bel Geddes office followed its standard practice, and at the end of the project produced an official job summary, which was normally used to reflect on the successes and failures of the job, generate publicity, and attract new clients. The Philco job summary ignored the results of the survey and suggested that improved visual design had substantially increased the company's sales.[37] According to Bel Geddes, his designs for Philco helped the company gain 50 percent of US radio sales, reach peak production of 4,000,000 sets, and resulted in the building of a new factory by the end of 1932.[38] This boast, of course, did not acknowledge Philco's recent aggressive advertising, marketing, and promotion of smaller radios. In 1940, Bel Geddes would achieve another commercial success in radio design, the "Patriot" plastic radio for Emerson, which employed an American flag motif, with stars as dial indicators and stripes as the speaker baffle (Plate 23). Bel Geddes would soon develop and refine his consumer research as he moved from the design of domestic products to the planning of domestic dwellings.

In 1934, the Bel Geddes office produced a market research and design study aimed at reviving the upper-income Forest Hill residential development outside Cleveland, Ohio.[39] The contract for the Abeyton Realty Corporation and John D. Rockefeller, Jr. required sketches, drawings, models, and a detailed marketing study. The study aimed to pinpoint the "sociological makeup of the market," using demographic information to identify the ideal purchaser of a Forest Hill house, the earliest such study by the Bel Geddes office.[40] Information gathered on the potential buyer included income, occupation, education, "race," and family size. In addition, statistics regarding local population trends, and commercial and utility infrastructures were collated. The study was consistent with Bel Geddes's modern image and his efforts to sell to a middle-class market. It recommended selling medium-priced "modern" houses to culturally educated middle-class consumers.[41] The report pointed to "similar developments" in modern residential housing, including the socially idealistic "garden cities" of England, and those of Holland and Belgium, praised for their use of innovative funding schemes, including joint stock societies and government supported loans.[42] Despite an interest in social housing and politically liberal financing, the study presented the "poor" as a "serious problem" and excluded them as a potential consumer group.[43]

This type of study represented a substantial shift from Bel Geddes's more prosaic consumer and dealer surveys and coincided with a broader national trend in social research.[44] Much of the credit for the transformation in research at the Bel Geddes office belongs to Earl Newsom. With a doctorate in English from Columbia, Newsom became Bel Geddes's partner and business manager in 1933. He began a career in market research in 1925, working first for *Reader's Digest*, and then in 1927 for the Oil Heating Institute, where his job was to "help change the public's fears of converting from coal to oil."[45] Newsom was interested in mass behavior and the emotional response of "the crowd mind."[46] The idea of the "people" became a rhetorical tool for cutting radio cabinet should be designed as of a definite period, that is, Tudor, or Louis XIV, or Jacobean. It is hardly reasonable, however, to assume that a respectable piece of furniture can be a combination of all three. On the other hand, it might be assumed that a radio need reflect none of these periods, but have a form that would be appropriate anywhere, due to its simplicity and dignity.[1*] Instead of accepting this point of view, some manufacturers reason that if a radio were designed as simply as a grand piano, for instance, it would not appeal to popular taste. Hence, a style of a purely mongrel nature which few persons of taste can tolerate.[1*] There is a still stranger point of view in the industry at the moment — to disguise the fact that a radio is a radio.

Many manufacturers are designing clocks and putting radio chassis and speaker inside them. They are doing the same thing with desks and tables. It is contrary to all principles of good design to represent an object on the outside as something other than it really is. Essentially the radio is one of the most representative products of the modern era, an era in which the mechanistic and the æsthetic are related. Its future design will proceed upon this basis.

190 · PHILCO RADIO   DESIGNED BY NORMAN BEL GEDDES 1931

FIGURE 6.2 Philco Radio Model 270 Lazyboy by Bel Geddes, 1931. Photograph by Maurice Goldberg reproduced in *Horizons*, 1932. Harry Ransom Center, University of Texas, and the Edith Lutyens and Norman Bel Geddes Foundation, Inc. 2016.

across class, ethnic, and ideological lines to create a sense of national unity and culture.[47] The concepts of the "people" and the "Average American" were manufactured in part through the practice of mass polling and opinion surveys, pioneered after 1935 by George Gallup's American Institute of Public Opinion.[48] Bel Geddes's office developed its use of consumer surveys during this period. Bel Geddes, however, didn't construct the "people" as a unified and homogenous mass, but with Newsom's help, as a large middle class, which could be divided into different consumer segments.

"Tomorrow's Consumer," 1943

By the 1940s, the Bel Geddes office had acquired substantial experience in consumer research, an activity now central to the design firm. In 1943, Bel Geddes publicized his consumer research expertise at Philadelphia's Annual Meeting of the American Society of Refrigerator Engineers. He informed his audience, "For 25 years I have been investigating consumer psychology . . . . The most significant results of that work are now functioning successfully as a technique of interpreting consumer needs and wants considerably in advance of production."[49] Bel Geddes's paper, "Tomorrow's Consumer," presented "the people" as a transformed and powerful consumer force, demanding both function and style in postwar products. Borrowing the potent phrasing of Abraham Lincoln's *Gettysburg Address*, Bel Geddes celebrated the emergence of "a nation of design and industry, as well as government—by the people, for the people," where "the people will speak up about the details of everyday living."[50] The use of Lincoln's famous words equated the national unification of the nineteenth century with the rise of the consumer in the twentieth century. Recalling the "1929 fiasco," the paper warned of an equivalent economic crisis if manufacturers did not satisfy consumer desires. "Until you . . . act upon the fact that you have a mass of people who want the best they can buy, you are in danger of making the same mistake again."[51] Tomorrow's consumer, Bel Geddes warned, "will not take excuses from an industrial system that has proved it can perform miracles for war and destruction. They will expect those miracles for peace."[52] "This consumer . . . has been inarticulate except in terms of sales and results."[53] The message was clear: that now more than ever, manufacturers must turn to consultant designers to interpret consumer longings.

The notion of the inarticulate consumer helped to develop significant roles for design consultants, advertisers, and marketers as consumer mediators, providing a raison d'être for these new professions. In 1924, Lois Arderly of the J. Walter Thompson advertising agency published "Inarticulate Longings" in the company's *News Bulletin*. Referring to consumer goods, Arderly's article asserted that the female consumer "wants it but she doesn't know it—yet."[54] By 1929, Christine Frederick, the well-known home economist and marketing consultant, described the consumer as a capricious female whose material wishes needed constant monitoring. In her book *Selling Mrs. Consumer*, a popular guide for advertisers, she wrote, "Mrs. Consumer can kick the whole program out of the kitchen window . . . if she decides that in some lines she wants more rather than less variety . . . . When she isn't consulted, she takes her unconscious revenge by her usual deadly weapon, her failure to buy."[55] Although men significantly participated in consumption at the time, the notion of the female consumer was widely promoted by advertisers, marketers, and women's magazine editors, bolstering the myth that women shopped and men produced.[56]

Bel Geddes subscribed to this view, choosing housewives as respondents for his Philco and SGE surveys.[57]

The historical transformation of the customer into the consumer had occurred decades earlier with the demise of traditional retailing, which relied on face-to-face relationships, and the rise of a branded mass market, which was less personal, favored the seller, and required consumer trust.[58] However, in 1943 Bel Geddes claimed that a "revolution" was imminent—the passive "customer" of the prewar days would be "obsoleted" by an active postwar "consumer."[59] Bel Geddes claimed that the postwar consumer would become even more demanding and knowledgeable as a result of years of deferred consumption and wartime experience. During the 1930s, he noted, consumers suffered a "pent-up demand" that resulted in a "deep-rooted craving for satisfaction from the appearance of things around them."[60] For Bel Geddes, women's wartime manufacture of products had taught them not only "how it looks" but also "how it ticks." Bel Geddes's postwar consumer had learned the factory values of efficiency and technological progress and would now demand them in the home. "The new consumer" "is a woman" who believes "time-motion study" should be applied to "all equipment made for her use. She's crossed the threshold of the home to work in factories and business offices."[61] Bel Geddes argued that because competing products were equally technologically advanced "that leaves just one field—mine—design and consumer interpretation in terms of function, efficiency, and appearance" that "will determine buying in a competitive market."[62] "Tomorrow's Consumer," built upon the myth of the menacing and inarticulate consumer, positioned the designer as a necessary mediator between the manufacture and the masses, and presented Bel Geddes as an industrial savior and consumer visionary—albeit a visionary guided by the scientific expertise of his staff. This picture of a constantly shifting consumer landscape provided an important interpretative role for the Bel Geddes firm and for the industrial design profession as a whole.

Designing for the postwar consumer: Shell Oil, Radio Corporation of America, and Rittenhouse Chimes

Bel Geddes's postwar consumer research was his most sophisticated. It continued the pattern set by the Abeyton Realty surveys, and exemplified the tendency of the Bel Geddes office to offer products targeted at mass consumer segments of average taste and middle incomes. Prior to 1942, the size of Bel Geddes's staff grew from fifty to eighty persons.[63] By 1942, Bel Geddes had seventy-five staff working in his Rockefeller Center office, "experts in every phase of creative design—color, line, functionalism, merchandising, engineering, and manufacturing," primarily engaged in "production planning for the post-war period." Bel Geddes explained "business has never been better in our field."[64] However, he found the firm's increased design activity and emphasis on consumer research a distraction from his greater interest—unbridled visionary design.[65] The office would soon attempt to streamline its operations, perhaps in response to Bel Geddes's dissatisfaction with its research focus and increased size.

By the early 1940s, the Bel Geddes office had refined its operations, codifying them in its four-volume *Standard Practice* handbook of 1944. The handbook reflected Bel Geddes's mania for order, especially in its emphasis on office efficiency (Figure 6.3). However, it also announced a new departure for the office, a focus on retaining "a selected number of clients."[66] This latter goal

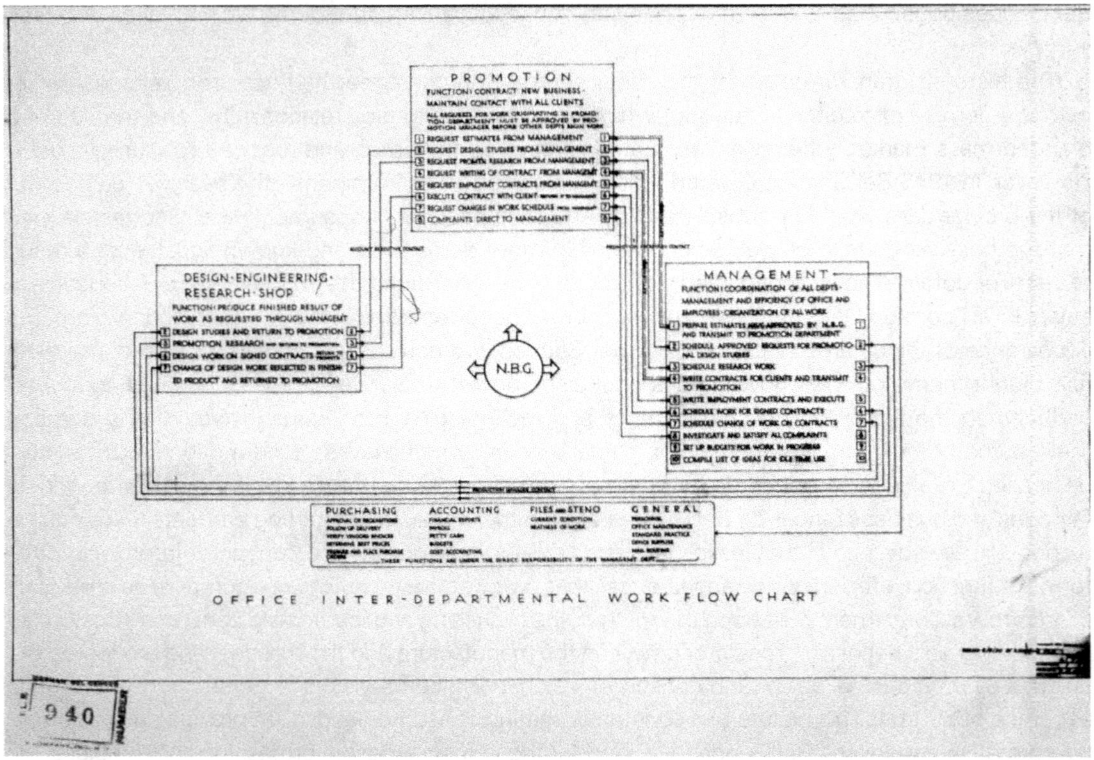

FIGURE 6.3 "Office Inter-Departmental Work Flow Chart," showing Bel Geddes at the center. No date. Harry Ransom Center, University of Texas, and the Edith Lutyens and Norman Bel Geddes Foundation, Inc. 2016.

would be achieved by the coordinated operations of the office's three departments: management, service, and production. The task of client relations was the province of the service department, whose key staff included the service director, who procured design accounts, and the press relations representative, who publicized the work of the Bel Geddes office. The service director ensured that the firm did "everything possible to hold all business and continue all contracts,"[67] and oversaw two "salesmen" working in its "No-Sales Department," so named to highlight the office's goal of "maintaining a small group of clients," as opposed to growth for its own sake.[68] Employees were informed that since the office's inception "we have wasted a large amount of our time in [the] wrong fields of activity" and on numerous "trivial" jobs. The new "policy" was to concentrate on "selected fields of activity and above a minimum price range of a $10,000 per contract." Compared to its 1934, fees of $1,000 to $100,000 plus royalties, the office manual presented an image of consistency and moderation.[69] Even as late as 1941 "the bulk" of Bel Geddes's business was made up of "bread-and-butter jobs in the $5,000-fee class."[70] The new policy was for the Bel Geddes office to "stop being a little business ... and think and perform as a big business." "In the past we have solicited nearly 1,000 accounts. In the future we will concentrate on less than 100."[71] The new policy may have pacified clients who feared the exorbitant fees of the Bel Geddes office, which had recently charged General Motors $200,000 for the design of the Futurama.[72] In actuality, Bel Geddes's wartime jobs ranged from a one-week assignment for Emerson Radio, costing $381.66, to a job for Shell Oil, which paid around $2,000 per month over roughly two years.[73]

During the months leading up to America's entry into the Second World War in December 1941, the Bel Geddes office was involved in numerous design jobs, including costume jewelry for Trifari, Krussman & Fishel, a stapler for Markwell Manufacturing Company, electric cooking ranges for Nash Kelvinator Corporation, and cigarette vending machines for U-Need-A-Pak Products Corporation. As the war progressed, the Bel Geddes office increasingly engaged in consumer research, postwar studies, and government contracts. Exemplifying the office's new direction, Bel Geddes and his staff began an ambitious postwar consumer research job for RCA, eventually leading to a major design assignment that would last from the end of 1942 into 1944. The RCA job may have been recommended to the Bel Geddes office by the Lord and Thomas advertising agency. A 1942 memo notes that Rebecca Hamilton, one of Bel Geddes's senior employees, visited the Lord and Thomas agency with one of the agency's partners, Albert Lasker. Lasker said he had been recommending Loewy to his clients. Hamilton replied that the Bel Geddes office was different than Loewy, "emphasizing the research and engineering facilities here—our more logical approach to a problem."[74] Meikle has observed that advertising agencies helped to link industrial designers with clients, noting that admen considered industrial design a "subsidiary" of advertising.[75] The contract required the Bel Geddes office to study the "post-war problem" and develop design recommendations for radios, electronics, televisions, phonograph records and players, transmitter sound systems, and electron microscopes.[76] In a series of detailed "quarterly reports," the designer and his team presented rigorous consumer research and completed designs.

During 1943, the Bel Geddes office produced similar reports for Shell Oil.[77] Both the Shell and RCA studies claimed that the tastes of postwar consumer groups would become increasingly homogenous, witnessing a "[d]ecrease in sectional differences in consumer taste."[78] Accordingly, clients would require the services of those who could interpret and design for the greatest market segment. This perception of a decrease in "sectional difference" pointed to the need for an aesthetic with mass appeal, as did arguments against selling to the poorer groups, which were considered too impoverished to make frequent major purchases. Bel Geddes's populist aims were consistent with those of the RCA representative Mr. Bonfig, who, echoing long-standing concerns within the home furnishings market, required Bel Geddes "to satisfy the post-war taste [of the middle-class consumer] without shocking it."[79]

Informed by both a desire to sell progressive design to middle America and recent marketing strategies, Bel Geddes's RCA study created four income groups: the "poor," the "getting by," the "comfortable," and the "prosperous."[80] In the study, conclusions were developed after reviewing prewar information on the four groups' tastes and "living conditions," investigating housing, work, and leisure.[81] The study found that furnishings of the "getting by" were "inexpensive, neat, and clean," while those of the "comfortable" were "modern and moderately priced," reflecting an "interest in home appearance and maintenance." On the other hand, the decor of the "poor" was "cheap" and "old-fashioned," while that of the "prosperous" was "expensive" and "luxurious." The report concluded that the former valued affordability, while the latter sought ostentation: "Neither group could be considered to have outstanding good taste."[82] Guided by Bonfig's comments, but seeking the "average mass viewpoint," the design office recommended designs for those

of median taste and incomes—the middle groups of the "getting by" and the "comfortable."
Bel Geddes's design of radio and phonograph combinations for RCA illustrated the unassuming
middlebrow aesthetic, and employed styles on a continuum from, what the report termed, the
"Contemporary Modern," through "Conservative Modern," to "Modified Period." "Contemporary
Modern" was the most progressive, having "No ornaments or design detail. Light modern
wood finish and fabrics. Color accents," while "Hardware [was] concealed or inconspicuous."
The "Conservative Modern" style took the middle road, allowing for a mixture of simple details
and materials, including wood veneer. "Modified Period," on the other hand, sported simplified
period styles, dark wood finishes, "conservative fabric," and "stylized hardware."[83] Thus, the style
spectrum mixed modern and conservative, and the restrained and the popular (Figure 6.4). The 1943
report also forecast technological modernization in housing, home furnishings, and transportation.
Homes would be functionally planned and employ prefabricated components, while simply styled
home furnishings would employ new materials. Recommending a conservative, yet progressive,
aesthetic, Bel Geddes's world of tomorrow would appear neither shocking nor staid.

FIGURE 6.4 Federal Telephone and Radio Corporation Model 5000-CP combination radio-phonograph.
Photograph by unidentified photographer. The use of contemporary design (bent plywood) and materials
(blonde wood) illustrates the application of Bel Geddes's notion of "Contemporary Modern" developed
for RCA. Harry Ransom Center, University of Texas, and the Edith Lutyens and Norman Bel Geddes
Foundation, Inc. 2016.

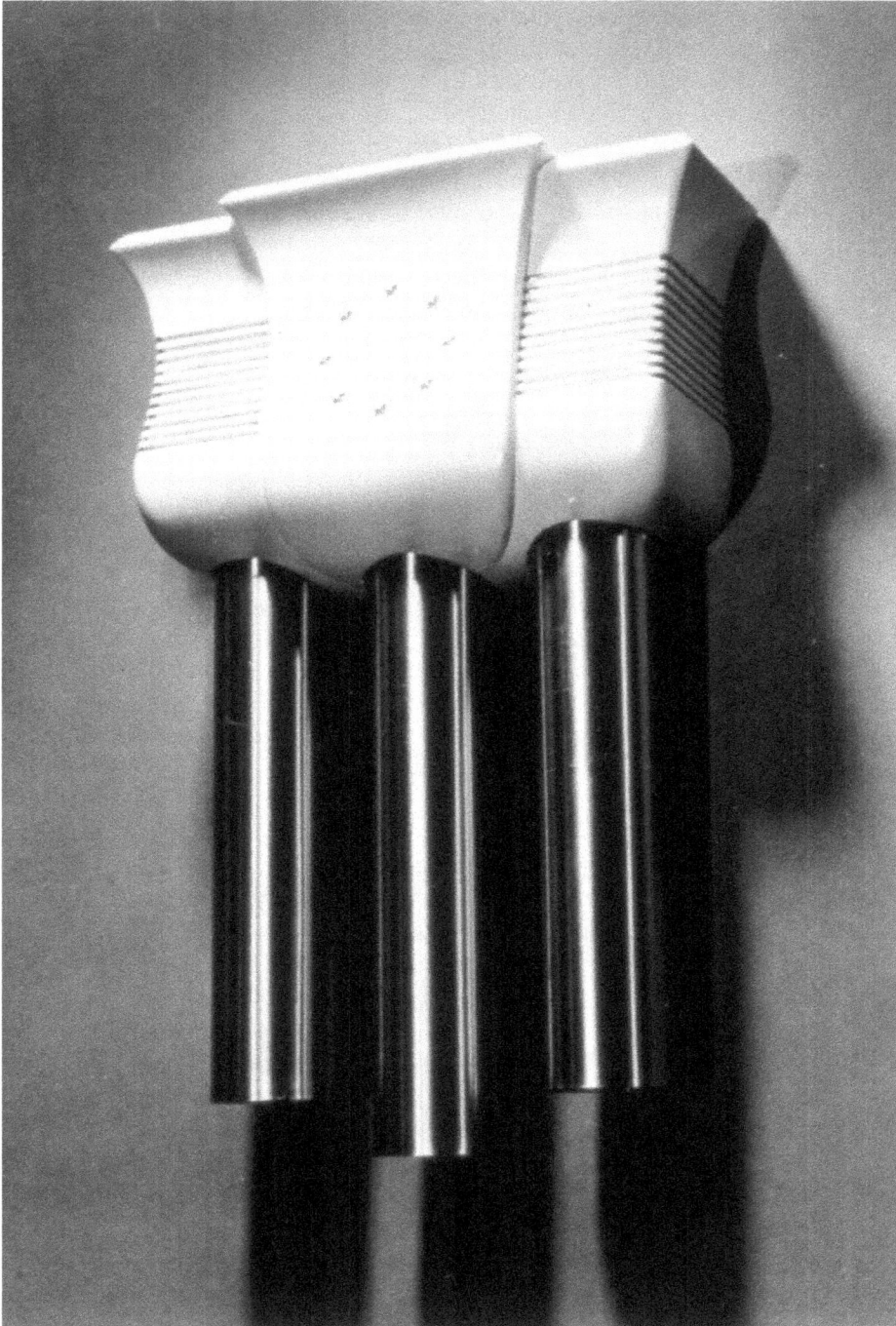

FIGURE 6.5 Period-style door chime by Bel Geddes for Rittenhouse Chimes, 1943. Photograph by unidentified photographer. Harry Ransom Center, University of Texas, and the Edith Lutyens and Norman Bel Geddes Foundation, Inc. 2016.

The use of consumer research strengthened the independent position of the designer in relation to the client. Clients did not always appreciate this. The Bel Geddes office insisted that research precede product design, and that it was essential in "eliminating ... the hit and miss selection of gadgets, models and designs."[84] This methodical approach often led to client frustration. During the research stage of the RCA job, Bonfig complained that the Bel Geddes staff "have not done the job," and that the RCA "boys" had come to New York City expecting to find something "they could get their teeth into" and had twice gone away disappointed.[85]

In mid-1943, the Bel Geddes office began a door chime study for the A. E. Rittenhouse Company continuing its practice of consumer research developed in the RCA and Shell Oil projects during that year. Rittenhouse had a history of employing industrial designers, having previously engaged the services of Russel Wright.[86] The Bel Geddes office was to test the consumer acceptance of a group of Bel Geddes-designed door chimes. With its emphasis on period styling the job challenged Bel Geddes's preference for modernist design. The study aimed to discover which market segments preferred "period" and which desired "universal" design, described as "modern in character"[87] (Figure 6.5). Bel Geddes's consumer preference study of December 1943 reported on 253 housewives who fell within the top three of the four income brackets used in the RCA study: the "getting-by," "comfortable," and the "prosperous." Again, "Poor people were omitted because it was felt they constitute only a minor part of the door chime market." The results of the survey found that the "prosperous-comfortable" group preferred the "universal" design, while the "getting-by" accepted the "period" style.[88] The term "universal" was used to indicate modern styling in the chime study. However, the term "modern" was often employed in the RCA job, perhaps because modern design was an established style in the home furnishings market.[89] The term "universal" may have acted as camouflage for those averse to modern design. The RCA and Rittenhouse projects illustrate Bel Geddes's ability to negotiate both the popular and the modern depending on the job.

Postwar and prewar consumer studies often responded to specific historic circumstances, including the stock market crash and economic depression, as well as uncertainty regarding postwar consumption. To convince clients of the value of design consultancy Bel Geddes preyed on their anxieties, rehearsing scenarios of rebellious consumers who could bring manufacturing to its knees. Bel Geddes's stories of consumer capriciousness protected his professional position. His contention that economic crises, such as the 1929 crash, were the result of overproduction and consumer rejection of poorly designed goods presented the industrial designer as an economic savior. Bel Geddes developed a myth of scientifically predictable consumer preferences, which presented the designer-researcher as a rational expert, thus legitimating the industrial design profession and helping to sell its services.[90] By describing his marketing research in almost scientific terms, Bel Geddes constructed a professional and logical self-image, appealing to clients who believed that consumer desire could be rationally calculated. However, his forays into consumer research defined him less as a visionary and more as a scientist of consumption, thus continuing his uneasy transformation from science fiction utopian to rational expert. Perhaps more significantly, consumer research helped Bel Geddes define consumer segments of average tastes, which he could sell a narrow range of styles. Bel Geddes's ability to imagine consumers was consistent with his General Motors Futurama exhibit, an ideological assembly line for manufacturing consumers of automobiles and superhighways.

7

The Production and Consumption of Model Worlds: Futurama and "War Maneuver Models" Exhibition, 1937–1944

Bel Geddes was one of the most important creators of visions of modernity. His models of futuristic cities cast him as a technocratic modernist, while his battle dioramas fashioned his image as armchair general and military prophet. Such projects presented the future as rational and predictable and Bel Geddes as logical and progressive. For the Shell Oil advertising campaign (1937), the Bel Geddes firm created a six-foot triangular model of a city of 1957. This concept was later expanded for General Motors, into the vast model for the Futurama of 1939–1940, considered Bel Geddes's "industrial masterpiece."[1] Both models illustrated how cities of the future could be planned to increase the smooth flow of automobile traffic. In the early 1940s, Bel Geddes's modeling work continued with his miniaturized recreations and forecasts of Second World War battles. The war models project was published in *Life* magazine in 1942 and exhibited as the "War Maneuver Models" at the Museum of Modern Art in January 1944, where two model battles were exhibited in finished form and a third, which predicted the outcome of the war, was displayed under constant construction (Figures 7.1 and 7.2). The models created for Shell Oil, General Motors, *Life* magazine, and MoMA presented an optimistic vision of a controllable future. Like his streamlined designs, these models offered images of historical continuity and control—futures that contained neither technological fallibility nor historical rupture. This view of tomorrow would have had great appeal after the economic hardship of the 1930s and during the political uncertainty of the Second World War. These imaginative projects allowed audiences to share a common positive belief. They can be viewed as analogous to the Christian Science practice of therapeutic thinking: rather than prayer offered to an ailing individual, such mass meditation on the world of tomorrow provided Mind-cure for the country, directed at the health of the nation after the economic depression.

Prior to the 1930s, models had long been used for promotional purposes, whether to fascinate or to educate. However, during the depression, the display of miniaturized products,

FIGURE 7.1 Bel Geddes and two women with Futurama model segment, *c.* 1939. Photograph by Richard Garrison. Harry Ransom Center, University of Texas, and the Edith Lutyens and Norman Bel Geddes Foundation, Inc. 2016.

technologies, and images of the future was urgently advocated as an effective form of merchandising. Accordingly, in the early 1930s America's largest corporations vigorously competed in the display of extravagant models: General Motors revealed a detailed miniature of its automotive testing grounds at Atlantic City, New Jersey, while Chrysler toured its replica De Soto factory across the country, where it was viewed by an estimated 5,000,000 people. A *Printers' Ink* report of 1932 observed: "Interest in models is naturally growing in these times, for when buyers become reticent and adopt a 'show me' attitude there is nothing like the three-dimensional way of doing it."[2]

While models developed as important merchandising tools for American industry, they became significant in defining Bel Geddes's public image. Miniature versions of Bel Geddes's streamlined designs were prominently displayed in his office foyer, illustrating the company's imaginative power and progressive identity while choreographing the viewer's experience (Figures 7.3–7.5). An

FIGURE 7.2 Model shop with war models construction, June 24, 1942. No photographer identified, probably Richard Garrison. Harry Ransom Center, University of Texas, and the Edith Lutyens and Norman Bel Geddes Foundation, Inc. 2016.

article of 1939, "Practical Showman," described the office as "Square, bare and off-white. Here and there in glass cases are models of yachts and automobiles. Occupying a prominent ledge is a miniature of his famous 'tear-drop' car."[3] Bel Geddes's emphasis on the exhibition of models cast him in the role of modernist entertainer. A reviewer of the Futurama recognized this duality.

> He combines the thrills of Coney Island with the glories of Le Corbusier. He functions at one time as the generous owner of a toy train from Schwarz's and as Jules Verne, H. G. Wells and Hugh Ferris [sic]. His vision is as all embracing in its scale as it is unanswerable in its smallest details.[4]

Greatly influenced by both avant-garde design and science fiction, Bel Geddes's world of tomorrow fused rational modernism with childlike playfulness.

Bel Geddes's model constructions as well as his constructed identity were products created for public consumption—goods which spectators could both enjoy and transform. Viewers delighted in the accuracy of the models and found pleasure in deciphering their illusions. Thus, audiences actively engaged in producing the model's meanings, rejecting some messages, and modifying

FIGURE 7.3 Sitting area of Norman Bel Geddes & Co. offices, Rockefeller Center, Wenner-Gren yacht in foreground, *c.* June 24, 1940. Photograph by Richard Garrison. Harry Ransom Center, University of Texas, and the Edith Lutyens and Norman Bel Geddes Foundation, Inc. 2016.

FIGURE 7.4 Sitting areas and displays of Bel Geddes designs, Norman Bel Geddes & Co. offices, Rockefeller Center, June 27, 1940. Photograph by Richard Garrison. Harry Ransom Center, University of Texas, and the Edith Lutyens and Norman Bel Geddes Foundation, Inc. 2016.

others. Bel Geddes's miniature worlds emphasized logic and fantasy, science, and spectacle. Consistent with his former incarnation as Zedsky the Boy Magician, his models provided a magical escape from a world increasingly disenchanted by science.

As a seasoned showman, Bel Geddes relied on spectacle and illusion to produce deceptively entertaining models, exhibits, and theater, paving the way for the Disneyfication of commercial environments.[5] He, however, also provided tools to decode these deceptions. In the case of the Futurama and the "War Maneuver Models" exhibits, he offered the public technical details of his models' construction through press releases and photographs. Journalists realized that audiences enjoyed deciphering the trick as much as being fooled by it, and eagerly published the details of the models' fabrication. This collaborative process opened up the models to new meanings, made the construction of their messages transparent, and arguably diminished

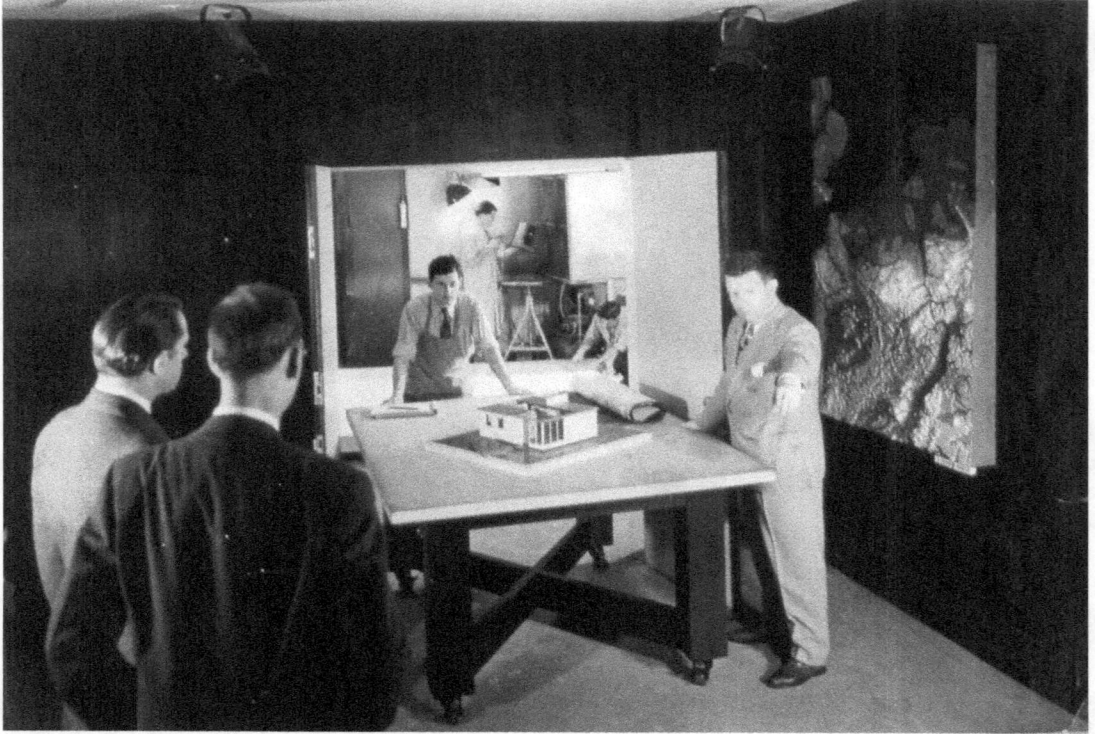

FIGURE 7.5 Bel Geddes orchestrating a busy model photography session of a Revere Copper and Brass house, *c.* 1940. Image also shows one of Bel Geddes's topographical war models and a modelmaker in the background using an airbrush. Photograph by unidentified photographer. Harry Ransom Center, University of Texas, and the Edith Lutyens and Norman Bel Geddes Foundation, Inc. 2016.

Bel Geddes's image as a visionary planner of tomorrow. The laboriously handcrafted dioramas depended on simulation and deception, and thus contradicted modernist tenets of mass production and honesty in design—values Bel Geddes nurtured in his modernist image. Furthermore, for many observers the models were understood as entertaining toys rather than blueprints for tomorrow.

Miniature games: The origins of Bel Geddes's modeling and futurology

Bel Geddes's modeling work for Shell Oil, General Motors, *Life* magazine, and MoMA evolved from a variety of interests, including the reading of fantasy literature, the practice of stage set design, and the creation and playing of model-based parlor games. Bel Geddes's childhood reading of *Gulliver's Travels* and *Alice in Wonderland*, with their themes of miniaturization and imaginary environments, provided an early source for his Lilliputian worlds. As a boy Bel Geddes's mother encouraged him to make model stage sets and cardboard characters.[6] As a young man his use of models to "map" out theatrical staging became increasingly advanced. At first he employed a "simple drawing board with a few chessmen for characters." Later, the chessmen were substituted with "blocks" whose movements were tracked on sheets of paper, while scenery was fashioned from "folded bits of heavy papers."[7]

Bel Geddes had long been interested in creating fantasy worlds through the production of miniature parlor games, including golf, baseball, football, horse racing, and war games, which he made in his spare time between design jobs (227). Such games were realistic, played with groups of friends, and often employed mechanical components to aid in verisimilitude. In his studio in 1915, he constructed a miniature war game that he played with companions including a five-star general. In operation as late as 1933, Bel Geddes considered his war game his favorite recreational project (231–233). The rules for the game were written during the First World War. Again, realism within a miniaturized cosmos was emphasized. Reminiscent of the contoured features of the *Divine Comedy* stage and a precursor to the topographical surfaces of the Futurama, the game used a 24 x 40-foot relief map and textured materials to represent geographical and natural features, and was installed in Bel Geddes's Manhattan home. Up to 12,000 tacks representing military units might appear on the board at one time. As many as thirty-eight people played the game through the night: the atmosphere was often intense. Consistent with Bel Geddes's mania for organization and detail, each team had its own staff of field commanders, advisors, clerks, and the accoutrements of battle planning, including maps, charts, and typewriters. The play of the war game was reported in the local press, which called it "chess on a heroic scale" (231–233). Bel Geddes's war game and war models for *Life* and MoMA may have been inspired by his copy of H. G. Wells's *Little Wars* (1913). The book provided rules for a miniature war game that Wells called a "homeopathic remedy" for "Garden Napoleons" (Figure 7.6).[8] Bel Geddes later described himself

FIGURE 7.6 Illustration from *Little Wars*, H. G. Wells, 1913.

as a "pacifist" who was "unsympathetic to warfare" except in its technological contributions. He intimated that war had kept his more imaginative designs from being accepted and produced. If his life had not been interrupted by the two world wars, he mused, his "state of imagination" and appreciation by "the masses" would have "developed entirely differently."[9]

Bel Geddes also developed a horse racing game and played it with friends until around 1931. A colossal and complex project, it took up a large portion of the groundfloor of his home. Its use of electric motors, threads, and other machinery to move brass horses along a track was a precursor to the mechanical animation of the streamlined cars in the Futurama. Boxes, grandstands, stables, and brass rails were built, owners traded hundreds of brass horses while racing programs were printed weekly.[10] Bel Geddes's games were extremely popular among New York's social set and creative community, attracting leading cultural figures, including writers (Wilder Hobson of *Fortune*, Gilbert Seldes, and Alexander Woollcott), editors (Harold Ross of the *New Yorker*), actors (Douglas Fairbanks, Charlie Chaplin Sr.), advertising men (Ralph Barton), various celebrities (Amelia Earhart, the pioneering pilot), the American chess champion (Edward Lasker), and numerous high-ranking military men.[11] His games simultaneously presented Bel Geddes as a skilled innovator while nurturing essential professional contacts. One journalist wrote, "It can be said that, to a large extent, his business has grown out of his hobbies."[12] As industrial culture was increasingly understood as dehumanizing, Bel Geddes's promotion of the eternal boy in the world of tomorrow provided an appealing rebuff to the critics of modernity.[13]

Shell Oil "City of Tomorrow" advertisement, 1937

While modelmaking became an important part of American merchandising and a significant aspect of Bel Geddes's self-promotion and design development, it wasn't until 1937 that the design firm embraced it as *the* central component of a major industrial assignment. Between 1936 and 1937, Bel Geddes began his first attempts to construct an ideal city of the future for the Shell Oil Company. The result was an advertising campaign using a series of separate ads to represent the "City of Tomorrow." The ads relied on Bel Geddes's reputation as a technological visionary, depicted a miniature tower city crisscrossed by motorways, and presented an ideal image of smooth-flowing automobile traffic of 1957.[14] The resulting illusion was offered as a blueprint for the future—the city in twenty years. Bel Geddes would later produce a similar futuristic forecast in his "Toledo Tomorrow" City Plan of 1945, a promotional scheme designed to encourage public support for urban development. The Shell Oil agreement of September 1936 with the J. Walter Thompson advertising agency required the production of a model depicting traffic solutions of 1957 for a Shell Oil institutional advertising campaign.[15] The project was developed in partnership with the advertising agency, who handled the Shell Oil Company account, and Miller McClintock, director of the Bureau of Street Traffic Research, Harvard University, who promoted a theory of nonstop, frictionless traffic.[16] The final model comprised a six-foot triangle depicting the city of the future. It mixed tower blocks with low-rise structures, and relied on modernist design sources for inspiration, including Le Corbusier's *Towards a New Architecture*, Frank Lloyd Wright's *The Disappearing City* (1932), and Hugh Ferriss's *The Metropolis of Tomorrow* (1929) (Figure 7.7).[17] After the middle of 1937, the Shell advertisements appeared in America's leading picture magazines, including the *Saturday Evening Post*, *Life*, and *Collier's*.[18] The "City of Tomorrow" ad used the model to illustrate traffic solutions of the future and read: "In the

FIGURE 7.7 Linear view of Shell Oil "City of Tomorrow" model, *c.* 1936–1937. Photograph by Norman Bel Geddes & Co. Harry Ransom Center, University of Texas, and the Edith Lutyens and Norman Bel Geddes Foundation, Inc. 2016.

"City of Tomorrow"—you'll breeze right over cross-town traffic"; "You won't have to slow down at intersections on tomorrow's 'Main Street.'"[19] In coordination with the advertising campaign, and in an effort to bolster a national highway scheme, Shell made a series of slide films of the model city available to chambers of commerce across the country.[20] By May 1938, Bel Geddes had sold an expanded version of the Shell idea to General Motors, whose president Alfred P. Sloan had since 1932 longed for a federally funded highway system in order to increase car sales.[21] While it is not clear what Shell representatives thought of Bel Geddes recycling and expanding the "city of tomorrow" plan for General Motors, it can be assumed that the oil company would have appreciated and greatly benefitted from the project's aim of an improved transport infrastructure and increased traffic capacity.

Publicity for the Shell ad presented Bel Geddes as a planner of immense vision. At a 1937 National Planning Conference, McClintock described Bel Geddes as a planning "prophet" and "master of functional shape and form," and invoked the title of Bel Geddes's prophetic monograph: "he has looked over the horizon of today to glimpse the automotive 'city of tomorrow.'"[22] An example of the publicity writing for Bel Geddes's traffic plan took the form of a short story which depicted a fanciful encounter between Dr. Pottlesmith, a planning skeptic, and Bel Geddes, the traffic visionary. Bel Geddes's studio was described as an "impressive" laboratory of "calm surroundings," full of "blue prints … models and … photographs."[23] He was presented as a genius, whose remarkable talents raised him above the common fray. The exaggerated characterization virtually transported him into his own traffic fantasy. "Here busied [Geddes] not as one of the myriads of scurrying ants who succeeded only in dragging home a bit of sustenance," but one "whose active mind" "was bubbling, sizzling and bursting with ideas which would transform the nightmare of traffic into a pleasant dream or perhaps even an actual experience."[24] The colorful characters and images were consistent with Geddes's vaudevillian past.

Such exuberance and caricature were absent from the Shell Oil project, which, in the tradition of science fiction, sought a simulation of utmost plausibility. Despite Geddes's wish to create an effective illusion, publicity for the miniature city provided a detailed description of the tricks employed. In July 1938, the company periodical *Shell Progress* informed readers of Geddes's skyscrapers cast in plaster, cars molded from metal, and figures formed from "short bits of wire pushed through long steel strips" representing "elevated sidewalks." Foliage was fashioned from sponge rubber died green, while areas of water were made of reflective blue metal (Figure 7.8).[25] The emphasis on construction techniques was consistent with Geddes's vision of a modern world subject to constant improvement, and reflected the depression-era popularity of hobbies, which were encouraged as an antidote to idleness among boys and men.[23]

The Shell Oil ad was widely discussed in America's newspapers, Shell trade publications, and the architectural press.[27] Most unquestioningly accepted the monumental planning of the traffic forecast. Others, however, were more skeptical. The author of a *Worcester Telegram* article worried that the model provided a too-prescriptive vision which "does leave a little room for anxious speculation."[28] The writer feared that steady-stream traffic would reduce the human element in driving: "There will be no place for sudden, spontaneous decisions to stop for a hamburger or a hitch-hiker."[29] The writer was equally suspicious of the motivations of Bel Geddes's collaborator in the project. "Surely the J. Walter Thompson agency is surprised to find itself like this, plunking for the Revolution and the triumph of Right and Reason."[30] The *New York Times* hinted its concern about a future dominated by cars and suffocating engine exhaust, in "Make Traffic Photo Wearing Gas Masks: Photographers Obtain Effects in Geddes Design of 'City of Tomorrow,'" which described the use of smudge pots to create the effect of "thick,

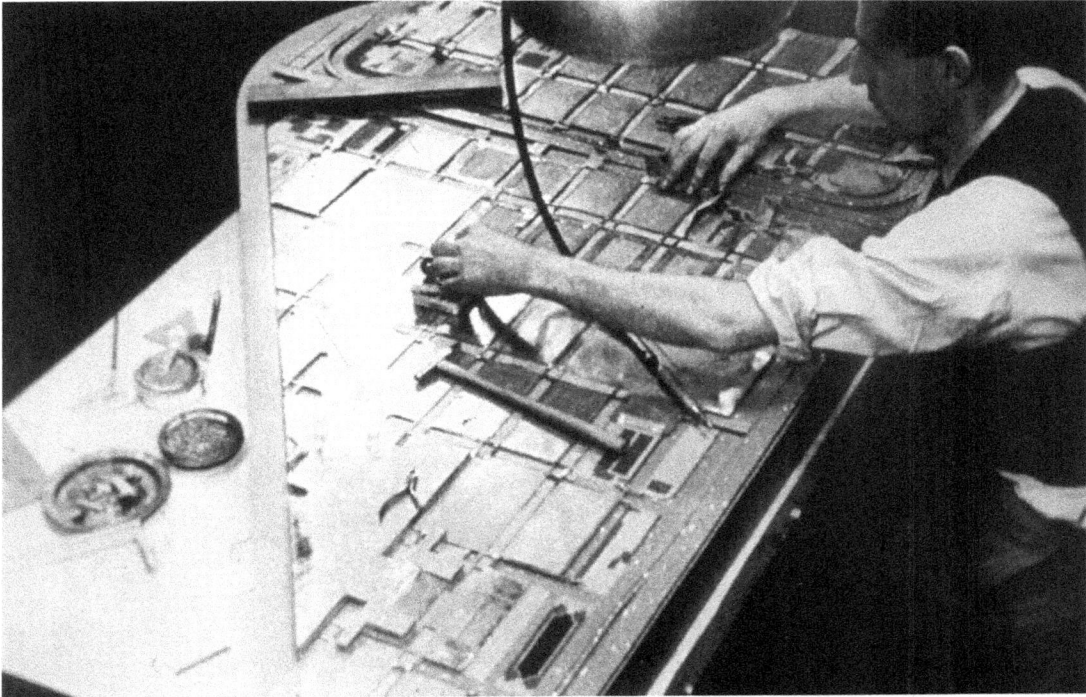

FIGURE 7.8 Man working on Shell Oil "City of Tomorrow" model, *c.* 1937. Photograph by Frances Waite. Harry Ransom Center, University of Texas, and the Edith Lutyens and Norman Bel Geddes Foundation, Inc. 2016.

choking smoke" (Figure 7.9).[31] *Architectural Forum* invoked Aldous Huxley's novel *Brave New World* of 1932, describing the deserted "downtown of Geddes's 'brave new city,'" a result of the segregation of work and living zones.[32] Zoning was, however, not a far-fetched idea in 1937. In the United States, the support for allocating different parts of the city for specific uses took off after 1916 and became accepted practice by the late 1920s.[33] Questions regarding the imposition of regimented living and its effect on American life were also raised in the Bel Geddes office. The anxieties regarding standardization echoed those raised at the dawn of the decade concerning machine-age living. These concerns anticipated a more vocal critique of the most significant assignment of Bel Geddes's career, the General Motors Futurama, at the New York World's Fair.

The General Motors Futurama exhibit, New York World's Fair, 1939–1940

The New York World's Fair was a celebration of American business and provided an opportunity for companies to advertise their goods and images as the depression decade came to a close. The fair's theme, planning the world of tomorrow, was developed by Walter Dorwin Teague, who

FIGURE 7.9 Shell Oil "City of Tomorrow" model, men with smudge pots. Photograph by Frances Waite. Harry Ransom Center, University of Texas, and the Edith Lutyens and Norman Bel Geddes Foundation, Inc. 2016.

served with a group of architects on the fair's Board of Design. Recognized as "the designer's fair," many of its exhibits and buildings were conceived by America's leading industrial designers, including Teague, Bel Geddes, Dreyfuss, and Loewy. Dominating the center of the fairground, the fair's focal buildings were the Trylon, a 610-foot triangular tower, and the Perisphere, an orb of 180 feet in diameter. Designed by Wallace K. Harrison and André Fouilhoux, the structures reinforced the fair's themes of imaginative flight and the ideal future. Housed in the Perisphere was Dreyfuss's theme exhibit, Democracity, which displayed a model metropolis based on garden city ideas, where business, leisure, and homes were spatially separated and green belts and parks were liberally employed.[34] The classical forms of the triangle and the sphere contrasted with the streamlined façade of the General Motors Futurama building, reflecting both the popularity of the streamlined style and Teague's preference for geometric shapes.

The General Motors Futurama exhibit further developed the ideas, images, and techniques of the Shell Oil ad. It offered spectators a sixteen-minute amusement ride that simulated an airplane flight over a hi-tech world of 1960, a world dominated by radio-controlled traffic, superhighways, scientific farming, skyscraper cities, and pastoral villages—merging the decentralism of Wright's *Broadacre City*, the rigid order of Le Corbusier's *Ville Contemporaine*, and the science fiction imagery of H.G. Wells.[35] This illusion was created through the production of a series of vast and meticulous dioramas (Figures 7.10 and 7.11). A press release of April 1939 noted that the

FIGURE 7.10 Futurama publicity photo of modelmaker installing bridge. Photograph by Richard Garrison. Harry Ransom Center, University of Texas, and the Edith Lutyens and Norman Bel Geddes Foundation, Inc. 2016.

FIGURE 7.11 Futurama model segments under construction at the Futurama model workshop, *c.* 1939. Photograph by unidentified photographer. Harry Ransom Center, University of Texas, and the Edith Lutyens and Norman Bel Geddes Foundation, Inc. 2016.

35,000-square-foot model extended one-third of a mile and contained around 500,000 buildings, 1,000,000 trees, and 50,000 automobiles, 10,000 of which were in motion.[36] General Motors officials and Bel Geddes hoped the Futurama would promote the idea of an immense American highway system. In fact, by the 1950s traffic solutions similar to the Futurama's were accepted by the US government.[37] Though offered to the public as an educational exhibit, the project was essentially a three-dimensional goodwill advert that presented General Motors as a benevolent institution.[38] Advertising that promoted a company image of service was widely adopted in the early twentieth century, a time when rapidly expanding American corporations appeared to threaten the traditional institutions of church, family, community, and the economy.[39] Such public relations efforts were often spurred by fears of government interference in American business, including public ownership, federal control, increased taxes, and tighter employment regulations. In 1938, the trade journal *Product Engineering* reflected such worries in its promotion of a nationwide strategy for the manufacturing industry: "a properly conceived and intelligently executed public relations program [that] offers business the means of counteracting unjust suspicions, unfair political attack,

[and] unwarranted outside dictation."[40] Articles from the same year, such as "Business Finds Its Voice" in *Harper's Magazine*, echoed such messages, neatly encapsulated in General Motors's slogan, "Who Serves Progress-Serves America."[41] General Motors's ambitious project spared no expense, and eventually cost the automobile giant over $7 million, while earning Bel Geddes $200,000.[42] During a two-year period around twenty-four million people experienced General Motors's education exhibit, the most popular at the fair.[43] A significant cultural event, the Futurama profoundly influenced the popular image of the future, technology, and the American corporation.

The Futurama helped Bel Geddes craft a self-image as a technological prophet and creator of futuristic worlds, and associated him with progress, order, and omnipotent vision. An article for the architectural magazine *Pencil Points,* produced through the Bel Geddes office, presented the designer as a God-like creator: "A practical poet's dream has come true before your eyes ... It was as though Norman Bel Bel Geddes were presented with a new firmament, and told to separate day from night."[44] The Futurama exhibit provided General Motors with an image of competence and beneficence, offering a corporate vision of perpetual progress centered upon prodigious planning and the mass consumption of automobiles. In the guidebook for the Futurama Alfred P. Sloan identified the central theme as one of possibility. He stated that "the world, far from being finished, is hardly yet begun; that the job of building the future is one which will demand our best energies."[45] This emphasis on the process of constructing the future may have helped viewers to imagine utopias of their own creation.

Futurama—planning and research: Creating a theatrical simulation

The designers of the Futurama hoped to create a model world that was an authentic microcosm. Bel Geddes knew that to be both plausible and visionary his world of tomorrow must abide by the tenets of science fiction—it must reflect the world of today while evoking the future of 1960. For "the entire ride," Bel Geddes wrote, the spectator "will live in that future—but a future that retains enough of 1939 to keep it from being fantastic."[46] The Futurama exhibit further developed the research of the Shell Oil job and Bel Geddes's traffic research, which had begun in the early 1930s,[47] employing the traffic expert McClintock, while taking advantage of the generous resources of General Motors. To get some perspective on the actual look of the American landscape, the automotive company took the Bel Geddes team on an airplane flight piloted by Eddie Rickenbacker, a hero of the First World War.[48] The trip, a memo explained, "was valuable in deciding, for maximum realism, detailed topographical features."[49] Observed during the flight were "mess in back yards ... Piles of dirt ... [and] junk around railroad sidings." Ironically, for a project emphasizing logic and order, the disorder of the built environment was thought to add authenticity: "The model must not be too clean—it must be junked up."[50] In a meeting to discuss the mechanical animation of the model, verisimilitude was considered a primary goal. To achieve it, the Bel Geddes team decided to add "human interest" details, such as people walking into shops, men repairing streets, stoplights blinking, or cars parking under buildings. The human interest scenes were to be "accurate enough to photograph faithfully in a close-up, in spite of the fact that they might only be seen from 20 or 30 feet."[51] This requirement underlines the importance of dioramas as publicity tools: readers of magazines and newspapers viewed a constant stream of photographs of the model. In keeping with Sloan's theme of possibility, it was suggested that buildings be shown under construction, including a crane lifting steel girders.[52] A special department was set up to help decide how many of the "buildings in the Futurama should be under construction, to give it a realistic touch."[53] "[T]here definitely must be enough action outside of the street, or it would look as if the automobiles were moving on highways running through a cemetery."[54] Thus, viewers were invited to imagine the ultimate "city of tomorrow". This was to be a lifelike city in the process of completion.

Despite the aim of authenticity, its attainment was elusive, "poor results with color values followed any attempt to duplicate actual conditions. The colors needed slight exaggeration and some theatrical brilliance."[55] In some situations, it was felt that "to give the model life it would be wise to forget naturalism." Therefore, the designers agreed to "increase the speed of everything so that motion which would not, under actual circumstance, be visible, will be definitely apparent."[56] A resemblance to the present was needed to conjure a believable fantasy of tomorrow: "anything unusual must not be beyond the realm of common sense."[57] The rejection of "naturalism" and the "unusual," while embracing "theatricality" and plausibility, created the image of a utopian world grounded in the knowledge of today. This tightrope act, between the present and the future, allowed viewers to imagine a world in the process of becoming. This aim for balance is notable in the discussion of landscaping. "While modern landscaping should not be universal throughout, it should be predominant. [It] Should not be conspicuous for its wildness. It must be well inhabited."[58] The future would be a middle landscape that balanced the natural and the modern, the past and the future.[59] It would be neither too startlingly progressive nor too similar to the present day. It would be today with more brilliant sunrises, faster cars, and wider highways.

Constructing the future: The publicity and the press

The emphasis on Bel Geddes as a visionary architect of the world of tomorrow was a constant theme in the Futurama's publicity and reviews. An article from the *Christian Science Monitor* read: "There is a saying in architectural and other circles that Norman Bel Geddes … is an orderly thinker and workman; that he admires and practices thoroughness in everything he does; and that he has both vision and practicality."[60] Much of this writing focused on how the model's lifelike qualities were achieved. *Pencil Points* outlined the Bel Geddes team's use of angled lights and colored filters to mimic nature: "the edge of the ravine was seared with brilliant orange," "a small town in the distance gleamed in white-yellow light," while "grey-blue and cool green was applied as back-light."[61] Another writer was awed by the illusion of the diorama: "the model landscape is what strikes the armchair audience dumb with amazement and admiration."[62] More than any of his projects the Futurama brought together Bel Geddes's knowledge of theatricality, design, and salesmanship, relying on his considerable skills as a set designer, lighting pioneer, and consumer engineer.

Aware of the public fascination with the exhibit's construction, journalists across the country described its secrets, including polished steel rivers, rubber roads, and cornflake terrain. One writer described the layering of plastic and plaster to simulate landscape and the use of velour to duplicate the pastureland. The public's education on model construction was further informed by the reports of Bel Geddes's staff of some 3,000 workers, including sculptors, painters, model-makers, carpenters, and lighting and sound engineers. The same journalist described the crew of thirty who serviced and cleaned the exhibit every night, washing lakes, and installing thousands of trees, "treading cautiously in sneakers, [and] run[ning] vacuum cleaners over vast areas of foliage and fields." While war raged in Europe, the Futurama provided an appealing fantasy of peace and prosperity, with Bel Geddes commanding an army of workers who constructed the world of tomorrow (Figure 7.12 and Plate 24).

To experience the Futurama viewers joined enormous queues, which snaked around the perimeter of the building. As they wound their way up the pair of undulating ramps and through a glowing red shaft in the towering hook-shaped façade, the queuing mass of spectators became a significant theatrical element in Bel Geddes's production. It is perhaps no surprise that Bel Geddes sought out Eero Saarinen to assist him with the design of the General Motors building. A key contributor to the collaborative design of the structure, Saarinen believed that modern architecture required drama, a notion that would have found great sympathy with Bel Geddes (Figure 7.13).[63] Once in the exhibit lobby, visitors viewed a huge map of the United States that compared 1939 traffic to the predicted volume of 1960, forecasting a traffic calamity only superhighways could avert (Figures 7.14 and 7.15). Visitors were then seated in plush chairs that conveyed them through a series of dioramas, while a gentle, but authoritative, voice described future miracles of planning and science. Viewers witnessed highways, scientific farms, quiet villages, suburban communities, and modern cities. The successive models increased in size to simulate an airplane descent into the world of 1960 (Figure 7.16). At the end of the ride, the spectator stepped into a futuristic stage set—a life-sized urban intersection of tomorrow—and received a badge announcing, "I have seen the future." Affirming their participation in General Motors's commercial vision of tomorrow, they viewed a static display of GM's latest automobiles in the streets below (Figure 7.17 and Plate 25).[64] Because the visitor to the Futurama effectively assumed the guise of both performer and viewer, the ramp and intersection materialized Bel Geddes's stage design goal of uniting masses of actors with a mass audience. The intersection segregated pedestrians and automobile: an established urban planning concept that had been promoted in the United States by Harvey Wiley Corbett in 1923 as chair of the architect's subcommittee of *The Regional Plan of New York and Its Environs* (1924) and was depicted in Ferriss's *The Metropolis of Tomorrow*.[65]

While the details of the model's illusion were made public in newspapers and magazines, viewers of the Futurama discovered disorder and mechanical breakdowns within its model world of 1960. Some criticisms were petty: model boats faced the wrong way, their sails billowing into the wind.[66] Other comments were more pointed: one reviewer proclaimed that the Futurama was far from self-regulating, that problems with maintenance and heat effectively destroyed the illusion of a tidy future, "grease [dripped] from the overhead wiring system to the miniature cities and countryside below."[67] The irony of mechanical breakdowns in the world of tomorrow was noted by another critic who described a massive pile-up on the miniature, animated motorway:

One of the little cars stalled on that mountain road and another piled into it behind. Along came another and then there were two or three hundred of the little cars plowing in and kicking hell out of each other. Then something snapped and they all tumbled down over the cliff.[68]

FIGURE 7.12 Man preparing streamlined cars. Photograph by Richard Garrison, *c.* 1939. Harry Ransom Center, University of Texas, and the Edith Lutyens and Norman Bel Geddes Foundation, Inc. 2016.

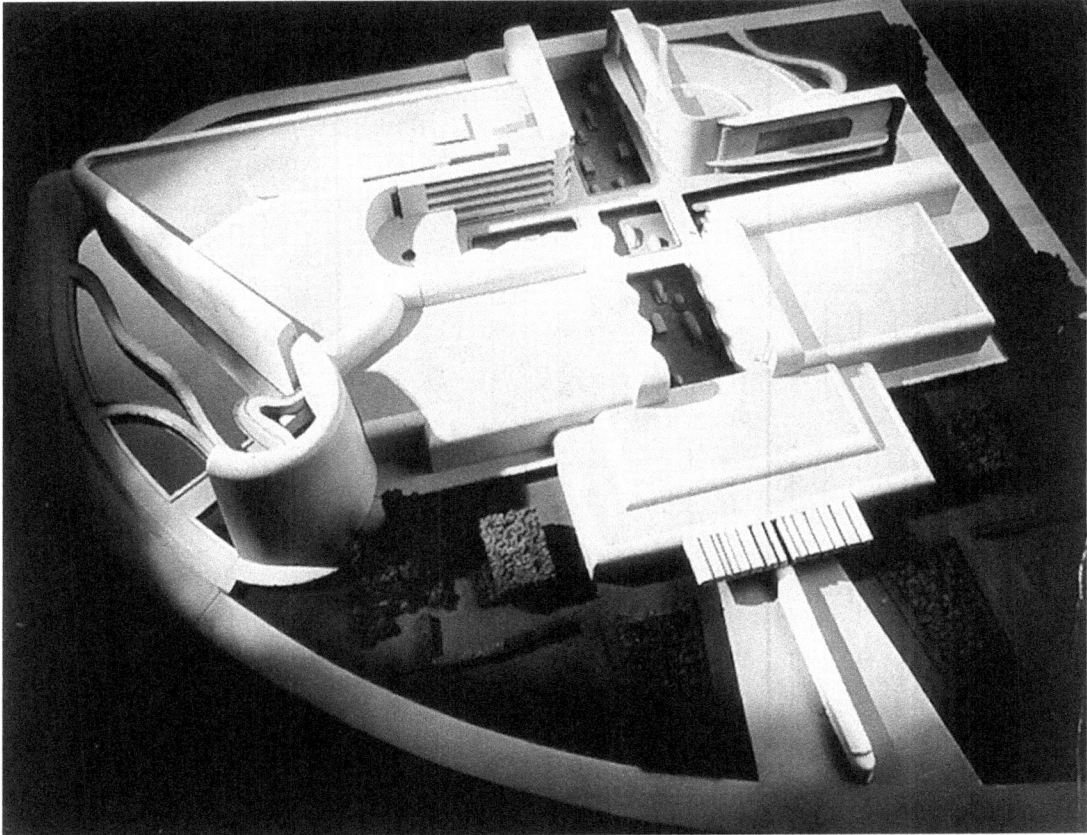

FIGURE 7.13 Aerial view of General Motors building model showing curved façade, entry ramp, and intersection, *c.* 1939. Photograph by Richard Garrison. Harry Ransom Center, University of Texas, and the Edith Lutyens and Norman Bel Geddes Foundation, Inc. 2016.

When mechanical problems in the ride arose, the futuristic illusion was effectively shattered. Highlighting the disjunction between the present and future, reality and fiction, a *New York Times* headline read: "Accidents of Today Halts Futurama... Chair Mechanism Breaks Down ... Spectators, Roused From 1960 Dream of Super-Highways, Walk to Nearest Exit."[69] Though viewers took great pleasure in experiencing the duplicity of Bel Geddes's models, they often resisted the narratives of progress these fantasies offered. Some ridiculed the notion of futuristic livestock: "There's something moving into the picture. Little hoofs stamping, head bobbing, tail flying round and round. Do you recognize it? That's the Cow of Tomorrow."[70] Others, such as the essayist E. B. White, considered the seductive association of progress and automobility both intoxicating and repugnant:

When night falls in the General Motors exhibit and you lean back in the cushioned chair ... and hear ... the soft electric assurance of a better life—the life which rests on wheels alone—there is a strong, sweet poison which infects the blood. I didn't want to wake up.[71]

FIGURE 7.14 Curved façade and visitors queueing to enter General Motors building. Photograph by Richard Garrison, *c.* 1939. Harry Ransom Center, University of Texas, and the Edith Lutyens and Norman Bel Geddes Foundation, Inc. 2016.

FIGURE 7.15 Visitors in conveyor chairs at the General Motors Futurama exhibit, 1939. Photographer not credited. Getty Bettmann/Contributor.

The consumer advocate Stuart Chase, though amused by the model, resented the seductive and didactic narration, what he referred to as the "soft-voiced loud-speaker—if you see what I mean." He wasn't exactly sure why people liked the exhibit, whether it was the animated diorama's sheer charm or its message of national potential.

The amazing success of the exhibit indicated that citizens either were keenly interested in the future of their country, or were delighted in little cars running over little bridges and disappearing into little tunnels. Perhaps they were both interested and delighted. I was.[72]

Despite its optimistic outlook, its overemphasis on order at a high financial cost worried Chase. "Granted that we can build and pay for it, is it the kind of world we should really enjoy living in? Or is it too clean, too fast, too neatly planned?"[73] Chase's comments reflected wider concerns regarding the costs of large-scale public works projects and the rationalization of everyday life in the wake of the New Deal. Bel Geddes and General Motors's vision of tomorrow was immediately recognized as oppressive precisely because it was understood as a narrow and prescriptive blueprint of the future. This view was neatly summed up by E. B. White, who described the

FIGURE 7.16 Futurama model of downtown intersection, *c.* 1939. Photograph by Richard Garrison. Harry Ransom Center, University of Texas, and the Edith Lutyens and Norman Bel Geddes Foundation, Inc. 2016.

FIGURE 7.17 General Motors building, life-size intersection, and concourse with cars at night, *c.* 1939–1940. Unidentified photographer. New York World's Fair 1939–1940 records. Manuscripts and Archives Division, The New York Public Library, Astor, Lenox and Tildon Foundations.

exhibit as an authoritarian fantasy where a cult of order had sapped the world of spontaneity and humanity.

> In Tomorrow everything is lit from below—people, trees even the cow on the rotolactor is lit from below.
> In Tomorrow one voice does for all.
> Rugs do not slip in Tomorrow.
> There is no talking back in Tomorrow.
> In Tomorrow, most sounds are not the sounds themselves but a memory of sounds, or an electrification.
> … It is all rather impersonal, this dream.[74]

Was the Futurama disparaged for its message as well as its medium? Was the viewer held hostage to a corporate narrative of progress and consumption through sophisticated and constraining machinery? At a time when Europe's totalitarian leaders wielded mass spectacle as a weapon of war, intimations of social engineering would have been met with great anxiety. Even Bel Geddes recognized the model's potential to unnerve viewers. In a press release he related how an exhibit guide took control of the sound system, and in a "very sinister fashion" "chortle[d]." "This is the mysterious Dr. Fu Man Chu." "The visitors jumped a mile."[75]

Evidence of the public concern regarding mass media and mass consumption appeared with the emergence of the consumer movement in the late 1920s and 1930s. Muckraking writing such as *Your Money's Worth* (1927), by Stuart Chase and F. J. Schlink, led to the development of Consumers' Research, a national consumer organization that quickly expanded during the depression years and spawned the Consumers' Union (CU) in 1936.[76] Concerned by the manipulation of spectators by American manufacturers at the fair, the CU set up its own exhibit that claimed to be the event's only noncommercial display. Publicity for their exhibit advised pointedly, "A quick look at CU's World's Fair exhibit where crowds come to see the guinea pigs, and learn how not to be one."[77] Other critics of the fair parodied the exhibit buildings. The popular satirical magazine *Ballyhoo* published its own designs of fairground buildings, including banana and leg-shaped spoofs of the Futurama and the Crystal Lassies exhibit, Bel Geddes's mirrored peep show. Suggestive of humbug and the excesses of modern design, the caption read, "The Banana Oil Building, designed by Norman Belch Geddys," with its "banana skin doormat" and a "chromium plated entrance" "is one of the finest examples of modernistic architecture."[78] The often-discordant contrast between the high-minded and crassly commercial at the fair was neatly lampooned in "The Chorus Girls building," a leg-shaped structure housing the "Leg of Nations" (Figure 7.18).

THE BANANA OIL BUILDING, designed by Norman Belch Geddy, is one of the finest examples of modernistic architecture, says Mr. Geddy. A touch of Old World Artistry is the banana skin doormat at the chromium-plated entrance, says Mr. Geddy.

FIGURE 7.18 "Banana Oil Building" in *Ballyhoo* magazine, February 1939.

FIGURE 7.19 Alexander Leydenfrost rendering of unbuilt version of Crystal Lassies building, *c.* 1939–1940. Harry Ransom Center, University of Texas, and the Edith Lutyens and Norman Bel Geddes Foundation, Inc. 2016.

Ballyhoo was the perfect satirical vehicle for what was arguably the advertisers' world's fair. The iconoclastic magazine contained only tongue-in-cheek spoofs of well-known advertisements. Begun in 1932, it was a depression-era success and offered clear evidence of the public's skepticism toward advertising and consumer culture.[79] While *Ballyhoo* emphasized the titillating intent of the Crystal Lassies exhibit, a rejected Bel Geddes design revealed a possibly more profound motive (Figure 7.19). The radiant rendering of the crystalline building echoed a range of avant-garde aesthetics and ideas: the utopian glass architecture of Taut, theosophical geometry of Bragdon, and the futurism of Ferriss. The design, a faceted gemlike form, materialized the show's title. It parroted Taut's Glass Pavilion (Figure 7.20), a dome of glass diamonds built for the Cologne Deutscher Werkbund Exhibition, 1914, in collaboration with author and mystic Paul Scheerbart, who considered glass to be a material of great spiritual potential. It also seemed to suggest Claude Bragdon's understanding of the Platonic solids as theosophical forms associated with humanity's link with the universe (Figure 7.21).[80] Bel Geddes's luminous illustration mirrored Ferriss's radiant diamond tipped skyscrapers seen in *The Metropolis of Tomorrow* (1929), referencing his thrusting and romantic futurism (Figure 7.22). The rendering encapsulated Bel Geddes's diverse interests ranging from the utopian strains of the European avant-garde to the spiritual attitude of Claude Bragdon and Ferriss's aerial fantasies. The result

FIGURE 7.20 Bruno Taut with Franz Hoffmann, Glass House, Werkbund Exhibition, 1914. Appears in *Jahrbuch des Deutschen Werkbundes*, 1915.

presents a remarkable contrast: a unique pastiche of early twentieth-century avant-garde ideas and aesthetics employed to house a fairground peepshow.

Futurama as an advertisement

Bel Geddes understood the Futurama essentially as a clever advertisement for General Motors. In the *Retail Executive*, he wrote of the exhibit's innovative strategy—that a concept rather than a product was being sold. Referring to the thousands who endured lengthy queues, he noted the way in which selling a concept was essential in selling a product. "They wait to be 'sold' an

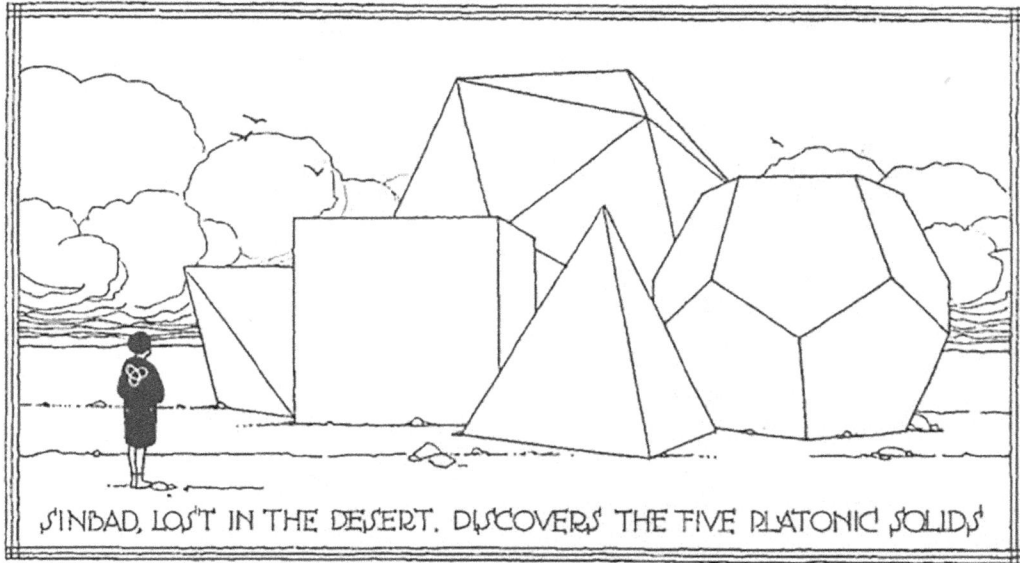

ORNAMENT 87

SINBAD, LOST IN THE DESERT, DISCOVERS THE FIVE PLATONIC SOLIDS

FIGURE 7.21 "Sinbad, lost in the desert, discovers the five Platonic solids," illustration from *The Frozen Fountain*, by Claude Bragdon, 1932. Courtesy of the Department of Rare Books, Special Collections and Preservation, University of Rochester River Campus Libraries.

idea of better, straighter, faster highways which equal better, faster, more comfortable motor cars." Bel Geddes believed that dramatic advertising was essential in stimulating such desire; it sold unnecessary things, yet was fundamental to the American economy and way of life. A contrast to his usual functionalist rhetoric, Bel Geddes proclaimed: "The wheels of industry and business do not turn on what we need, but what we want. That is why the standard of living of the American public is the highest in the world. To sell people what they 'want' rather than what they 'need' requires drama to make them want."[81] He wrote that the Futurama would put spectators in a "favorable frame of mind to examine the client's products and send them out of the Fair zone talking about it."[82] His notion of consumer influence was built on his long-standing study of the mechanics of the mind, whether advertising psychology, the clarity of thought promoted in Christian Science, or the persuasive power of dramatic performance. Building on this diverse knowledge and continuing his approach used in the J. Walter Thompson assembly hall, the Futurama exhibit was designed to put audiences in a "receptive mood" and in a "frame of mind conditioned" to spread a word-of-mouth campaign, thus creating "good will toward the client."[83] As he had done throughout his industrial design career, Bel Geddes combined the skills of theater and design to sell a product. He used his theatrical knowledge, of telling a story in a dramatic fashion, to sell a progressive image of General Motors.

A theater critic visiting the Futurama recognized the ride as a new form of theater, where the audience was placed in a restrictive and passive position, noting that throughout Bel

FIGURE 7.22 "Night in the Science Zone," Hugh Ferriss rendering from *The Metropolis of Tomorrow*, 1929. © Christopher M. Leich 2016.

Geddes's theater career he "has moved nearly everything portable in the theatre, [and] has at last succeeded in moving the audience. I mean physically as well as emotionally." The critic, perhaps more accustomed to reviewing plays than amusement rides, resented the Futurama's compliant spectatorship and imagined how Bel Geddes might industrialize the theater of 1960, envisaging a mechanized and manipulative playhouse "in which a revolving audience meets a revolving stage in a sort of giddy repertory system, with nobody ever seeing the same thing twice... Critics, I suppose, will be merely wheeled out into the daylight now and then to see if they are still breathing and then put back on the treadmill."[84] Bel Geddes may have found this idea completely reasonable. He had designed innovative theaters since 1914 and numerous revolving structures, including a garage, airport, and restaurant. In *Horizons*, his chapter, "Industrializing the Theater," proclaimed that "the quality of our drama would be enhanced if the theatre were industrialized" in the same fashion as "a factory, an office, a man's desk," or "the most efficient kitchen."[85]

Another critic of the Futurama observed the mechanical way in which viewers were processed. He considered the Futurama to be remarkably similar to the factory, creating an assembly-line production of tomorrow's consumers.[86]

> The engineer familiar with the design of modern continuous manufacturing processes will realize that the basic idea of such methods has been applied to this exhibit. It is, in effect, a continuous assembly line with the exception that nothing happens to the unit moving along the line—the spectator—other than the information poured into him via his eyes and ears... The desirability of applying such methods to the handling of large crowds must have occurred to many engineers upon numerous occasions.[87]

The author perceptively linked the technique at the core of automotive production with the process at the heart of the advertising industry; the Futurama brought both together under one roof. From this vantage point, consumer engineering had been successfully achieved. At previous world's fairs manufacturers had displayed their assembly lines and focused on their products. General Motors had done so at the Chicago World's Fair, 1933–1934. At the New York fair, however, General Motors's focus was not on the product, but on selling the company image. Illustrating the shift from a culture of production to one of consumption, visitors who once viewed demonstrations of factory production were now the products of consumer engineering; they had become vessels for corporate messages. Bel Geddes's heavily underscored copy of Arens and Sheldon's *Consumer Engineering* described the need to mass-produce consumers in order to absorb the flood of mass-produced goods.[88] In the introduction the machine metaphor was applied to the manufacture of desire. "We engineered an adequate supply of goods. We can engineer an adequate supply of customers" (12). The book presented consumer research, "fashion promotion," obsolescence, and product styling as essential in differentiating products, generating novelty, and thereby stimulating consumption and the economy (210). "Does there seem to be a sad waste in the process? Not at all. Wearing things out does not produce prosperity, but buying things does" (7).

The Shell Oil advertisement and the Futurama exhibit relied on Bel Geddes's knowledge of entertainment, his interest in games, and his belief in modernism. The Futurama adapted the metaphor of assembly-line production to a three-dimensional advertisement. It created an image of Bel Geddes as a modernist and a visionary, as well as a salesman and entertainer. The Futurama and the Shell Oil advertisement produced a modern image rooted in both rationality and play. At the same time, the exhibit presented an optimistic vision of the future in accord with the Pollyanna positivity of Mind-cure writing. Bel Geddes's audiences didn't always accept his fantastic images of the world of tomorrow, or his self-presentation as a practical visionary. Critiques of the Shell Oil advertisement and the Futurama revealed the fallibility of Bel Geddes's orderly world and effectively undermined his image as a modernist planner and technocrat. Despite the phenomenal popularity of the Futurama, at the end of its first year in 1939 it was reported that the fair itself grossed half of what was expected: "the radio and automobile have made people familiar with so many wonders that they are no longer awed by such spectacles."[89] Ironically, the overriding concern of the Futurama, modern technology, was the very thing that diminished the fair's attraction.

War Models in *Life* Magazine, 1942, and at The Museum of Modern Art, New York, 1944

While Bel Geddes's war models project continued his modelmaking work after the Futurama closed in 1940, they grew out of a deeper and prolonged fascination and engagement with military strategy and model war games.[90] For the war models project, Bel Geddes fabricated three dioramas of miniaturized Second World War battles (Figure 7.23). He published photos of the scenes for a *Life* magazine assignment in May 1942 and exhibited models and photomurals at MoMA in January 1944. After nearly a decade of exhibits of Bauhaus-inspired industrial products and avant-garde painting, sculpture, photography, and architecture, the museum's engagement in propaganda and spectacle may have taken some by surprise (Figure 7.24). However, during the Second World War, MoMA sponsored a diverse range of patriotic activities, including educational and social events and numerous war-related exhibitions at the museum and abroad.[91] In addition, the museum brought in prominent artists and designers to create its wartime exhibitions, including photographer Edward Steichen, poet Carl Sandburg, and designer Herbert Bayer. Often comparing such patriotic work to the great art of peacetime, MoMA presented Steichen's exhibit "Road to Victory" (1942), and its numerous Farm Security Administration photos,[92] "as instruments or records of war, [which] will hold their own as excellent works of art when the war is over."[93] Through their wartime exhibits, MoMA promoted propaganda as art, while legitimating its continued existence in a time of national crisis.

Bel Geddes's war models project served a variety of purposes. It was designed as propaganda and aimed at a mass audience. It provided a patriotic aura for the museum and *Life*, two of America's prestigious and influential cultural institutions. The museum lent its stamp of good taste, while *Life* magazine provided a certification of broad appeal. *Life*'s circulation rose from 2.86 million in 1940 to 5.45 million in 1948, while its readership remained largely middle and upper class.[94] The "War Maneuver Models" exhibit created a sense of historical continuity, an image of future victory during a time of uncertainty. Like the Futurama, the war models exhibit fostered an image of Bel Geddes as a rational prophet, both armchair general and military visionary. The understanding that such work originated from his leisure activities legitimated the hobbyist craft of modelmaking, while adding a playful dimension to Bel Geddes's modernist image.

Combining the utility of documentary with the fantasy of fiction, the MoMA exhibit recreated three battles, two of which were based on actual military engagements, while a third envisioned

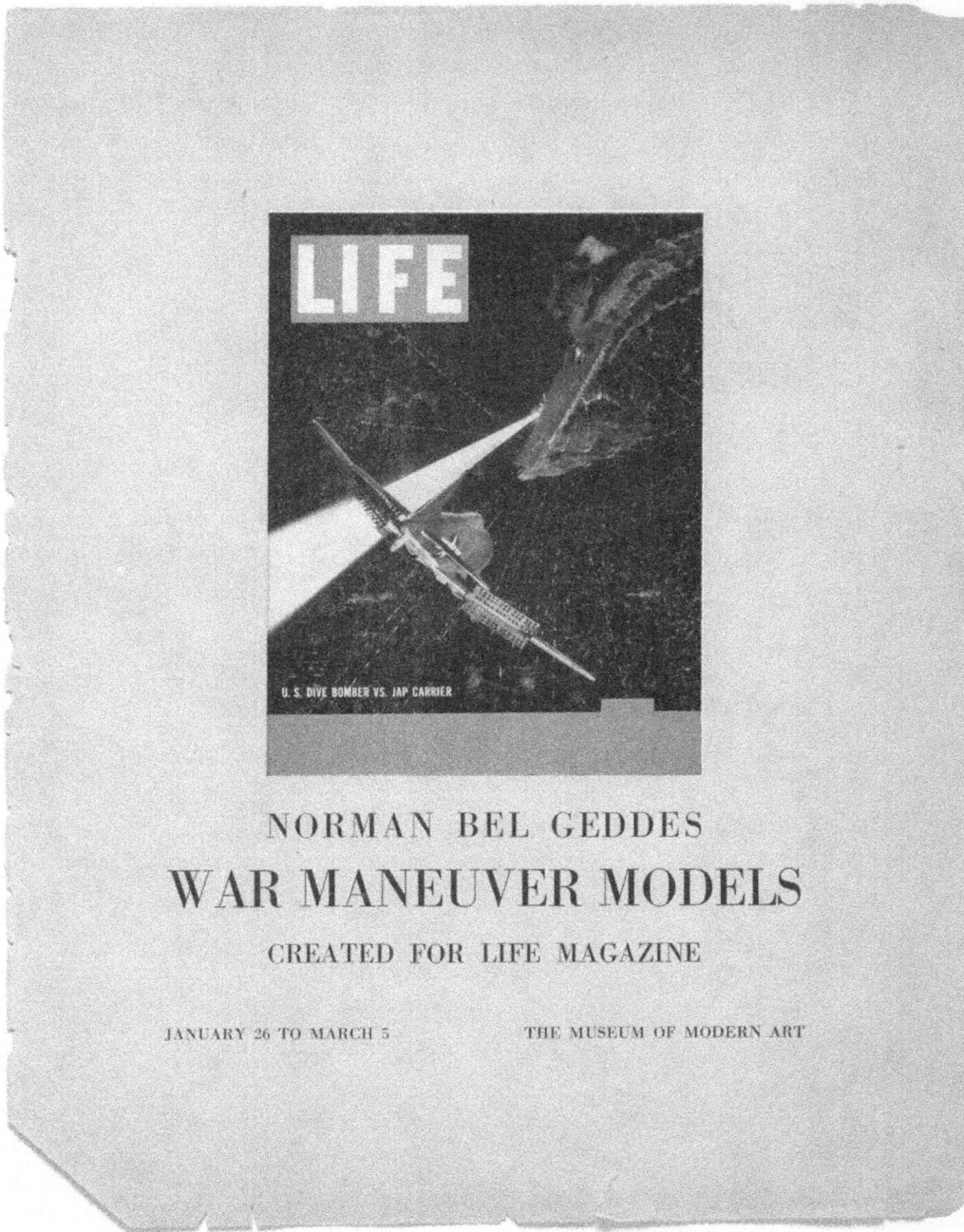

FIGURE 7.23 "Norman Bel Geddes: War Maneuver Models Created for *Life* magazine, 1944," exhibition catalog cover of plane dive-bombing aircraft carrier. New York, MoMA. © 2017. Digital image. The Museum of Modern Art, New York/Scala, Florence.

FIGURE 7.24 Four figures seated with numerous die-cast aircraft carriers. From the New York, MoMA exhibition catalog, "Norman Bel Geddes: War Maneuver Models Created for *Life* Magazine, 1944." © 2017. Digital image. The Museum of Modern Art, New York/Scala, Florence.

an Allied victory, bringing an end to the war. Like the Futurama, the exhibit offered an imagined future, which would bring order out of chaos. While the Futurama's dream of prosperity closed the depression decade, the MoMA exhibit's imagined peace coincided with the last years of the Second World War. Visitors viewed the exhibition from suspended ramps to see the daily fabrication of the war models by workers below (Figure 7.25). A MoMA press release read: "Perhaps the most interesting part of the exhibition is a large model of an invading army coming up against a river defense line. Model makers ... will build this day by day under the eyes of the spectators who look down from runways above" (Figure 7.26).[95] Like the Futurama the war models exhibit engaged in prophecy and amusement, albeit within the hallowed halls of America's leading modernist cultural institution. Yet, MoMA's display contrasted with General Motors in one very significant way: audiences viewed the constant construction of a model that would forecast the outcome of the war. Contemporary critics, such as Clement Greenberg, thought mass art or kitsch required little interpretative work, while fine art demanded viewer engagement.[96] In 1939, Greenberg wrote that kitsch "pre-digests art for the spectator and spares him no effort, provides him with a short cut to the pleasure of art that detours what is necessarily difficult in genuine art."[97] MoMA's focus on fabrication may have helped to remove the stigma cultural critics associated with mass art and propaganda, and distinguished the "War Maneuver Models" exhibit from both the fun fair quality of the Futurama and the mass culture associations of *Life* magazine, where two years earlier Bel Geddes's war models dazzled millions of readers.

At the museum's war models exhibit, spectators could simultaneously enjoy the realistic fantasy and understand its construction as fiction. The museum's press release highlighted the excitement of experiencing the hoax, writing that the "sense of realism is so great" that it's "almost impossible for the spectator not to believe he is seeing by means of the camera the actual event taking place."[98] The museum's strategy of mixing the thrill of illusion with the fun of discovery is evident in the narration of an invented attack on the Rock of Gibraltar. The battle description carries the reader into a fiction that it abruptly dispels.

> The third picture shows the Rock at twilight, looking north from Spanish Morocco. The attackers are withdrawing, the shell fire abates and the smoke drifts away. The photographs of the Gibraltar models were never published in *Life* because the attack did not take place.[99]

At odds with the stark realities of wartime, Bel Geddes's visionary fantasies were sharply criticized. We "found ourselves resenting the huge photomurals," wrote one reviewer. Seeming to critique the Christian Science notion of thought effecting life, the same reviewer added: "The pictures seemed too lulling ... [and] the most dangerous wishful thinking."[100]

MoMA developed Bel Geddes's militaristic identity through its press releases, which observed, "shortly before the United States entered the war, Bel Geddes had begun building our fleet in miniature. With Pearl Harbor his organization started a ship building race with our own Navy."[101] Despite this approach, Bel Geddes's modern and military identities were demystified by the disclosure of modeling methods, which revealed him as a hobbyist, effectively domesticating his heroic fantasies. As with the Futurama publicity, the method of the artifice was divulged to readers, who were shown that the model's illusions were crafted from things you could find around the house. "Some of the effects achieved in the Norman Bel Geddes models are ship wakes made of soda, distant rain simulated by a screen of slanting wire threads, long smoke trails

MODEL BUILDER RECLINES on board catwalk while setting single figure in place. This model shows advanced phase of an amphibious operation. Attackers have landed in force and are pressing forward to penetrate the echeloned enemy positions.

CRAFTSMEN RETOUCH EDGES of breakers for model of amphibious attack. Geddes originally used powdered sugar for white-capped waves and wakes of ships, had to stop because of wartime shortage. Now he uses table salt for same purpose.

FIGURE 7.25 Modeler on board and two modelers painting sea wakes. From the New York, MoMA exhibition catalog, "Norman Bel Geddes: War Maneuver Models Created for *Life* magazine, 1944." © 2017. Digital image. The Museum of Modern Art, New York/Scala, Florence.

FIGURE 7.26 Close-up of war model setup 04, take 11, *c.* 1942 for *Life* magazine. Model created by Bel Geddes. Photograph by Norman Bel Geddes and Co. Harry Ransom Center, University of Texas, and the Edith Lutyens and Norman Bel Geddes Foundation, Inc. 2016.

of cotton-batting on a framework of wire; clouds are often nothing but studio lighting."[102] Such an understanding dispelled the illusion of the model and by implication suggested that audiences could create their own visions of tomorrow from ordinary materials in the privacy of their own homes.

An enthusiastic review of the war models pictured in *Life* magazine was printed in the 1942 issue of *Model Photography Magazine*. The author praised Bel Geddes for ushering in a new age for "tabletop" modeling and encouraged readers to create similar bold constructions in their garages and workrooms. The article revealed the significance of Bel Geddes's role as hobbyist and attached manly attributes to his modelmaking: "Don't let [the] magnitude of Gedde's [*sic*] battle tabletops put your own sorties with scissors, glue and gadgets in the category of cutting paper dolls."[103] Underlining the masculine image of men's war modeling by opposing the supposedly feminine craft of paper dolls, the author insisted that Bel Geddes's creation of "super tabletops" had lent vigor to modelmaking, formerly considered mere "tricks indulged in by amateurs." "Geddes silenced once and for all those sobersies who scoffed at the business of fiddling with small models and gadgets in imitation of nature."[104]

The modeling projects for Shell Oil, General Motors, *Life*, and MoMA promoted the therapeutic ethic associated with Mind-cure thinking: both projects presented optimistic images of an improved world and both relied on the positive thinking of mass audiences. Likewise, the viewer's imaginative transportation from the real world to a vision of tomorrow was not so different from the theosophical practice of the spiritual evolution of the self to access higher dimensions achieved through disciplined thought. The Shell Oil advertisement and the Futurama fashioned an image of Bel Geddes as technological seer and practical visionary. *Life* magazine and the "War Maneuver Models" exhibit enhanced his prophetic and military image. While contemporary critics may have understood his models as manipulative propaganda, audiences made up their own minds. While many were thrilled by the consumer fantasy the Futurama offered, others enjoyed finding flaws in its rigid planning. Though some viewers of the "War Maneuver Models" exhibit were delighted by its artistry and craft, many found models of war both childish and distasteful. Bel Geddes's love of visionary planning resulted in the triumph of his career—the Futurama. Yet, it left him susceptible to public criticism and may have significantly contributed to the demise of his office.

Conclusion

The Second World War provided numerous design contracts for the Bel Geddes office, including government war assignments and commercial postwar forecasting. However, it would prove to be an emotional and professional trial for Bel Geddes. In January 1943, Gedess's wife of ten years, Frances Resor Waite, died.[105] The resulting emotional strain, poor health, and disagreements with his partners, Roger Nowland, Peter Schladermundt, and Katherine B. Gray, profoundly affected his professional life.[106] He became increasingly unhappy with what he considered his partners' emphasis on consumer research at the expense of design.[107] Deeply upset with a change in contractual terms in which a new client was given ownership of the firm's designs, Bel Geddes called his partners "rigid" and "unswerving,"[108] telling them, "You people can obviously go ahead and sign it without me."[109] He subsequently broke from his partners,[110] who joined the Harold Van Doren office to become by 1944 Van Doren, Nowland & Schladermundt.[111]

Despite the departure, Bel Geddes continued to run a bustling office. Design jobs included: the lobby of the Commonwealth Edison building, Chicago (1941–1947); luggage for Atlantic Products Corporation, New Jersey (1944–1945); model construction and photography for *Encyclopaedia Britannica* (1944–1945); calculating machines, typewriters, furniture, and vehicles for International Business Machines, IBM (1944–1947); an Airport Service Station for Texaco (1945); vending machines for U-Need-A Vendors, New Jersey (1945); boats for Gar Wood Industries, Michigan (1945–1946); radios for Federal Telephone and Radio, New Jersey (1945–1946); consultation on the lobby of Webb & Knapp, New York (1947–1951); and consultation with Edward D. Stone for Arkansas University Theater (1948). Regardless of such activity, the office suffered financially due to tax problems, late payments by the US government on wartime projects and a tendency toward extravagant expenditure where "profits often went for models of projects for which he had no commissions and little chance of selling."[112]

With the death of his wife, differences with partners, lethal high blood pressure, and an annual overhead of $884,000,[113] Bel Geddes was forced to close his Rockefeller Center office in 1946, take a six-month convalescence, and open a smaller office with a staff of twelve devoted to "design" rather than "administration," as Bel Geddes put it.[114] He wrote that during the war "industrial design ha[d] become a volume business—growing much too fast." Because of the large size of the Rockefeller office, Bel Geddes explained, he entered a vicious cycle of taking every assignment to keep his employees busy, resulting in mostly "uninteresting jobs and purely to produce income."[115] By early January 1947, he had reduced the volume of his business by 50 percent.[116] By the end of 1947, he sought a loan to "get on his feet."[117] In 1948, *Time* magazine announced Bel Geddes's "comeback," and listed his recent assignments, including the design of shoe stores, a Manhattan office façade, silverware patterns, a million-dollar nightclub in Miami, and a five-year plan for the Ambassador Hotel, Los Angeles.[118] In the 1950s, Bel Geddes viewed his decision to close his Rockefeller office as one of "self protection," a result of "animal instinct," believing that if he had continued he would either be "doing [that] which you hate" or "probably not be alive today."[119]

By 1952, Bel Geddes returned to what he enjoyed most—visionary design. Though not as grandiose as his *Divine Comedy*, Air Liner Number 4, or the Futurama, his space-saving ideas for the home of tomorrow reflected postwar hopes for a push-button future and included: the Living Room Kitchen, a movable appliance wall unit which expanded the area of the adjacent living room; the Expand-a-House, which employed sliding walls and hideaway furniture; and the Wall-less House, where, at the touch of a button, garage doorlike exterior walls opened onto outside terraces. As the office's only designer, salesman, and client contact,[120] Bel Geddes had now reduced his staff to five people (one draftsman and four clerical staff): research, engineering, modelmaking, and rendering were handled on a subcontract basis.[121]

After 1956, Bel Geddes spent much of his time in Jamaica writing his autobiography. He and his publishers agreed that the book should cover his boyhood, ten contributions in the fields of theater, industrial design, and architecture, and conclude with a recent "highly imaginative" project, such as the Wall-less House.[122] Unfortunately, Bel Geddes's tendency for grandiose projects applied to his own autobiography, which quickly snowballed. Having winnowed it from 1,000,000 to 250,000 words, his publisher warned that its enormous scope would require three separate volumes.[123] The publisher told him that he was "too close to the material to have any objectivity."[124] The proposed title, *Miracle in the Evening*, reflected the editorial cuts and the emphasis on a single aspect of Bel Geddes's career. The focus on theater elicited disgust from Bel Geddes, who told his publisher

I don't wish to have my life identified with ... one field of activities. I have done equal amounts of work in the theatre and in industries and in architecture... Since this is the autobiography of someone, should the title be concerned with Norman Bel Geddes?[125]

Whereas his efforts to achieve the "ultimate" designs of vehicles and buildings ensured they remained ideals, his compromised autobiography appeared in bookstores in 1960, two years after Bel Geddes's sudden fatal heart attack of May 9, 1958. Reviewers were surprised by the book's narrow outlook. Kenneth MacGowan's *Los Angeles Mirror* review was typical. "Few autobiographies published after a man's death have been so disappointing as Norman Bel Geddes's ... [which] covers only half his life ... 10 of his more than 30 years of brilliant creativeness."[126]

Why did Bel Geddes's publisher only focus on his theater career? There are numerous reasons outside that of the problematic manuscript, including his inability to intervene, a busy editor, and, perhaps more importantly, the fading appeal of the flamboyant first generation of industrial designers. By 1958, industrial design had discarded the visionary image that Bel Geddes was so instrumental in forging. The theatrical, celebrity-driven era of industrial design had passed. Yet, the duality of his practical and visionary professional persona informed posthumous appraisals of his work. Niels Diffrient, a second-generation industrial designer and partner at Henry Dreyfuss and Associates, explained the change:

> judging from what I've seen of Loewy's work, and Bel Geddes's work, and Teague's, I think that they were used to the flourish, and it was drama, it was high drama to them, and they played it like theater. And they wanted to be stars in their own rights. And when the star era began to wane, I think they all generally lost an interest in it.[127]

An obvious inheritor of Bel Geddes's legacy is found in the theme park industry. Walt Disney's concept of "imagineering" encompassed practical vision, Bel Geddes's motto "imagination makes the actual," and the designer's embrace of consumer engineering. "Imagineering," a portmanteau of imagination and engineering, is associated with the use of technology to create seamless illusions, whether on Hollywood sets, in American shopping malls, or at Disneyland's Main Street USA, a 7/8-scale model of the main street of Marceline, Missouri, Disney's hometown. Furthermore, Disney took inspiration for Disneyland, its rides, and especially its future-themed environment, Tomorrowland, from the 1939 fair—its "stage set" portrayals of technology and abundance found in the Futurama.[128]

In his tribute to Bel Geddes, Dreyfuss summed up the "tremendous influence" the flamboyant designer had exerted over him and "will continue to exert over all designers." Dreyfuss, who had apprenticed for three years with Bel Geddes, explained that "To be an industrial designer is to breathe an atmosphere that Norman Bel Geddes helped to create." He "was the modern counterpart of the 15th century master craftsman. To back his often grandiose schemes, he turned to today's businessmen just as the master craftsmen turned to the Medici. And like his 15th century predecessor, Norman could turn his talents in any direction." "He was both a practical man and a visionary." His ideas "were built, manufactured, staged. And their impact was unforgettable. But equally powerful were the ideas that never left the drawing board, the dreams that remained dreams ... somehow they got into the air and were absorbed by hundreds of other designers, who drew inspiration, in some unaccountable way, from a man they may never have known."[129]

Over the course of Bel Geddes's career, the deployment of his practical visionary image—essentially a 1930s science fiction utopian with a modernist streak—was met with varying degrees of success. In the years following the 1929 Wall Street Crash, this image found an eager audience that desired fantasy and distraction. The application of vision and pragmatism was appropriate for some design projects such as stage design that could employ simplicity in sets and lighting to seek a psychological or spiritual transformation in its audience. However, the rigid application of the supposedly ideal form—the teardrop or egg shape—to streamlined vehicles did not translate into commercial success. Maintaining the image of the practical visionary in the postwar years proved even more difficult as such a persona had little relevance and even less resonance. Developments within the Rockefeller office further challenged Bel Geddes's persona as the firm increasingly employed social science techniques to sell its services and interrogate its consumers. It is perhaps this transformation from utopian visionary to scientific consumer expert that proved most problematic in the years following the Second World War. While the notion of the practical visionary could embrace both, it could not escape its own internal tensions–unbridled vision versus statistical accounting of the average consumer. Perhaps the ultimate barrier to Bel Geddes's postwar success was his 1930s approach to the aesthetic of streamlining, which presented a kind of caricature of scientific fact in material form—the teardrop shape applied to both static and moving objects—yet was presented as based on hard science. This could not be sustained during the postwar period, when exuberant consumers sought a notion of streamlining as both frivolous and fun. It is, perhaps, for these reasons that Bel Geddes's notion of the practical visionary lost its appeal.

Notes

Introduction

1 Bel Geddes's cultural significance has been recognized in numerous publications. See, for example, Donald Albrecht (ed.) *Norman Bel Geddes Designs America: I Have Seen the Future* (New York: Abrams, 2012); Christopher Innes, *Designing Modern America: Broadway to Main Street* (New Haven, CT: Yale University Press, 2005); Nicolas P. Maffei, "Designing the Image of the Practical Visionary: Norman Bel Geddes, 1893-1958," Ph.d. diss., Royal College of Art, London, 2000; Jeffrey L. Meikle, *Twentieth Century Limited: Industrial Design in America, 1925-1939* (Philadelphia, PA: Temple University Press, 1979).

2 Andrew Ross, "Getting Out of the Gernsback Continuum," in *Strange Weather: Culture, Science and Technology in the Age of Limits* (London and New York: Verso, 1991), 101–135.

3 Arthur J. Pulos, *The American Design Ethic: A History of Industrial Design* (Cambridge, MA: The MIT Press, 1986), 346–347.

4 Christin Essin, "Designing American Modernity: David Belasco's *The Governor's Lady* and Robert Edmond Jones's, *The Man Who Married a Dumb Wife Theatre History Studies,* Vol. 29 (2009), 32–51.

5 "Selected Biographical Data," June 18, 1946, AP1-AP12, Bel Geddes Papers.

6 "NBG Biographical Sketch," AP1-AP12, Box 16, Bel Geddes Papers.

7 G. D. (Probably Associate Editor, Gregory Dunne, with contributions from Gilbert Seldes and Henry Dreyfuss), "Norman Bel Geddes (1893–1958)," *Industrial Design*, June 1958, 51.

8 Bel Geddes to Howard Church, Dean, Art Department, Michigan State College, East Lansing, Michigan, May 8, 1946, Job 972, Syracuse Industrial Design Course, Bel Geddes Papers.

9 Russell Flinchum, *Henry Dreyfuss, Industrial Designer: The Man in the Brown Suit* (New York: Rizzoli International Publications, Inc., 1997), 27.

10 George Nelson, "Both Fish and Fowl," *Fortune,* Vol. 9, No. 2 (February 1934), 90, 40–43, 90, 94, 97, 98.

11 Hellman, "Profiles: Design for a Living-I," *New Yorker* (February 8, 1941), 25, 24–28.

12 Meikle, *Twentieth Century Limited,* 48; Geoffrey T. Hellman, "Profiles: Design for a Living – III," *New Yorker* (February 22, 1941), 26–30, 32, 35.

13 See, for example, Richard G. Wilson, Diane H. Pilgrim, and Dick Tashjian, *The Machine Age in America 1918–1941* (New York: Abrams, 1986) and the accompanying exhibition October 17, 1986 to February 16, 1987, at the Brooklyn Museum, New York.

14 Danielle Brune Sigler, "Norman Bel Geddes and a Spiritual Philosophy of Art and Inspiration," in Albrecht, *Norman Bel Geddes Designs America*, 41–53.

15 Frank Zelko, "'A Flower Is Your Brother!': Holism, Nature, and the (Non-Ironic) Enchantment of Modernity," *Intellectual History Review*, Vol. 23, No. 4 (2013), 517–536; J. Landy and M. Saler eds., *The Re-Enchantment of the World: Secular Magic in a Rational Age* (Stanford, CA: Stanford

University Press, 2009); J. Cook, *The Arts of Deception: Playing with Fraud in the Age of Barnum* (Cambridge, MA: Harvard University Press, 2001); C. Treitel, *A Science for the Soul: Occultism and the Genesis of the German Modern* (Baltimore, MD: Johns Hopkins University Press, 2004); A. Owen, *The Place of Enchantment: British Occultism and the Culture of the Modern* (Chicago, IL: University of Chicago Press, 2004). M. Saler, "Modernity and Enchantment: A Historiographic Review," *American Historical Review*, Vol. 111, No. 3 (2006), 692–716. See also R. Laurence Moore, "Spiritualism and Science: Reflections on the First Decade of the Spirit Rappings," *American Quarterly*, Vol. 24, No. 4 (Oct. 1972), 474–500.

16 Daniel Herman, "Whose Knocking? Spiritualism as Entertainment and Therapy in Nineteenth Century San Francisco," *American Nineteenth Century History*, Vol. 7, No. 3 (September 2006), 417–442, 417.

17 Herman, "Whose Knocking?" 419.

18 John M. Jordan, *Machine-Age Ideology: Social Engineering and American Liberalism, 1911–1939* (Chapel Hill: The University of North Carolina Press, 1994).

19 Stuart Chase, *Men and Machines* (London: Jonathon Cape, 1929); S. Chase and F. J. Schlink, *Your Money's Worth: A Study in the Waste of the Consumer's Dollar* (New York: The Macmillan Company, 1935 [1927]); Thorstein Veblen, *The Engineers and the Price System*, with an introduction by Daniel Bell (rpt., 1921; New Brunswick and London, Transaction Publishers, 1990), Veblen's book was reprinted in 1932 when it became a best seller.

20 Roland Marchand, *Creating the Corporate Soul: The Rise of Public Relations and Corporate Imagery in American Big Business* (Berkeley, Los Angeles and London: The University of California Press, 1998); Richard S. Tedlow, *Keeping the Corporate Image: Public Relations and Business* (Greenwich, CT: JAI Press, 1979); Terry Smith, *Making the Modern: Industry, Art, and Design in America* (Chicago and London: University of Chicago Press, 1993).

21 T. J. Jackson Lears, *Fables of Abundance: A Cultural History of Advertising in America* (New York: Basic Books, A Division of HarperCollins Publishers, Inc., 1994), 9.

22 Lears, *No Place of Grace: Antimodernism and the Transformation of American Culture, 1880–1920* (Chicago and London: University of Chicago Press, 1983), 37; Douglas Kellner, "Popular Culture and the Construction of Postmodern Identities," in Scott Lash and Jonathan Friedman, eds., *Modernity and Identity* (Oxford: Blackwell, 1992), 141–177; Quote from David Riesman in Lears, *No Place of Grace*, 37.

23 Bel Geddes, *I Designed My Life: The Autobiography of Norman Bel Geddes,* August 27, 1954, Job 653, Biography, folder 653.6, Bel Geddes Papers.

24 In the 1930s, Bel Geddes avoided calling himself an architect for fear it would anger registered architects and thus compromise his efforts at architectural registration. The title of Bel Geddes's Standard Gas Equipment pamphlet from around 1933 presents Bel Geddes as a chameleonlike figure who could tackle any design problem: *Architecturalist ... Designer ... Artist Industrialist ... Painter With Light ... Dramatizer of the Grounds, Chicago's 1933 Century of Progress ... Believer in the Natural Beauty of Industrial Objects—That's Norman Bel Geddes*, Box 982.1a, Philco, Bel Geddes Papers.

25 The cultural influence of Frederick Jackson Turner's claim that the American frontier closed in 1893 is discussed in Mark Seltzer, *Bodies and Machines* (New York and London: Routledge, 1992), 150.

26 "General Electric Hour over NBC" (radio script?), December 19, 1932, NBG Scrapbook, 982, Philco, Bel Geddes Papers.

27 E. Gordon Craig, "Imagination" (1912), in *The Theatre Advancing* (London: Constable, 1921), 72, 73.

28 Bel Geddes, "Meanwhile," folder k.1 *InWhich*, no. 3–4 (August–September 1915), Bel Geddes Papers.

29 "IV Visualizing Setting," Chapter 4, Stage Design Course and Book, folder k.32 (undated), Bel Geddes Papers.

30 Design Course/SC-6/y.–2., quoted in Meikle, *Twentieth Century Limited*, 50.

31 Le Corbusier, *The City of To-morrow and Its Planning*, trans. for the 8th edition of Urbanisme with an introduction by Frederick Etchells (New York: Payson & Clarke, 1929?), p. 139, stamped: "this vol. belongs in the library of Bel Geddes Papers."

32 Research for this book is based on the vast Norman Bel Geddes Papers (referred to as the Bel Geddes Papers throughout) at the Harry Ransom Center, Austin, Texas. The archive includes rough sketches, final renderings, photographs of finished models, as well as memoranda charting the complete development of most every Bel Geddes job. In addition, it holds clippings covering the launch of designs, correspondences with friends, family, and colleagues, and a draft of Bel Geddes's autobiography, as well as Bel Geddes's personal collection of books on everything from scientific management to Theosophy and from consumer forecasting to Fordism. On the Bel Geddes archive, see K. Feo Kelly, and H. Baer 2012. "A Visionary's Archive, The Norman Bel Geddes Papers at the Harry Ransom Center," *Journal of Design History*, advance access publication August 7, 2012, Oxford University Press. http://jdh.oxfordjournals.org/content/early/2012/07/31/jdh.eps020.full.pdf. For an in depth discussion of Bel Geddes and subjectivity see Maffei, N. P. "Norman Bel Geddes: The Rise and Fall of Subjective Vision," in "Special Issue: It's Personal: Subjectivity in Design History," Fallan K. and Lees-Maffei, G. eds., *Design and Culture*, Vol. 7, No. 1 (2014), 29–50.

Chapter 1

1 Lears, *No Place of Grace: Antimodernism and the Transformation of American Culture, 1880-1920* (Chicago and London: University of Chicago Press, 1983), xvi.

2 Warren I. Susman, *Culture as History: The Transformation of American Society in the Twentieth Century* (New York: Pantheon Books, 1984), 280, 276, 275.

3 Ann Douglas, *Terrible Honesty: Mongrel Manhattan in the 1920s* (London: Papermac, 1997), 32–33.

4 "First Whack," August 27, 1954, AE-5, "Autobiography, by Norman Bel Geddes," Bel Geddes Papers. Bel Geddes used the terms "reason" and "instinct."

5 "First Whack," Bel Geddes Papers.

6 Folder AE-6, Autobiography, Bel Geddes Papers.

7 William Kelley, ed., *Miracle in the Evening* (Garden City, NY: Doubleday, 1960), 9–13.

8 "93-6, Father and Mother," December 8, 1951, folder AE-89, Autobiography; folder AE-6, Autobiography, Bel Geddes Papers.

9 "93-6, Father and Mother," Bel Geddes Papers.

10 Lears, *No Place of Grace,* xvi.

11 Ibid.; Kelley, *Miracle in the Evening*, 26–29.

12 Kelley, *Miracle in the Evening,* 26–29.

13 "93-6, Father and Mother," Bel Geddes Papers; *Miracle*, 17–21.

14 Ibid.; Meikle email to author, January 2004; Jeffrey L. Meikle, "Technological Visions of American Industrial Design, 1925-1939," Ph.D. diss., University of Texas, 1977.

15 George Edwin Bogusch, "Unity in the New Stagecraft: A Study of Productions Designed and Directed by Norman Bel Geddes," Ph.D. diss., Indiana University, 1968, 2.

16 Observation made by Meikle, email to author, January 2004.

17 Charlotte Himber, *Famous in Their Twenties* (New York: Association Press, 1942), 25–26.

18 Kelley, *Miracle in the Evening*, 12.

19 Anthony E. Rotundo, *American Manhood: Transformations in American Masculinity from the Revolution to the Modern Era* (New York: Basic Books, 1993), 227–232; Jay Mechling, "'Playing Indian' and the Search for Authenticity in Modern White America," *Prospects*, Vol. 5 (October 1980), 18–33.

20 Kelley, *Miracle in the Evening*, 22.

21 Jonathan Swift, *Gulliver's Travels into Some Remote Regions of the World* (New York: G. H. McKibbin, *c.*1900), published anonymously by Swift in 1726; Lewis Carroll, *Alice in Wonderland* (London and New York: R. Tuck & Sons, 1910?), originally published as *Alice's Adventures Underground* (1865); L. Frank Baum, *The Wonderful Wizard of Oz* (Chicago and New York: G.M. Hill Co., 1900). Kelley, *Miracle in the Evening*, 21, 22.

22 William Leach, *Land of Desire: Merchants, Power, and the Rise of a New American Culture* (New York: Vintage Books, 1993), 226, 227, 246–260.

23 Douglas Gilbert, *American Vaudeville: Its Life and Times* (New York: Dover Publications, 1963 from reprint of 1940, Whittlesey House), 306, 309; Albert F. McLean, Jr., *American Vaudeville as Ritual* (Lexington: University of Kentucky Press, 1965), 54; Folder AE-89, *Chapter* 88, Autobiography, Bel Geddes Papers.

24 John F. Kasson, *Houdini, Tarzan and the Perfect Man: The White Male Body and the Challenge of Modernity* (New York: Hill and Wang, a Division of Farrar, Straus and Giroux, 2001), 77.

25 Gilbert, *American Vaudeville,* 220.

26 Kelley, *Miracle in the Evening*, 84.

27 Himber, *Famous in Their Twenties*, 25.

28 Kasson, *Houdini, Tarzan and the Perfect Man.*

29 Chapter 1, folder "237.12 Horizons Manuscript, Ch. 1–4, 1st Draft with Autograph Corrections," 7, Bel Geddes Papers.

30 Simon During, *Modern Enchantments: The Cultural Power of Secular Magic* (Cambridge, MA/ London: Harvard University Press, 2002), 1.

31 Kelley, *Miracle in the Evening*, 92.

32 Kelley, *Miracle in the Evening*, 93; offprint of "Bel-Geddes, Norman," in *National Cyclopedia of American Biography*, folder "982.3, Biographical Data," Bel Geddes Papers.

33 M. O. Hammond diary notes, April 6, 1913, Archives of Ontario website, http://www.archives.gov .on.ca/english/exhibits/hammond/portraiture.htm.

34 Walter McClintock, *The Old North Trail or Life, Legends and Religion of the Blackfeet Indians* (Nebraska: University of Nebraska Press, 1968); Mick Gidley, *Edward S. Curtis and the North American Indian, Incorporated* (Cambridge: Cambridge University Press, 1998), 3–13.

35 Edward S. Curtis, *The North American Indian*, ed. Frederick Webb Hodge, 20 vols., 20 portfolios (Cambridge, MA: University Press, then Norwood, Mass.: The Plimpton Press, 1907–1930)

36 Kelley, *Miracle in the Evening*, 111.

37 Russell Thornton, *American Indian Holocaust and Survival: A Population History since 1492* (Norman and London: University of Oklahoma Press, 1987), xv, xvii.

38 Bel Geddes quoted from a 1913 *Detroit News* article, in Hellman, "Profiles: Design for a Living-II," *New Yorker* (February 15, 1941), 23.

39 Leach, *Land of Desire,* 228. In October 1921, Bel Geddes received from the author a signed presentation copy of Claude Bragdon's *Oracle* (Rochester, NY: Manas Press, 1921) a collection of spirit communications received by Bragdon's wife, Eugenie, through automatic writing.

40 "Sixth Lecture—December 3, 1927," folder "K-4c, SC-4, Design Course, Lesson 1–6 w/ms revisions *c.* 1922 & 1927," Bel Geddes Papers.

41 Bel Geddes Diary (1912–13), "NBG 960.1 Family Correspondence, NBG Notes, Diaries, etc. 1901-1913"; "Adrian Degree, Letter from Hardon L. Freeman, President—(1936?)," Autobiography, folder AE—79, chapter 75, Bel Geddes Papers.

42 Mark Seltzer, *Bodies and Machines* (New York and London: Routledge, 1992), 149.

43 *InWhich*, no. 3 (August 1915), Bel Geddes Papers.

44 Kelley, *Miracle in the Evening*, 39. During his industrial design career Bel Geddes collected and filmed reptiles and other creatures as a hobby.

45 The relation between evolutionary theory and modernist design is explored in: Philip Steadman, *The Evolution of Designs: Biological Analogy in Architecture and the Applied Arts* (Cambridge: Cambridge University Press, 1979).

46 A link between Bel Geddes's streamlined design and eugenics is asserted in: Christina Cogdell, *Eugenic Design: Streamlining America in the 1930s* (Philadelphia: University of Pennsylvania Press, 2004)

47 Offprint of "Bel-Geddes, Norman," Bel Geddes Papers. B. Bliven, "Norman-Bel Geddes: His Art and Ideas," *Theatre Arts*, Vol. 111, No. 3 (July 1919), 179–190, 182.

48 Kelley, *Miracle in the Evening*, 118.

49 Carl Laurin, Emil Hannover, and Jens Thiis, with an introduction by Christian Brinton, *Scandinavian Art* (New York and London: Benjamin Blom, 1968, first published 1922), 608.

50 Iris Müller-Westermann, *Munch by Himself* (London: Royal Academy of Arts, 2005); Reinhold Heller, *Edvard Munch: The Scream* (London, Allen Lane the Penguin Press, 1973).

51 Notes on Lund and Munch, n.d., Biography/Clippings, Job 653, Bel Geddes Papers.

52 Kelley, *Miracle in the Evening*, 119–121.

53 *InWhich*, no. 2 (July 1915), Bel Geddes Papers.

54 Michele Helene Bogart, *Artists, Advertising, and the Borders of Art* (Chicago: University of Chicago Press, 1995), 26.

55 Kelley, *Miracle in the Evening*, 124; Arthur Strawn, "Norman Bel Geddes," *Outlook and Independent*, Vol. 154, No. 7 (February 12, 1930), 273.

56 Meikle, "Weighing the Difference: Industrial Design at the Toledo Scale Company, 1925–1950," in Dennis P. Doordan et al., eds., *The Alliance of Art and Industry: Toledo Designs for a Modern America* (New York: Toledo Museum of Art and Hudson Hill Press, 2002), 133.

57 Bel Geddes Diary (1912–13), Bel Geddes Papers.

58 Offprint of "Bel-Geddes, Norman," Bel Geddes Papers.

59 Otis Pease, *The Responsibilities of American Advertising* (New Haven, CT: Yale University Press, 1958), 10.

60 Bel Geddes was with the Barnes Crosby Company (*c.* 1912, Chicago; *c.* 1914–1916, Detroit), the Peninsular Engraving Company (late 1913, Detroit), the commercial art firm, Apel-Campbell (*c.* 1914, Detroit), and the publicity agency Thorson-Seelye (*c.* 1914–1915, Detroit). Dates during this period are approximate, as many of Bel Geddes's biographical accounts contradict each other. Offprint of "Bel-Geddes, Norman," Bel Geddes Papers; Kelley, *Miracle in the Evening*, 126–131.

61 Kelley, *Miracle in the Evening*, 130–131; F. J. Hunter, *Catalog of the Norman Bel Geddes Theater Collection, Humanities Research Center University of Texas at Austin* (Boston: G. K. Hall & Co.,1973), 2. On Bel Geddes's production and strategic use of models in his design work, see Andrea Gustavson, "The Bel Geddes Process" in Albrecht, *Norman Bel Geddes Designs America*, 340–353.

62 Bogusch, "Unity in the New Stagecraft."

63 Kelley, *Miracle in the Evening*, 130–131.

64 Bogart, *Artists, Advertising, and the Borders of Art*, 20–23.

65 Ibid.

66 Walter Dill Scott, "The Psychology of Advertising," *The Atlantic Monthly,* 93 (1904), 29–36; Walter Dill Scott, *The Psychology of Advertising: A Simple Exposition of The Principles of Psychology in Their Relation to Successful Advertising* (London: Sir Isaac Pitman & Sons, Ltd., 1909), published in the United States in 1908. Bel Geddes owned many books on advertising and psychology spanning 1914–1932.

67 "Insert 41," May 17, 1954, Autobiography, AJ-7 chapters 41–43, Bel Geddes Papers.

68 Mary Baker Eddy, *Science and Health: With a Key to the Scriptures* (Boston: A. V. Stewart, 1914), NBG collection signed presentation copy to Bel Geddes from his mother, Luella, Christmas 1913; Edwin Björkman, *Gleams: A Fragmentary Interpretation of Man and His World* (New York and London: Mitchell Kennerley, 1912); Alexander Cannon, *Powers That Be (The Mayfair Lectures)* (New York: E. P. Dutton, 1936).

69 Charles H. Lippy, *Being Religious, American Style: A History of Popular Religiosity in the United States* (Westport, CT and London: Greenwood Press, 1994).

70 Leach, *Land of Desire,* 226–229; The influence of Christian Science on Bel Geddes is discussed in: Meikle, "Technological Visions."

71 William James, *The Varieties of Religious Experience: A Study in Human Nature [1902]* (New Hyde Park, New York: University Books, 1963), 96.

72 Ibid., 95–96.

73 Ellen Kappy Suckiel, *The Pragmatic Philosophy of William James* (Notre Dame, IN: University of Notre Dame Press, 1982).

74 "Insert 41," Bel Geddes Papers.

75 Kelley, *Miracle in the Evening*, 28–29.

76 Florence (probably his mother Flora Luella Yingling) to Bel Geddes, Detroit, November 30, 1915, folder "8 960.23. 138, 142–143, 148—[158] Aug-Sept 1915"; Correspondence between Bel Geddes and William Spratling, 1943–47, Job 957, Correspondence & Autographs, Bel Geddes Papers.

77 Helen Belle Sneider to Bel Geddes, Toledo, Ohio, 5 February 1915, folder "960.16 1, 3, 9, 14–18, Oct. 1914—Feb. 1915," Bel Geddes Papers.

78 Eddy, *Science and Health*, 261; In addition to writing by Eddy, Bel Geddes also owned the Swedish émigré and editor Björkman's *Gleams*, which offered a series of aphorisms in accord with Christian Science on the evolution of thought, the collective mind, and the need for clean thoughts to achieve a healthy body.

79 Eddy, *Science and Health*, 248.

80 E. St. Elmo Lewis, *Getting the Most Out of Business: Observations of the Application of the Scientific Method to Business Practice* (New York: The Ronald Press Company, 1917), inscribed "Norman-Geddes, 1917" and stamped "this vol. belongs in the library of Norman Bel Geddes"; Henry Ford, *My Philosophy of Industry, Henry Ford* (New York: Coward-McCann Inc., 1929), stamped "this vol. belongs in the library of Norman Bel Geddes."

81 Ibid., 37. The phrase, "an industrial or domestic life a successful one," is not underlined.

82 Himber, *Famous in Their Twenties*, 25–31.

83 *InWhich* appears alongside hundreds of little magazines spanning the first half of the twentieth century in Frederick J. Hoffmann, Charles Allen, and Carolyn F. Ulrich, *The Little Magazine: A History and a Bibliography* (Princeton, NJ: Princeton UP, 1947), 2, 4, 5.

84 *InWhich*, no. 11 (April 1916), Bel Geddes Papers.

85 On the history of little magazines and their relation to modernism, see: Mark S. Morrison, *The Public Face of Modernism: Little Magazines, Audiences, and Reception, 1905–1920* (Madison, WI: The University of Wisconsin Press, 2001); Adam McKible, *The Space and Place of Modernism: The Russian Revolution, Little Magazines and New York* (New York and London: Routledge, 2002) and Shari Benstock and Bernard Benstock, "The Role of Little Magazines in the Emergence of Modernism," *The Literary Chronicle of the University of Texas at Austin*, Vol. 20, No. 4 (1991), 69–87.

86 *InWhich*, no. 1 (June 1915), Bel Geddes Papers.

87 Adnan Morshed, "The Aviator's (Re)Vision of the World: An Aesthetics of Ascension in Norman Bel Geddes's Futurama," Ph.D. diss., Massachusetts Institute of Technology, 2001. Morshed explores aerial vision within the work and ideas of Bel Geddes, including a detailed discussion relating Nietzsche and modernist design citing, Wolfgang Pehnt, *Expressionist Architecture*, trans., J. A. Underwood and Edith Küstner (New York and Washington: Praeger Publishers, 1973); Fritz Neumeyer, *The Artless Word, Mies van der Rohe on the Building Art*, trans., Mark Jarzombek (Cambridge, MA: The MIT Press, 1991; originally published in 1986); Iain Boyd Whyte, *Bruno Taut and the Architecture of Activism* (Cambridge, England: Cambridge University Press, 1982). Geddes, *Horizons* (Boston: Little, Brown, 1932).

88 Leach, *Land of Desire*, 41.

89 Lears, *No Place of Grace,* 69. Bel Geddes owned Elbert Hubbard's, *Little Journeys to the Homes of Great Philosophers, Vol XIV* (East Aurora, New York: The Roycrofters, 1904), stamped "this vol. belongs in the library of Norman Bel Geddes," Bel Geddes Papers.

90 Helen Belle Sneider Diary, folder "960.27 Helen Belle Sneider [Geddes], Diary 24 July 1915—31 Jan 1916," Bel Geddes Papers.

91 For a corrective of the view that the Arts and Crafts Movement rejected the machine, see Jonathan Clancy, "Elbert Hubbard, Transcendentalism and the Arts and Crafts Movement in America," *The Journal of Modern Craft*, Vol. 2, No. 2 (2009), 143–160.

92 William Morris, *Hopes and Fears for Art* (London: Ellis and White, 1882), 108.

93 Bel Geddes to Jacob Weitz, Business Manager of *InWhich*, September, 29 (*c.* 1915), folder "j.2 *InWhich* WM-1 Correspondence May 1915–1916," Bel Geddes Papers.

94 Those who received copies included Margerette Whitmore—"Suffrage Leader," George Stevens, "Director of the Toledo Museum of Art," Edward Penfield—"Father of Posters," Oliver Morosco— "Theatrical Producer," Hiram Kelly Moderwell, "Author—Critic Boston Transcript," Hon. Newton D. Baker, "Mayor of Cleveland," Maurice Browne, "Manager Little Theatre—Chicago," Winthrop Ames, "Mgr. Little Theatre—NY," Aline Barnsdall, "Manager—Players Producing Co.," "A FEW OF THE PEOPLE ON THE *INWHICH* SUBSCRIPTION LIST," folder "j.3 *InWhich* WM-1 Subscriber's Correspondence n.d., June–Dec. 1915," Bel Geddes Papers. On Bel Geddes's role at Barnsdall's Los Angeles Little Theatre, see Kathryn Smith, "Frank Lloyd Wright, Hollyhock House, and Olive Hill, 1914-1924," *The Journal of the Society of Architectural Historians*, Vol. 38, No. 1 (March 1979), 15–33.

95 Bel Geddes to Weitz, September, 29 (*c.* 1915), Bel Geddes Papers.

96 Hubbard, *Little Journeys*; David Arnold Balch, *Elbert Hubbard, Genius of Roycroft; a Biography by David Arnold Balch* (New York: Frederick A. Stokes Company, 1940); Ford, *My Philosophy of Industry*; Sydney George Fisher, *The True William Penn* (Philadelphia: J.B. Lippincott, c.1899); Sigmund Freud, *Leonardo da Vinci: A Psychosexual Study of an Infantile Reminiscence* (New York: Dodd, Mead, 1932); Ralph Fox, *Lenin: A Biography* (New York: Harcourt, Brace, 1934); William Roscoe Thayer, *Theodore Roosevelt, an Intimate Biography* (Boston and New York: Houghton Mifflin Company, 1919).

97 *The Education of Henry Adams: An Autobiography* (Boston: Houghton Mifflin, 1918); *An Autobiography: Frank Lloyd Wright* (London and New York: Longmans, Green and Co., 1932); *The Private Life of the Late Benjamin Franklin, LL.D* (London: J. Parsons, 1793); Meikle email to author, January 2004.

98 Folder "653.9a NBG's Literary Clippings, 1916–1917," Box 52, Job 653, Biography NBG, 1882–1961, Bel Geddes Papers.

99 Romain Rolland, *Michelangelo* (New York: Duffield & Company, 1915), unpaginated, 54.

100 Susman, *Culture as History*, 282.

101 Walter Lippmann, *Public Opinion* [1922] (New York: Penguin Books, 1946), 4.

102 Bel Geddes to Weitz, September, 29 (*c*.1915), Bel Geddes Papers.

103 *InWhich*, no. 1 (June 1915), Bel Geddes Papers.

104 *InWhich*, no. 8 (January 1916), Bel Geddes Papers.

105 The *InWhich* manuscripts includes the love poem "The Dream" signed, "Maq Yohaan," with a margin notation by Geddes, folder g.1, *InWhich* Manuscript Material [WM-1 g-1] 4, Bel Geddes Papers.

106 Ibid.

107 Friedrich Nietzsche, *Beyond Good and Evil: Prelude to a Philosophy of the Future*, 2nd ed. (Edinburgh: T. N. Foulis, 1909); *Thus Spake Zarathustra: A Book for All and None* (New York: Macmillan, 1911); *Twilight of the Idols, or, How to Philosophise with the Hammer; The Anti-Christ; Notes to Zarathustra and Eternal Recurrence* (New York: Macmillan, 1911); Bel Geddes Papers.

108 "Insert 41"; *InWhich*, nos. 16–17 (September–October 1916), Bel Geddes Papers.

109 Morshed, "The Aviator's (Re)Vision of the World," 95.

110 In a clipping Bel Geddes saved on Nietzschean thought, *c*. 1916, he underscored the following modernist notion: "If your course of conduct is stunting and withering your power of life…. Strength and courage to command and change your world, are what the voice of nature demands of you." Max Eastman, "What Nietzsche Really Thought," *Everybody's Magazine*, 703, 704, clipping *c*. 1916–1917, Job 653, Biography, Bel Geddes Papers.

111 Eddy, *Science and Health*, 57.

112 Sneider to Bel Geddes, Toledo, March 12, 1915, folder "960.16 1,3, 9, 14–18, Oct. 1914–Feb 1915," Bel Geddes Papers.

113 Bel Geddes to Sneider, February 22, 1916, folder "960.26 NBG Letters sent to BS 22 Feb 1916," Bel Geddes Papers.

114 Ibid., Bel Geddes Papers.

115 *InWhich*, no. 11 (April 1916), Bel Geddes Papers.

116 Hellman writes that Bel Geddes dropped the hyphen in 1932 upon his divorce, Hellman, "Profiles: Design for a Living-II," 22; Bel Geddes says he removed the hyphen in the late teens, "84-3 The Name, Dec. 2, 1951," Autobiography, AE85, Ch. 81, Bel Geddes Papers.

117 Draft article on art and creativity by Bel Geddes, folder "g.1 *InWhich* Manuscript Material [WM-1 g-1] 4," Bel Geddes Papers.

118 Bel Geddes, "Meanwhile," Bel Geddes Papers.

119 Sandra Lee Underwood, *Charles H. Caffin: A Voice for Modernism* (Ann Arbor: UMI Research Press, 1983), 24; Charles Henry Caffin, *Art for Life's Sake; An Application of the Principles of Art to the Ideals and Conduct of Individual and Collective Life* (New York: The Prang Company, 1913), 137; Caffin, *Art for Life's Sake*, 9,10,14, 256.

120 Dudley Geddes to Bel Geddes, Detroit, November 27, 1916, folder "j.2 *InWhich* WM-1 Correspondence May 1915–1916," Bel Geddes Papers.

121 Kelley, *Miracle in the Evening*, 151.

122 Meikle, *Twentieth Century Limited,* 48.

123 Himber, *Famous in Their Twenties*, 18; Bel Geddes to Bragdon, October 2, 1922, Job 957, "Correspondence & Autographs," Job 95, Bel Geddes Papers; Meikle, *Twentieth Century Limited,* 48.

124 Bogusch, "Unity in the New Stagecraft," 19.

125 "54 Barnsdall Theatre," "Chapter 24 part II, 54 Barnsdall Theatre, pp. 54-4-54-6," folder AJ 10, Bel Geddes Papers.

126 In September 1922, the Viennese émigré architect Rudolph Schindler wrote to Bel Geddes's friend Claude Bragdon explaining that "Frank Lloyd Wright … designed a theatre two years ago, which embodies the essential ideas of Mr. Geddes's plan: one ceiling for stage and auditorium, three dimensional settings and the curtainless change of scenery in the basement." Schindler to Bragdon September 18, 1922, Job 957, "Correspondence & Autographs," Job 95, Bel Geddes Papers. In a letter to Claude Bragdon of October 2, 1922, Bel Geddes explained that his theater design ideas first appeared in *InWhich* of June 1915, published before he met Barnsdall or Wright. Bel Geddes explained that Wright started work on the theater five years ago and that Barnsdall asked for the *InWhich* article in 1916. "I am not certain he [Wright] is aware of the part I have played with regard to his theatre." "All of mine [ideas] that reached him went through Miss Barnsdall." Schindler to Bragdon September 18, 1922; Bel Geddes to Bragdon 2 October 1922, Bel Geddes Papers.

127 Hellman, "Profiles: Design for a Living-II," 24.

128 Offprint of "Bel-Geddes, Norman," Bel Geddes Papers; Bogusch, "Unity in the New Stagecraft," 19.

129 Hellman, "Profiles: Design for a Living-II," 24.

130 Himber, *Famous in Their Twenties*, 32.

131 Ibid., 32–33.

132 "94-5 Insect Movies," December 9, 1951, AE-89, Ch. 88, Autobiography, Bel Geddes Papers; author's discussion Steve Wilson, film curator, HRC, Summer 2002; Hellman, "Profiles: Design for a Living—III," 34.

133 "510-1-mjg 6/10/52 Los Angeles 1917, House (6), Letter to mother from Bel," folder "AP-21 Dupes, NBG corres., Sources," Bel Geddes Papers.

Chapter 2

1 See, for example, Hugh Ferriss, *The Metropolis of Tomorrow* (New York: Ives Washburn, 1929); Claude Bragdon, *Architecture and Democracy* (New York: Alfred A. Knopf, 1918); Sheldon Cheney, *The New World Architecture* (London: Longmans, Green and Co., 1930).

2 Charlotte Himber, *Famous in Their Twenties* (New York: Association Press, 1942), 34–35; Bel Geddes to his mother, New York, probably late November 1917, folder "960.6 Family Correspondence, Letter sent, memo 1917; Correspondence 1946–1956," Bel Geddes Papers; Bel Geddes may have stretched the truth in this tale, as the trip East was additionally funded by his graphic work, ten covers at $50 each, countering his rags-to-riches life story. "510-1-mjg 6/10/52 Los Angeles 1917, House (6), Letter to mother from Bel," folder "AP-21 Dupes, NBG corres., Sources," Bel Geddes Papers.

3 George Edwin Bogusch, "Unity in the New Stagecraft: A Study of Productions Designed and Directed by Norman Bel Geddes," Ph.D. diss., Indiana University, 1968.

4 Claude Bragdon, *The Secret Springs: An Autobiography* (London: Andrew Dakers Ltd., 1938), 93; Bragdon to Bel Geddes, April 29, 1921, Job 957, Bel Geddes Papers.

5 Thomas Bender, *New York Intellect: A History of Intellectual Life in New York City, from 1750 to the Beginnings of Our Own Time* (New York: Alfred A. Knopf, 1987), 228. See also Henry F. May, *The Discontent of the Intellectuals: A Problem of the Twenties* (Chicago: University of California, RAND McNally & Company, 1963); Christopher Lasch, *The New Radicalism in America: [1889–1963] The Intellectual as a Social Type* (New York: Alfred A. Knopf, 1966); Ann Douglas, *Terrible Honesty: Mongrel Manhattan in the 1920s* (London: Papermac, 1997). Robert Crunden, *Body and Soul: The Making of America Modernism: Art, Music, and Letters in the Jazz Age 1919–1926* (New York: Basic Books, 2000).

6 Ferriss, *The Metropolis of Tomorrow*, 60, 61, stamped "this book belongs in the library of Norman Bel Geddes," Bel Geddes Papers.

7 Egmont Arens and Roy Sheldon, *Consumer Engineering: A New Technique for Prosperity* (New York: Harper and Brothers, 1932), 97–100, 19, miscellaneous markings by Bel Geddes throughout, Bel Geddes Papers.

8 Meikle, *Twentieth Century Limited*, 183–184. Bel Geddes owned the following books by Claude Bragdon: *A Primer of Higher Space (the Fourth Dimension)* (Rochester, NY: The Manas Press, 1913); *Projective Ornament* (Rochester, NY: The Manas Press, 1915); *Four-Dimensional Vistas,* 2nd ed. (New York: A. A. Knopf, 1923), contains miscellaneous notes by Bel Geddes; *The New Image* (New York: A. A. Knopf, 1928), inscribed "F. R. Waite"; *Old Lamps for New: The Ancient Wisdom in the Modern World* (New York: A. A. Knopf, 1925) author's signed presentation copy to Norman and Belle, November 13, 1925; *The Arch Lectures, Eighteen Discourses on a Great Variety of Subjects Delivered in New York, During the Winter of 1940* (New York: Creative Age Press, 1942), author's inscribed copy.

9 Claude Bragdon, *The Frozen Fountain: Being Essays on Architecture and the Art of Design in Space* (New York: Knopf, 1932), 6; Bragdon, *The Frozen Fountain*, 8; Bragdon, *The Secret Springs*, 181. On Bragdon and the embrace of mysticism, the unconscious, and the fourth dimension by modernist artists including the Cubists, Kazimir Malevich and Piet Mondrian, see Linda D. Henderson, *The Fourth Dimension and Non-Euclidean Geometry in Modern Art* (Princeton, NJ: Princeton University Press, 1983).

10 B. F. Campbell, *Ancient Wisdom Revived: A History of the Theosophical Movement* (Berkeley: University of California Press, 1980), 9, 14, 63; Romesh C. Dutt, *The Ramayana and the Mahabharata* (London and Toronto, New York: J. M. Dent & Sons Ltd., E. P. Dutton & Co.,1915), stamped with "NG" monogram and "1916" inside cover.

11 Bragdon continued to offer such concepts in his 1920 translation of the mystic P. D. Ouspensky's book *Tertium Organum*, 1923 (originally published by Bragdon in 1920 for his Manas Press), and his own *Four-Dimensional Vistas*, 2nd ed. (New York: A. A. Knopf, 1923), which Bel Geddes filled with notations. Bragdon, *Four-Dimensional Vistas*; Bragdon, introduction to *Tertium Organum: The Third Canon of Thought A Key to The Enigmas of the World*, by P. D. Ouspensky, translated by N. Bessaraboff and Bragdon (1923; rpt., London: Routledge & Kegan Paul, 1981), 3. Ouspensky was a disciple of the Greco-Armenian mystic G. I. Gurdjieff (1872?–1949)

12 Bragdon, *A Primer of Higher Space*, 21.

13 Eugenia Victoria Ellis, "Man: The Magic Square," in *Oriental-Occidental: Geography, Identity, Space,* Proceedings of the XXX ACSA International Conference, 315–319.

14 Linda Dalrymple Henderson, "The Artist, 'The Fourth Dimension,' and Non-Euclidian Geometry 1900-1930: A Romance of Many Dimensions," Ph.D. Diss., Yale University, 1975, 298–299, 304.

15 Henderson, 307, 308.

16 Ouspensky, *Tertium Organum*, 161–162.

17 C. W. Leadbetter, *Man Visible and Invisible: Examples of Different Types of Men as Seen by Means of Trained Clairvoyance* (London: Theosophical Publishing House, 1920), with sticker "Philosophers Book Shop, Inc. Theosophical and Esoteric Books, 441 Madison Ave., at 50th St., New York" and stamped "this vol. belongs in the library of Norman Bel Geddes." Annie Besant and C. W. Leadbetter, *Thought-Forms* (London: The Theosophical Publishing Society, 1905).

18 Henderson, *The Fourth Dimension and Non-Euclidean Geometry in Modern Art.*

19 "Artist and Society," p. 2, Stage Design Course and Book, Job 79; "Draft of Stage Design Book,' *c.* 1927, Stage Design Course and Book, Job 79, Bel Geddes Papers.

20 The theatrical presentation of an alternate psychological reality had been central to German expressionist theater of the 1910s and 1920s. S. Behr, D. Fanning, and J. Douglas, *Expressionism Reassessed* (Manchester: Manchester University Press, 1993), 2.

21 Stage Design Course and Book, *c.* 1929, Job 79, Bel Geddes Papers.

22 Cheney, *Stage Decoration* (London: Chapman & Hall, Ltd., 1928), 10. Cheney was born in 1886. In 1916, he founded *Theatre Arts Magazine*, which was the main disseminator of new theater ideas until 1948; Bogusch, "Unity in the New Stagecraft," 15.

23 R. Leacroft and H. Lea, *Theatre and Playhouse: An Illustrated Survey of Theatre Building from Ancient Greece to the Present Day* (London: Methuen, 1984); O. G. Brockett, *History of Theatre* (1968; rpt. Boston: Allyn and Bacon, Inc., 1982), 625–627.

24 Bogusch, "Unity in the New Stagecraft."

25 Christin Essin Yannacci, "Landscapes of American Modernity: A Cultural History of Theatrical Design, 1912-1951," Ph.D. diss., The University of Texas at Austin, December 2006, 8.

26 Ibid., 13.

27 Ibid., 14; Hiram K. Moderwell, *The Theatre of Today* (New York: John Lane, 1914).

28 By 1958, Bel Geddes boasted of having "designed" 63 theatres between 1914 and 1956, "Theatres Designed by Norman Bel Geddes," Job 653.7, Bel Geddes Papers. In 1957 Bel Geddes noted that his "theatre plans" had been referenced in over 200 books on "Theatre Architecture," that he was the author of "the article" on theater architecture in the *Encyclopedia Britannica*, and that twenty-eight of his "plans" for theatres had been built, including the Duplex Movie Theater, Detroit (1914), the Century Roof Theater, New York (1918), Earl Carroll Theater, New York (1923), The Guild Theater, New York (1925), and Paul Poiret's Theater on two barges in the Seine at the Paris Exposition of 1925; Bel Geddes to Wallace K. Harrison, April 27, 1957, "Selected Bio. Data," Job "AP-4 Chronology," Bel Geddes Papers.

29 Bragdon, "Towards a New Theatre," *Architectural Record,* Vol. 52 (September 1922), 182, 170–182. A summary of Bragdon's article appears in Theater Number 6 clippings, Job 15, Bel Geddes Papers. It is possible that Bel Geddes collaborated with Bragdon on this article, following his established practice of working with "ghost writers."

30 Bel Geddes, *Horizons* (Boston: Little, Brown, 1932), 158.

31 Bragdon, "Towards a New Theatre."

32 Ibid., 174, 176.

33 Bel Geddes to T. Helburn, April 8, 1924; Helburn to Bel Geddes, April 10, 1925, Job 89, Bel Geddes Papers. Bel Geddes's designs for Theatres were reproduced and celebrated in many contemporary and recent Theatre histories, including W. R. Fuerst and S. J. Hume, *Twentieth-Century Stage Decoration*, Vol. 1 (New York: Benjamin Blom, 1967 [1929]); Sheldon Cheney, *The Theatre: Three Thousand Years of Drama, Acting and Stagecraft* (1929; rpt., New York: Longmans, Green and Co.,

1952); Brockett, *History of Theatre*; Ian Mackintosh, *Architecture, Actor and Audience* (London: Routledge, 1993), 47, 48.

34 Bogusch, "Unity in the New Stagecraft," 379, 6, 8.

35 Ibid., 417.

36 Ibid., 380.

37 Bragdon, *Architecture and Democracy*, 68; Cheney, *The New World Architecture*. Cheney thought highly of Bragdon's architectural and theatrical work. Cheney, *Stage Decoration*, 215–218. Bel Geddes owned Cheney's, *New World Architecture*, which has tipped in notes from Cheney dated May and June 1931, Bel Geddes Papers.

38 Bragdon, *Four-Dimensional Vistas*, includes miscellaneous notations by Bel Geddes, 9.

39 Claude Bragdon, *Merely Players* (New York: Alfred A. Knopf, 1929), 39, a collection of Bragdon's writing spanning 1905–1929.

40 Bragdon, *The Frozen Fountain*, 66.

41 Ibid., 182.

42 Oliver M. Sayler, "The New Movement in the Theater," *The North American Review*, clipping *c.* 1922, Job 15, Bel Geddes Papers.

43 Stephen Eskilson, "Color and Consumption," *Design Issues*, Vol. 18, No. 2 (Spring, 2002, The MIT Press), 17–29, 19.

44 E. Gordon, Craig to the editors of *Architectural Record*, October 27, 1922, Job 15, Bel Geddes Papers.

45 Ernst Wasmuth to Bel Geddes, June 8, 1923, Job 15, Bel Geddes Papers.

46 Frank Lloyd Wright, *Ausgeführte Bauten und Entwürfe von Frank Lloyd Wright* (Berlin: Ernst Wasmuth, 1910).

47 Oskar Fischel, *Das Moderne Buhnenbild* (Berlin: Ernst Wasmuth, 1923).

48 An advanced course may have been run as late as the Fall of 1929, Bogusch, "Unity in the New Stagecraft," 344. The exact dates of Bel Geddes's lectures are difficult to ascertain, as much material is undated and mixes a stage design book project with the stage course lectures. Students who went on to make significant contributions in their respective careers of industrial design, stage design, and costume design included Henry Dreyfuss, Aline Bernstein, Mordecai Gorelick, and Constance Ripley. Stage Design Course and Book, 1929, Job 79, Bel Geddes Papers.

49 Flinchum, *Henry Dreyfuss*, 26–27.

50 Ibid., 27.

51 Kelley, *Miracle in the Evening*, 258.

52 Bogusch, "Unity in the New Stagecraft," 343.

53 File #SC-3, i.–2, Bel Geddes Papers.

54 Bogusch, "Unity in the New Stagecraft," 348.

55 Ibid., 350, 351.

56 Files #SC-4, k.–5 and k.–6, Bel Geddes Papers.

57 Lecture II, Hollywood lectures, summer of 1924, Job #SC-4, k.–7, Bel Geddes Papers.

58 Ibid.

59 File #SC-4, y.–1, Bel Geddes Papers.

60 Elementary Lecture IV, "Visualizing the Costume," November 19, 1927, pp. 6–8, file #SC-4, k.–13, Bel Geddes Papers.

61 Elementary Lecture V, "Visualizing the Lighting," November 1927, 3–4, file #SC-4, k.–14, Bel Geddes Papers.

62 File #SC-4, y.–1, Bel Geddes Papers.

63 Stage Design Course and Book, 1929, 2, Job 79, Bel Geddes Papers.

64 "Advanced Course—Drama, Its Form and Quality—Lesson III (Play & the Stage)," Stage Design Course and Book, *c.* 1929, Job 79, Bel Geddes Papers.

65 Bel Geddes, *Horizons*, 156.

66 G. Wilson, *The Psychology of the Performing Arts* (New York: St. Martin's Press, 1985), 3; "The Objective 4," Stage Design Course and Book, Job 79, Bel Geddes Papers.

67 Cheney, *The Theatre,* [1929] (1952) 537. In 1916 Cheney founded *Theatre Arts Magazine*, the main disseminator of new theater ideas until 1948.

68 Bel Geddes, Notes on Lighting and Costume, file #SC-6 y.–7, Bel Geddes Papers.

69 "Color," Stage Design Lectures, Bel Geddes Papers. Claude Bragdon, *The Beautiful Necessity, Seven Essays on Theosophy and Architecture* (Rochester, NY: The Manas Press, 1910), author's inscribed copy to Bel Geddes. Frances Resor Waite's class notes, 1927–1928, Stage Design Course, Cabinet (SC-6), Folder y.3, Job 79, Bel Geddes Papers.

70 W. Moritz, "Abstract Film and Color Music," in M. Tuchman et al., *The Spiritual in Art: Abstract Painting, 1890–1985* (New York: Abbeville Publishers, 1986), 298, 299; "Machine Mimics Glow of Fireplace," *Popular Science Monthly,* July 1930, 33.

71 Chapter "Prohibition," folder "AJ-8 Ch. 44–47, Autobiography Jamaica," Bel Geddes Papers.

72 "Insert 59–17 74 45," September 25, 1954, folder "AJ-8 Ch. 44–47, Autobiography Jamaica," Bel Geddes Papers.

73 Bragdon to Bel Geddes, Rochester, N.Y., April 29, 1921, Correspondence & Autographs, Job 957, Bel Geddes Papers.

74 "Prometheus," *Oxford English Dictionary*, http://www.oed.com/view/Entry/152416#eid28173996 (accessed March 2, 2017).

75 James Billington, *The Icon and the Axe: An Interpretive History of Russian Culture* (New York: Alfred A. Knopf, 1968), 478.

76 Billington, 478.

77 "Insert 59–17 74 45," Bel Geddes Papers.

78 "93-6, Father and Mother," Bel Geddes Papers.

79 Chapter "Prohibition," Bel Geddes Papers.

80 "Biography 1926, 83, Mar. 4, 1952," folder "AJ-20 Ch. 80–83, Autobiography Jamaica," Bel Geddes Papers; Bogusch places the divorce in 1925, Bogusch, "Unity in the New Stagecraft," 12.

81 "10 56 To be added to the autography [*sic*] notes on Charlie Chaplin," folder "AJ-5 Ch. 33–37 Autobiography Jamaica," Bel Geddes Papers.

82 Simonson quoted in Lee Simonson, *The Stage Is Set* (New York: Theatre Arts Books, *c.* 1963), 62, 327.

83 Bragdon, *Merely Players*, 39.

84 Bragdon, "Towards a New Theatre," 180.

85 Bogusch, "Unity in the New Stagecraft," 28, 38.

86 Albrecht, "Introduction," 2012, 15.

87 Ibid., 30.

88 Ibid., 41.

89 M. Banham, *The Cambridge Guide to Theater* (Cambridge: Cambridge University Press, 1995), 83. Cheney, *The Theatre*, 534.

90 Bogusch, "Unity in the New Stagecraft," 47.

91 Essin Yannacci, "Landscapes of American Modernity," 133.

92 Norman Bel Geddes, *A Project for the Theatrical Presentation of The Divine Comedy of Dante Alighieri* (New York: Theatre Arts Guild, 1924), photographs by Francis Bruguière. Anne McCauley, "Francis Bruguière and Lance Sieveking's *Beyond This Point* (1929): An Experiment in Abstract Photography, Synaesthesia, and the Cinematic Book," *Record of the Art Museum*, Princeton University, Vol. 67 (2008), 46–65, 47, 52.

93 McCauley, "Francis Bruguière and Lance Sieveking's *Beyond This Point* (1929)," 47.

94 McCauley, "Francis Bruguière and Lance Sieveking's *Beyond This Point* (1929)," 94

95 Bogusch, "Unity in the New Stagecraft," 39, 43.

96 Ibid., 69.

97 Brockett, *History of Theatre*, 627. Cheney, *The Theatre*, 534.

98 Bel Geddes, *Horizons*, 157.

99 Donald Albrecht, Robert Schonfield, and Lindsay Stamm Shapiro, *Russel Wright: Creating American Lifestyle* (New York: Harry N. Abrams, Inc., in association with The Cooper-Hewitt, National Design Museum, Smithsonian Institution, 2001), 13.

100 "Uniqueness of Theater We Are Going Toward," Stage Design Course and Book, Job 79, Bel Geddes Papers.

101 Joseph Breuer and Sigmund Freud, *Studies in Hysteria* (1895; rpt., Boston: Beacon Press, 1960). In their book Freud and Breuer developed the cathartic method of curing hysteria. Rachel Bowlby, *Shopping with Freud* (London: Routledge, 1993), 109.

102 Himber, *Famous in Their Twenties*, 36.

103 Frederick Kiesler, *Contemporary Art Applied to the Store and Its Display* (New York: Brentano's Publishers, 1930), *passim*, 67–68.

104 Kiesler, *Contemporary Art*, 66, 67.

105 William Leach, "Strategists of Display and the Production of Desire," in Simon J. Bronner, ed., *Consuming Visions: Accumulation and Display of Goods in America, 1880–1920* (New York: W. W. Norton and Co., 1989), 100, 110.

106 Bel Geddes, *Horizons*, 259.

107 Ibid.

108 By 1928, the analogy of the window as a stage could be found in work on illumination engineering. Bel Geddes to Mr. Adam Gimbel, Saks & Company, NY, April 18, 1927, Job 653; article on Bel Geddes's Franklin Simon window displays *c.* 1927, no other information, "All the Window Is a Stage – the Merchandise Merely Player," (probably a version of Bel Geddes's "The Store Window a Stage: Merchandise the Actors," *Women's Wear Daily*, November 19, 1927, which was the basis for his chapter on window display in *Horizons*), quote from "Section 1," 18, folder "653.106 Press Clippings of Scrapbook pages for Autobiography Ch. 70 Store Display, Franklin Simon, etc.," Bel Geddes Papers.

109 Francis E. Cady and Henry B. Dates, *Illuminating Engineering* (New York: John Wiley & Sons, Inc., 1928) stamped: "this vol. belongs in the library of Norman Bel Geddes." Includes a section on commercial lighting and "Show Windows," 385; Kiesler, *Contemporary Art*.

110 William Leach, *Land of Desire: Merchants, Power, and the Rise of a New American Culture* (New York: Vintage Books, 1993), 56–61.

111 Robert A. M. Stern, Gregory Gilmartin and Thomas Mellins, *New York 1930: Architecture and Urbanism between the Two World Wars* (New York: Rizzoli International Publications, 1987), 318.

112 Himber, *Famous in Their Twenties*, 36.

113 Bel Geddes, *Horizons*, 268.

114 Leach, *Land of Desire*, 65–66.

115 Bel Geddes, *Horizons*, 263.

116 "Bel Geddes, Looking Back, Sees His Simple Motif the Vogue," *Retailing*, July 1, 1935, executive edition, Franklin Simon clippings, Bel Geddes Papers.

117 Franklin Simon display, AE75, Ch. 71, Autobiography, Bel Geddes Papers.

118 Bel Geddes, *Horizons*, 271.

119 Contractual letter written by Bel Geddes and signed by Earle Heard (sp.?) treasurer, J. Walter Thompson, June 4, 1928, folder 133.1 J. Walter Thompson Correspondence, Bel Geddes Papers.

120 Stephen R. Fox, *The Mirror Makers: A History of American Advertising and Its Creators* (New York: Morrow, 1984), 90.

121 Jennifer Scanlon, *Inarticulate Longings: The* Ladie's Home Journal, *Gender, and the Promise of Consumer Culture* (New York and London: Routledge, 1995), 174–175.

122 "74-K," March 9, 1953, folder "AJ-20 Ch. 80–83, Autobiography Jamaica," Bel Geddes Papers.

123 Meikle, *Twentieth Century Limited*, 51.

124 "Norman Bel Geddes Weds His Partner," *Morning Telegraph*, March 4, 1933, Scrapbook "Industrial Design Publicity, Personal," Job 982, Bel Geddes Papers.

125 Transcripts of articles on J. Walter Thompson assembly room, August 26, 1954; transcript of R. Peters article in *N.Y. Evening Post*, in Autobiography, AE75, Chapter 71, Bel Geddes Papers.

126 Ibid.

127 J. W. Thompson Office, May 11, 1955, Autobiography, AE75, Chapter 71, Job 71, Bel Geddes Papers.

128 Transcript of article from *Theatre Arts Monthly*, Autobiography, AE75, Chapter 71, Bel Geddes Papers.

129 Himber, *Famous in Their Twenties*, 29.

130 "Draft of Stage Design Book," 1927, Stage Design Course and Book, Job 79, Bel Geddes Papers.

131 Cheney, *Stage Decoration*, 119, 98.

132 Simonson, *The Stage is Set*, 62, 344. Simonson was referring to Bel Geddes's stage designs of the 1920s, such as *Joan of Arc*, *Lazarus Laughed* and *Divine Comedy*.

133 Meikle, *Twentieth Century Limited*, 49; Erich Mendelsohn, *Structures and Sketches* (Berlin: Ernst Wasmuth, n.d.). The book and pasted-in 1919 sketch of the Einstein Tower are dated November 25, 1924.

134 Reyner Banham, "Review: *Amerika, Bilderbuch Eines Architekten* by Erich Mendelsohn," *Journal of the Society of Architectural Historians*, Vol. 38, No. 3 (October 1979), 300–301.

135 Meikle, *Twentieth Century Limited*, 49.

136 A. D. Albert, to Bel Geddes, July 11, 29, Chicago World's Fair Advisory Commission correspondence, Bel Geddes Papers.

137 A. D. Albert to Bel Geddes, July 2, 1929, Chicago World's Fair Advisory Commission correspondence; Bel Geddes to all "outstanding individuals of the world whose work ... points toward the future of theater in its finest creative form," October 23, 1929; letters to Bel Geddes, August 1929–March 1930, Bel Geddes Papers.

138 The list of those who were sent letters also included, Harley Granville Barker, Paul Green, Sidney Howard, Leopold Jessner, Louis Jouvet, Georg Kaiser, Emil Pirchan, Georges Pitoëff, and Alexander Tairov, ibid., Bel Geddes Papers.

139 Ibid.

140 Bel Geddes, *Horizons*, 161.

141 Cheney to Bel Geddes, November 23, 1929, Chicago World's Fair Advisory Commission correspondence, Bel Geddes Papers.

142 W. R. Fuerst to Bel Geddes, Paris, September 22, 1929, Chicago World's Fair Advisory Commission correspondence, Bel Geddes Papers.

143 H. W. Corbett to Bel Geddes, February 10, 1930, Chicago World's Fair Illuminating Plans, Job 182, Bel Geddes Papers. The letter asked Bel Geddes to work as a lighting consultant for the fair. Bel Geddes outlined his responsibilities and his invitation to participate in the fair in *Horizons*, 161.

144 Bel Geddes, *Horizons*, 161; Corbett to Bel Geddes, February 10, 1930, Chicago World's Fair Illuminating Plans, Job 182, Bel Geddes Papers.

145 M. K. Wisehart, "Are YOU Afraid of the Unexpected," *American Magazine* (July 1931): 71–73, 85. Publicity, Job 937, Bel Geddes Papers.

146 Folder 182 "Chicago World's Fair, Illuminating Plan Ideas – Lighting Buildings, Grounds, Landscaping," Bel Geddes Papers.

147 Preliminary Sketches, Illumination Plan, Job 182, Bel Geddes Papers.

148 Ibid.

149 In these unpublished drafts, it is often impossible to separate the contributions of Bel Geddes from France Resor Waite. For the purposes of his essay, they are treated as coauthored. Waite and Bel Geddes, "Upstairs, Downstairs and in My Lady's Chamber," *Ladies' Home Journal* project, *c.* May 1931, Job 206.1, Bel Geddes Papers.

150 Bel Geddes and Waite, "Article Number 3," p. 13, Job 206.1, Bel Geddes Papers.

151 Bel Geddes and Waite, "Article Number 7," pp. 10, 11, 12 (May 11, 1931), Job 206.1, Bel Geddes Papers.

152 Selim Omarovich Khan-Magomedov, *Pioneers of Soviet Architecture: The Search for New Solutions in the 1920s and 1930s, Part 1* (New York: Rizzoli, 1987), 459, 465, 466, 477.

153 May, *The Discontent of the Intellectuals*; Lasch, *The New Radicalism in America*; see also Daniel Bell's introduction to Veblen's *The Engineers and the Price System*.

154 Books owned by Bel Geddes included: E. Toller, *Man and the Masses a Play of the Social Revolution in Seven Scenes. The Theater Guild Version, with Six Photos from the Theater Guild production* (Garden City: Doubleday, Page and Co., 1924); W. C. White, *Lenin* (New York: H. Smith and R. Haas, *c.*1936), miscellaneous notes by Bel Geddes throughout; R. Fox, *Lenin: A Biography* (New York: Harcourt, Brace, 1934), miscellaneous markings by Bel Geddes; L. Trotsky, *The History of the Russian Revolution* (New York: Simon and Schuster, 1932); Valeriu Marcu, *Lenin*, trans. E. W. Dickes (New York: Macmillan, 1928); H. Johnson, *The Soviet Power: The Socialist Sixth of the World* (New York: International Publishers, 1941).

155 "Chapter 36, September 5, 1951," Folder "AJ-5 Ch. 33–37 Autobiography, Jamaica," Bel Geddes Papers.

156 Bel Geddes, *Horizons*, 289.

157 Bel Geddes continued to be drawn to socialist ideas. The underlined passages in his 1933 copy of H. G. Well's, *The Shape of Things to Come* (New York: The Macmillan Company, 1933) describes a history of the future where a modern state provides many of life's necessities, freeing people to engage in leisure.

158 Translations of Frederick W. Taylor's writing on scientific management spread throughout Europe prior to the First World War. Fordism was even more popular, especially in Russia in the 1920s. J. Cohen, *Scenes of the World to Come: European Architecture and the American Challenge, 1893–1960* (Paris: Flammarion and the Canadian Centre for Architecture, 1995), 68–70. On the diffusion of Fordism through the European continent, see Daniel T. Rogers, *Atlantic Crossings: Social Politics in a Progressive Age* (Cambridge: Belknap Press of Harvard University Press, 1998), 368–375.

159 This quote has been underscored by Bel Geddes. Prospectus for the International Competition in Composing a Project for the State Ukrainian Theater Mass Musical Stage with 4,000 Seat Capacity, *c.* June 1931, p. 117, Job 203, Bel Geddes Papers.

160 Ibid., 119, 128.

161 *Horizons* Manuscript, Chapter 7, p. 5, folder "237.3 Ch. 5–9," Bel Geddes Papers.

162 Bel Geddes, *Horizons*, 156.

163 M. Liubtchenko to Bel Geddes, June 31, 1931, Job 203, Bel Geddes Papers.

164 Bel Geddes, *Horizons*, 140.

165 "A Project for the State Theater of the Ukraine," Job 203, Bel Geddes Papers.

166 Bel Geddes to Wallace K. Harrison, April 27, 1957, Bel Geddes Papers.

167 Margaret Bourke-White informed Bel Geddes of the Palace of the Soviets design competition in a letter *c.* September 1931; Bel Geddes was asked to submit a proposal by P. E. Nitkin, Representative of All Building Industry of the U.S.S.R. (AUBI), in a letter to Bel Geddes from P. E. Nitkin, C.E., October 1, 1931, Palace of Soviets, Job 238.1, Bel Geddes Papers; Stanislaus von Moos, *Le Corbusier: Elements of Synthesis* (Cambridge, MA: The MIT Press, 1982), 245–246.

168 Kenneth Frampton, *Modern Architecture: A Critical History* (London: Thames and Hudson, 1987), 213–214.

169 "Announcement concerning a Contest for Architectural Designs for the Palace of Soviets," August 4, 1931, p. 8, Job 238.1, Bel Geddes Papers.

170 Ibid.

171 Bel Geddes, *Horizons*, 157; Khan-Magomedov, *Pioneers of Soviet Architecture*, 459.

172 Gilbert Seldes, *The Seven Lively Arts* (New York: Harper & Brothers Publishers, 1924), list taken from index. Bel Geddes's copy includes tipped in notes from Seldes to Bel Geddes dated April and May 1930, Bel Geddes Papers.

173 Bel Geddes, *Horizons*, 186. Bel Geddes directed and designed Seldes's version of *Lysistrata*, which opened in Philadelphia on April 28, 1930. Hunter, *Catalog of the Norman Bel Geddes Theater Collection*, 13.

174 Michael Kammen, *The Lively Arts: Gilbert Seldes and the Transformation of Cultural Criticism in the United States* (Oxford: Oxford University Press, 1996), 25, 9; Seldes, *The Seven Lively Arts*, 318.

175 Seldes, *The Seven Lively Arts*, 313.

176 Seldes, Gilbert, "Industrial Design" *Saturday Evening Post*, Philadelphia, May 28, 1932, from NBG Scrapbook "Industrial Design Publicity, Personal," in box 982.1a, Philco, Bel Geddes Papers.

177 Meikle, *Twentieth Century Limited*, 43.

178 Untitled sheet on Bel Geddes's visionary work, 1928 (probably written after the early 1940s), AE78Ch74 Autobiography, Bel Geddes Papers.

179 *InWhich*, no. 5 (October 1915).

180 Untitled chapter draft, folder "j.3 SC-3, Correspondence and draft, stage design book 1927," Job 79, Bel Geddes Papers.

181 Ibid.

182 Nelson, "Both Fish and Fowl," 94.

183 Hand written note, "Book One" "WHO AM I?" AE-1 Preface, Autobiography, Bel Geddes Papers.

184 Untitled page: "it was during…," folder "AP-15, Memoranda, I Autobiography, Sources." AP1-AP12, Bel Geddes Papers.

Chapter 3

1 Promoting Bel Geddes as a technological prophet became a significant aspect of the office's output and an important source of income and publicity. "19. Books and Articles," September 4, 1945, "Office Procedures—Publicity," Office Procedures, Job 940, Bel Geddes Papers.

2 Henry Dreyfuss, *Ten Years of Industrial Design: 1929–1939* (New York: Pynson Printers, 1939), the first of a series of privately published books of his designs updated in 1947, 1952, and 1957; Walter Dorwin Teague, *Design This Day: The Technique of Order in the Machine Age* (New York: Harcourt, Brace, 1940); Raymond Loewy, *Never Leave Well Enough Alone* (New York: Simon and Schuster, 1951). Teague's 1940 book *Design this Day* had the most in common with *Horizons*. It expressed sympathy with classical Greece, associated technology with progress, and defined design as a civilizing and improving force.

3 In 1933, *Horizons* won plaudits as one of the forty best books of the year from the American Library Association. It was named one of the "fifty best" books by the American Institute of Graphic Arts and *Printing Magazine*, the design credit going to Bel Geddes and Arthur Williams, Clippings on *Horizons*, including *Savannah (GA) News*, June 1933 on ALA award, "Biography," Job 653, folder 653.8, Bel Geddes Papers.

4 SGE agreement December 1930, Job 267, Bel Geddes Papers.

5 "Geddes and Art in Life," *Cincinnati Enquirer*, December 31, 1932; "A Streamlinear Book," *Baltimore Evening Sun*, December 31, 1932; R. L. Duffus, "A Designer's 'Brave New World,'" *The New York Times Book Review* (December 18, 1932); Box 11a, Publicity Clippings 1932–1933, folder 237.8, Bel Geddes Papers. Frank Lloyd Wright, "On Popular Mechanics," *The Saturday Review of Literature* (December 31, 1932), 351; Lewis Mumford, "The Second Wave," *The New Republic* (May 17, 1933), 26.

6 Publicity pamphlet from publishers of *Horizons*, Little, Brown and Co., n.d., *c.* 1932, Job 237, Bel Geddes Papers.

7 H. G. Wells books Bel Geddes owned included, *Little Wars: A Game for Boys…* (Boston: Small, Maynard and Co., *c.* 1913); *The Science of Life* (Garden City, NY: Double-Day, Doran, 1931); *The Shape of Things to Come* (New York: Macmillan, 1933); *The Way the World Is Going: Guesses and Forecasts of the Year-Ahead* (Garden City, NY: Doubleday, Doran and Co., 1929); and *A Year of Prophesying* (New York: Macmillan, 1925).

8 Gernsback quoted in Ross, "Getting Out of the Gernsback Continuum," 108. The roots of *Horizons* extend to the late-nineteenth-century utopian novelists and technological romantics, such as the social reformer Edward Bellamy, whose proto-science fiction emphasized the progressive use of technology. Ruth Schwartz Cowan, *A Social History of Technology* (New York and Oxford: Oxford University Press, 1997), 209–211; Howard P. Segal, *Technological Utopianism in American Culture* (Chicago and London: University of Chicago Press, *c.* 1985), 22–31; Edward Bellamy, *Looking Backward* (1888; rpt., New York: New American Library of World Literature, Inc., 1960).

9 George Nelson, "Both Fish and Fowl," *Fortune,* Vol. 9, No. 2 (February 1934), 94. Those who owned copies of *Horizons* included, H. Earl Hoover, vice president, The Hoover Company, Ohio; M. Luckiesh, director, Lighting Research Laboratory, Incandescent Lamp Department, General Electric; M. Luckiesh to Bel Geddes, December 4, 1934; H. Earl Hoover to Bel Geddes, December 5, 1934, "Correspondences—Replies to Mailing of Articles ('Streamlining' in *Atlantic Monthly*), November 1934–January 1935," folder WA-14b; "19. Books and Articles," Bel Geddes Papers.

10 Meikle, *Twentieth Century Limited*; Donald J. Bush, *The Streamlined Decade* (New York: George Braziller, 1975); Claude Lichtenstein and Franz Engler, *Streamlined: A Metaphor for Progress: The Esthetics of Minimized Drag* (Baden, Switzerland: Lars Müller, 1993?).

11 Nelson, "Both Fish and Fowl," 94. Nelson was probably referring to the original publication of the chapters as essays in the magazine *L'Esprit Nouveau* from 1921. These were then published in French as the book *Vers une Achitecture* (1923) and in English as *Towards a New Architecture* (1927).

12 David Hounshell, *From the American System to Mass Production, 1800-1932: The Development of Manufacturing Technology in the United States* (Baltimore and London: Johns Hopkins University Press, 1984); Ford introduced the assembly line in 1913 and the Five Dollar Day in 1914. Cowan, *A Social History of American Technology*, 228–230.

13 Bel Geddes, *Horizons* (Boston: Little, Brown, 1932), 4.

14 Le Corbusier, *Towards a New Architecture* (New York: Payson & Clarke, 1927), 227.

15 Stephen Kern, *The Culture of Space and Time, 1880–1918* (London: Weidenfeld and Nicolson, 1983); Richard G. Wilson, Diane H. Pilgrim, and Dick Tashjian, *The Machine Age in America 1918–1941* (New York: Abrams, 1986); Cecelia Tichi, *Shifting Gears: Technology, Literature, Culture in Modernist America* (Chapel Hill: University of North Carolina Press, 1987); Gillian Darley, *Factory* (London: Reaktion Books, 2003). On the contemporary notion of "cultural lag," "a period of dislocation when changes in social practice have not yet accommodated the new material culture," popularized by the American academic William F. Ogburn in the 1920s, see Claude S. Fischer, *America Calling: A Social History of the Telephone to 1940* (Berkeley: University of California Press, 1992), 8.

16 Charles Henry Caffin, *Art for Life's Sake; An Application of the Principles of Art to the Ideals and Conduct of Individual and Collective Life* (New York: The Prang Company, 1913), 178; Sandra Lee Underwood, *Charles H. Caffin: A Voice for Modernism* (Ann Arbor: UMI Research Press, 1983), 30.

17 Stuart Chase, *Men and Machines* (London: Jonathon Cape, 1929), 263.

18 Lewis Mumford, "The Drama of the Machines," *Scribner's Magazine*, Vol. 88, No. 2 (August 1930), 156, 159.

19 Sheldon Cheney, *The New World Architecture* (London: Longmans, Green and Co., 1930), 75.

20 "Bel Geddes," *Fortune* 2 (July 1930), 51–57, quotes from 52, 51.

21 "Dollars and Cents in Design," *Printers' Ink* (November 10, 1932), 77.

22 William A. Lydgate, "Romantic Business," *Scribner's Magazine*, Vol. 104, No. 3 (September 1938), 57, 17; Michael Augspurger, *An Economy of Abundant Beauty:* Fortune *Magazine and Depression America* (Ithaca and London: Cornell University Press, 2004), 4.

23 Augspurger, *An Economy of Abundant Beauty*, 3, 12.

24 Phyllis Ross, "Merchandising the Modern: Gilbert Rohde at Herman Miller," *Journal of Design History*, Vol. 17, No. 4 (2004), 359–376.

25 "Bel Geddes," Fortune, 51.

26 Nelson, "Both Fish and Fowl," quotes from 41.

27 Harold Van Doren, *Industrial Design* (New York: McGraw-Hill, 1940), 17.

28 Nelson, "Both Fish and Fowl," 88.

29 Ibid., 40.

30 Richard S. Tedlow, *Keeping the Corporate Image: Public Relations and Business* (Greenwich, Connecticut: JAI Press, 1979); Terry Smith, *Making the Modern: Industry, Art, and Design in America* (Chicago and London: University of Chicago Press, 1993), 160–166.

31 "Bankrupt Business Leadership" *The New Republic*, Vol. 65, No. 833 (November 19, 1930), 4.

32 Smith, *Making the Modern*, 164.

33 Roland Marchand, *Creating the Corporate Soul: The Rise of Public Relations and Corporate Imagery in American Big Business* (Berkeley, Los Angeles and London: The University of California Press, 1998), 1.

34 Ibid., 1–2.

35 "19. Books and Articles," Bel Geddes Papers.

36 The book's edited proofs show the active editing roles of Bel Geddes, Frances Waite, and Worthen Paxton, folder "237.8 Horizons 1st page proofs with autograph corrections by Bel Geddes, Frances Waite, Worthen Paxton, Ch. 1–5," Bel Geddes Papers.

37 Bel Geddes, *Horizons*, 4.

38 During a visit to France in 1928, Frances Resor Waite found a similar correlation between the machinery of aviation and gothic architecture, reveling in the intricate "tracery" of each, Frances Waite's Paris sketchbook 1928, Family Correspondence, Job 960, Bel Geddes Papers.

39 Bel Geddes, "Modern Theory of Design," in "Theatre" section, *Encyclopaedia Britannica* (London: Encyclopaedia Britannica Co., *c*. 1929), 14th ed., p. 5. This is similar to Le Corbusier's notion of the architect-engineer promoted in *Towards a New Architecture*.

40 Bel Geddes, *Horizons*, 25.

41 Van Doren, *Industrial Design*, 16.

42 Mumford, "The Drama of the Machines," 160.

43 Edwin T. Layton Jr., *The Revolt of the Engineers: Social Responsibility and the American Engineering Profession* (Cleveland and London: The Press of Case Western Reserve University, 1971), 57.

44 Tichi, *Shifting Gears*.

45 See Haber, Jordan, Layton, on the efficiency movement and the role of engineers. Samuel Haber, *Efficiency and Uplift: Scientific Management in the Progressive Era, 1860–1920* (Chicago: University of Chicago press, 1964); Suellen Hoy, *Chasing Dirt: The American Pursuit of Cleanliness* (New York: Oxford University Press, 1995), 154–55.

46 Haber, *Efficiency and Uplift*, 56.

47 Bel Geddes, *Horizons*, 7.

48 Robert McDonnell, "Art for Sales' Sake," *Radio Industry*, May 1932, 30, 42, NBG Scrapbook "Industrial Design Publicity, Personal," Bel Geddes Papers.

49 Mary Jacobs, "How Shall We Live in the Future?," *Scientific American*, Vol. 146, No. 1 (January 1932), 71–74; Bel Geddes, "Ten Years from Now," *Ladies' Home Journal*, No. 48 (January 1931), reprinted in *The Readers' Digest,* May 1931, pp. 19–20.

50 Folder 169.5, cover of *Popular Mechanics*, July 1930; *Popular Science* cover, Job 653, n.d., Bel Geddes Papers.

51 Russell Flinchum, *Henry Dreyfuss, Industrial Designer: The Man in the Brown Suit* (New York: Rizzoli International Publications, Inc., 1997), 43.

52 Walter Dorwin Teague, "The Artist in Industry: What He Does and How He Works," *Product Engineering*, Vol. III, No. 6 (June 1932), 245.

53 Such mediation is recognized as a key component of industrialized society. Roger Horowitz and Arwen Mohun, eds., *His and Hers: Gender, Consumption and Technology* (Charlottesville and London: University Press of Virginia, 1998), 3, *passim*; Regina Lee Blaszczyk, *Imagining Consumers: Design and Innovation from Wedgwood to Corning* (Baltimore and London: Johns Hopkins University Press, 2000).

54 Bel Geddes, *Horizons*, 5.

55 The nine buildings he designed for the fair included the Aquarium Restaurant, Repertory Theater, Water Pageant Theater, Island Dance Theater, Aerial Restaurant, the Divine Comedy Theater, Open Air Cabaret, Seats Surrounded by Stage Theatre, and the Temple of Music. Barnhardt to Bel Geddes, August 10, 1929, Box 95, Folder 957.22, Job 957, Bel Geddes Papers.

56 Morshed, "The Aviator's (Re)Vision of the World," 157.

57 El Lissitizky, *Russland: die Rekonstruktion der Architektur in der Sowjetunion* (Wien: A. Schroll, 1930).

58 On the technological sublime see: David Nye, *American Technological Sublime* (Cambridge, MA MIT Press, 1994); Leo Marx, *The Machine in the Garden: Technology and the Pastoral Ideal in America* (London: Oxford University Press, 1964).

59 Summary transcript of untitled and undated newspaper article, *c.* 1930–1933, Publicity Clippings, Job 147, Bel Geddes Papers.

60 Ibid.

61 Bel Geddes, *Horizons*, 162.

62 Chad Randl, *Revolving Architecture: A History of Buildings That Rotate, Swivel, and Pivot* (New York: Princeton Architectural Press, 2008), 93.

63 Bel Geddes, *Horizons*, 110.

64 Ibid., 115, 117.

65 Le Corbusier, *Towards a New Architecture*, 283.

66 Lichtenstein and Engler, *Streamlined*, 240.

67 Bel Geddes, *Horizons*, 111.

68 Ibid., letter of agreement between Bel Geddes and Dr. Otto A. Koller, January 1, 1932, Job 328, Bel Geddes Papers.

69 Koller to Bel Geddes, January 1, 1932; Bel Geddes to Koller, June 14, 1932, Job 328, Bel Geddes Papers.

70 Bel Geddes, *Horizons*, 222.

71 W. Frank Roberts, "How Modern Gas Range Fits into the New Scheme of Things," *American Gas Association Monthly* (November 1932), 481, 481, 482; a reprint of an address at the American Gas Association Convention, Atlantic City, New Jersey, October 10–12, 1932.

72 Bel Geddes, *Horizons*, 249–258. Untitled transcript of *Printers' Ink* article, April 1933; AE80 Ch. 76, Bel Geddes Papers. Nelson, "Both Fish and Fowl," quote from 94; "Oriole Geddes Continues to Create Interest," *The American Enameler*, May 1934, Job 653, Bel Geddes Papers.

73 The Oriole appeared in *House and Garden, American Home, Field and Stream, Arts and Decoration, Stylist, American Builder, Fortune, Better Homes and Gardens*, and many others. "Oriole Geddes Continues to Create Interest," Job 653, Bel Geddes Papers.

74 "Bel-Geddes Plans Streamline Range," *Philadelphia Record*, March 18, 1933, "Chapter 36: Better Living for Everybodies," Autobiography, AE80, Ch. 76, Bel Geddes Papers.

75 Meikle, *Twentieth Century Limited*, 101; "Appendix 81," March 19, 1952, NBG Autobiography AE-1-2, AE72-92, Job 653, Bel Geddes Papers.

76 "31.6 Press Schedule Planned," *Standard Practice*, "Service Department," Job 940, Bel Geddes Papers.

77 Nelson, "Both Fish and Fowl," 42.

78 Ibid.

79 W. Frank Roberts to Bel Geddes, September 5, 1933, Job 267, Bel Geddes Papers.

80 Nelson, "Both Fish and Fowl," 42.

81 Wigley writes that in avant-garde architecture the trend for white walls had begun in the late nineteenth century and only around forty years later did a consensus occur. Mark Wigley, *White Walls, Designer Dresses: The Fashioning of Modern Architecture* (Cambridge, MA: The MIT Press, 1995), xiv.

82 Loos quoted in Wigley, p. 10. Adolf Loos, "Ornament und Verbrechen," lecture of 1908, translated as "Ornament and Crime" by Wilfred Wand in *The Architecture of Adolf Loos* (London: The Arts Council, 1985).

83 Le Corbusier, *Towards a New Architecture*, 143.

84 Bel Geddes, "Upstairs, Downstairs and in My Lady's Chamber" #3 ("Final"), *c.* 1931, 206, Bel Geddes Papers.

85 Bel Geddes, *Horizons*, 250.

86 Ibid., 258; despite Bel Geddes's description of his "all white" kitchen, the stove could be purchased in "white and a color." Transcript from *Springfield New Leader*, December 1933, "Chapter 36: Better Living for Everybodies," Bel Geddes Papers.

87 Bel Geddes, *Horizons*, 251.

88 Ibid., 223.

89 Le Corbusier, *The Decorative Art of Today* (London: Architectural Press, 1987), originally published as *L'Art decoratif d'aujourd'hui* in 1925.

90 Bel Geddes, *Horizons*, 3, 189.

91 Ibid., 251.

92 Transcript from *Springfield New Leader*, Bel Geddes Papers.

93 Meikle, *Twentieth Century Limited*, 101–109.

94 *Sales Management*, clipping, n.d., Job 653, Bel Geddes Papers; Leroy M. Edwards, "Legislation Prohibiting Utility Companies Selling Gas Appliances," *American Gas Association Monthly* (September 1932), 383–385.

95 "New Design Opens New Outlets," *Printers' Ink,* April 1933, Job 653; SGE pamphlets included: "Architecturalist... Designer... Artist Industrialist... Painter With Light... Dramatizer of the Grounds, Chicago's 1933 Century of Progress... Believer in the Natural Beauty of Industrial Objects—That's Norman Bel Geddes," "The Many Shapes of a Triangle," Scrapbook, "Industrial Design Publicity, Personal," Job 982; "Here Is the Modern Gas Range Designed by Norman Bel Geddes to Meet Today's Competition," Job 653, Bel Geddes Papers.

96 "New Design Opens New Outlets," Bel Geddes Papers.

97 Roberts to NBG & Co., September 5, 1933, Bel Geddes Papers.

98 Roberts to NBG & Co., September 1, 1933, Job 267, Bel Geddes Papers; *Fortune*, 42.

99 Roberts to Earl Newsom, December 14, 1933, Job 267, Bel Geddes Papers.

100 Bel Geddes made a similar arrangement regarding the design of radios for the Philadelphia Storage Battery Company in 1930. See Meikle, *Twentieth Century Limited*, 85, 102; contract between SGE and Bel Geddes, December 1930, Job 267, Bel Geddes Papers.

101 30.8 "Press Relations," Box 940 Office Procedures, Job 940.6, Office Procedures, *Standard Practice*, Bel Geddes Papers.

102 G. D. "Norman Bel Geddes (1893–1958)," 48.

103 "Memorandum on *Horizons* by Norman Bel Geddes," April 22, 1932, Folder 237.3, *Horizons* correspondence, Job 237, Bel Geddes Papers.

104 Earnest Elmo Calkins, "Advertising, Builder of Taste," *American Magazine of Art*, Vol. XXI, No. 9 (September 1930), 497–502, quotes from 498.

105 Chapters in *Horizons* included: "Industrializing the Theater"; "Architecture for the Amusement Industry"; and "In Window Display the Play's the Thing."

106 Reyner Banham, *Theory and Design in the First Machine Age* (1960; rpt., Cambridge, MA: The MIT Press, 1992), 14–15.

107 Le Corbusier, *Towards a New Architecture*, 113, *passim*. In the first few decades of the twentieth century, the desire to give the products of the machine an emotional appeal was not confined to Le Corbusier, but was a concern of many designers, ranging from members of the Deutscher Werkbund to the Norwegian Applied Art Association. See Kjetil Fallan, *Designing Modern Norway: A History of Design Discourse* (London and New York: Routledge, 2017), 40–45.

108 Bel Geddes, *Horizons*, 202.

109 Ibid., 20.

110 Bel Geddes may have visited the Freysinnet hangar. A short film of a dirigible hangar is held in the Bel Geddes Papers.

111 Francis S. Oderdonk, *The Ferro-Concrete Style: Reinforced Concrete in Modern Architecture* (New York: Architectural Book Publishing Co., 1928), 196.

112 Bel Geddes, *Horizons*, 293–294.

113 Patricia Johnston, *Real Fantasies: Edward Steichen's Advertising Photography* (Berkeley, Los Angeles, London: University of California Press, 1997), 1.

114 "Editorial: Designers—European and American," *Good Furniture Magazine*, April 1929, 167, 172.

115 Smith, *Making the Modern*, 194.

116 *Fotografía Pública: Photography in Print 1919–1939* (Madrid: Museo Nacional Centro de Arte Reina Sofià, 1999), 72.

117 Bel Geddes, *Horizons*, 293.

118 Le Corbusier, *Towards a New Architecture*, 289.

119 Bel Geddes, *Horizons*, 289.

120 Haber, *Efficiency and Uplift*, 55–57; Harrington Emerson, *The Twelve Principles of Efficiency*, 5th ed. (1913; rpt., New York: Engineering Magazine, 1917), v, vi, xviii, 423, includes Bel Geddes's personal library stamp and is dated November 1911.

121 Veblen, *The Engineers and the Price System*, *passim*.

122 The Technocracy movement coincided with the reissue of *The Engineers and the Price System*, which became a best seller. Bell's introduction to Veblen, *The Engineers and the Price System*, 2.

123 Allen Raymond, *What Is Technocracy* (New York: Whittlesey House, McGraw-Hill Book Co., 1933); Harold Loeb, *Life in Technocracy: What It Might Be Like* (New York: The Viking Press, 1933); Howard Scott et al., *An Introduction to Technocracy* (New York: The John Day Company, 1933); Meikle, *Twentieth Century Limited*, 69.

124 Veblen, *The Engineers and the Price System*, 70.

125 Ibid., 28.

126 Bel Geddes, *Horizons*, 291, 292.

127 Reviews of *Horizons* appeared in the *Baltimore Evening Sun*, *Christian Science Monitor*, *The Power Specialist*, *The Chronicle* (San Francisco), *Daily Times Herald* (Dallas), *Brooklyn Daily Eagle*, *New York Sun*, *Cincinnati Enquirer*, *Canadian Motorist*, *Philadelphia Inquirer*, *Milwaukee Journal*, and others, Box 11a, Publicity Clippings 1932–1933, Folders 237.7-8, Bel Geddes Papers.

128 Meikle, *Twentieth Century Limited*, 48.

129 Chapters in *Horizons* which addressed architecture included: "New Houses for Old," "Industrializing the Theater," "Architecture for the Amusement Industry," "Restaurant Architecture," and "What Price Factory Ugliness."

130 Mumford, "The Second Wave," 26; Douglas Haskell, "A 'Stylist's' Prospectus," *Creative Art* 12, February 1933, 126, 132–133, both quoted from Meikle, *Twentieth Century Limited*, 148.

131 Lewis Mumford, *Technics and Civilization* (1934; rpt., New York and London: Harcourt Brace Jovanovich, 1963), 457.

132 F. L. Wright, "On Popular Mechanics," 351.

133 Duffus, "A Designer's 'Brave New World,'" Bel Geddes Papers.

134 Nelson, "Both Fish and Fowl," 94.

135 Duffus, "A Designer's 'Brave New World,'" Bel Geddes Papers.

136 Ibid.

137 "Art for Utility's Sake," *Christian Science Monitor*, January 3, 1933, Box 11a, Publicity Clippings 1932–1933, Folders 237.7-8, Bel Geddes Papers.

138 *Horizons: Excerpts from "Horizons" by Norman Bel Geddes* (New York: Institute of Aerodynamic Research, *c*. 1932–1933), Box 11a, folder 237.6, Bel Geddes Papers.

139 "Horizons," *The Power Specialist*, Vol. 9, No. 1 (January 1933), Bel Geddes Papers.

140 "Memorandum on *Horizons* by Norman Bel Geddes," Bel Geddes Papers.

141 "Geddes and Art in Life," Bel Geddes Papers.

142 Duffus, "A Designer's 'Brave New World,'" Bel Geddes Papers.

143 Bel Geddes, *Horizons*, 16.

144 *Forbes* clipping, n.d., Job 161, Bel Geddes Papers.

145 Ibid., 81.

146 Ibid., 292.

147 Ibid.

148 Ibid.

149 Bel Geddes, "Ten Years from Now," 3.

150 See Cogdell 2004.

151 Bel Geddes, "Ten Years from Now," 3.

152 Andrew Ross, "Getting Out of the Gernsback Continuum," 102, 103.

153 "Edison Opinions on Future of Science and Invention Revealed in Interviews Published for the First Time," *New York Herald Tribune*, October 25, 1931, Job 206, Bel Geddes Papers.

154 "The Shape of Things to Come, by NBG Internationally Famous Industrial Designer—Aug. 6, 1942," AE75, Ch. 71, Autobiography, Bel Geddes Papers.

155 Warren I. Susman, *Culture as History: The Transformation of American Society in the Twentieth Century* (New York: Pantheon Books, 1984), 156.

156 Arthur J. Pulos, *The American Design Ethic: A History of Industrial Design* (Cambridge, MA: The MIT Press, 1986), 401.

157 Ibid., 402.

158 Bel Geddes's wartime design jobs almost always included detailed forecasts of both technology and postwar consumer preferences.

159 Transcript of a *San Francisco Chronicle* article by Joseph H. Jackson, 1932, Autobiography, AE80, Ch. 76, Bel Geddes Papers.

160 Bel Geddes, *Magic Motorways* (New York: Random House, 1940); Publicity for *Magic Motorways*, Job 384, Bel Geddes Papers.

161 Pulos, *The American Design Ethic*, 402.

162 Van Doren, *Industrial Design,* 29.

163 Leah Armstrong outlines the codification of the British design profession in the decades after 1945 where constraints on commercialism were a central concern in "Steering a Course between Professionalism and Commercialism: The Society of Industrial Artists and the Code of Conduct for the Professional Designer 1945-1975," *The Journal of Design History,* Vol. 29, No. 2 (2015), 161–179.

Chapter 4

1 Robert A. M. Stern, Gregory Gilmartin and Thomas Mellins, *New York 1930: Architecture and Urbanism between the Two World Wars* (New York: Rizzoli International Publications, 1987), 29.

2 Bel Geddes claimed that "several years" after 1929 his Toledo factory plans were "altered slightly" by Albert Kahn, the material changed from concrete to brick, and "the buildings are standing today ninety five percent as I designed them." Untitled notes on designs, n.d., AP1-AP12; only one "experimental" service station was built, according to Bel Geddes, Socony-Vacuum Service Station, report, Job 322, Bel Geddes Papers.

3 Lindy Biggs, "The Engineered Factory," *Technology and Culture*, Vol. 36, No. 2 (April 1995): S174–S188, quote from S. 174; Mauro F. Guillén, *The Taylorized Beauty of the Mechanical: Scientific Management and the Rise of Modernist Architecture* (Princeton, NJ: Princeton University Press, 2008).

4 F. L. Wright, "The Art and Craft of the Machine," 1901 in F. L. Wright, ed., *Frank Lloyd Wright, Modern Architecture; Being the Kahn Lectures for 1930* (Princeton, NJ: Princeton University Press, 1931), inner page reads "this vol. belongs in the library of NBG, BB," Bel Geddes Papers.

5 Wright, *Frank Lloyd Wright*, 5.

6 Le Corbusier, *Towards a New Architecture* (New York: Payson & Clarke, 1927), 227. Despite his goal of mass-production housing, Le Corbusier produced a number of luxurious villas during the 1920s.

7 Gillian Darley, *Factory* (London: Reaktion Books, 2003), 8–10.

8 Biggs, "The Engineered Factory," S179.

9 Reyner Banham, *Theory and Design in the First Machine Age* (1960; rpt., Cambridge, MA: The MIT Press, 1992), 79.

10 Le Corbusier, *Towards a New Architecture*, 41.

11 G. H. Edgell, *The American Architecture of To-day* (New York and London: Charles Scribner's Sons, 1928), 289.

12 S. Cheney, *New World Architecture* (London: Longmans, Green and Co., 1930), 292–293.

13 Ibid., 293.

14 Bel Geddes, *Horizons* (Boston: Little, Brown, 1932), 126.

15 Amy Bix, *Inventing Ourselves Out of Jobs? America's Debate over Technological Unemployment, 1929–1981* (Baltimore and London: Johns Hopkins University Press, 2000), 1.

16 Smith has suggested that after the stock market crash an iconography of modernity was used to reimage industry in the United States as a responsible and moral community. Such an iconography was dependent on the production and distribution of visual pairings of the worker and factory; the product and the consumer; and the city and the crowd in *Making the Modern*, introduction.

17 Bel Geddes, *Horizons*, 206; agreement between Bel Geddes and The Toledo Scale Co., April 10, 1929, Job 153, Bel Geddes Papers; the skyscraper architect, Harvey Wiley Corbett, who had already completed designs for their new factory, had been removed from the project, Jeffrey L. Meikle, "Weighing the Difference: Industrial Design at the Toledo Scale Company, 1925-1950," in Dennis P. Doordan et al., eds., *The Alliance of Art and Industry: Toledo Designs for a Modern America* (New York: Toledo Museum of Art and Hudson Hill Press, 2002).

18 "Wonder How the Scale Business Is in Denver," *Automatic Age*, April 1932, 129.

19 Photo captions of Toledo Scale Co. Store Fixtures, Job 152, Bel Geddes Papers.

20 Meikle, "Weighing the Difference."

21 Ibid.

22 Bel Geddes, *Horizons*, 208.

23 Ibid., 220.

24 Ibid., 214.

25 "Bel Geddes," *Fortune*, 56.

26 Oud quoted by Henry-Russell Hitchcock, *Modern Architecture*, 1921 from "Bel Geddes," *Fortune*, 51.

27 Ibid., 204.

28 Bel Geddes, *Horizons*, 200.

29 Ibid., 206.

30 Ibid., 200, 204; Edgell, *The American Architecture of To-day*, 289.

31 William Blake, "Milton [Preface]," 1804, in Geoffrey Keynes, ed., *Blake: Complete Writings with Variant Readings* (Oxford: Oxford University Press, 1991), 481.

32 Whyte, *Bruno Taut and the Architecture of Activism*, 12, 32.

33 Ibid., 12.

34 Bruno Taut, *Modern Architecture* (London: The Studio Ltd., *c.* 1929), 8–9.

35 Cheney, *The New World Architecture*, 296.

36 Bel Geddes, *Horizons*, 206.

37 Cheney, *The New World Architecture*, 76, 89–90.

38 Ibid., 300–308.

39 Alan Windsor, *Peter Behrens: Architect and Designer* (London: The Architectural Press, 1981), 77–105.

40 Cheney, *The New World Architecture*, 356.

41 These influences have been noted in: Jeffrey L. Meikle, *Twentieth Century Limited: Industrial Design in America, 1925-1939* (Philadelphia: Temple University Press, 1979), 53. Books on and by Wright in Bel Geddes's book collection included: *Frank Lloyd Wright: (new and unpublished works)* (New York: Time Inc., 1938); Hendricus Theodorus Wijdeveld, ed., *The Life-Work of the American Architect, Frank Lloyd Wright, with Contributions by Frank Lloyd Wright, an Introduction by Architect H. Th. Wijdeveld and Many Articles by Famous European Architects and American Writers* (Santpoort, Holland: C.A. Mees, 1925); Wright, *An Autobiography: Frank Lloyd Wright* (London and New York: Longmans, Green and Co., 1932), inset letter to Norman Bel Geddes from Wright and letter from Bel Geddes to Wright, December 1929; Wright, *Modern Architecture; Being the Kahn Lectures for 1930* (Princeton, NJ: Princeton University Press, published for the Department of Art and Archaeology of Princeton University, 1931); Wright, *The Natural House* (New York: Horizon Press, 1954).

42 Kathleen James, *Erich Mendelsohn and the Architecture of German Modernism* (Cambridge: Cambridge University Press, 1997), 57–58. James writes that in the early 1920s European architects like Mendelsohn looked to the United States, Americanism, and Fordism as an answer to their economic problems.

43 James, *Erich Mendelsohn*, 69.

44 Meikle, *Twentieth Century Limited*, 49.

45 Erich Mendelsohn, *Structures and Sketches*, inscribed "to Norman Bel Geddes, New York, 25. 11. 24." Meikle, "'A Few Years Ahead': Defining Modernism with a Popular Appeal," 114–134 in Albrecht, *Norman Bel Geddes Designs America*

46 Meikle, "Weighing the Difference," 137; Katherine Feo Kelley, "Workplaces," in Albrecht, pp. 276–287.

47 Meikle, "Weighing the Difference."

48 By 1933, there were 1,000 foreclosures per week, and residential building had dropped from 937,000 units in 1925 to 93,000 in 1933. Gwendolyn Wright, *Building the Dream: A Social History of Housing in America* (New York: Pantheon, 1981), 240. By the late 1930s, housing had begun to rally from the depression. Ronald C. Tobey, *Technology as Freedom: The New Deal and the Electrical Modernization of the American Home* (Berkeley, Los Angeles and London: University of California Press, 1996), 105; Peter Rowe, *Modernity and Housing* (Cambridge, MA: The MIT Press, 1993), 177.

49 Bel Geddes, "The House of Tomorrow," 12.

50 His five points were published in 1926. Frampton, *Modern Architecture: A Critical History*, 157.

51 Bel Geddes to Wallace K. Harrison, April 27, 1957, Bel Geddes Papers; Bel Geddes's production of *Jeanne d'Arc* opened as Jehanne d'Arc in Paris on June 25, 1925 at the Porte St.-Martin Theatre, Bogusch, "Unity in the New Stagecraft," 85.

52 John A. Jakle and Keith A. Sculle, *The Gas Station in America* (Baltimore and London: Johns Hopkins University Press, 1994), 62.

53 Meikle, *Twentieth Century Limited*, 129; Jakle and Sculle; Chester H. Liebs, *Main Street to Miracle Mile: American Roadside Architecture* (Baltimore: Johns Hopkins University Press, [1985] 1994).

54 Jakle and Sculle, The Gas station in America, 60.

55 "Report on Service Stations Prepared for the Socony-Vacuum Oil Company, Inc.," Vol. 1, 1934 pp. 3, 5. Socony-Vacuum Service Station, Job 322, Box 17, Folder 322.1, report, 1934, Bel Geddes Papers.

56 Liebs, 104.

57 Ibid., 69.

58 Ibid., 65.

59 Ibid., 58, 65–66.

60 Ibid., 65.

61 "Report on Service Stations Prepared for the Socony-Vacuum Oil Company, Inc.," p. 56, Bel Geddes Papers. Postmodern design, on the other hand, employed denotation, where explicit meaning, such as an explanatory signage, was employed, Robert Venturi, "The Duck and the Decorated Shed," in Thomas Docherty, ed., *Postmodernism: A Reader* (New York: Simon and Schuster, 1993), 295–307. Originally printed in Robert Venturi, Denise Scott-Brown and Steven Izenour, *Learning from Las Vegas* (Cambridge, MA: MIT Press, 1972).

62 Ibid., 59.

63 Ibid., 8.

64 "Outdoor Interests Offer Plan for State Regulation," *Printers' Ink*, October 27, 1932, 49; "Outdoor Industry Submits a Code," *Printers' Ink*, September 14, 1933, 88; On the history of American outdoor advertising, see Catherine Gudis, *Buyways: Billboards, Automobiles and the American Landscape* (New York and London: Routledge, 2004).

65 Ibid., 59.

66 In the photographs of his model, however, the Socony-Vacuum name appears on the vertical uprights of the pump islands but not on the building.

67 Gilbert Herbert, *The Dream of the Factory-Made House: Walter Gropius and Conrad Wachsmann* (Cambridge, MA: The MIT Press, 1984).

68 "Report on Service Stations Prepared for the Socony-Vacuum Oil Company, Inc.," p. 44, Bel Geddes Papers.

69 Daniel I. Vieyra, *Fill 'er Up: An Architectural History of America's Gas Station* (New York: Collier Books, 1979), 56–58.

70 Ibid., 45.

71 Liebs, 106.

72 Liebs, 107.

73 The article profiled Bel Geddes's design and theater work and included six images and a lengthy description of the Socony station. Reid, Kenneth, "Master of Design 2- Norman Bel Geddes," *Pencil Points*, January 1937, 1–32.

74 Each laborer would earn $2,000 a year—twice their usual wage. Houses would sell for $2,500 each, "Housing Corporation of America: Presentation to the President," December 1939. Job 400.1; "House by Geddes," *Business Week*, January 13, 1940, 35–36, Bel Geddes Papers.

75 "Housing Corporation of America: Presentation to the President," December 1939, Job 400, Bel Geddes Papers.

76 Bel Geddes to Theresa Helburn, Executive Director of the Theatre Guild Incorporated 7 June 1923, Job 89; Helburn to Bel Geddes, June 27, 1924, Job 89, Bel Geddes Papers.

77 Bel Geddes from Helburn, June 27, 1924, Job 89, Bel Geddes Papers.

78 Bel Geddes to Helburn, April 8, 1924, Job 89, Bel Geddes Papers. William C. Young, *Famous American Playhouses, 1900–1971*, Documents of American Theatre History, Vol. 2 (Chicago: American Library Association, 1973), 65.

79 Helburn to Bel Geddes April 10, 1925, Job 89, Bel Geddes Papers.

80 "Application of Norman Bel Geddes for Certificate as Registered Architect," Job 314, Bel Geddes Papers.

81 "Geddes' [sic] explanation of Architectural Registration Difficulty," December 4, 1940, Job 314, Bel Geddes Papers.

82 "Application of Norman Bel Geddes for Certificate as Registered Architect," Job 314, Bel Geddes Papers.

83 Ibid.; Herbert J. Hamilton, Chief at the University of the State of New York, The State Education Department, to Bel Geddes, Albany, February 4,1931, Job 314, Bel Geddes Papers.

84 Bel Geddes quoting Ralph T. Walker's letter of support for his architectural registration, n.d., Job 314. Bel Geddes Papers.

85 Ibid.; Hamilton letter, February 4, 1931, Job 314, Bel Geddes Papers.

86 Bel Geddes to Ben Wasson, Manager, Literary Department, American Play Company, August 17, 1931, Job 237, Bel Geddes Papers.

87 "Memorandum on *Horizons* by Norman Bel Geddes," Bel Geddes Papers.

88 Bel Geddes, "House of Tomorrow," 1; "House of Tomorrow," *Reader's Digest*, May 1931, 19–20.

89 Kathryn Dethier, "The Spirit of Progressive Reform: the *Ladies' Home Journal* House Plans, 1900–1902," *Journal of Design History*, Vol. 6, No. 4 (1993), 247.

90 Meikle, *Twentieth Century Limited*, 49–50; Robert A. M. Stern "Relevance of the Decade," *Journal of the Society of Architectural Historians*, Vol. 24 (March 1965), 7.

91 Bel Geddes to Mrs. Henry Breckinridge, February 28, 1935, Job 314, Bel Geddes Papers.

92 Nelson, "Both Fish and Fowl," 43.

93 Hellman, "Profiles: Design for a Living – III," 28; Meikle, *Twentieth Century Limited*, 86.

94 "Geddes' [sic] explanation of Architectural Registration Difficulty," Bel Geddes Papers.

95 "Architecture: Old Friends Plan to Soar on Building Boom," *The Arts*, June 8, 1935, 18; *New York Times*, May 29 (*c.* 1935), Bel Geddes Papers.

96 Norman Bel Geddes & Howe Partnership Company Brochure, Job 331, Bel Geddes Papers.

97 "Geddes' [sic] explanation of Architectural Registration Difficulty," Bel Geddes Papers.

98 Ibid.

99 Ibid.

100 "FROM ARCHITECTURE MAGAZINE – JANUARY 1935," September 13, 1951, Autobiography, folder AJ – 10, Bel Geddes Papers.

101 James B. Sullivan, *Industrialization in the Building Industry* (New York: Van Nostrand Reinhold, 1980), 18–19.

102 "Tomorrow's Homes for the Many," Job 290, Bel Geddes Papers.

103 Stanley Abercrombie, *George Nelson: The Design of Modern Design* (Cambridge and London: The MIT Press, 1995), 186–187.

104 "For us the Living … Better Homes," Revere Copper and Brass, *c.* 1941–1945.

105 Donald F. Haggerty, Assistant Advertising Manager, Revere Copper and Brass, to Bel Geddes, August 22, 1945, Prefab House Correspondence, Job 400, Bel Geddes Papers.

106 Sullivan, *Industrialization in the Building Industry*, 18–21.

107 Ibid.

Chapter 5

1 Advanced course lessons I-X, 1929, pp. 2–3, Stage Design Course and Book, Job 79, Bel Geddes Papers.

2 In *Towards a New Architecture*, Le Corbusier repeatedly noted the efficiency of the streamlined form in nature and in vehicle design. Le Corbusier returned to the subject of aerodynamic design in his book *Aircraft* (New York: Studio Publications, 1935). Walter Gropius's design of a car body for Adler Cabriolet (1930) provides another example of a modernist architect involved in streamlining in Banham, *Theory and Design in the First Machine Age* (1960; rpt., Cambridge, MA: The MIT Press, 1992), 304.

3 Le Corbusier, *Towards a New Architecture* (New York: Payson & Clarke, 1927), 146.

4 S. Cheney, *The New World Architecture* (London: Longmans, Green and Co., 1930), 80.

5 Bel Geddes, "Modern Theory of Design," *Encyclopaedia Britannica*.

6 Samuel R. Calthrop patented an "air-resisting train" with tapered front and rear in 1865. By the end of the nineteenth century, the teardrop form had been accepted as the ideal air-resistant shape. Some early examples of European streamlining include Edmund Rumpler's Tropfenauto (1921) and Paul Jaray's Lay T6 (1922). In Britain, Sir Charles Burney's Streamliner was produced around 1930. In the United States, Buckminster Fuller's Dymaxion Cars were built after 1933. Donald J. Bush, *The Streamlined Decade* (New York: George Braziller, 1975), 99. In 1930, Bel Geddes did consider his contribution to streamlining significant and recognized that he did not "originate streamlining," but did the "original creative work on them [streamlined designs] and published it in a complete drawings-plans specifications, making it available to any one…" '626-2 wh," AP1-AP12, Bel Geddes Papers.

7 Nelson, "Both Fish and Fowl," *Fortune,* Vol. 9, No. 2 (February 1934), 94. Auguste Piccard (1884–1962) was a Swiss physicist known for his explorations of the stratosphere and the deep sea. He made the first ascent into the stratosphere reaching an altitude of 51,800 feet in 1931. "Picard, Auguste" *World Encyclopedia*. Philip's, 2004. *Oxford Reference Online* (Oxford University Press). Hertfordshire University. January 16, 2005 http://www.oxfordreference.com.views/ENTRY .html?subview=Main%entry=t105.e9033.

8 James J. Flink, *The Automobile Age* (Cambridge, MA: The MIT Press, 1990), 237.

9 Bel Geddes, "Streamlining," *The Atlantic Monthly*, November 1934, 553–568.

10 *Horizons: Excerpts from "Horizons" by Norman Bel Geddes*, Job 237, Bel Geddes Papers.

11 Harold Van Doren, *Industrial Design* (New York: McGraw-Hill, 1940), 147–148.

12 Paul Frankl, *Form and Re-form: A Practical Handbook for Modern Interiors* (New York: Harper and Brothers, 1930), 51.

13 S. Cheney and Martha Candler Cheney, *Art and the Machine: An Account of Industrial Design in 20th-Century America* (New York: Whittlesey House, 1936), 64.

14 Ibid., 102.

15 Pulos, "Dynamic Showman: Norman Bel Geddes," *Industrial Design*, Vol. 17 (July 1970), 60–64. Pulos notes that it was unfortunate that Bel Geddes became associated with stylistic streamlining and that "his designs became paradigms of the mania for speed and the progress it implied that ruled the early thirties," 64.

16 Bel Geddes continued to present himself as a streamlining pioneer even as the popularity of the style decreased. See "Low Cost Houses-Presentation Book," n.d., *c.* 1946–54, p. 51, Job 460, Bel Geddes Papers.

17 Van Doren, *Industrial Design*, 180. A fuller discussion of the origins of streamlining, aerodynamics, and hydrodynamics appears in Bush, *The Streamlined Decade*.

18 Jeffrey L. Meikle, *Twentieth Century Limited: Industrial Design in America, 1925-1939* (Philadelphia: Temple University Press, 1979), 160.

19 Flink, *The Automobile Age*, 237.

20 "Graham-Paige Announcement Dinner," Job 161, Bel Geddes Papers.

21 "Selected Biographical Data," June 18, 1946, AP1-AP12; "Agreement Norman Bel Geddes and Ray A. Graham, May 21, 1929," May 21, 1929, Job 161, Bel Geddes Papers. Nelson, "Both Fish and Fowl," 94; Bel Geddes, *Horizons* (Boston: Little, Brown, 1932), 52.

22 Bel Geddes to R. Graham, January 22, 1929, Job 161, Bel Geddes Papers.

23 "Agreement," Job 161, Bel Geddes Papers.

24 "Ray Graham Ends Life by Drowning," *New York Times,* n.d., Bel Geddes Papers.

25 Flink, *Automobile Age*, 242.

26 David Gartman, *Auto Opium: A Social History of American Automobile Design* (London and New York: Routledge, 1994), 120.

27 Ibid., 79.

28 Bel Geddes to Graham, January 22, 1929, Geddes Papers.

29 Minutes of conference with Bel Geddes, W. L. Graham, and R. Graham, May 21, 1929, Job 161; *Automobile Topics* article draft by Munroe Innes in collaboration with Bel Geddes office used as publicity, Job 161, Bel Geddes Papers.

30 Memo regarding Graham-Paige case history to Bel Geddes and Miss Maxon from M. Steffens, November 1, 1945, Job 161; "The Automobile of the Future," draft of publicity by Bel Geddes and Chritchell Rimington (Director of Public Relations), 1942, Job 161, Bel Geddes Papers; Pioneers of streamlined automotive design included, Count Ricotti (1914) and Paul Jaray, who filed patents for his streamlined car bodies in 1922 (Germany) and in 1927 (the United States) Bush, *The Streamlined Decade*, 99.

31 Bel Geddes to Mrs. Ray Graham, August 18, 1932, Job 161, Bel Geddes Papers.

32 *Automobile Topics* article draft, Job 161, *Bel Geddes Papers*.

33 Bel Geddes, *Horizons*, 54.

34 Minutes of meeting with W. Graham and Bel Geddes, August 7, 1929, Job 161, Bel Geddes Papers.

35 Le Corbusier, *Towards a New Architecture*, 133.

36 Ibid., 128.

37 Bel Geddes, *Horizons*, 48.

38 Letter to Bel Geddes from Innes, March 4, 1929. Bel Geddes Papers.

39 *Automobile Topics* article draft, Job 161, *Bel Geddes Papers*.

40 Ibid.

41 Le Corbusier, *Towards a New Architecture*, 177.

42 Ibid.

43 *Automobile Topics* article draft, Job 161, Bel Geddes Papers; Bel Geddes, *Horizons*, 55.

44 Minutes of meeting with R. Graham, W. H. Neely, and Bel Geddes, September 11, 1929, Job 161. In 1933, Bel Geddes was contracted by the Graham-Paige Motor Car Company to design an automobile radiator ornament and interiors and exteriors. Bel Geddes Papers.

45 Memo regarding Graham-Paige case history to Bel Geddes and Miss Maxon from M. Steffens, November 1, 1945, Job 161; Bel Geddes and Rimington, "The Automobile of the Future," Job 161, Bel Geddes Papers; *Horizons*, 54.

46 *Automobile Topics* article draft, Job 161.

47 "1138/vb/3/19/56 Autobiography—653 Chapter 71," p. 1, AE75, Ch. 71, Autobiography, Bel Geddes Papers.

48 Bel Geddes, *Horizons*, 50.

49 Raymond Loewy, *Never Leave Well Enough Alone* (Baltimore: Johns Hopkins University Press, 2002), originally published in 1951. In 1951, Raymond Loewy presented the egg as "the perfect functional shape," 200.

50 Page beginning: "summer at Southampton 80," folder "AJ-20 Ch. 80–83, Autobiography Jamaica," Bel Geddes Papers.

51 Bel Geddes, *Horizons,* 58.

52 Motor Car Number 8's obvious predecessor was Giuseppe Merosi's pioneering aerodynamic teardrop car of 1913. Penny Sparke, *A Century of Car Design* (London: Mitchell Beazley, 2002), 26. Likewise, Car Number 8 mimics the form of Buckminster Fuller's teardrop-shaped Zoomobile design of 1927. Fuller would develop this shape and vehicle concept further in his Dymaxion Car Number One, 1933. Bush, *The Streamlined Decade,* 41, 105.

53 Le Corbusier, *Towards a New Architecture*, 128.

54 Paul Jaray, "Teardrops, Aerodynamics and Motor Cars: The Falling Drop—Not a 'Teardrop,'" from *Deutsche-Motor-Zeitschrift*, 1924, in Lichtenstein and Engler, *Streamlined*, 264.

55 Caption from GM medal record book, Job 262, Bel Geddes Papers.

56 Clyde C. Trees, President of Medallic Art Company, to Bel Geddes, July 9, 1940, Job 262, Bel Geddes Papers.

57 Caption from GM medal record book, Job 262, Bel Geddes Papers.

58 Nicolas P. Maffei, "The Search for an American Design Aesthetic, from Art Deco to Streamlining," in C. Benton, T. Benton, and G. Wood, eds., *Art Deco: 1910–1939* (London: Victoria and Albert Museum Publications, 2003).

59 Philip Johnson, "History of Machine Art," in Museum of Modern Art, *Machine Art, March 6 to April 30, 1934* (1934; rpt., New York: Published for The Museum of Modern Art by Arno Press, 1969), unpaginated. The nationalistic emphasis of the catalog is ironic considering that the ball bearing on its cover was produced by the Swedish firm SKF. Thanks to Kjetil Fallan for this observation.

60 Ibid.

61 Ibid.

62 Plato's *Philebus 51c*, quoted in *Machine Art*.

63 Le Corbusier, *Towards a New Architecture*, 158.

64 Ibid.

65 Van Doren, *Industrial Design*, 187.

66 Ibid., 179.

67 Alfred Barr Jr. in *Machine Art*.

68 John McAndrews, "'Modernistic' and 'Streamlined'," *The Bulletin of the Museum of Modern Art*, Vol. V, No. 6 (December 1938), 2.

69 "Airflow: A New Kind of Motor Car," publicity by Chrysler Corporation, 1933, Job 271, Bel Geddes Papers; Advertisement, "I salute Walter P. Chrysler and Fred Zeder FOR BUILDING THIS AUTHENTIC AIRFLOW CAR," December 16, 1933, *Saturday Evening Post*, Bel Geddes Papers. Streamlining definitions from Richard Burns Carson page 237 in Flink. From Carson, *The Olympian Cars: The Great American Luxury Automobiles of the Twenties and Thirties* (New York: Knopf, 1976), 37.

70 Kettering to Bel Geddes, July 27, 1933, Job 957, Bel Geddes Papers.

71 Memo from Bel Geddes to Newsom regarding visit to Chrysler factory on October 24, 25, and 26, 1933, Autobiography, AE- 79, Ch. 75, Bel Geddes Papers.

72 Meeting minutes of Chrysler ("Q") account, January 17, 1934, Job 271, Bel Geddes Papers.

73 Kettering to Bel Geddes, July 27, 1933, Bel Geddes Papers.

74 "Airflow: A New Kind of Motor Car," Bel Geddes Papers.

75 Bel Geddes, *Horizons*, 63.

76 Advertisement, "I salute Walter P. Chrysler and Fred Zeder FOR BUILDING THIS AUTHENTIC AIRFLOW CAR," Bel Geddes Papers.

77 "Present and Future," *New York American*, January 4, 1934, Job 271, Bel Geddes Papers.

78 Advertisement, "I salute Walter P. Chrysler and Fred Zeder FOR BUILDING THIS AUTHENTIC AIRFLOW CAR," Bel Geddes Papers.

79 Ibid.

80 Carolyn Edmundson, "It's a Great Thing That Chrysler Has Done," *Chrysler News*, Job 271, Bel Geddes Papers.

81 Meeting minutes of Chrysler ("Q") account, January 17, 1934, Bel Geddes Papers.

82 Carl Breer, "Airflow Styling Brings New Beauty: Airflow Is First Car Built around Fundamental Requirements," Job 271, Bel Geddes Papers.

83 Ibid.

84 Breer, "Airflow Styling Brings New Beauty," Bel Geddes Papers.

85 Sparke, *A Century of Car Design*, 26–29; Bush, *The Streamlined Decade*, 99–102.

86 An important contemporaneous streamlined design was the Jaray-influenced 1934 Tatra 77 by Hans Ledwinka. Gartman, *Auto Opium*, 118–121. William Stout's streamlined Scarab car of 1935 provides a useful comparison to the Airflow.

87 Meikle, *Twentieth Century Limited*, 86.

88 Minutes, October 10, 1933, Job 271, Bel Geddes Papers.

89 Gartman, *Auto Opium*, 121–125.

90 Meikle, *Twentieth Century Limited*, 148.

91 Minutes, October 24 & 25, 1933, Job 271, Bel Geddes Papers.

92 Minutes, October 10, 1933, Bel Geddes Papers.

93 Meikle, *Twentieth Century Limited*, 148–151.

94 Minutes, October 10, 1933, Bel Geddes Papers.

95 Ibid.

96 Minutes Q Account, November 6 & 7, 1933, Job 271, Bel Geddes Papers.

97 Ibid.; Meeting minutes, October 10, 1933, January 17, 1934, Bel Geddes Papers.

98 Gartman, *Auto Opium*, 121.

99 Minutes Q Account, November 6 & 7, 1933, Bel Geddes Papers.

100 Ibid.

101 Ibid.

102 Minutes, November 10, 1933, Bel Geddes Papers.

103 Minutes, November 15, 1933, Bel Geddes Papers.

104 Ibid.

105 Minutes, January 10, 1934, Job 271, Bel Geddes Papers.

106 Meeting minutes of Chrysler ("Q") account, January 17, 1934, Bel Geddes Papers.

107 Chrysler Corporation, *Story of the Airflow Cars*, 9–10, in Meikle, *Twentieth Century Limited*, 150.

108 Ralph Nader, *Unsafe at Any Speed: The Designed-In Dangers of the American Automobile* (New York: Grossman, 1965); Flink, *The Automobile Age*, 268.

109 "19. Books and Articles," Bel Geddes Papers; H. D. Bennett, President, Toledo Scale Company, Toledo, to Bel Geddes, December 12, 1934; Referring to the "streamlining" article, Bennett wrote "you will pardon my suspicions of a 'ghost' since I quite distinctly recall you once saying that you never wrote anything, although the 'ghost' has expressed your ideas well." Box 175, Job WA-14b, replies to "Streamlining" article, Bel Geddes Papers.

110 Bel Geddes, "Streamlining," *The Atlantic Monthly*.

111 H. G. Weaver, General Motors Corp., Detroit, to Earl Newson, December 14, 1934, Box 175, Job WA-14b, Replies to "Streamlining," Bel Geddes Papers.

112 The last sentence was underscored in the letter from Alfred Barr Jr. to Bel Geddes, December 4, 1934, Box 175, Job WA-14b, Replies to "Streamlining," Bel Geddes Papers. Nicolas P. Maffei, "Streamlined Pencil Sharpener, USA," in *Iconic Design: 50 Stories about 50 Things* (Bloomsbury: London, 2014), 122–125.

113 Ely Jacques Kahn to Bel Geddes, New York, NY, November 28, 1934, Box 175, Job WA-14b, Replies to "Streamlining," Bel Geddes Papers.

114 Fred L. Palmer, Distributors Group, Inc., to Bel Geddes, New York, NY, November 30, 1930. Box 175, Job WA-14b, Replies to "Streamlining," Bel Geddes Papers.

115 30.8 "Press Relations," Bel Geddes Papers.

116 Lippmann, *Public Opinion*; Susman, *Culture as History*, 158.

117 30.8 "Press Relations," Bel Geddes Papers.

118 Hellman, "Profiles: Design for a Living—III," 27.

119 "Quackery Dies While Art Endures," *Product Engineering*, Vol. V, No. 4 (April 1934), 121.

120 "Report on Vacuum Cleaner: Prepared for Electrolux, Inc., Norman Bel Geddes & Company, 1934," Job 301, Electrolux Vacuum Cleaner, Bel Geddes Papers.

121 Meikle, *Twentieth Century Limited*, 125.

122 Meeting minutes, September 26, 1945, Job 562, Bel Geddes Papers.

123 "Estimating Data," client survey for Globe Slicing Machine, November 25, 1940, Job 493, Bel Geddes Papers.

124 Meeting minutes, July 29, 1941, Job 493, Bel Geddes Papers.

125 "Estimating Data," Bel Geddes Papers.

126 Ibid.

127 "American Industrial Design," *The Bulletin of the Museum of Modern Art*, Vol. VIII, No. 1 (November 1940), 11.

128 Ibid., 9.

129 Siegfried Giedion, *Mechanization Takes Command* (New York: Oxford University Press, 1948), 611.

130 Nelson, "Both Fish and Fowl," 40. Illustration credit is given to Kemp Starrett and the *New Yorker*.

131 Publicity writing, "Norman Bel Geddes to Design for Loose-Wiles Biscuit and Cracker Company of Long Island City," January 1, 1940; Loose-Wiles to J. L. Brent, April 11, 1941, Job 430, Bel Geddes Papers.

132 "Press Release: A Superior Product + Improved Package Design = Increased Sales, by Critchell Rimington," March 24, 1942; Preliminary Draft of Job Program: Loose Wiles, January 14, 1941, Job 430, Bel Geddes Papers.

133 Howard A. Weiner to Bel Geddes, November 28, 1949; Rice-Weiner and Co. to Bel Geddes, November 30, 1949, Job 630, Bel Geddes Papers.

134 Howard A. Weiner to Bel Geddes, November 28, 1949, Bel Geddes Papers.

135 "Here's what the Press Have to Say About…" *Herald Tribune*, June 15, 1950, Job 630, Bel Geddes Papers.

136 "Flow-Motion" catalog, 1950, Job 630, Bel Geddes Papers.

137 Eliot F. Noyes, *Organic Design in Home Furnishings* (New York: The Museum of Modern Art, c. 1941); Kathryn B. Heisinger and George H. Marcus, *Landmarks of Twentieth Century Design* (New York: Abbeville Press, 1993), 368. "Employees, Applications and Subcontractors," Job 927, Bel Geddes Papers. John Harwood, "The White Room: Eliot Noyes and the Logic of the Information Age Interior," *Grey Room*, No. 12 (Summer 2003, The MIT Press), 5–31, 9.

138 Harwood, 10.

Chapter 6

1 Egmont Arens and Roy Sheldon, *Consumer Engineering: A New Technique for Prosperity* (New York: Harper and Brothers, 1932), 2, 14, 19.

2 Ben Nash, "Selling What the Consumer Wants," *Printers' Ink Monthly*, Vol. XXI, No. 5 (November 1930), 36, 85.

3 Roger Horowitz and Arwen Mohun, eds., *His and Hers: Gender, Consumption, and Technology* (Charlottesville and London: University Press of Virginia, 1998), 2–3.

4 Jennifer Scanlon, *Inarticulate Longings: The "Ladies' Home Journal," Gender, and the Promise of Consumer Culture* (New York and London; Routledge, 1995), 10; Lois Arderly, "Inarticulate Longings," J. Walter Thompson *News Bulletin*, 1924; quote from Bel Geddes to Montague Charman, Head of Design, Art Department, Syracuse University, Syracuse NY, March 11, 1946, Job 972, Bel Geddes Papers.

5 "Quarterly Report to RCA Victor Division: Insurance Line Combination Study-Stage 1," Job 481, *c.* 1943, Bel Geddes Papers.

6 Bel Geddes to Charman, March 11, 1946, Job 972, Bel Geddes Papers.

7 Bel Geddes, *Horizons* (Boston: Little, Brown, 1932), 230.

8 Bel Geddes to Charman, March 11, 1946, Job 972, Bel Geddes Papers.

9 Shelley Kaplan Nickles, "Object Lessons: Household Appliances and the American Middle Class," 1920–1960 Ph.D. diss., University of Virginia, 1999, 10.

10 Colin K. Lee, "An Engineer Considers Art in Engineering," *Product Engineering*, Vol. III, No. 5 (May 1932), 201.

11 Quoted in Jeffrey L. Meikle, *Twentieth Century Limited: Industrial Design in America, 1925-1939* (Philadelphia: Temple University Press, 1979), 134. Van Doren, *Industrial Design*, 45–46, 54.

12 Raymond Loewy, *Never Leave Well Enough Alone* (New York: Harcourt, Brace, 1940), 278.

13 In *Keeping the Corporate Image*, Tedlow writes that Fordism was dominant in the 1910s and 1920s during the rise of a national mass market where a number of firms, including Ford, General Electric, Coca-Cola and many others, developed dominant positions, national brands, and increased in scale through mass production of inexpensive goods. At this time, firms began systematically collecting marketing data, while organizing and educating the mass market, 6–7.

14 Richard S. Tedlow, *Keeping the Corporate Image: Public Relations and Business* (Greenwich, CT: JAI Press, 1979), 4–6.

15 Roland Marchand, *Creating the Corporate Soul: The Rise of Public Relations and Corporate Imagery in American Big Business* (Berkeley, Los Angeles and London: The University of California Press, 1998), 230. See also Sally H. Clarke, *Trust and Power: Consumers and the Making of the United States Automobile Market* (Cambridge: Cambridge University Press, 2007).

16 Meikle, *Twentieth Century Limited*, 16, 17, 70.

17 Bel Geddes to Charman, March 11, 1946, Job 972, Bel Geddes Papers.

18 Bel Geddes, *Horizons*, 225–227.

19 Ibid., 231.

20 Ibid., 230–231.

21 "Cost data on Philco and Standard Gas Equipment Surveys, May 22, 1931," Job 199, Bel Geddes Papers.

22 Meikle, *Twentieth Century Limited*, 8; Joel Kimball, "Do You Own a Radio?" *The New Republic*, Vol. LXIII, No. 815 (July 16, 1930), 231–233.

23 Sayre M. Ramsdall, "How Philco Doubled Sales during the Depression," *Printers' Ink* (October 22, 1931), 17–19.

24 Ramsdall, "How Philco Doubled Sales during the Depression," 17–19.

25 "Philco Ready to Challenge 1932," *Printers' Ink*, December 31, 1931, 69.

26 Philco contract, September 28, 1930, Job 199, Bel Geddes Papers.

27 "Cost Data on Philco and Standard Gas Equipment Surveys, May 22, 1931," Job 199, Bel Geddes Papers.

28 "Reports on Conversations Held with Various People Concerning Radio;" Philco Survey, Job 199, Bel Geddes Papers. Helen Lansdowne Resor would later become the first woman in the Advertising Hall of Fame. Susan Strasser, *Satisfaction Guaranteed: The Making of the American Mass Market* (New York: Pantheon Books, 1989), 10.

29 Ibid.

30 Bel Geddes, *Horizons*, 231.

31 Ibid., 241.

32 Robert McDonnell, "Art for Sales' Sake," Bel Geddes Papers. Charles R. Richards, "Sane and Insane Modernism in Furniture," *Good Furniture Magazine*, Vol. 32 (January 1929), 8–14.

33 "Norman Bel Geddes," *Product Engineering*, May 1931, 222, clipping, Box 173, File WA-1, Bel Geddes Papers.

34 Bel Geddes, *Horizons*, 240.

35 "Case History-File 199, Philco Radio, 1931, 1932," January 23, 1946, Job 199, Bel Geddes Papers.

36 "The Engineer Meets the Consumer," *Product Engineering,* Vol. II, No. 2 (February 1931), 51.

37 "Case History-File 199, Philco Radio, 1931, 1932," January 23, 1946, Job 199, Bel Geddes Papers.

38 Philco Case History, 1943, Job 199, Bel Geddes Papers.

39 Agreement with Abeyton Realty Corp., July 20, 1933, Job 263; Meikle, *Twentieth Century Limited*, 132.

40 "A study leading to the development of Forest Hill, 1934 vol. 2," Job 263, Bel Geddes Papers.

41 Ibid.

42 Ibid.

43 Christina Cogdell, "The Futurama Recontextualized: Norman Bel Geddes's Eugenic World of Tomorrow," *American Quarterly,* Vol. 52, No. 2 (2000), 193–245.

44 *Recent Social Trends in the United States, A Report of the President's Research Committee on Social Trends* (1933; rpt., New York, McGraw-Hill, 1970).

45 "PR Counselor Earl Newsom: Management Is Happier When It's a 'Good Citizen,'" *Printers' Ink*, February 14, 1958, 70, 70–74, Job 927, Bel Geddes Papers.

46 Newsom's notion of mass behavior was influenced by Le Bon and Martin. Le Bon viewed the crowd as a single "organism" which was characterized by "barbarian" "spirit" and "unconscious" action. Martin believed that a crowd had a "psychotic nature." Gustave Le Bon, *The Crowd: A Study of the Popular Mind* (1896; rpt., London: Ernest Benn Limited, 1952), 155, 7; Everett Dean Martin, *The Behavior of Crowds: A Psychological Study* (New York: Harper, 1920).

47 During his career, Newsom used information services such as the Elmo Roper opinion surveys and Link Audit, which was started in 1937 and attempted to chart the "climate" of public opinion through interviews. In the 1930s, he focused on selling products; in the 1940s, he concentrated on fashioning corporate images, identifying, and molding a company's "personality picture." "PR counselor Earl Newsom: Management is happier when it's a 'good citizen,'" *Printers' Ink,* February 14, 1958, 70–74. Bel Geddes Papers. Warren I. Susman, *Culture as History: The Transformation of American Society in the Twentieth Century* (New York: Pantheon Books, 1984), 212.

48 Ibid., 213, 217.

49 Bel Geddes, "Tomorrow's Consumer," a speech presented at the 39th Annual Meeting of the American Society of Refrigerator Engineers in Philadelphia, Pennsylvania, December 9, 1943, Theatre Box 175, Folder WA20, Bel Geddes Papers.

50 Bel Geddes, "Tomorrow's Consumer," Bel Geddes Papers.

51 Ibid.

52 Ibid.

53 Ibid. The speech's sophistication suggests it is by Newsom rather than Bel Geddes.

54 Quoted in Scanlon, *Inarticulate Longings*, 10; Arderly, "Inarticulate Longings."

55 Christine Frederick, *Selling Mrs. Consumer* (New York: The Business Bourse, 1929), 5.

56 Mark A. Swiencicki, "Consuming Brotherhood: Men's Culture, Style and Recreation as Consumer Culture, 1880–1930," *Journal of Social History*, Vol. 31 (Summer 1998). Reprinted in *Consumer Society in American History: A Reader*, Lawrence B. Glickman, ed. (Ithaca and London: Cornell University Press, 1999), 207–240. Swiencicki notes that women weren't the only significant consumers of the first decades of the twentieth century. Men tended to consume commercialized leisure, entertainment, and recreation, while women consumed domestic and family goods.

57 Ibid.

58 Strasser, *Satisfaction Guaranteed*, 26.

59 Bel Geddes, "Tomorrow's Consumer," Bel Geddes Papers.

60 Ibid.

61 Ibid.

62 Ibid.

63 Hellman, "Profiles: Design for a Living—III," *New Yorker* (February 22, 1941), 24.

64 Charlotte Himber, *Famous in Their Twenties* (New York: Association Press, 1942), 26, 38, 38.

65 Letter from Katherine B. Gray of Van Doren, Nowland & Schladermundt, May 2, 1944, Nash Car, 415, Box 26, folder 415.1, agreements, Bel Geddes Papers.

66 "30.1 Client Service," Box 940 Office Procedures, File 940.6, Office Procedures, *Standard Practice*, Bel Geddes Papers.

67 Section 30.3, Box 940 Office Procedures, File 940.6, Office Procedures, *Standard Practice*, Bel Geddes Papers.

68 "Standard Practice 31. 31 Prospective Client Service. 31.1 No-Sale Department," Box 940 Office Procedures, File 940.6, Office Procedures, *Standard Practice*, Bel Geddes Papers.

69 George Nelson, "Both Fish and Fowl," *Fortune* 9, no. 2 (February 1934), 43.

70 Hellman, "Profiles: Design for a Living—III," 24.

71 31.2 "Concentration versus Dispersion," Box 940 Office Procedures, File 940.6, Office Procedures, *Standard Practice*, Bel Geddes Papers.

72 Hellman, "Profiles: Design for a Living—III," 29.

73 Emerson Radio, Job 414; Agreement between NBG & Company and the Shell Oil Company, January 7, 1943, Shell Oil Service Station, Job 471, Bel Geddes Papers.

74 Contract between Bel Geddes and RCA, December 2, 1942, Job 481, Bel Geddes Papers. "Memo to NBG from Mrs. Hamilton 9/28/42," Job 481, Bel Geddes Papers.

75 Meikle, *Twentieth Century Limited*, 73.

76 RCA contract, December 2, 1942, Job 481, Bel Geddes Papers.

77 "Shell Oil Service Station Report May 6, 1943," Job 47, Bel Geddes Papers.

78 "Quarterly Report to Shell Oil Company: Retail Service Center Study-Stage 1," Job 471, Bel Geddes Papers.

79 Meeting minutes, December 30, 1942, Job 481, Bel Geddes Papers.

80 "Quarterly Report to RCA Victor Division: Living Conditions—Stage 1," Job 481, Bel Geddes Papers.

81 Ibid.

82 Ibid.

83 "Quarterly Report to RCA Victor Division: Insurance Line Combination Study-Stage 1," Job 481, Bel Geddes Papers.

84 "Quarterly Report to RCA Victor Division: Living Conditions—Stage 1," Bel Geddes Papers.

85 Meeting minutes, RCA and NBG & Co., August 17, 1943, RCA Radio Cabinets, Job 481, Bel Geddes Papers.

86 "Catalogue for Rittenhouse Electric Door Chimes, Vol. 40, 1943," Job 494, Bel Geddes Papers.

87 Agreement, A. E. Rittenhouse Co. Inc. and NBG & Co. Inc., July 20, 1943, Job 494; "Door Chime Survey," December 14, 1943, Job 494, Bel Geddes Papers.

88 "Door Chime Survey," Bel Geddes Papers.

89 Thomas Hine, *Populuxe* (New York: Alfred A. Knopf, 1987), *passim*.

90 On the construction of the powerful, imaginary consumer, see Celia Lury and Alan Warde, "Investments in the Imaginary Consumer: Conjectures Regarding Power, Knowledge and Advertising," in Mica Nava et al., eds., *Advertising and Consumption* (London and New York: Routledge, 1997).

Chapter 7

1 Geoffrey T. Hellman, "Profiles: Design for a Living-III," *New Yorker* (February 22, 1941), 28. Scholarship on the Futurama is profuse and includes: William Stott, "Greenbelt and Futurama: The Heavenly Cities of the 1930's," *The Journal of American Studies Association of Texas*, Vol. 4 (1973), 18–29; Jeffrey L. Meikle, *Twentieth Century Limited: Industrial Design in America, 1925-1939* (Philadelphia: Temple University Press, 1979), Terry Smith, *Making the Modern: Industry, Art, and Design in America* (Chicago and London: University of Chicago Press, 1993); Roland Marchand, "The Designers Go to the Fair, II: Norman Bel Geddes, the General Motors 'Futurama,' and the Visit to the Factory Transformed," *Design Issues*, Vol. 8 (Spring 1992), 23–40; David E. Nye, *The American Technological Sublime* (Cambridge and London: MIT, 1994).

2 "Models, Large and Small," *Printers' Ink* (April 14, 1932), 82.

3 Shelton Davis August, "Practical Showman," 1939, 21–22, publicity clipping, Job 381, Bel Geddes Papers.

4 "Two on the Aisle: Norman Bel Geddes' [sic] Addition to the Fair," *New York Post*, May 11, 1939, Bel Geddes Papers.

5 Around 1941, Bel Geddes would design a pole-less tent, cages, trucks, costumes, feature acts, and midway, for Ringling Brothers Barnum & Bailey Circus.

6 F. J. Hunter, *Catalog of the Norman Bel Geddes Theatre Collection, Humanities Research Center University of Texas at Austin* (Boston: G. K. Hall & Co.,1973), 2.

7 William Kelley, *Miracle in the Evening* (Garden City, NY: Doubleday, 1960), 131–132.

8 H. G. Wells, *Little Wars: A Game for Boys…* (Boston: Small, Maynard and Co., *c.* 1913), 152–153, 10.

9 From MS "War—unproduced designs," and 1135/vb, March 15, 1956, Autobiography, Jamaica Version, Chs. 33–37, Bel Geddes Papers.

10 Kelley, *Miracle in the Evening*, 228–230.

11 "Games worth a Candle," Autobiography, Jamaica Version, Ch. 44, Bel Geddes Papers.

12 August, "Practical Showman," 21–22, Bel Geddes Papers.

13 On eternal boyhood as an element of masculine consumerism, see Woody Register, *The Kid of Coney Island: Fred Thompson and the Rise of American Amusements* (Oxford: Oxford University Press, 2001), 12–14.

14 Emmet Crozier, "Success of Futurama, Which 2,000,000 Have Visited, Is Tribute to Geddes," *New York Herald Tribune*, July 1939, Job 381, Bel Geddes Papers.

15 Agreement between Bel Geddes and J. Walter Thompson regarding Shell Oil "City of the Future" advertisement, September 2, 1936, Job 356, Bel Geddes Papers. Sandy Isenstadt, "The Future Is Here: Norman Bel Geddes and the Theater of Time," in Albrecht, *Norman Bel Geddes Designs America*, 136–153.

16 Miller McClintock, "Of the Things to Come," publicity writing for the National Planning Conference, Detroit, June 1, 1937, from J. Walter Thompson Press Bureau, Job 356; Meikle, *Twentieth Century Limited*, 206–207.

17 Meikle, *Twentieth Century Limited*, 206–207. The Shell advert is discussed in terms of smooth traffic flow in: Meikle, *Twentieth Century Limited*; A detailed analysis of the Shell job, examining both its construction and representation is provided in: Meikle, *The "City of Tomorrow," Model 1937*, Pentagram Papers no. 11 (London: Pentagram Design, 1983); Meeting minutes, November 10, 1936, Job 356, Bel Geddes Papers. A list of research material sent to the J. Walter Thompson agency by Bel Geddes included: Cesare Chiodi, *La Citta Moderna: Technica Urbanista* (Milano, Italy: Ulrico Hoepli Editore, 1935); Le Corbusier et P. Jeanneret, *L'Architecture Vivante* (Cinquieme and Troisieme Serie and Zoning) (Paris: Albert Morance, 1932); Le Corbusier, *Towards a New Architecture* (New York: Payson & Clarke, 1927); F. L. Wright, *The Disappearing City* (New York: William Farquhar Payson, 1932). Bel Geddes also owned a copy of Le Corbusier's *The "City of Tomorrow" and Its Planning* (New York: Payson and Clarke, 1929), with stamp of the library of Bel Geddes, Bel Geddes Papers.

18 *Shell Progress*, July 8, 1937, Job 356, Bel Geddes Papers; Meikle, *Twentieth Century Limited*, 207.

19 Shell Oil "City of Tomorrow" ad, *Saturday Evening Post*, November 13, 1937, Job 356, Bel Geddes Papers. The ad also appeared in the *Saturday Evening Post* on July 10, 1937, 40–41 and July 17, 1937, 71.

20 *Shell Progress*, Job 356, Bel Geddes Papers.

21 Meikle, *Twentieth Century Limited*, 207.

22 McClintock, "Of the Things to Come," Bel Geddes Papers.

23 Ibid.

24 "Pottlesmith, On Traffic," publicity writing, Job 356, Bel Geddes Papers.

25 "Shell Presents Tomorrow to Make Sales for Today," *Shell Progress*, July 1937, Job 356, Bel Geddes Papers.

26 Steven M. Gelber, *Hobbies: Leisure, and the Culture of Work in America* (New York: Columbia University Press, 1999), 224, 231.

27 Untitled article from *Worcester (MA) Telegram*, October 2, 1937; "Make Traffic Photo Wearing Gas Masks: Photographers Obtain Effects in Geddes Design of 'City of Tomorrow,'" *New York Times*, August 1, 1937; "Model City of Future Built: Facilities for Traffic Shown," *Los Angeles Examiner*, July 13, 1937; *Shell Progress*, July 8, 1937; "Shell Presents Tomorrow to Make Sales for Today"; "Predicts 24-Hour Journey to Coast: Norman Bel Geddes Sees Safety Factor Chief Obstacle" *New York Times*, July 15, 1937; "Making Streets Safe," *Perth Amboy (New Jersey) News*, June 8, 1937; "Designs Future Traffic Lanes: Geddes's 'Model City of 1960' Shown at National Planning Conference," *New York Sun*, June 1, 1937, "City 1960: Norman Bel Geddes Designer," *Architectural Forum*, July 1937, clippings in Job 356, Bel Geddes Papers.

28 Untitled article, *Worcester (MA) Telegram*, Bel Geddes Papers.

29 Ibid.

30 Ibid.

31 "Make Traffic Photo Wearing Gas Masks," Bel Geddes Papers.

32 "City 1960," Bel Geddes Papers.

33 Barry Cullingworth, *Planning in the USA: Policies, Issues and Processes* (London and New York: Routledge, 1997), 59–63.

34 Meikle, *Twentieth Century Limited*, 187–210.

35 Transcript of article by Waldemar Kaempffert in *New York Times*, n.d., Job 653, Bel Geddes Papers. On the influence of modernism and science fiction on Bel Geddes's vision of the future, see Morshed, "The Aviator's (Re)Vision of the World," 21 and *passim*.

36 "Spectacular View in the World of the Future," press release for April 29, 1939, Job 381, Bel Geddes Papers.

37 Stott, "Greenbelt and Futurama," 25.

38 Bel Geddes, "A Theatre That Stimulates Desire," *The Retail Executive*, June 21, 1939. Bel Geddes Papers.

39 Roland Marchand, *Creating the Corporate Soul: The Rise of Public Relations and Corporate Imagery in American Big Business* (Berkeley, Los Angeles and London: The University of California Press, 1998), 3.

40 "Why a Public Relations Program," *Product Engineering*, Vol. III, No. 11 (October 1938), 363, 365.

41 S. H. Walker, Paul Sklar, "Business Finds its Voice," *Harper's Magazine* 176 (January 1938), 113–123, quote from 118.

42 Hellman, "Profiles: Design for a Living-III," 29.

43 Polling by the American Institute of Public Opinion found that Fair visitors considered the Futurama their favorite exhibit, transcription of *New York Times* article, n.d., pp. 33–34, Autobiography AE-1-2, AE72-92, Job 653, Bel Geddes Papers.

44 Robert Henri Mutrux, "The World's Largest Rendering," draft of article for *Pencil Points*, May 17, 1939, Job 381, Bel Geddes Papers.

45 Futurama exhibit guide 1940, p. 1, Job 381, Bel Geddes Papers.

46 "Description of G.M. Building…," September 8, 1939, Job 381, Bel Geddes Papers.

47 Bel Geddes explained that the Futurama was the outcome of a fallow period at the office in 1933 when he paid his staff to develop traffic solutions, Crozier, "Success of Futurama," 11, 18, Job 381, Bel Geddes Papers.

48 Bel Geddes staff included on the flight were Roger Nowland, Thomas Farrar, and Peter Schladermundt; memo to Bel Geddes from Paxton, November 1, 1938, Job 381, Bel Geddes Papers.

49 Interoffice memo, November 2, 1938, case history of the General Motors intersection, Job 381, Bel Geddes Papers.

50 Memo from J. G. to Paxton, November 2, 1938, production specifications, Job 381, Bel Geddes Papers.

51 Case History of the GM Intersection, *c.* 1941, Job 381, Bel Geddes Papers.

52 Meeting notes regarding animation of traffic model sequence, November 1, 1938, with Bel Geddes, Paxton, and Nowland present, production specifications, Job 381, Bel Geddes Papers.

53 Transcript, "Futurama Requires Constant Rebuilding to Keep it Star Hit of World's Fair," Publicity Clippings, Job 381, Bel Geddes Papers.

54 Meeting notes regarding animation of traffic model sequence, Bel Geddes Papers.

55 Case History of the GM Intersection, Bel Geddes Papers.

56 Meeting notes regarding animation of traffic model sequence, Bel Geddes Papers.

57 Case History of the GM Intersection, Bel Geddes Papers.

58 Ibid.

59 On the middle landscape, see Leo Marx, *The Machine in the Garden: Technology and the Pastoral Ideal in America* (London: Oxford University Press, 1964).

60 Transcript of article by Janet Mable, *Christian Science Monitor*, no other information, Autobiography AE-1-2, AE72-92, Job 653, Bel Geddes Papers.

61 Mutrux, "The World's Largest Rendering," Bel Geddes Papers.

62 Transcript editorial, *New York Sunday News*, June 18, 1939, Autobiography AE-1-2, AE72-92, Job 653, Bel Geddes Papers.

63 Saarinen worked forty-six days on the GM building, and was involved in the majority of sketches, layouts, and final drawings of the building's exterior. Meikle in Albrecht, "'A Few Years Ahead:' Defining Modernism with a Popular Appeal," 130; David P. Handlin, *American Architecture* (London: Thames and Hudson, 2004), 249.

64 "Fair Called Model for City Planners: Chief Examples of Permanent Contributions Win Praise of Regional Association," *New York Times*, June 25, 1939, Sunday, Job 381, Bel Geddes Papers.

65 Sandy Isenstadt, footnote 24, in Albrecht, *Norman Bel Geddes Designs America*.

66 Leonard Lyons, "The Lyons Den," *New York Post*, October 14, 1939, publicity, Job 381, Bel Geddes Papers.

67 "Futurama Requires Constant Rebuilding to Keep It Star Hit of World's Fair," Bel Geddes Papers.

68 Crozier, "Success of Futurama," 11, 18, Bel Geddes Papers.

69 "Accidents of Today Halts Futurama: 3,000 Waiting in Line to Exhibit as Moving Chair Mechanism Breaks Down: Out of Order for Two Hours: Spectators, Roused from 1960 Dream of Super-Highways, Walk to Nearest Exit." *New York Times*, October 13, 1939, Job 381, Bel Geddes Papers.

70 Transcript, "World's Fair Section," *New York Sun*, April 29, n.d., Job 381, Bel Geddes Papers.

71 E. B. White, "A Reporter at Large: They Come with Joyous Song," *New Yorker*, May 13, 1939 publicity, Bel Geddes Papers.

72 Stuart Chase, "Pattern for a Brave New World," *Cosmopolitan*, January 1940, 38, Bel Geddes Papers.

73 Ibid.

74 E. B. White, "A Reporter at Large," Bel Geddes Papers.

75 "Press Release to *World Telegram*, from NBG & Co.," n.d., Job 381, Bel Geddes Papers.

76 Roland Marchand, *Advertising the American Dream: Making Way for Modernity* (Berkeley, Los Angeles and London: University of California Press, 1985), 314; Susie McKellar, "'Seals of Approval:' Consumer Representation in 1930s America," *Journal of Design History*, Vol. 15, No. 1 (2002), 1–13.

77 "Don't Be a Guinea Pig," caption for an illustration in *Consumers Union Reports*, August 1939, 16.

78 "A Preview of the World's Exhibits," *Ballyhoo*, February 1939, Job 381, Bel Geddes Papers.

79 Marchand, *Advertising the American Dream*, 312–313. Ballyhoo anticipated *Adbusters* magazine (founded in 1989) and its subvertisements, fake advertisements which appropriated and critiqued the images and messages of big brands.

80 Bragdon considered the triangle, square, and circle to have theosophical implications, relating to the body, the universe and a "higher trinity," Donovan A. Shilling, *They Put Rochester on the Map: Personalities of Rochester's Past* (place of publication not identified, Pancoast Publishing: 2012), 37–38.

81 Bel Geddes, "A Theatre That Stimulates Desire," Bel Geddes Papers.

82 Memo to Bel Geddes, regarding Futurama case history, September 29, 1941, Job 381, Bel Geddes Papers.

83 Memo, Mr. Brent to Bel Geddes, regarding Futurama case history, August 14, 1941, Autobiography, Jamaica, Ch. 80–83, Bel Geddes Papers.

84 John Anderson, "Mr. Anderson Soliloquizes on the Fair and a B'way Heartache," *New York Journal*, June 11, 1939, Job 381, Bel Geddes Papers.

85 Bel Geddes, *Horizons*, 140, 142.

86 The factory analogy is further developed in Marchand, "The Designers Go to the Fair, II."

87 David Dietz, "Vast Panorama, Fair Exhibit," *World Telegram*, January 18, 1939, Job 381, Bel Geddes Papers.

88 Egmont Arens and Roy Sheldon, *Consumer Engineering: A New Technique for Prosperity* (New York: Harper and Brothers, 1932).

89 "The World's Fair Closes," *Utica Daily Press*, November 1, 1939, Job 381, Bel Geddes Papers.

90 For a detailed overview and analysis of Bel Geddes's contradictory attitude toward war—he was both a self-proclaimed pacifist but a dedicated student of military strategy—and his career-long development of his war models project and its links with the military, see Cogdell, "Theater of War," Albrecht, *Norman Bel Geddes Designs America*, 317–339.

91 Smith, *Making the Modern*, 400.

92 Ibid.

93 "The Museum and the War," *The Bulletin of the MoMA*, 10, no. 1 (October–November 1942), 3.

94 James L. Baughman, "Who Read *Life*? The Circulation of America's Favorite Magazine," in Erika Doss, ed., *Looking at* Life *Magazine* (Washington and London: Smithsonian Institution Press, 2001), 41–51, 44.

95 "MoMA Press Release—War Maneuver Models Shown at MoMA," n.d., *c.* January 1944, Job 499, Bel Geddes Papers.

96 Clement Greenberg, "Avant-Garde and Kitsch," in Bernard Rosenberg and David Manning White, eds., *Mass Culture: The Popular Arts in America* (Glencoe, IL: The Free Press and the Falcon's Wing Press, 1957). This article was originally published in the *Partisan Review* (Fall 1939).

97 Greenberg, "Avant-Garde and Kitsch," 105.

98 "MoMA Press Release—War Maneuver Models Shown at MoMA," Bel Geddes Papers.

99 Ibid.

100 "One More River to Cross," *Cue*, February 5, 1944, Job 499, Bel Geddes Papers.

101 "MoMA Press Release—War Maneuver Models Shown at MoMA," Bel Geddes Papers.

102 Ibid.

103 Bruce Downes, "Seeing the War in Tabletops," *Model Photography Magazine*, October 1942, 21, 90–91, Bel Geddes Papers.

104 Downes, "Seeing the War in Tabletops," Bel Geddes Papers.

105 "Mrs. Norman Bel Geddes," *New York Star*, January 21, 1943. Chapter 87, Autobiography, Bel Geddes Papers.

106 Ibid.

107 Letter from Katherine B. Gray of Van Doren, Nowland & Schladermundt, May 2, 1944, Nash Car, Job 415, Box 26, folder 415.1, agreements, Bel Geddes Papers.

108 Memo to Mr. Lance and Miss [Katherine B.] Gray from Bel Geddes, December 1, 1943, in reference to the Nash-Kelvinator contract as arranged by Schladermundt, Agreements, Job 415, Bel Geddes Papers.

109 Ibid.

110 Bel Geddes to G. Mason, President, Nash-Kelvinator, March 15, 1944, agreements, Job 415, Bel Geddes Papers.

111 Letter from Gray, May 2, 1944, agreements, Job 415, Bel Geddes Papers.

112 AJ-20, Ch. 80–83, Autobiography Jamaica, Bel Geddes Papers; G. D. "Norman Bel Geddes (1893–1958)," 48.

113 "Comeback," *Time*, December 13, 1948, 98.

114 Bel Geddes to Mr. and Mrs. Windsor Lewis (Barbara Bel Geddes), August 7, 1952, Family Correspondences, Job 960, Bel Geddes Papers.

115 "1138/vb/3/19/56," Autobiography, Job 653, Chapter 87, Bel Geddes Papers.

116 Meeting minutes, Bel Geddes and Mr. Wolf of Federal Telephone and Radio, January 17, 1947, Washer Diary, Job 551, Bel Geddes Papers.

117 Mr. Zeckendorf of Webb & Knapp, Inc. New York City, to Bel Geddes, October 24, 1947, Autobiography, AE 89, Job 653, Chapter 88, Bel Geddes Papers.

118 "Comeback," *Time*.

119 "AUTOBIOGRAPHY-RETROSPECT 88," *c.* 1956, Autobiography, AE89 Chapter 88, Job 653, Bel Geddes Papers.

120 "Office Procedure," Drafting Instructions, December 3, 1953, Job 940, Bel Geddes Papers.

121 Bel Geddes to George Fowler, Cunningham & Walsh, New York City, August 27, 1952, Living Room Kitchen correspondence, Job 650, Bel Geddes Papers.

122 "Biography-Book 653, 1302/1 bd," *c.* September 20, 1957, folder AM-8, Job 653, Bel Geddes Papers.

123 Page "1298/1—bd 653 (continued from 1941)," September 12, 1957, Folder AM-8, Job 653, Bel Geddes Papers.

124 Elizabeth Otis to Bel Geddes, New York, January 2, 1958, Folder AM-8, Job 653, Bel Geddes Papers.

125 Bel Geddes to Kenneth McCormick, Doubleday & Company, Inc. New York, May 6, 1958, Correspondence with Publisher 1957, Folder AM-8, Job 653, Bel Geddes Papers.

126 Kenneth MacGowan, "Norman Bel Geddes' Only Fault: He Just Skimmed the Surface: Great Book Tells Only Half the Story," *Los Angeles Mirror*, March 6, 1961, part 3, Folder AM-9, Reviews 1960–61, Bel Geddes Papers.

127 Diffrient interviewed March 1, 1991, in Flinchum, *Henry Dreyfuss*, 126.

128 Miles Orvell, *After the Machine: Visual Arts and the Erasing of Cultural Boundaries* (Jackson: University of Mississippi Press, 1995), 155–156.

129 G. D. "Norman Bel Geddes (1893–1958)," 48–51.

Index

Notes:
1. NBG is the abbreviation for Norman Bel Geddes.
2. Page numbers in **bold** denote images.
2. A page number followed by n denotes a footnote on that page.
3. *P* followed by a number in *italics* denotes the number of a Plate.

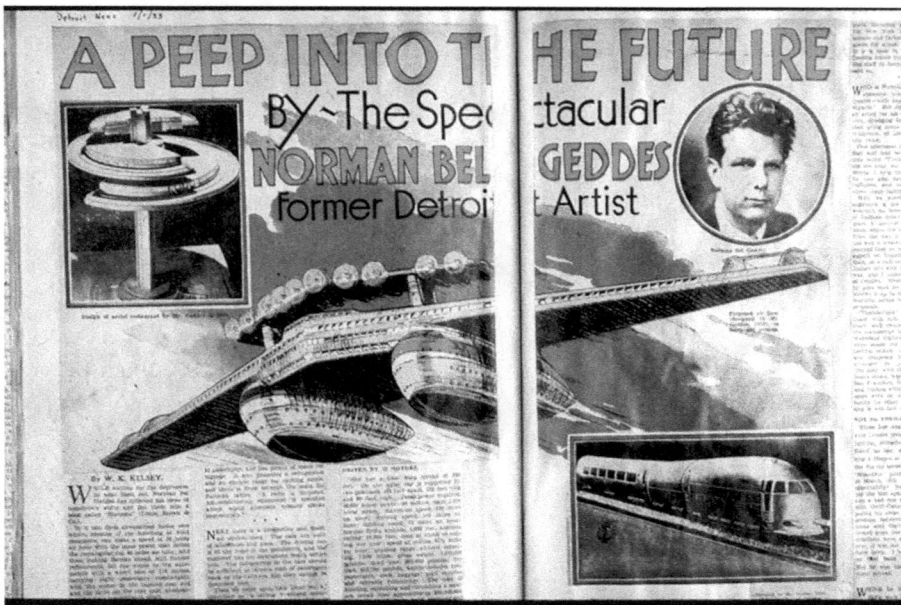

PLATE 1 W. K. Kelsey article, "A Peep into the Future by the Spectacular Norman Bel Geddes" in the *Detroit News*, January 1, 1933. Detroit News, Inc.

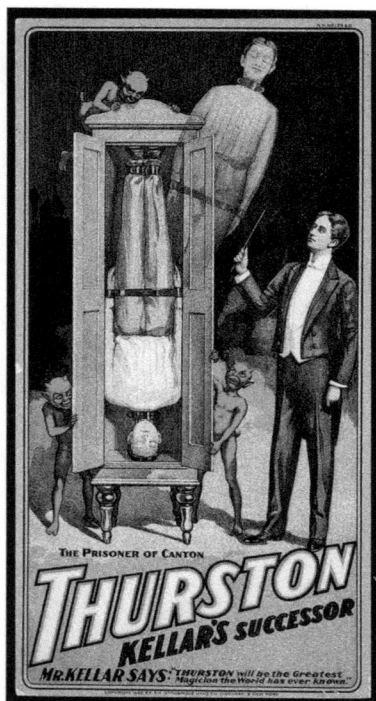

PLATE 2 American magician Howard Thurston. Color lithographic poster, 1908, 14 × 7 in. (35 × 18 cm). Library of Congress Prints and Photographs Division, Washington, DC.

A · S I O U A N · T Y P E
RED CHALK STUDY BY NORMAN GEDDES
ENGRAVED FOR INWHICH BY DAVID PARKINSON.

PLATE 3 Bel Geddes's "A Siouan Type" red chalk drawing in *In Which*. Harry Ransom Center, University of Texas, and the Edith Lutyens and Norman Bel Geddes Foundation, Inc. 2016.

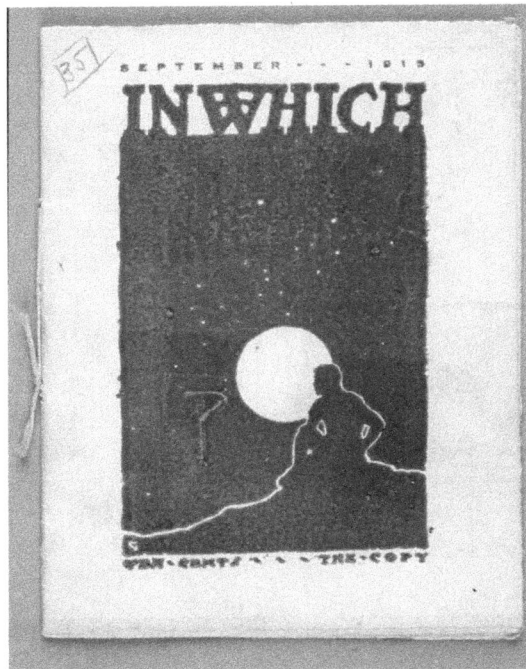

PLATE 4 Cover of *In Which* by Bel Geddes, September 1915. Harry Ransom Center, University of Texas, and the Edith Lutyens and Norman Bel Geddes Foundation, Inc. 2016.

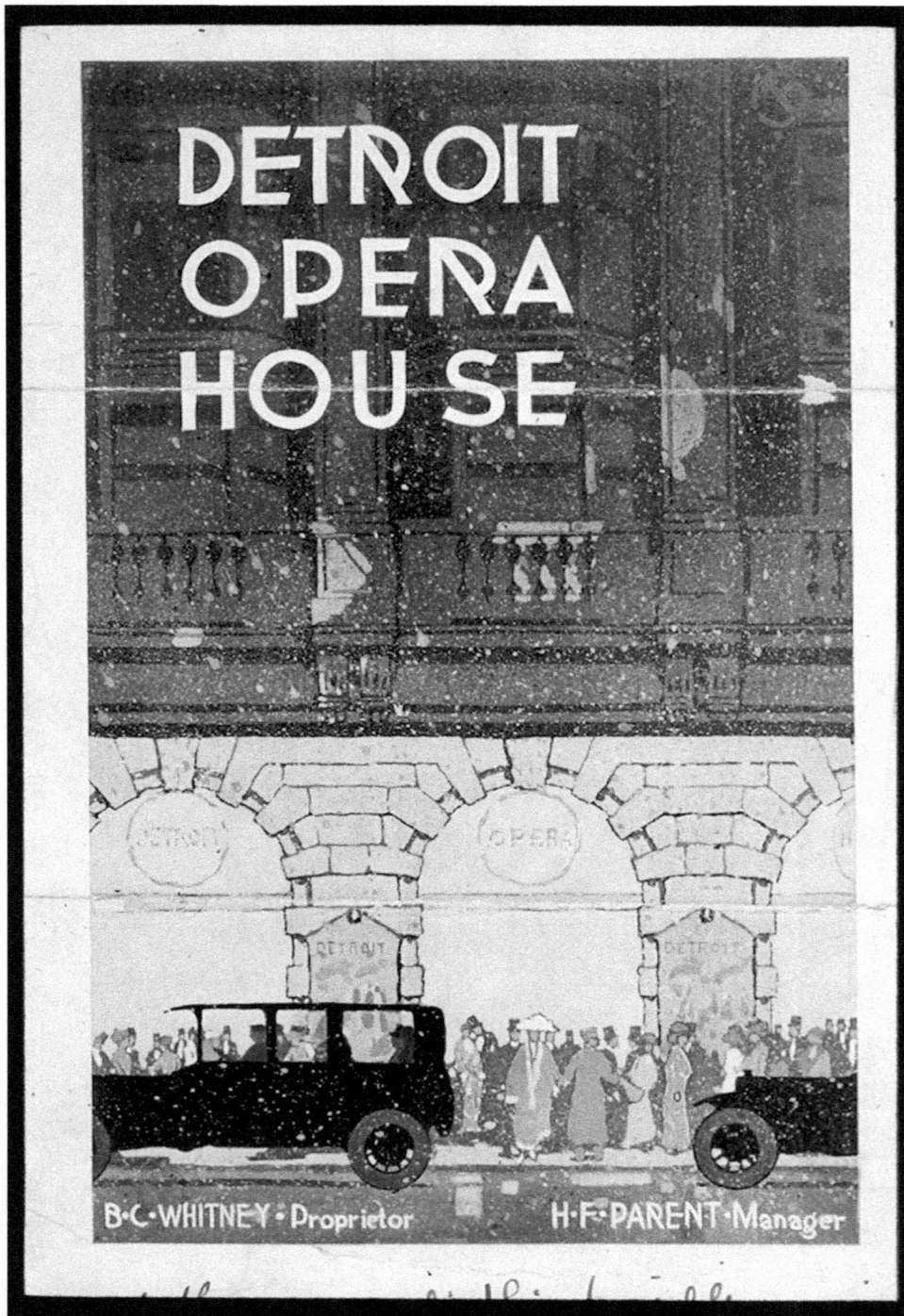

PLATE 5 Detroit Opera House poster by Bel Geddes, n.d. Harry Ransom Center, University of Texas, and the Edith Lutyens and Norman Bel Geddes Foundation, Inc. 2016.

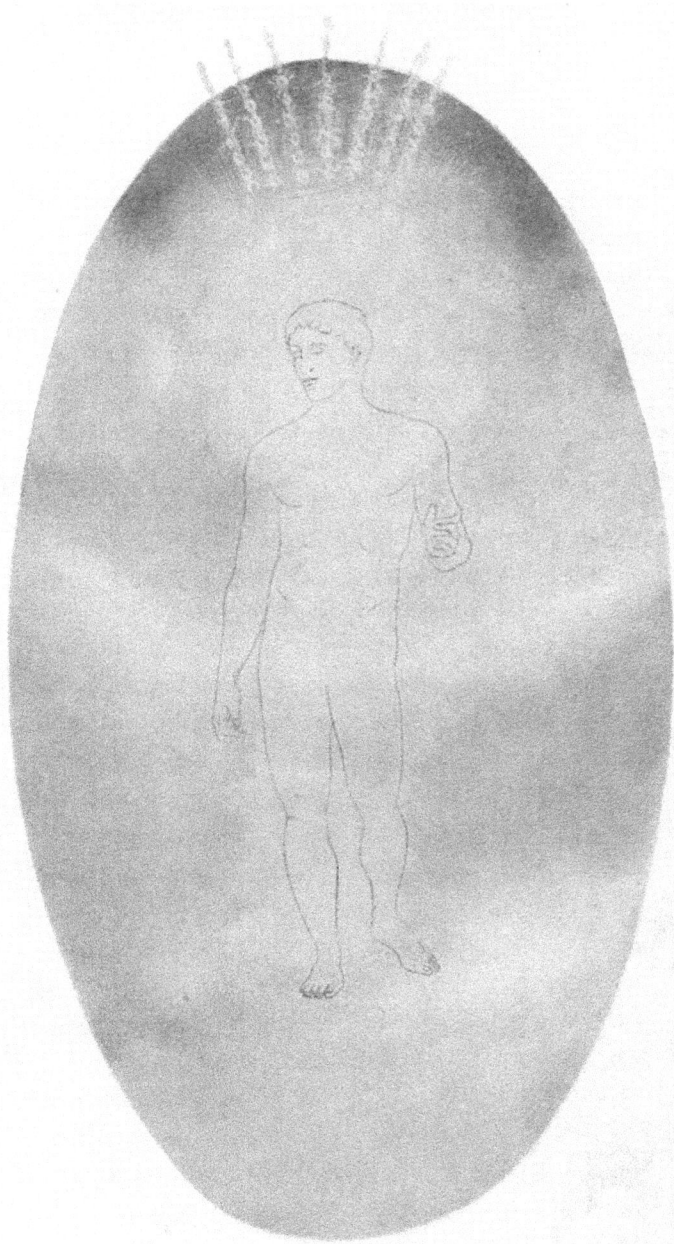

The Mental Body of the Developed Man.

XXII

PLATE 6 "The Mental Body of the Developed Man," in C. W. Leadbetter's *Man Visible and Invisible: Examples of Different Types of Men as Seen by Means of Trained Clairvoyance*, 1920.

17

PLATE 7 "Response to Devotion" in Annie Besant and Leadbetter's *Thought Forms,* 1905.

PLATE 8 Bel Geddes scene rendering for Dante Alighieri's *The Divine Comedy*, "Dante meets Beatrice," watercolor on paper, 23 × 20 in. (58.4 × 50.8 cm), 1920–1924. Harry Ransom Center, University of Texas, and the Edith Lutyens and Norman Bel Geddes Foundation, Inc. 2016.

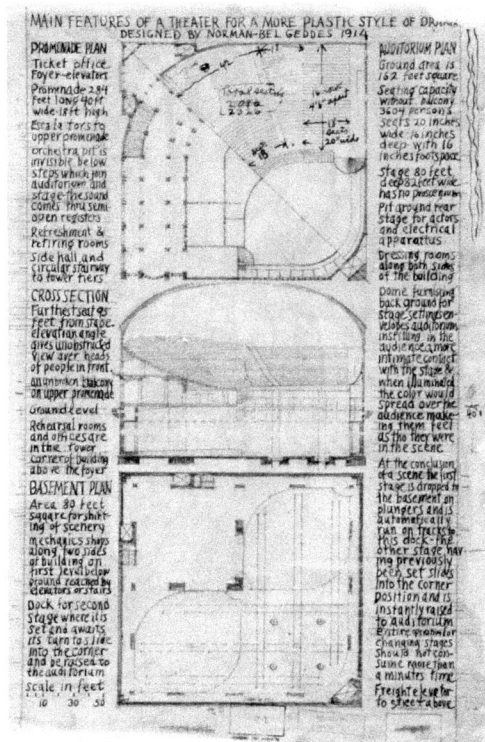

PLATE 9 "Theatre for a more plastic style of drama," Bel Geddes's earliest theatre design, dated 1914. Probably drawn and written by Bel Geddes. Harry Ransom Center, University of Texas, and the Edith Lutyens and Norman Bel Geddes Foundation, Inc. 2016.

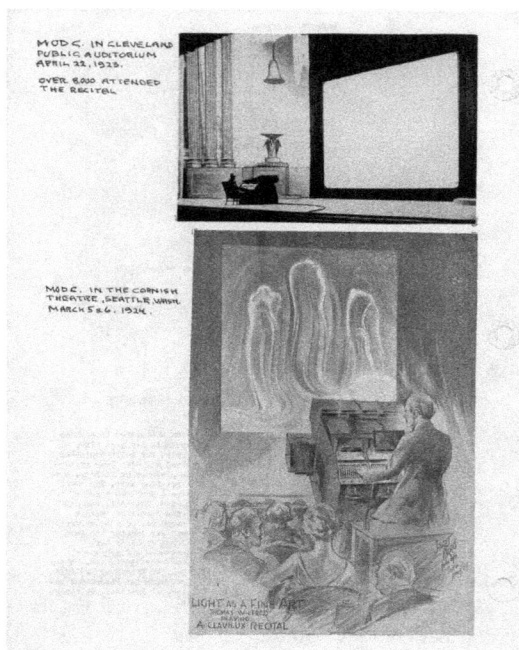

PLATE 10 Images of Thomas Wilfred's "color organ," or "Clavilux," performances 1923 (Cleveland) and 1924 (Seattle). Thomas Wilfred Papers (MS 1375). Manuscripts and Archives, Yale University Library.

PLATE 11 Bel Geddes with Frances Resor Waite, March 1, 1938. Bel Geddes's pencil on board sketches of masks for an unrealized production of Eugene O'Neil's *Lazarus Laughed*, 1927, in background. Harry Ransom Center, University of Texas, and the Edith Lutyens and Norman Bel Geddes Foundation, Inc. 2016.

PLATE 12 Bel Geddes-designed Simmons furniture rendering, *c.* 1928–1929. Harry Ransom Center, University of Texas, and the Edith Lutyens and Norman Bel Geddes Foundation, Inc. 2016.

PLATE 13 Sketch by Erich Mendelsohn of his Einstein Tower, originally dated 1919. Given to Bel Geddes by the architect on November 25, 1924. Ink on paper. Harry Ransom Center, University of Texas, and the Edith Lutyens and Norman Bel Geddes Foundation, Inc. 2016.

PLATE 14 *Horizons* (1932), by Norman Bel Geddes, cover. Harry Ransom Center, University of Texas, and the Edith Lutyens and Norman Bel Geddes Foundation, Inc. 2016.

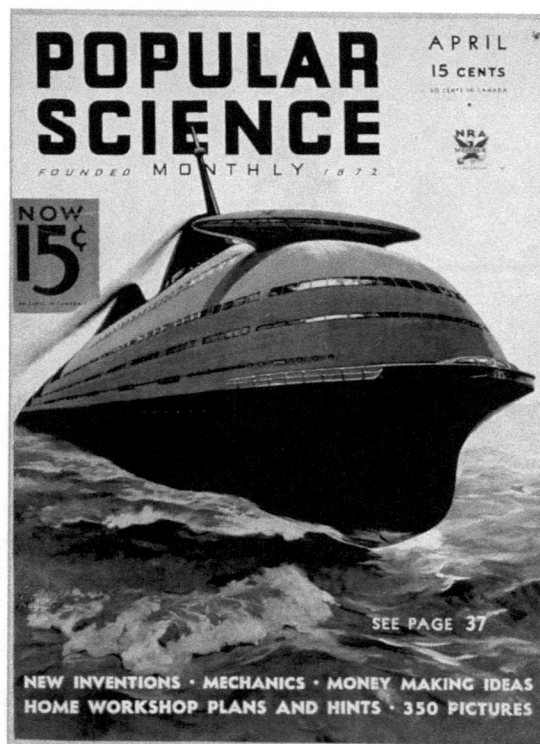

PLATE 15 Cover illustration of Bel Geddes's Ocean Liner, *Popular Science*, April 1934.

PLATE 16 Cover illustration of Bel Geddes's Aerial Restaurant, *Popular Mechanics*, July 1930. Hearst Communications Inc.

PLATE 17 Aerial Restaurant sketch, *c.* 1929. Harry Ransom Center, University of Texas, and the Edith Lutyens and Norman Bel Geddes Foundation, Inc. 2016.

PLATE 18 Drawing of Theater Number 14, frontal view, n.d. Harry Ransom Center, University of Texas, and the Edith Lutyens and Norman Bel Geddes Foundation, Inc. 2016.

PLATE 19 Bel Geddes's article, "The House of Tomorrow" in the *Ladies' Home Journal*, April 1931.

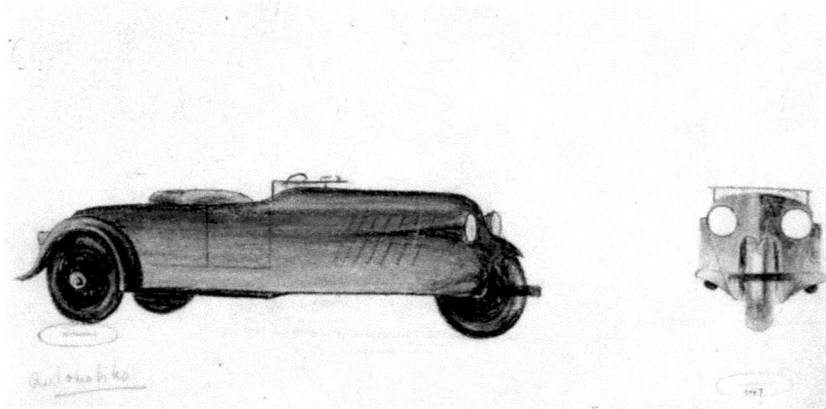

PLATE 20 Undated, unsigned rendering of car, possibly by Bel Geddes for Graham-Paige, n.d. Harry Ransom Center, University of Texas, and the Edith Lutyens and Norman Bel Geddes Foundation, Inc. 2016., c. 1928.

PLATE 21 Painted sketches of female head pendants, Rice-Weiner, *c.* 1949. Harry Ransom Center, University of Texas, and the Edith Lutyens and Norman Bel Geddes Foundation, Inc. 2016.

PLATE 22 Bel Geddes-designed Philco Lazyboy, *c.* 1931. Wood, 23 × 23 × 13 3/4 in. (58.5 × 58.5 × 35 cm). Harry Ransom Center, University of Texas, and the Edith Lutyens and Norman Bel Geddes Foundation, Inc. 2016.

PLATE 23 Bel Geddes's FC-400 Patriot Radio for Emerson, *c.* 1940–1941. Plastic, 11 × 6 × 9 in. (27.9 × 15.2 × 22.9 cm). Harry Ransom Center, University of Texas, and the Edith Lutyens and Norman Bel Geddes Foundation, Inc. 2016

PLATE 24 Streamlined model cars for the Futurama exhibit, *c.* 1939. Mixed media, 6 × 3 × 3 in. (15.2 x 7.6 x 7.6 cm) Harry Ransom Center, University of Texas, and the Edith Lutyens and Norman Bel Geddes Foundation, Inc. 2016.

PLATE 25 Theodore Kautzky drawing of visitors exiting Futurama exhibit from moving chairs and entering the life-size intersection of the General Motors building, *c.* 1939–1940. Manuscripts and Archives Division, The New York Public Library, Astor, Lenox and Tildon Foundations.